Comparing Post-Socialist Media Systems

This book explains divergent media system trajectories in the countries in Southeast Europe and challenges the presumption that the common socialist experience critically influences a common outcome in media development after democratic transformations by showing different remote and proximate configuration of conditions that influence their contemporary shape.

Applying an innovative longitudinal set-theoretical methodological approach, the book contributes to the theory of media systems with a novel theoretical framework for the comparative analysis of post-socialist media systems. This theory builds on the theory of historical institutionalism and the notion of critical junctures and path dependency in searching for an explanation for similarities or differences among media systems in the Eastern European region.

Extending the understanding of media systems beyond a political journalism focus, this book is a valuable contribution to the literature on comparative media systems in the areas of media systems studies, political science, Southeast and Central European studies, post-socialist studies and communication studies.

Zrinjka Peruško is Full Professor of Sociology of Media and Communication in the Faculty of Political Science at the University of Zagreb, Croatia.

Dina Vozab is Assistant Professor in the Faculty of Political Science at the University of Zagreb, Croatia.

Antonija Čuvalo is Assistant Professor in the Faculty of Political Science at the University of Zagreb, Croatia.

Routledge Advances in Internationalizing Media Studies
Edited by Daya Thussu
Hong Kong Baptist University

Everyday Media Culture in Africa
Audiences and Users
Edited by Wendy Willems and Winston Mano

Children and Media in India
Narratives of Class, Agency and Social Change
Shakuntala Banaji

Advancing Comparative Media and Communication Research
Edited by Joseph M. Chan and Francis L.F. Lee

Childcare Workers, Global Migration and Digital Media
Youna Kim

Media Imperialism in India and Pakistan
Farooq Sulehria

Global Convergence Cultures
Transmedia Earth
Edited by Matthew Freeman and William Proctor

The International Photojournalism Industry
Cultural Production and the Making and Selling of News Pictures
Jonathan Ilan

Internet Memes and Society
Social, Cultural, and Political Contexts
Anastasia Bertazzoli

Comparing Post-Socialist Media Systems
The Case of Southeast Europe
Zrinjka Peruško, Dina Vozab and Antonija Čuvalo

For more information about this series, please visit: www.routledge.com

Comparing Post-Socialist Media Systems
The Case of Southeast Europe

Zrinjka Peruško, Dina Vozab and Antonija Čuvalo

LONDON AND NEW YORK

First published 2021
by Routledge
2 Park Square, Milton Park, Abingdon, Oxon OX14 4RN

and by Routledge
52 Vanderbilt Avenue, New York, NY 10017

Routledge is an imprint of the Taylor & Francis Group, an informa business

© 2021 Zrinjka Peruško, Dina Vozab and Antonija Čuvalo

The right of Zrinjka Peruško, Dina Vozab and Antonija Čuvalo to be identified as authors of this work has been asserted by them in accordance with sections 77 and 78 of the Copyright, Designs and Patents Act 1988.

All rights reserved. No part of this book may be reprinted or reproduced or utilised in any form or by any electronic, mechanical, or other means, now known or hereafter invented, including photocopying and recording, or in any information storage or retrieval system, without permission in writing from the publishers.

Trademark notice: Product or corporate names may be trademarks or registered trademarks, and are used only for identification and explanation without intent to infringe.

British Library Cataloguing-in-Publication Data
A catalogue record for this book is available from the British Library

Library of Congress Cataloging-in-Publication Data
A catalog record for this book has been requested

ISBN: 978-0-367-22677-0 (hbk)
ISBN: 978-0-367-22678-7 (ebk)

Typeset in Sabon
by Apex CoVantage, LLC

Contents

List of figures ix
List of tables x
Foreword by Paolo Mancini xii
Preface xv

1 **Introduction** 1
  Three approaches to comparing the media systems of CEE countries 3
  The media systems of CEE countries cluster with those of Western European countries 5
  The impact of socialism on media systems 7
  Plan of the book 9

2 **Explaining the transformations of post-socialist media systems** 13
  The problem of studying media change 14
    Change in communication research 14
    Social theories on change 15
      Social change as evolution 17
      The processual approach to social change 18
      Change or continuity? The role of culture 20
  The problem of periodization: critical junctures and path dependencies in media systems change 22
    The first juncture: modernization 25
    The second juncture: socialism 26
    The third juncture: post-socialist democratizations 27
    The communication juncture 28
  The problem of comparison 32
  A set theoretic research approach: fuzzy set qualitative comparative analysis (fsQCA) 33
    Conditions shaping outcomes in media systems 34
      The political field 35

vi *Contents*

        The socio-economic field 36
        The cultural and symbolic field 37

3   **Prelude to modernity**   40
    Transformations of the political field 43
      Habsburg and Ottoman Empires 43
      Kingdom of Serbs, Croats, and Slovenes/Kingdom of Yugoslavia 46
    Transformations of the economic field 48
    Transformations of the cultural field 51
      States' evolving relationships with the media 52
        Habsburg and Ottoman Empires 52
        Kingdom of SHS/Yugoslavia 54
      Development of media markets 56
        Differences in the spread of printing 56
        Newspapers and the political public sphere 59
          Habsburg and Ottoman Empires 59
          Kingdom of SHS/Yugoslavia 62
        Radio 66
      Political parallelism 67
        Habsburg and Ottoman Empires 67
        Kingdom of SHS/Yugoslavia 70
      Journalistic professionalism and autonomy 71
      Globalization and communication flows 72
    Conclusion 73

4   **Media systems in socialist modernity**   76
    Transformations of the political and economic fields 78
      The idea of socialism 79
      Economic transformations: real existing socialism versus self-management socialism 82
      Transformations of the state and the political field 84
      Pluralism, polarization, and cleavages of the political field 86
    Transformations of the cultural field 88
      Socialist values and modernization 89
      The role of the state: making the socialist media 92
        The administrative period: 1945–1952 93
        Self-management of the socialist media market: 1950s and 1960s 95
        The mature period of decadent socialism: 1970s and 1980s 98

Journalistic professionalism and autonomy 99
Political parallelism in a one-party system 102
  The socialist public sphere 103
Self-management of the media market in a socialist society 111
  The press: profit, advertising, and audiences 111
  Developing television in self-management socialism 114
Media culture and global communication flows 122
Conclusion 125

5 **Toward democracy: Post-socialist media systems in digital modernity**   132
Transformations of the political field 134
  First transition: exiting socialism 136
  War and the collapse of Yugoslavia 137
  State building and institutions 139
  What divides the polities? 140
  Consolidation of democracy or hybrid regimes 145
Economic transformation: (re)turn to market economy 147
Transformations of the cultural field 149
  The role of the state: creating democratic media systems 151
    Post-socialist makeovers 152
    Freedom of expression and its restrictions 158
    Regulatory system for broadcasting 161
    Media pluralism policy 162
    Digital media policy 164
    Governance of public service media 166
  Political parallelism 168
  Media market after self-management socialism 173
    Media audiences, advertising, and digital media 174
  Journalistic autonomy 177
  Media culture and global communication flows 183
Conclusion 188

6 **Why the media systems are the way they are**   194
Calibrating the conditions within media systems across three temporal frameworks: the design of the fsQCA 195
Space-time transformations of media systems and the concepts that describe them 200

    The political field 201
    The socio-economic field 206
    The cultural and symbolic field 208
        The state and the media 209
        Political parallelism 212
        Media market 214
        Journalistic autonomy and professionalism 218
        Globalized media culture 220
    Causal configurations and paths of media systems transformations in Southeast Europe 224
    Modernization path of developing media systems 226
    Media systems during socialism 229
    Media systems in digital modernity 232
        Necessary conditions and different paths to the development of the media market 232
            Sufficient media system conditions for media market development 233
            Sufficient structural and macro conditions for media market development 233
        Necessary conditions and different paths to media freedom 235
            Sufficient media system conditions for media freedom 235
            Sufficient macro and structural conditions in the path to media freedom 236
    The longue durée in media freedom and media market development 237
    The missing pieces and directions for future research 242

Methodological Appendix   245
References   263
Index   291

Figures

4.1	Main types of programs on republic TV channels (1979) (% of daily minutes, one-week composite sample)	116
5.1	Audience use of different media platforms (%) (2018)	176
5.2	Maximum potential reach for different media platforms (2018)	176
5.3	Media market inclusiveness toward education and gender segments (2018)	177
5.4	Distribution of information, fiction, and entertainment programming on commercial and PSB TV in 2016 (% daily minutes, one-week consecutive sample)	185
6.1	Media system conditions in the digital modernity temporal framework	237

Tables

1.1	Three empirical models of media systems in Western, Central, and Eastern Europe	6
3.1	Newspapers and journalists (19th & early 20th century)	64
3.2	Parties and their newspapers (19th & early 20th century)	68
4.1	Society, politics, and culture: the SFRY and its republics	77
4.2	Media legislation timeline (SFRY federal level)	96
4.3	Media in SFR Yugoslavia	104
4.4	Young workers as audiences for the printed press (regular use, personal or family)	113
4.5	Genre distributions on republican TV stations (1979) (% of daily minutes, one-week composite sample)	118
4.6	Origins of prime-time TV (1979) (% of daily minutes, one-week composite sample)	119
4.7	A day in the life of socialist TV broadcasting (1979)	120
4.8	Young workers as audiences for television	122
5.1	Comparative overview of SEE social, economic, political, and cultural/media statistical indicators	141
5.2	Comparative SEE media policy and regulation	154
5.3	Main media outlets in Southeast Europe	178
5.4	Genre distribution on commercial and PSB TV channels 2016 (% of daily minutes, one-week consecutive sample)	184
5.5	Origins of broadcasts on commercial and PSB TV in 2016 (% daily minutes, one-week consecutive sample)	187
6.1	Fuzzy set calibrated values	222
6.2	Sufficient conditions for a developed print market in modernization	227
6.3	Sufficient conditions for a highly developed journalism profession in modernization	228
6.4	Sufficient conditions for a developed media market in the era of socialism	230
6.5	Sufficient conditions for a developed journalism profession in socialism	231

6.6	Sufficient conditions for political parallelism in socialism	231
6.7	Sufficient media system conditions for a developed media market in digital modernity	233
6.8	Sufficient conditions for a developed media market in digital modernity – structural and agency conditions	234
6.9	Sufficient media system characteristics for media freedom in digital modernity	235
6.10	Sufficient conditions for media freedom in digital modernity – structural and agency conditions	236
6.11	Sufficient conditions for media freedom in digital modernity – contextual, socio-economic, and political system conditions	238
6.12	Sufficient conditions for media freedom in digital modernity – remote contextual and media systems conditions	240
6.13	Sufficient remote and media system conditions explaining the media market in digital modernity	240

Foreword

The publication of *Comparing Media Systems. Three Models of Media and Politics* raised a large interest among scholars in Eastern Europe. As authors of the book, we were asked a frequent question: which of your models applies to my country? This question was asked in many other parts of the world as well, but we were sincerely struck by the frequency of this question in Eastern Europe. The reasons for this frequency may be various, but there is no doubt that the ambiguous perception of being part of Europe, sharing therefore a close culture and a close historical evolution with the other countries of the same continent but at the same time passing through a very diverse experience linked to the Communist regime, motivated the interest of scholars in Eastern Europe. This interest raised suddenly when the separation between the two "Europes" (East and West) collapsed, scientific and academic circulation rapidly developed, and curiosity and the search for new subjects and innovative methods finally had open space in Eastern Europe: the possibility to compare and to understand the own country in relation to others, coming from different experiences, became a welcome reality.

There is no doubt, indeed, that the Communist period left a strong and well-established legacy: the book by Peruško, Vozab, and Čuvalo insists on this. The interplay between path dependence that, at least in part, marks the persistence of some Communist legacy, and critical junctures, such as the fall of the Berlin Wall, constitute a major plot of their book; moving from the existing literature in this regard, it offers empirical evidences on how and when path dependence meets critical junctures.

This book helps to answer the question that was asked frequently when our book came out as it secures an important initial point: if one intends to compare Western Europe with "the other Europe," that is that part of the continent that for more than 50 years passed through the Communist experience, it is necessary to speak of "other Europes" and not just of one single "other Europe." For example, looking essentially at Western Europe we suggested the existence of three models of professional journalism, in the same way Eastern Europe is featured by important differences of economic, historical, and political character that surely affect the relationship between media and politics. Southeast Europe itself, which is the subject of this book, includes countries marked by important and dramatic specificities that do not allow one to speak of one single geographical area. This book by Peruško and colleagues is about these differences.

More in particular, the authors of this volume underline an important point that, in some way, we underestimated in *Comparing Media Systems*. This is the question of historical periodization: in our book we treated historical evolution more largely, and in some way more superficially, without distinguishing different periods. The way in which the authors of this book treat this issue, beyond the complex theoretical framework they refer to, is stimulating and allows to place the study of professional journalism and its relationship to politics in a more complete interpretative framework. The periodization question becomes even more crucial if one considers the very particular and often dramatic changes that marked the more recent historical evolution of the countries of Eastern Europe after the fall of the Berlin Wall and that undoubtedly represents a major difference with Western Europe. It would be very interesting to check if, and which, different periodizations could be applied to each country, or at least to different geographical areas of Eastern Europe.

Nevertheless, the quest for periodization may involve a risk: it may privilege micro studies that, being very strictly focused on single aspects or periods, often do not allow comparisons among different realities undermining the possibility too of more general pictures able to offer a comprehensive understanding of the main important characterizations affecting the structure and the usual procedures of the news media.

Beyond the main question on which model does apply to East Europe, this book by Peruško and colleagues rightly reiterates another question that has been the focus of many discussions about *Comparing Media Systems*: is it possible to use the same dimensions proposed in our book to observe realities that are different from the ones considered in the original book? I am very interested in this question first because, such as we wrote many times, the main aim of our book was that of compiling a list of dimensions able to help and to address comparative studies rather than designing possible professional models of journalism. Unfortunately, this latter reading of our book prevailed over the former. The present book rightly starts with what was our originally suggested question: what are the dimensions to observe in a study on the relationship between media and politics in East Europe, and in Southeast Europe in particular?

I am not afraid to say that the similar paths that Western and Eastern European countries, with the possible exception of Russia, passed through long periods of their history suggest that analytical dimensions may be very similar. Some others have to be added: in particular, the question of ethnicity and religious affiliation represents in many parts of Eastern Europe an important feature that directs the contents and the structure of media systems. Such as we spoke of political parallelism, media systems may divide among the lines of ethnical and religious affiliation. As is well known, this is an important differentiating feature as to several countries in Southeast Europe.

The legacy of the Communist experience, even if with important differences among the countries, as already said, suggests placing particular attention to the theme of formality/informality too. This is a theme strictly linked to the everyday life and culture during the Communist period: indeed, in face of a tendency toward "hyper-formalism" in terms of norms and legislations, everyday life was featured by an attempt to solve informally a vast range of social occasions and behaviors and this applies to the field of news media as well. This produces consequences that may be defined as positive for civil life but negative as well, as informality has often facilitated unethical behaviors in the field of journalism such as in many other social environments.

The present book refers several times to the issue of hybridization that is the attempt to talk of media systems in Eastern Europe, and in Southeast Europe as well, as hybrid systems that mix together characterizations that, as from *Comparing Media Systems*, could be observed in each of the three models that the book describes. In several of the works that try to apply to Eastern Europe the schema proposed in our book, hybridization is referred in particular to the mixture of commercialization featuring the liberal model of journalism and the instrumentalization that is typical of the polarized-pluralist model. On one side, this is a correct description of the situation in several of the countries in Eastern Europe, but at the same time this risks being a sort of residual category in which to place subjects that scholars are not able to define more precisely and to name after major characterizing features.

Peruško and colleagues support their discussion of the media systems in Southeast Europe with a rich and often complex interpretative apparatus deriving both from media studies and political science. Undoubtedly this mixture represents a major enrichment of their attempt that opens the doors to other possible applications, avoiding the frequent self-reference that often characterizes media studies.

Paolo Mancini

Preface

The idea for this book began to germinate in 2011 following the launch of UNESCO's (the United Nations Educational, Scientific and Cultural Organization) regional project on media development indicators, which was designed to compare three countries in Southeast Europe. The project represented the continuation of an earlier study of Croatia (Peruško 2011; Peruško et al. 2011), which was conducted at the newly established Centre for Media and Communication Research at the Faculty of Political Science, University of Zagreb. We are grateful for this early support from Wijayanandae Jayaweera, Saorla McCabe, and Guy Berger of UNESCO (Paris) and from the Croatian Commission for UNESCO. Thanks are also due to the Faculty of Political Science, University of Zagreb, for the research leave provided to Zrinjka Peruško, as well as to the University of Zagreb for the series of small grants that supported the research for this project. We are grateful to Paolo Mancini for his encouragement and generous support to this book project.

Some of the arguments developed in this book have previously been published elsewhere. We are grateful to the relevant publishers for granting permission to reprint certain parts of the following publications:

Parts of Chapters 1 and 2 have previously appeared in Peruško, Z. (2016) Historical institutionalist approach in comparative media systems research: The case of post Yugoslavia. *Javnost – The Public*. 23 (3), 255–272; and Peruško, Z. and Čuvalo, A. (2014) Comparing socialist and post-socialist television culture: Fifty years of television in Croatia, View. *Journal of European Television, History & Culture*. 3 (5), 131–150. Parts of Chapter 5 have been published in Peruško, Z. (2014) Great expectations: On experiences with media reform in post-socialist Europe (and some unexpected outcomes). *Central European Journal of Communication*. 7 (2), 241–252; and in Peruško, Z. (2013) Media pluralism policy in a post-socialist Mediterranean media system: The case of Croatia. *Central European Journal of Communication*. 6 (2), 204–218.

We benefited from the feedback offered by colleagues at different conferences and workshops where we presented our ideas as they were developing, including the European Communication Research and Education

Association (ECREA) 2012 conference in Istanbul; the Comparing Media Reforms Trans-Regional Conference at the Peace Institute, Ljubljana, in 2012; the Conference on Media and Democracy: Central and Eastern Europe in a Comparative Context at the University of Oxford in 2013; the Central and Eastern European Communication and Media (CEECOM) 2012 conference in Kaunas and 2014 conference in Warsaw; the Panel: 25 Years of Media Freedom and Democracy in Central and East Europe at the International Communication Association (ICA) conference in Seattle in 2014; the ECREA 2018 Panel on Communication and Social Change in Lugano, and the Censorship in Central and Eastern Europe and Russia: Comparative historical perspectives workshop at the University of Copenhagen in 2019. The developing ideas were also discussed in the context of the yearly meetings of the Spring School on Comparative Media Systems held at the Interuniversity Center in Dubrovnik. We are grateful for all the feedback provided by our colleagues and by the participating students.

We would also like to thank the students who attended Zrinjka Peruško's 2015/16 Media and Popular Culture course for comparatively trying out our television genre coding matrix as well as the students from the University of Zagreb who performed a similar task later on in relation to the newspaper article content analysis. The final coding, the results of which are included in this book, was performed by the authors and Ana-Maria Kezerić, Eduard Petranović, and Marija Rihtarić, who has our thanks for coding the Macedonian-language newspapers. We would also like to thank Monika Valečić for assisting in building a list of sources and documents early on in the research process.

We wish to acknowledge with gratitude those colleagues, experts, and informants from different fields of media production, policy, and academia who generously shared their insights with us: in Bosnia and Herzegovina, Mirna Buljugić and Borka Rudić; in Croatia, Paško Bilić and Hrvoje Zovko; in North Macedonia, Besim Nebiu and Snežana Trpevska; in Montenegro, Marijana Camović and Vladan Mićunović; in Serbia, Dragan Janjić, Snežana Milivojević, Saša Mirković, Antonela Riha, and Aleksandar Todorović; and in Slovenia, Boris Bergant, Igor Vobič, and Brankica Petković.

We are also grateful to the colleagues who took the time to read and comment on earlier drafts of individual chapters – Andrea Feldman, Tihomir Cipek, Halliki Haro Loit, Dejan Jović, Miklós Sükösd, and Mikhail Suslov. Special thanks are owed to Gvozden Flego who provided insightful comments and who is always the first reader of Zrinjka's work. Any remaining mistakes are, of course, on us. The historical ground covered in this book is quite large. While we employed every effort to include national literature on specific topics in addition to internationally published sources, we are certain to have missed important works and insights. We hope that colleagues with specific expertise in particular areas, or temporal frameworks, will wish to apply our approach to build a more complete and detailed picture of media system development in Southeast Europe.

The South Slavic national appellations used in this book follow the standard and examples set out by Banac (1984/1991, pp. 17–18). The adjectives "Slovene," "Croat," and "Serb" refer to people (i.e., Slovene audiences, Serb student, Croat politician), while the adjectives "Slovenian," "Croatian," "Serbian," "Macedonian," "Bosnian," and "Montenegrin" refer to lands or language and other things with a long history (Croatian Sabor, Serbian history, Slovenian language) as well as to institutions and things within the relevant countries, such as Macedonian media, Montenegrin press, and Bosnian and Herzegovinian journalism. All the acronyms are provided in their original languages, for example, SKJ for the League of Communists of Yugoslavia (Savez komunista Jugoslavije). The only exception is the acronym SFRY (i.e., the Socialist Federal Republic of Yugoslavia, rather than the original SFRJ), which is widely accepted in the English-language literature. All the acronyms from the Cyrillic script (i.e., from Macedonian or Serbian) are given in the Latin alphabet.

Zrinjka Peruško, Zagreb, March 2020

1 Introduction

Today, hardly anyone remembers the song *Rock Me*, which was performed by the Croatian group Riva and which won the Eurovision Song Contest for Yugoslavia in 1989. That year is far better known for the fall of the Berlin Wall – a clear signal that socialism had collapsed in Central and Eastern Europe. The following year (and one day after the Eurovision Song Contest was held in Zagreb in May 1990), the final round of the first post-socialist multi-party parliamentary election was held in Croatia, which at that time was still part of Yugoslavia. Despite many Central and Eastern European (CEE) countries having held their first democratic elections in the same year, Europe was still divided in terms of the Eurovision Song Contest. The only socialist country to participate in that year's contest was Yugoslavia, which had been a member of the European Broadcasting Union (EBU) since 1961. Unlike audiences in Poland, Czechoslovakia, or other Eastern European countries that were members of the Soviet controlled Warsaw Pact, audiences in socialist yet non-aligned Yugoslavia had for several decades shared in the experience of the network of associations and practices of simultaneity, sharing, and belonging represented by the Eurovision's logo and theme tune (including what is often referred to as the greatest-ever Eurovision song: ABBA's performance of *Waterloo* during the 1974 contest).

During the 30 years that have now passed since Yugoslavia's Eurovision victory, many changes have taken place, including the fact that the country itself has withered away (Jović 2009), shifting from being the most developed, liberal, and progressive state in socialist Eastern Europe to the most troubled area of the Western Balkans. The winner of the 1990 Eurovision Song Contest was Toto Cutugno with *Insieme: 1992* (*Together: 1992*), a tribute to the then upcoming European unification, but somehow also a harbinger of the wider enlargement of the European Union (EU) that was to follow both the milder and the more violent processes of democratization and nation building that took place in the post-socialist part of Europe.

What happened to the media in those countries? The transformations of the media following the fall of socialism involved changes in the institutions – in the rules and values but also in the practices of media professionals (including journalists) and in the media-related practices of audiences.

While early research in this area focused on the common aspects of post-socialist transitions and transformations (Splichal 1994; Sparks 1998), later the focus shifted to the need to understand the diversity within the groups of post-socialist media systems. Why are the media systems in Central and Eastern Europe different from those in Western Europe? After 30 years of post-socialist media research, we are still unsure how to answer this question. Several flawed generalizations have contributed to this state of affairs: an overgeneralization of the socialist past, a narrow focus on media reforms during the post-socialist period, and a disregard for the importance of the formative period of modernization in relation to media development. This disregard for the long-term historical influences, or the *tabula rasa* hypothesis (Kitcshelt 1995), is responsible for many misunderstandings regarding media system and media policy development in the post-1989 CEE countries.

This book is motivated by the theoretical problem of how to explain the divergent media system trajectories observed in the new democracies of post-socialist Europe, with a focus on the least well known of them, namely the countries in Southeast Europe. The book aims to determine why the freedom of expression, independence, and autonomy of the media in countries in that region are consistently rated lower than in Central European countries, despite several decades having passed since the beginning of the post-communist democratic transition. How do these post-communist media systems compare to the media systems in Western democracies? Can sufficient commonalities be found that they could be included in the same typology? Or are these media systems so marked by their communist antecedents that they merit classification as a special type of "post-communist media system"?

From the first decade of the post-socialist transformations onwards, the media systems of CEE countries were analyzed in comparative terms to demonstrate (largely to Western audiences) how the media and their political context in Eastern Europe differed from those in the West, thereby implicitly continuing the normative classification of the Cold War era (Siebert et al. 1956). In an effort to identify commonalities in the media development trends in the CEE region, especially those that differentiated CEE media from Western media, the significant differences that existed in the institutional conditions and media manifestations between the countries were overlooked. This search for commonalities was often normatively framed in relation to the expected outcomes of media reform as a form of media democratization, and it focused on the gap between the empirical state of affairs in CEE countries and the desired outcome of democratic media and political communication/media system reform (cf. Peruško 2014). While normative approaches regarding media and democracy also predominated in much of the Western political communication research (Pfetsch and Esser 2012, pp. 26–28), having provided important insights into the gradual democratization of the CEE post-socialist media landscapes (Splichal 1994; Paletz et al. 1995; Paletz and Jakubowicz 2003; Sparks 1998; Petković

2004; Sükösd and Bajomi-Lázár 2003; Jakubowicz and Sükösd 2008; Czepek et al. 2009), such approaches do not clarify the processes and conditions that shape or produce specific media system characteristics.

The majority of studies concerning the media systems of CEE countries are either country studies, country-by-country monograph-style comparisons, or focused on specific issues. The predominant preoccupation with journalism, media and politics or media policy issues has been expanded to focus on culture, nation, and transnational trends (e.g., Downey and Mihelj 2012; Mihelj and Huxtable 2018). Prior comparative empirical research on media systems and/or their dimensions within CEE countries shares the trend of comparative research in the field of communication and media studies more generally (Esser and Hanitzsch 2012), with descriptive studies or monographic comparisons preceding theoretically shaped empirical analyses. Examples of country-by-country studies focusing on the macro level of media systems in cross-European research include the first EUROMEDIA studies conducted during the 1980s (Humphreys 2012, p. 160), while the CEE countries also appear in subsequent broader compendiums, such as the work by Terzis (2007) and the Open Society Institute's (2005, 2012) "Television Across Europe" and "Mapping Digital Media" projects. These provide interesting baseline comparative data, although they lack a theoretical framework. An interesting and useful comparative project is Popescu et al.'s (2011) "Media Systems in Europe" project, an expert survey conducted in 34 countries, although it shares the challenges (and advantages) of other data sets based on expert opinion, including the Freedom House Freedom of Expression Index and the Reporters Without Borders Index on Press Freedom (Maestas 2018).[1]

Hallin and Mancini's (2004) theory of three media systems in Western Europe and North America has provided a theoretical framework for comparative media system research in a disciplinary climate characterized by a growing interest in all kinds of comparative research in the field of communication and media studies (Esser and Hanitzsch 2012). Despite the many valid critiques of their model (Norris 2009; Hardy 2012; Humphreys 2012), as well as their own doubts regarding the usefulness of their theory with regard to non-Western systems (Hallin and Mancini 2004, 2012), for research into CEE media systems the original model also functioned as a useful empirical benchmark for broader theoretically informed comparisons (thereby replacing the earlier, normatively framed studies).

Three approaches to comparing the media systems of CEE countries

With regard to comparing the media systems of CEE countries, it is possible to identify three distinct approaches. The predominant approach involves their classification into a fourth type of "post-socialist," "transition," "mixed," or "hybrid" media system (Terzis 2007; Jakubowicz 2007, 2008;

Curran and Park 2000; Puppis et al. 2009; Elvestad and Blekesaune 2008; Voltmer 2008; Aalberg et al. 2013; Nimrod et al. 2015). This fourth "type" has never been empirically described, neither by Hallin and Mancini (2004) nor by any of the cited studies.

The second group of empirical studies, which were predominantly conducted by CEE scholars from Lithuania (Balčytiene 2009), Poland (Dobek-Ostrowska 2012), and Croatia (Peruško 2012, 2013a), highlight the differences in the cultural traditions and contexts of the investigated countries, in addition to identifying certain common trends. The initial expectation that the new CEE democracies would all fit into the Mediterranean polarized pluralist model due to them being the most polarized politically and having the lowest levels of professionalization of journalism was only partially supported, as Poland was already showing conflicting trends. An important exception in relation to the early studies is de Smaele's (1999) study of the Russian media system, in which she recognizes the cultural, political, and historical differences between Central European, Southeast European, and Eastern European countries and notes that differences should also be expected in their media systems.

An intermediate approach between a multi-country quantitative analysis and country studies involves comparative aggregate data, albeit in an interpretative fashion. This approach is exemplified by the work of Dobek-Ostrowska (2015), who proposes four types of media systems in the post-communist part of Europe – the hybrid liberal model, the politicized media model, the media-in-transition model, and the authoritarian model. The investigated countries were allocated to specific groups based on the interpretation of the country rankings within international indexes describing four dimensions – democracy, freedom of the press, gross domestic product (GDP) per capita, and Internet penetration with the most weight given to the character of the political system.

The third approach includes a handful of multi-country comparative studies that use aggregate data and statistical modeling (i.e., hierarchical cluster analysis, multidimensional scaling, multiple regression). To date, only two studies have investigated the media systems in CEE countries, namely the work by Peruško et al. (2013, expanded in Peruško 2016), who analyzed both Western and CEE countries, and that by Castro Herrero et al. (2017), who only studied CEE countries. All these studies primarily rely on the media systems survey data gathered by Popescu et al. (2011) in addition to aggregate data obtained from the European Audiovisual Observatory, World Press Trends data, and so forth. The studies operationalize the theoretical model proposed by Hallin and Mancini (2004) for quantitative analyses based on media systems, their dimensions, and their relationships. The four examined dimensions – the professionalization of journalism, political parallelism, media market development, and the role of the state – are intended to provide an account of a mass media system that pivots on the journalism-politics relationship. The fifth dimension (i.e., the political system) was not included in either of these studies.

The media systems of CEE countries cluster with those of Western European countries

The CEE media systems appear in two of the three empirical clusters/models obtained by means of hierarchical cluster analysis in the work by Peruško et al. (2013) and by Peruško (2016). The three empirical media system models resemble to some extent Hallin and Mancini's (2004) three models and the associated characteristics. The Mediterranean model derived from Hallin and Mancini's typology resembles the South/East European model proposed by Peruško et al. (2013) in terms of three media system dimensions: the media market (newspaper circulation is lower than average in the analyzed group of countries), higher political parallelism, and lower professionalization of journalism. The group also exhibits a lower to medium quality of public service television, which was the indicator used to show the role of the state. The democratic corporatist model derived from Hallin and Mancini's typology is similar to the empirical Nordic model proposed by Peruško et al. (2013), except in relation to political parallelism, which is found to be low in the empirical model (also found by Brüggemann et al. 2014), as opposed to the high political parallelism envisaged by Hallin and Mancini (2004). Low political parallelism was a characteristic of the liberal model included in Hallin and Mancini's typology. This finding might indicate developments in this dimension that were actually envisaged by Hallin and Mancini (2004) with regard to their expectation of convergence to the liberal model. The third empirical European mainstream model is differentiated by the moderate values of both political parallelism and journalistic professionalism. It includes countries from all three models featured in Hallin and Mancini's typology (Table 1.1). This cluster also includes several CEE countries.

When the analysis is extended to also include non-EU CEE countries for which data were available in the study by Popescu et al. (2011), we find that Macedonia, Serbia, Lithuania, and Russia all cluster in the South/East European model (Peruško 2016). While the clustering of Croatia, Lithuania, Hungary, Romania, and Bulgaria might be accepted from a theoretical point of view (all the data pertain to 2010, when the media systems survey was conducted [Popescu et al. 2011]), the inclusion of Serbia and Macedonia in the model is more problematic. The fact that among the six Southeast European countries, Slovenia clusters in the European mainstream model while Croatia, Serbia, and Macedonia cluster in the South/East model also requires further explanation. Additionally, the fact that Russia, as an authoritarian regime, clusters in the same group as Italy and Spain alerts us to the need to consider the regime type when employing media system classifications, as was originally done by Hallin and Mancini (2004). Clearly, the media

Table 1.1 Three empirical models of media systems in Western, Central, and Eastern Europe

	The South/East European model	*The European mainstream model*	*The Nordic model*
Countries	Greece, Spain, Lithuania, Croatia, Hungary, Italy, Romania, Bulgaria, Serbia, Macedonia, Russia	Austria, Poland, Belgium, Estonia, Czech Republic, Germany, France, Slovenia, Ireland, UK, Portugal, Slovakia	Finland, Sweden, Denmark, the Netherlands
Role of the state	Lower to medium quality of public television	*Public television quality is not a distinguishing factor*	Higher quality of public television
Media market	Lower newspaper circulation	*Public television quality is not a distinguishing factor*	Higher newspaper circulation
Political parallelism	Higher party influence	Moderate party influence	Lower party influence
Economic parallelism	Higher owner influence	Moderate owner influence	Lower owner influence
Professionalization of journalism	Lower professionalism and independence	Moderate professionalism and independence	Higher professionalism and independence

Source: Peruško (2016).

system characteristics alone, without the incorporation of the political system, only go so far in terms of differentiating media systems that lie at the edge of, or out of, the zone of democracy. The theoretical model proposed by Hallin and Mancini (2004), as operationalized by Peruško et al. (2013), does not sufficiently distinguish media systems in democracies from those in authoritarian regimes.

The study by Castro Herrero et al. (2017) adapted Brüggemann et al.'s (2014) operationalization of Hallin and Mancini (2004), as applied to Western European countries, and explored 11 CEE countries, members of the EU. They found that the media systems in CEE countries cluster into three distinct groups based on four key dimensions: political parallelism, public broadcasting, foreign ownership, and press freedom. The latter two dimensions, which were not used in the earlier study, were found to be particularly important in relation to differentiating the post-communist media systems. The grouping of the countries into three media systems (eastern, central, and northern) also supports the findings of earlier studies, which showed differences between the post-communist media systems.

While the present state-of-the-art theory of media systems provides a starting point for determining patterns of similarities or differences between contemporary Eastern and Western European media systems, it does not go far enough in terms of explaining the distinctions between the post-socialist media systems. Recent approaches to this issue include a shift from the idea of the media system to the media culture as the focus of research and comparison (Mihelj and Huxtable 2018), an approach that we find to be limiting because the media culture is just one part of a given media system (we will discuss this further in the subsequent chapter). We argue that there exists a need to develop a new approach for the analysis of post-socialist media systems that takes into account also the long-term institutional conditions that influence the processes of convergence or divergence in the media in post-socialist Europe.

The impact of socialism on media systems

The original classification of CEE media systems into a "post-socialist" category highlights an important related issue: What impact has socialism had on the media systems of the third-wave European democracies? Is there a common "post-socialist" media system model in Central and Eastern Europe, possibly some remnant of the Soviet media model proposed by Siebert et al. (1956)? Was there ever actually a common Soviet media system in Central and Eastern Europe with structural characteristics, practices, and/or a media culture that would be resistant to regime change? Was there a unique socialist political regime model, that is, was socialism the same in Czechoslovakia, Albania, and Yugoslavia?

The studies cited earlier show that post-socialist CEE media systems do not have identical characteristics but vary along several dimensions. This book aims to show why. The first reason for the original mistaken generalization concerns the "equalizing" of all socialist/communist conditions across the region in countries that made up the "communist oligarchy" (Voltmer 2008). An insufficient understanding of the relationship between contemporary CEE media systems and their historical origins in modernization also contributes to this. The historical characteristics of the political and social systems of the post-communist European countries, including the vitally important dimension of modernity, must be included in the study of postsocialist media systems in the European context. To base the analysis of these media systems solely on the period following the start of the transition is thus insufficient, as Ekiert and Ziblatt (2013) show in relation to the implementation of democracy in the CEE countries.

If the thesis concerning the common socialist experience critically influencing the future character of a media system more than its prior or subsequent developments is to be comparatively tested, we should look for countries that were parts of one state during socialism and then were separate states in the aftermath of socialism. In the most similar case design (Lijphart 1971), used also by Hallin and Mancini (2004), the post-Yugoslavian states of Southeast Europe provided an appealing testing ground.[2] They also form a logical set in terms of set theory as members in the same socialist state (Ragin 2000). The theoretical choice of this group of countries is reinforced by the distinctive position of Yugoslavia in relation to European socialism. As these countries have not shared the same pre-communist histories and have different post-communist trajectories, we can also investigate the variation on the influences of the long-term contextual conditions following different key historical junctures.

Yugoslavia was internally diverse and disproportionately developed. This included a split between the identity of Central Europe, as based on the "Habsburg factor" (Rizman 2001, in Jakubowicz 2004, p. 69), and the Balkan-Southeast-European identity, as based on the Ottoman legacy rejected by Slovenia and Croatia, who favored their Central European or Mediterranean identities over the imposed essentializing label (Todorova 2004, 2009) of a non-existent peninsula (Luketić 2013). In our study, we focus on the six countries in Central and Southeast Europe that used to be federal republics within the SFRY. They shared a common socialist federal state (although possibly not the same socialist experience) but they have followed different post-socialist paths. Of the six countries, Slovenia and Croatia are both members of the EU (since 2004 and 2013, respectively); Montenegro, Serbia, and Macedonia are candidate countries (since 2012 and 2014, respectively); and Bosnia and Herzegovina is a potential candidate. Kosovo, as the seventh successor state, is not included in the systematic comparison because it was not a republic within the SFRY but rather an autonomous province within Serbia, and the available comparative data were not sufficient for all the investigated temporal frameworks.

The aim of this book is not to attempt to fit the countries of this region into any of the particular types of media systems but rather to build on a familiar theoretical framework in order to develop an understanding of the changes that have taken place in post-socialist media systems as well as the dynamics that shape them in the digital media environment. Stepping away from the usual democratization reform approach, the five-dimensional theoretical framework proposed by Hallin and Mancini (2004) – the political history and context, media market development, the media and the state, political parallelism, and journalistic professionalism – is expanded with a set-theoretical research approach and historical institutionalism as a theoretical framework so as to explain the convergence and divergence of media systems in three key temporal frames.

The comparative method is clearly indicated, in this case with the explanatory design (Blumler 2012, p. xii). In our investigation, we combine a qualitative case study analysis with comparative quantitative indicators and the fuzzy set qualitative comparative analysis (fsQCA) approach (Ragin 1987,

2000; Downey and Stanyer 2010; Schneider and Wagemann 2012) to further investigate the relative importance of the conditions and influences on media systems in Southeast Europe. Our theoretical and methodological approaches start from the set-theoretical premises, that is, that the similar outcomes in the types of media systems can be reached by multiple and different paths, and that the outcomes are always caused by a combination of multiple conditions.

The focus of our book is thus broader than that of the prior research, not only in terms of the country focus. We analyze the media in the context of the wider social and political settings in which explanations for the outcomes are sought. The second broadening of scope relates to the historical perspective that forms the critical part of the new theoretical framework advanced in this book, that is, the contention that present-day media systems were shaped by the paths followed at three critical historical junctures.

We intend to show that the unsatisfactory state of the media in some of the countries under study is not the result of some historical "curse" but rather the outcome of decisions and policies, as well as the institutional context and conditions in which they occurred, both at the time and after each critical juncture. The cause, as well as the solution, we will argue, is not predominantly cultural but instead social, both in the structures and institutions and in the practice and implementation.

Plan of the book

Chapter 2 presents the theoretical and research approach employed in this book, structured around a new interpretative model for the analysis of post-socialist media systems in third-wave European democracies. We start with the notion, simple in hindsight, that in order to explain the contemporary institutional formations and the related practices of media systems in new democracies, the investigation should be extended to include the periods before the introduction of political pluralism. The socialist and pre-socialist institutional legacy thus influences contemporary media systems in Central and Eastern Europe. The model distinguishes between three distinctive historical periods associated with the development of media systems, the consequences of three critical junctures – modernization and the democratic revolutions from the 19th century until the end of World War II, the post-1945 socialist period, and the post-socialist period following 1989 (Peruško 2016). A multidisciplinary approach combining communication theory with political science, history, and sociology is necessary in order to grasp the relationships within media system construction and to benefit from theoretical and empirical knowledge relating to the post-communist/post-socialist environment and social change.

The institutional structures that frame the societies under analysis are the conditions that interact with the opportunity to change at the critical junctures affecting the media field. This non-media-centric (Morley 2009) position prevails in our analysis, which is of necessity anchored in different social science disciplines – sociology, political science, and communication and media studies. In this broad analysis of the macro- and meso-level circumstances, a complementary analysis relates to the media that were prominent during the respective historical periods. Media innovation itself can also be viewed as a kind of critical juncture that provides both the opportunity and the impetus for societal change.

Three key problems for comparing post-socialist media systems are identified, namely the problem of studying changes in media systems, the problem of the periodization of media and social change, and the problem of comparing. Historical institutionalism (HI) is identified as a primary approach for studying changes in media systems, as opposed to evolutionary theories. The question of culture as a form of path dependency and its role in continuity (as opposed to change) is tackled here. The question of the periodization of media and social change is discussed in relation to the critical junctures that mark the points of social rupture and precipitate regime changes, but also in terms of communication revolutions as a different kind of juncture. The problem of transposing known media system dimensions back and forth in time and space in the synchronic and the diachronic comparison of media systems is acknowledged, and its solving is defined as one of the theoretical aims of the book.

The research approach is the fuzzy set qualitative comparative analysis (fsQCA), which is in this book based on the qualitative comparative case studies that are necessary to understand the process of change and to explain the calibrations of conditions for comparison as well as for additional theory development in terms of explaining the convergence and divergence of media systems in Southeast Europe.

Chapters 3 through 5 are devoted to comparative studies of the six cases in the three temporal frameworks.

Industrialization and democratic revolutions (Moore 1966) represent the first critical juncture that shaped modernization and the ensuing conditions associated with the development of the mass media. The media's relationship to modernity has long been established, as has the relationship between modernization and democratization. The elements of the institutional structures that developed during that time will have been just as influential in terms of contemporary circumstance in the eastern part of Europe as they were in the western part. Chapter 3 explores the comparative positions of Slovenia, Croatia, Bosnia and Herzegovina, Serbia, Montenegro, and Macedonia in the lead-up to the end of the 19th century and during the first decades of the 20th century, including the interwar years. During this time, Western European modernization in relation to politics and society contributed to, and was spurred on by, the development of the press industry. The main expectation here is that belated modernizations and late press development negatively impacted today's media systems' autonomy and development.

The second critical juncture is World War II, after which a new geopolitical power balance was struck that allowed for the introduction of socialism as the dominant political and economic system in the eastern part of Europe. The second temporal framework starts in 1945 and ends in 1989. One could argue that the mass media in Eastern Europe actually came into existence during this period – television was certainly introduced then, and the press in many countries achieved its mass status for the first time after 1945. Chapter 4 examines the development of the media in the SFRY (1945–1990). The differences and similarities among the federal republics are analyzed, including the differences in the application of self-management socialism and the continuing development/modernization disparities. The focus of the chapter is broader than simply the issue of freedom of expression, and press, television, and other cultural industries are included, as is an examination of global cultural flows.

The third critical juncture changed the path toward democracy following the fall of the Berlin Wall in 1989, and it is considered the historical present, which is usually the only temporal framework seen in media systems comparisons and evaluations concerning Eastern Europe. Chapter 5 is focused on the post-1990 transition and the consolidation of the media systems into their present-day form. This third temporal framework includes the period of post-socialist transition and the introduction and consolidation of democracy (or other type of regime), and both market and individual freedoms. The processes of European integrations, which also had an important impact on the media systems of CEE countries, characterizes this period, too. In Southeast Europe, this is also the period of state independence and state building, which was further characterized in the 1990s by military conflict and authoritarian regressions. The manner in which these were overcome also played a part in media system developments in this part of Europe. The changes to the media environment that occur during this temporal framework mandate a revision of the concept of a media system, a revision that would both address the changed affordances of the new hybrid (Chadwick 2013) media landscapes and also recognize the need to shift the focus of media system analysis away from the media and politics and toward a broader understanding of what media landscapes are all about.

In Chapter 6, fsQCA is employed to explain which combinations of past conditions explain the contemporary shape of those media systems. This final chapter also discusses the findings in terms of the three theoretical challenges posited in Chapter 2. Our approach is intended to counter deterministic views regarding the "curse" of backwardness that disables any progress in the region, and it is explicitly multi-causal in terms of demonstrating the combination of conditions that influence the post-socialist democratization of media systems in relation to their prior histories.

This is a book about contemporary media systems that were shaped by their own contingent paths and changes during different historical epochs. It speaks to both change and continuity in terms of how the media are

12 *Introduction*

perceived and used, as well as to both convergence and divergence in relation to the contexts and conditions of media system development. The concluding chapter reviews how the theoretical framework explained our main substantive question, that is, why some media systems change in one way while others change in another way. Although this book began life as an attempt to show how best to compare post-socialist media systems, a larger theoretical question soon arose. The issue of change, and its opposite, namely continuity, kept coming up, which made our target much more ambitious. The last chapter of the book will review how we succeeded in explaining media system change, but now we want to introduce important issues that need to be tackled if we are to work our way to that ending.

Notes

1 Norris and Inglehart statistically compared the Freedom House Index of Press Freedom and the Press Freedom Index of the Reporters Without Borders and IREX Media Sustainability Index and showed significant statistical similarity of placement for most countries, even though the indicators were different (2009, pp. 143–144).
2 A similar theoretical case for the choice of a comparative subject could be made for Czechia, Slovakia, and the post-Soviet republics; however, the former two countries provide too few comparative subjects for our purpose, and the latter too many (in circumstances of missing prior research literature that could serve as the basis for comparative analysis). Our familiarity with the region and the languages of Southeast Europe was also a deciding factor.

2 Explaining the transformations of post-socialist media systems

Studying post-socialist media systems is associated with three particular problems. First, there is *the problem of studying change* when compared to an established media system. Although media systems are never actually static, they are predominantly treated as such, and the challenge is to reconcile new understandings of the field with the familiar empirical categories of the systems approach. Second, there is *the problem of the periodization of media and social change*. Here, the challenge is initially to identify specific times relevant to media system formation in specific historical and geographical places, and then to determine how to transpose the dimensions/variables necessary to compare media systems to a different historical period – to a past before media systems were formed, to a past with very different characteristics (i.e., socialism) than those seen in the media systems in the West during a comparable time. In addition, it is important to determine how to transpose the analysis of media systems to countries or regions that were not part of Western Europe, the geographic and cultural-historical area toward which all the existing theoretical models and the majority of empirical analyses incline, and where the identified relationships between the elements of the media system might not be present or important. This is, of course, only superficially a spatial problem, as it is actually a problem of, for example, how to conceive of the known idea of a democratic and capitalist media system in a one-party political regime with a socialist economy. This is linked to the third *problem of comparing*. Can the same dimensions and variables that describe and allow us to typify Western European media systems prove useful when studying media systems in those countries in which a significant historical period was spent under a different political and economic regime, or do we need completely new dimensions (and, if so, what are they)? Additionally, the problem of comparing is related to the method that can best rise to the challenge of explaining changes in media systems (post-socialist or otherwise). The significance of the different variables that explain political or social phenomena may be distorted when they are observed outside their original temporal context, as was convincingly argued by Pierson (2004). The focus should thus be extended to also include the temporal context of both the causation and the outcome conditions.

14 *Explaining the transformations*

Further, attention should be paid to the process of social change, not just to its outcome (or expected/desired outcome). This, of course, brings about new methodological challenges.

In this chapter, we first turn to the problem of studying media and social change, before moving on to introduce our proposal for approaching the temporal/longitudinal problem of media system analysis. After that, we discuss the methods and substance of comparison employed in this book. We primarily focus on the theoretical challenges posed by the three aforementioned problems, which we explore in an empirical fashion in the comparative studies of the six country cases in the three temporal frames examined in the following chapters.

The problem of studying media change

In approaching the issue of media change, we have two strands of literature to draw on: (1) media and communication theory, and (2) broader social theory, particularly sociology and political science. While the communication-theory-based approaches to analyzing communication change have only recently started to be systematically studied, meaning that the research concerning change is not plentiful in that regard (Stanyer and Mihelj 2016), in the fields of sociology and political science, social change and regime change are among the key theoretical (and also often empirical) topics.

Change in communication research

When we seek to investigate media or communication change, we must invariably also deal with social change, even if this is not often acknowledged by media researchers (with the notable exception of the mediatization approach; see Lundby [2014] for a comprehensive overview as well as a representative selection of approaches; also see the authors studying communication ages, as discussed later under "The Problem of Periodization"). Communication theory does, however, include a prominent stream of research investigating change, although it does not frame it in those terms. In the media effects research, different types of changes are defined as effects that either take a long time to manifest; are quickly noticeable, clearly visible, and easily noticed; or are unacknowledged by society or individual users (Bryant and Oliver 2009). In the case of media effects, the changing agent is conceived as coming from the media, most commonly the media message, while the effects are changes (or continuities) in actions, beliefs, or values in individuals or, consequently, the public sphere.

In the field of political science, two-thirds of the research focuses on the short-term causes of change and their effects (Pierson 2004). Although to the best of our knowledge no such comprehensive analysis has been performed in relation to communication studies, it is feasible to assume that the result would be similar, especially in terms of the media effects research.

Stanyer and Mihelj (2016) note that only about 1% of articles published in three leading communication journals over a 15-year period reflect temporal issues in their research designs. Research focusing on change over time focuses equally on media production (including media systems) and media text, while changes in audiences are less commonly studied diachronically. Stanyer and Mihelj (2016) further find that communication research involving change often falls short of explaining change, generally lacks temporal sensitivity, and is not clear on the reasons for the periodization of change that, when used, is mostly media-centric. Moreover, studies of media system change frequently employ the trend-mapping approach to communication change, which focuses on identifying the trends associated with a chosen phenomenon as well as how they change over time, while temporal comparisons (focusing on two or more discrete points in time and comparing the object of analysis) and turning points or critical junctures are not represented.

In our study of change in post-socialist media systems, we now turn to social science theories, on which we primarily draw in our effort to explain the mechanisms and substances of changes or continuities in media systems.

Social theories on change

The issue of how exactly social change occurs presents one of the key problems for social theory – a problem that has competing solutions (Weik 2015). Not all change happens at the same pace: some change happens slowly, incrementally, while some change is abrupt, sometimes disruptive, and more easily noticeable. The causes of change/transformation can come from within or without, although most large social transformations (such as revolutions) result from both exogenous and endogenous factors of change.

One set of social science approaches sees social change as occurring gradually in a linear fashion, while the other sees change as only coming about following moments of disruption. The most renowned theory from the first group is the modernization theory, which is arguably the most famous (or, indeed, infamous) evolutionary theory of social change. The second group of more recent sociological theories breaks with the notion of the linear evolutionary development of all societies as well as with functionalism and structuralism. Instead of linear evolution and the orderly progression of the "stages" of social development – traditional society, transitional society, modern society – these theories perceive historical development as being shaped by contingent and concrete historical circumstances, or "time-space edges" (Giddens 1981a, p. 96), where societies of different structural types can coexist. While new notions of social structuration and the role of human agency are gaining ground with new concepts and new understandings of social becoming, some of the "old" conceptions of social change and how best to study it remain relevant.

The prevalent contemporary method of studying social change[1] in diachronic empirical studies is a legacy of what Piotr Sztompka (1993) terms the original sin of sociology – the (artificial) division by Auguste Comte of the study of society into "social statics" and "social dynamics." Statics later became structures, while dynamics became functions. These concepts found full development within systems theory, functionalism, and structural-functionalist theories. Systems theory is a contemporary offshoot of this legacy, and it predominates in the study of change in the social sciences, including the fields of sociology, political science, and communication. Another well-known offshoot of this approach is modernization theory. Social development and social progress are specific types of social processes that are linked to the evolutionary, linear, modernization theory, which is still the dominant theory of social change. Structural and functional differentiation (processes that are well known in modernization and the theory of industrial society) are seen as the main drivers of evolution whereby progression moves from simpler to more complex states, to heterogeneity, and to system stability.

As we will show in the next section of this chapter, our study deals with the morphogenetic processes of social transformation, which result in both qualitative changes and new "social conditions, states of society, [and] social structure" that differ from the social processes of simple reproduction or social persistence (Sztompka 1993, pp. 17–18). The concept of social structure is an abstract one that is not available for empirical observation, meaning that it is notoriously difficult to define – in fact, its meaning changes depending on the applied theoretical approach. Two different levels of social reality intermesh – the level of individuals and the level of totalities made up of abstract social wholes of the supra-individual type. Social wholes, which are interpreted as structures, include societies (and social systems), cultures, civilizations, and socio-economic formations (Sztompka 1993, p. 213).

Social structures can be seen as "patterned relationships beyond the manipulative control of any single individual or group" (Skocpol 1985, p. 87). For Giddens (1984), structure means rules and resources that manifest in social systems as a form of reproduced social practices. Social systems extend in time and space as consequences of social actions, sometimes as the wished-for products of intentional action but sometimes as unexpected consequences. Structures combine the macro level of social systems and the micro level of individuals, as manifested in their actions (Giddens 1984, p. 17). The overcoming of the divide between structure (institutions) and agency (practice) is a staple of contemporary sociological theories, which have in their various renditions been employed to study media-related social change (especially in terms of the mediatization theory/approach; Hjarvard 2014). Roudakova (2012), in her study of the Russian media system, introduces change in terms of a sociological process that manifests in a relationship between the micro and macro aspects of media systems as well as in the relationship between structure and agency (cf. Peruško 2017). A complete sociological explanation of media system transformations should include both a structural analysis and an analysis of actions performed by individual or collective agents.

The issue of social change is necessarily related to the notion of *time*, its passage, and/or its length. Sociologists differentiate between several concepts that explain the various aspects of time-related social dynamics: the *durée* of activity (Schutz, as quoted in Giddens 1981a, p. 93) of everyday happening in society, as well as the *longue durée* of institutional time (Braudel, as quoted in Giddens 1981a, p. 93). For Giddens (1981a), "according to the theorem of the duality of structure, every moment of social interaction implies the *longue durée* of institutional time" (p. 93), which means that the past is always present in our actions, including past structures such as language. Sztompka (1993, p. 227) differentiates between social change as a transformation of one type of society into the next (i.e., involving one step of social change) and the *longue durée*, as the latter kind of social change includes multiple transformations of society or a series of social transformations.

Is it necessary to ask whether all types of changes can be explained by the same theory?

Social change as evolution

The classics of 19th-century sociology introduced the evolutionary theory of social development as modeled on the natural sciences. Even though these, albeit sometimes crude, ideas have since been discredited, some of them show a surprising tenacity. Talcott Parsons's (1971) neo-evolutionary theory of social change remains the standard for modernization as a form of social change. Four mechanisms of evolution – differentiation, adaptive upgrading (i.e., efficiency), inclusion, and value generalization – move a primitive society through two more stages so as to achieve the level of a modern society. This account, which clearly describes the evolution of Western European societies ("that area of Europe that fell heir to the western half of the Roman Empire north of the Mediterranean"; Sztompka 1993, p. 121) has, together with other iterations of modernization theory, been criticized for its Western bias. Despite such criticism, in one version or another, this understanding of social change persists in the majority of comparative accounts to date. Additionally, sociology originally developed (in Europe, not in the United States) to study the processes of modernization of society – industrialization, urbanization, secularization, and technological development, with secular and rational attitudes and differentiated social structures as well as the concurrent passing of traditional society,

Aside from the use of "modern" to identify any kind of progressive social change, modernity and modernization have different academic meanings: modernity is a historical epoch spanning four centuries (16th to 19th/20th), characterized by transformations in the socio-economic, political, and cultural fields in Western Europe, while modernization is a theory of social change applied to the post–World War II development of the third world in an attempt to catch up with the core developed societies (Sztompka 1993,

p. 129). The latter understanding of modernization as the emulation of developed, Western models predominates in the analyses of the transformations of media systems in CEE countries. The version of modernization theory applied to the post-socialist transformations of the 1990s, or to the transformations of the second (socialist) world, is known as convergence theory, with the idea being that the post-socialist states would "converge" with Western role models. The expectation was that the adaptation (as the main mechanism of social change according to the evolutionary theories) to the new conditions would also occur within the media system, following the path already taken by the developed industrial democracies in the West (cf. Jakubowicz [2004] on mimetic media policy transformation). The "transition" stage of social change, as the stage between premodern and modern society, thus became the key label.

As Sztompka (1993) argues, the neo-modernization theory applied to the post-socialist transition had a different starting point because the character of the zero-time society was not traditional but rather a socialist society in which a kind of modernization had been implemented for the past 45 or 70 years. Sztompka (1993) refers to this as fake modernity, as

> the incoherent, disharmonious, internally contradictory combination of three components: (1) imposed modernity in some domains of social life, coupled with (2) vestiges of traditional pre-modern society in many others, and all that dressed up with (3) the symbolic ornamentations pretending to imitate western modernity.
>
> (p. 137)

We show (in Chapter 4) that this sweeping generalization cannot be applied to all European socialist experiences, and further, that socialist modernization did indeed occur in the case of Yugoslavia, albeit incompletely in relation to the development of political pluralism, as it did not include multi-party democracy. The return to pre-modern attachments and values in the post-socialist temporal framework is sometimes explained by the freezing effect that socialism exerted on the state of values in societies that were unable to freely develop into the unified society promoted by a common market and pluralist democracy. This is certainly one of the paradoxes of post-socialist transformations, which should also be addressed in the study of media system change.

The processual approach to social change

Challenging approaches that question the systems approach to social change are gaining in prominence, primarily those sociological theories that pay more attention to human agency in social structuration (Giddens 1981a). These new approaches stress the ongoing nature of social change and attempt to de-reify social reality by employing the theory of the socio-cultural field.

In his critique of developmentalism, Charles Tilly (1997/1984) questions the assumptions of 19th-century sociology concerning social change, especially the idea that social change is one coherent phenomenon rather than a number of fragmentary processes, which run in the same or opposite directions, and the idea that there is something akin to overall social progress, which he finds to be contradicted by historical fact. He also questions the notion of differentiation as the main social process associated with modernization, showing how de-differentiation in the guise of society collapse or regression is evident. Contemporary sociological theories abandon the deterministic, linear, and developmental conceptions of social processes and replace them with conceptions of change that prioritize, in addition to human agency, historical contingency. While this new view of society as process, historical change as contingent, and social formation as structuration is also the view we adopt in this study, we continue to use the well-known and well-accepted terms from the times of the orthodox consensus (Giddens 1981a), including nation state, institutions, organizations, and systems, albeit with modified meanings reflecting the changed view of society.

The processual nature of society has an important implication for the study of social change because it "implies that the earlier phases are causally linked with the present phase, and that the present phase comprises the causally determining conditions for the next phase" (Sztompka 1993, p. 56). Therefore, Sztompka argues that historical sociology and new institutionalisms are, together with the theories of agency, the most authoritative theoretical conceptualizations that provide new tools for the interpretation of social transformations.

New institutionalisms are among the most important approaches for addressing social change as understood in a non-evolutionary way, although they are not commonly used in media and communication theory. While Hallin and Mancini (2004) stress the importance of the historical development of media systems, their approach does not explicitly include historical institutionalism (HI) (except for one path dependency reference; cf. Humphreys 2012, p. 170). In their reviews or critiques of the comparative media systems research, both Humphreys (2012) and Hardy (2012) point toward the use of HI for added depth and the grounding of the theoretical generalizations of media systems research. HI has, in prior communication research, been used in studies concerning digitalization policies (Humphreys 2012, pp. 170–171). More recently, HI and path dependency have also been employed in the analysis of media policy and media system development in the Netherlands (Lechner 2008), the United States and the UK (Ashley 2011), and Southeast Europe (Peruško 2016). The early work of McChesney (2000) highlights the importance of critical junctures for media policy change, while his later work on communication revolutions (2007) adds critical insights that figure importantly in our analysis. A recent study by Pickard (2015) of the American media reform movement also uses the path-dependent explanatory framework. A recent interpretation of historical institutionalism with regard to communication research was presented by Bannerman and Haggart (2015), and HI was employed for the analysis of media systems in Peruško (2013c, 2016).

The key characteristic of the historical institutionalist approach is the need to "analyze organizational configurations where others look at particular settings in isolation; and they pay attention to critical junctures and long-term processes where others look only at slices of time or short-term maneuvers" (Skocpol and Pierson 2002, p. 693). HI offers insight into the long-term consequences of the historical conditions of institutions (Hall and Taylor 1996; Mahoney 2000; Peters 2000; Humphreys 2012), and it enables the extension of the empirical field in which the social causality is located, not by presenting new cases for comparison in the present but rather by including processes from the past (Skocpol and Pierson 2002). Barrington Moore's (1966) structural account, for example, is based on the macrosocial variables that "predispose" countries to either dictatorship or democracy in the transformation from traditional to modern society.

Two concepts play a role in the historical institutionalist approach that allows for the focus to be on change or resilience in relation to media system development and transformation. The first is the concept of a critical juncture, which refers to the moment of the punctuated equilibrium of the institutional order. Such moments allow for a change in institutional frameworks, while path dependency and institutional inertia allow for the perpetuation of institutions in time and, therefore, work contrary to social change. Changes in the path are possible following critical junctures when space is provided for the articulation of new ideas that will bring about change. After the consequences of some critical junctures are socially accepted, path dependency comes into play and renders it difficult to change the direction of development. Through this inclusion of path dependency and the concept of critical junctures, the HI approach avoids historical determinism while also showing that path-dependent behaviors can survive even after an apparent change is introduced. Thus, the historical institutionalist approach provides a useful tool for unpacking the processes of long-term institutional change with regard to media systems.

Change or continuity? The role of culture

One common misconception is that with the passing of time, the social wholes we observe will necessarily exhibit some sort of change. Yet, continuity as an opposing process is equally evident. In the analysis of social and media transformations, we focus not only on discontinuities – the moments or periods of intense change and the ways they were used (or wasted) – but also on continuities and their intersection in specific country contexts (Ekiert and Ziblatt 2013). In Central and Eastern Europe, the frequency and revolutionary character of the observed discontinuities prevent, as Ekiert and Ziblatt (2013) argue, the full coalescence of institutions with culture (i.e., formal and informal institutions), and they allow for the retreat to the institutional and value formation of the previous historical period or the *longue durée*. Consequently, the experience of socialism in Eastern European countries has been shaped by their pre-communist experiences.

Culture is often invoked "to explain continuities in action in the face of structural changes" (Swindler 1986, p. 277). Following a lengthy debate on the meaning of culture among sociologists and anthropologists, the definition of culture as the "publicly available symbolic forms through which people experience and express meaning" has replaced the older definition whereby culture was seen as a whole way of life or as the totality of *things* everyone had to know to function in a given society (Swindler 1986, p. 273). According to Swindler (1986), these *things* include beliefs, formal rituals and ceremonies, and art forms, as well as informal cultural practices (e.g., language, everyday rituals). Stories, as cultural receptacles, are found in everyday talk but also in the media and popular culture. Following this definition, we might study practices that revolve around symbolic forms (i.e., media), although we could also study the type, shape, and form of the media content, or stories, as well as their meanings. In terms of the causal significance of culture, sociologists still focus on values as the "major link between culture and action" (Swindler 1986, p. 273). Swindler (1986) shows how Max Weber's understanding of culture, which rests on the notion that ideas, as historical constructions, motivate the interests that guide action, was modified by Parsons's use of abstract values in the place of ideas.

Ann Swindler's (1986) text on culture in action is one of the most influential sociological accounts of culture as practice, following the work of Clifford Geertz (1973), who redefines culture in terms of symbolic forms. Swindler (1986) defines culture in opposition to institutions insomuch that culture regulates "that part of social life which has to be continually created and recreated, not that part which is so institutionalized that it requires little active support by those it regulates" (p. 281 fn. 20). Contemporary sociological theory, as discussed earlier, sees action as part of institutional (re)structuration, and thus culture can be viewed as one part of the institutional field. Cultural elements include both "tacit culture" – attitudes and styles – and explicit cultural materials such as rituals and beliefs (Geertz 1973, p. 281). Swindler (1986) argues for the need to employ a different model of cultural influence during the unsettled times of social and cultural transformations as opposed to the model that fits the analysis during the usual times of regular cultural practice. In times of cultural change, ideologies, as explicitly articulated cultural models, shape action through symbols and rituals. Ideology is part of the cultural continuum that also includes tradition and common sense: "whatever the new ideology does not explicitly regulate still falls under the sway of the old order. Old orders are thus resilient, hiding their premises in the minutiae of daily life" (Swindler 1986, p. 279 n. 15). Swindler's unsettled culture manifests during critical junctures.

The predominant focus of cultural change is however (in terms of sociological analyses) on social values, with studies confirming that differences in social values interact differently with media domestication or diffusion; for example, openness to change as value predicted Internet diffusion into homes (Blekesaune 2019).

A model of institutional development that seems particularly well suited to the volatile histories of the CEE countries, and especially to the countries of Southeast Europe, is the dual model, which explains both the periods of regular institutional reproduction and the moments of rupture of the equilibrium, that is, both the path dependence and the critical junctures. While we structure the temporal aspect with the use of critical junctures, or the turning point as the moments (which can last for up to several decades; McChesney [2007a]) of regime (and media system) change, the focus of the historical institutionalist approach is also on the path-dependent future, or more precisely, "path dependence is a crucial causal mechanism for historical institutionalists, and critical junctures constitute the starting points for many path-dependent processes" (Capoccia and Kelemen 2007, p. 342). Critical junctures represent the focus of macro-historical analyses that analyze large-scale regime changes (Moore 1966; Mahoney 2001). While critical junctures point to moments/periods of social change – and we will argue that in all our identified critical junctures, change did occur at some level or in some aspect – it is also possible that the conditions enabling change are present, although that change does not occur. Critical junctures need not be periods in which all possible units of analysis (i.e., from individual organizations such as political parties, including public policy, to the political regime as a whole) will be affected (Capoccia and Kelemen 2007). The critical junctures identified and analyzed in this study, because they present regime changes that are linked to media systems, affect broad sets of political and economic issues and institutions. The society continues, however, because many other institutions remain. The discussion regarding how this affects the overall social change, as well as which areas (if any) of social life are unaffected by such sweeping regime change, is outside of the scope of this book.

Critical junctures, due to being qualitatively different from normal institutional settings (Capoccia and Kelemen 2007), are also periods in which agency has more influence on structure (Mahoney 2001) than during regular times of institutional stability, when the social structure changes only incrementally by way of changed practice that, in turn, influences the social institutions.

The problem of periodization: critical junctures and path dependencies in media systems change

Unlike mainstream political communication, which sees history as an inevitable result of events that happened in the past without questioning or investigating the relevant historical paths and events (Ryfe 2001), we employ the concept of turning points or critical junctures that shape periods for temporal comparison in the study of media systems change. The political and social system can be said to be in the moment of a critical juncture when both permissive conditions and conducive productive conditions exist (i.e., each is necessary and together they are sufficient for divergence; Soifer 2012). The events surrounding regime change and revolution, which we will encounter in our study, fulfill both conditions.

Some critical junctures are precipitated by exogenous factors that are reflected, sometimes with different consequent paths, for different countries. A case in point is the disruption caused by war during the period 1914–1945, which Hobsbawm (2011, loc. 4627) refers to as "capitalism's age of catastrophe." A similar exogenous impetus for change came about with the collapse of socialism in the Soviet Union, which brought about a critical juncture for political and economic revolutions (Huntington 1991) in Central and Eastern Europe.

Identifying the critical junctures relevant to the issue under analysis is one of the key steps in solving the temporal challenge. The all-European critical junctures include 1848, 1918, 1945, and 1989, while the important Eastern European junctures of de-democratization or failed democratization occurred in 1948, 1956, 1968, and 1980 (Ekiert and Ziblatt 2013). In Yugoslavia, however, the 1948 juncture represents the one whereby it diverged from the rest of Eastern European history, as it was at this juncture that the democratization (in socialist terms) and pluralization of both the political and economic fields began. Even the failed democratization of 1971/1972 in Croatia and Serbia in the SFRY was followed by actual increased federalization and an increase in the role of the republics, which contributed to the political diversity.

Critical junctures are those temporal frameworks, which can last for a shorter or longer time and sometimes for multiple decades (Capoccia and Kelemen 2007), during which the previous structural conditions, societal practices, and power relations are open to change in response to the appearance of new actors, processes, and conditions that allow for a renegotiation of the *status quo* (Mahoney 2000, 2001; Capoccia and Kelemen 2007). Some of these junctures can be explained in terms of proper revolutions or revolutionary situations that did not result in the transfer of state power (a distinction made by Charles Tilly). In this study, we encounter three social revolutions/critical junctures: the bourgeois revolution, the socialist revolution, and the democratic revolution, as well as multiple communication revolutions. We study all the ensuing temporal periods with regard to the structures of media systems as explanatory or exigent conditions for the present-day media systems. Thus we do not focus on how the critical junctures came about, or what actors, whether individual or institutional, participated, and with what aims, in the grand social change. We look to explain today's media systems by understanding the structural conditions or cultural models that enabled or constrained the successful democratization of the media and the implementation of a plural and open media system in the studied countries.

Robert McChesney (2007b) finds that critical junctures in media and communication occur when either of the three conditions are met:

> 1) there is a revolutionary new communication technology that undermines the existing system; 2) the content of the media system, especially the journalism, is increasingly discredited and seen as illegitimate; and 3) there is a major political crisis in which the existing order is no longer working and there are major movements for social reform.
>
> (pp. 1433–1434)

McChesney (2007a) identifies three critical junctures and periods in relation to the American media system: the progressive age of political reforms at the turn of the 20th century when journalism was at a low professional point, the 1930s and 1940s following the advent of radio, and today. The first era produced professional journalism in America, while the advent of radio ushered in the regulatory model of loosely regulated commercial networks that would also become a blueprint for television. The third communication revolution/critical juncture is evolving during the early 21st century as a result of the three conditions being met simultaneously: the digital revolution is challenging the business model of legacy media, journalism is in trouble, and the political system is creating growing inequalities and mistrust. The growing threat of fascism and the Great Depression influenced the second juncture, while the popular social movements of the 1960s and 1970s contributed to the third turning point in the global communication system, which gave rise to the neo-liberal character visible from the end of the 1980s (McChesney 2007a). The critical junctures in the history of the (US) press have also been identified as the rise of the penny press, the period of modernization and nationalism during the second part of the 19th century, the advent of commercial urban dailies, and the growth of multinational media conglomerates (Ryfe 2006).

The *longue durée* of the media, political, and economic fields in Western Europe also involves East Europe, albeit with different paths and outcomes following critical disruptions (Moore 1966; Acemoğlu and Robinson 2012). While European history includes several important watershed events, in relation to media system development in Southeast Europe three critical junctures seem to be the most important. All three critical junctures represent moments of regime change, followed by different paths in different parts of Europe. The differences in the patterns of modernization, cultural development, and political development of the six states prior to their common Yugoslav experience (which lasted less than 70 years, of which the latter 45 were socialist), their divergent contemporary political history following the dissolution of the SFRY, and their independent statehood after

1990 all contribute, we argue, to the diverse outcomes seen in media system development. Each of the three temporal frameworks that follow a critical juncture (presented below) also includes the communication juncture, the introduction of new media technology and institution that interplay with the changing social context. In our study of media system transformations, we are naturally disposed to take account of the communication junctures and the ways in which the social contexts in the respective temporal frameworks deal with them.

The first juncture: modernization

The first of the democratic revolutions, which occurred in 1789, can be seen as marking the critical juncture that shaped the different modernization trajectories (Moore 1966; Acemoğlu and Robinson 2012) as well as the ensuing conditions for the development of the mass media. The elements of the institutional structures that developed at this time would be equally influential in contemporary circumstance in Eastern Europe as they were in the West. As the mass media are the children of modernization, European style, the institutional conditions at that critical time are important for media development.

The importance of the original period of modernization to the history of media development in Central and Eastern Europe remains largely unexplored. Splichal (1994) and Gross (2002) are among the rare authors who underline the importance of the pre-democracy history in relation to understanding media development in contemporary Central and Eastern Europe. Despite finding differences across countries, Gross (2002) circles back to the common characteristics of the "communist political culture" and "communist media."

Ekiert and Ziblatt (2013) highlight the distinctly European character of the democratic transitions of the Eastern European countries (2003, p. 91), while also arguing that attention must be paid to the period of modernization during the 19th century when seeking to understand the contemporary democratic developments. The link between media and modernity has been well established from a theoretical perspective (J.B. Thompson 1995). Several institutional conditions are linked to the levels of modernization, which are in turn linked to media development. In Western European countries, increased literacy levels, industrialization, and urbanization went hand in hand with the rise of the mass press. While the modernization approaches to the post-communist transition were criticized in the early 1990s for their functionalism and evolutionism (Kollmorgen 2013), the historical institutionalist analysis highlights the possibility of different outcomes with regard to similar circumstances, depending on what other contextual circumstances are present (Bannerman and Haggart 2015, p. 5).

The six countries included in our analysis are on the periphery or semi-periphery of Europe. Modernization came late to them, meaning that in the early 20th century they still showed the marks of what were considered 19th-century developments in more developed European countries. For this reason, this initial period of media development is extended until World War II, when a new critical juncture permitted the socialist shift.

Two key events in the media world during this period draw our attention. The invention of movable printing technology enabled the institutions of book publishing, and newspapers become mass media. The mediation of communication signifies the greatest change between the traditional and the modern society. John B. Thompson (1995) describes the development of mass communication as a new range of communicative phenomena

> that emerged historically through the development of institutions seeking to exploit new opportunities for gathering and recording information, for producing and reproducing symbolic forms, and for transmitting information and symbolic content to a plurality of recipients in return for some kind of financial remuneration.
>
> (p. 26)

The second juncture: socialism

The second critical juncture with regard to the development of media systems in the CEE is the introduction of socialism, which further differentiated the eastern part of Europe from the western part. The second time frame is the socialist period, which in Central and Eastern Europe lasted from the end of World War II to 1989 (in Russia from 1917, in the SFRY from 1945, and in most of the CEE countries from 1948). During the second temporal framework, socialism was the dominant political and economic system in Eastern Europe. It was distinct from democracy due to its lack of political pluralism, as only communist/socialist parties were allowed; due to its central state economic planning based on nationalized property rather than on private property and free market capitalism; and due to the limitations placed on civil liberties, including the freedom of expression, assembly, and travel. Below, we will also consider how the differences between the types of socialism and the characteristics of regimes were of importance to media development both at the time and subsequently.

This post–World War II historical period in Western Europe and America is known to be characterized by the rise of television as the leading mass medium, the boom in mass communication and mass culture, and the development of the academic field of communication and media studies. However, there is still very little systematic knowledge regarding media and media systems in the CEE countries during the period of socialism/communism. Apart from the aforementioned work by Siebert et al. (1956) on normative media theories, the study by Gertrude Robinson (1977) on the media in Yugoslavia provides greater focus on the "maverick" self-managed media system. Little is known about the differences in the information flows in the different Yugoslav republics. Contemporary research offers increasing insight into television, its content and audiences during socialist times in Europe (Meyen and Scwer 2007; Pušnik and Starc 2008; Reifova and Pavličkova 2013; Peruško and Čuvalo 2014; Mihelj and Huxtable 2018), communication and media studies (Peruško and Vozab 2016) and media development (Bajomi-Lázár et al. 2020).

During the socialist period in Yugoslavia, we encounter several mini-junctures in which policy changes with long-term effects emerged. The first post-war period was marked by statist policies similar to the Soviet "real socialism" or state socialism. After this revolutionary phase ended, and by the early 1950s, social realism in the arts, culture, and science was abandoned and abstract art and art collectives became prominent, while in the field of architecture the rapidly developing urbanization of the socialist state was not shaped by the ornamental monumentalism of social realism but rather by the international style developing at the same time in Western Europe (Mrduljaš and Kulić 2012). It would be a mistake as well as a simplification to conflate all of socialism in Yugoslavia with its first, brutal yet brief, post–World War II period. Instead, we take into account the uneven expansions and constrictions of freedom and control in the decades following the 1950s, when the development of the media system of the federal state went hand in hand with developments at the level of the federal republics. We will show how even during the socialist period of federal Yugoslavia, the media landscape was changing in response to changing political power relations, thereby answering the increased federalization and power decentralization of self-management socialism with a combination of a common cultural space and distinctive public spheres in the federal republics.

The most interesting period of socialism with regard to the mass media occurred from the 1960s onwards, with the 1980s showing unprecedented plurality. This was the time when the media finally became mass media in terms of large audiences for radio, television, and print. A more in-depth analysis of this time frame and the position of the media field in relation to the fields of politics and economics, as well as the context of the cultural and social conditions, values, and institutional structures and dynamics, will help to refute the idea of a common "Soviet" media system (Siebert et al. 1956), which we still sometimes encounter.

The third juncture: post-socialist democratizations

The third critical juncture changed the path toward democracy following the "Fall of the Wall" in 1989, and it marks the beginning of the historical present, which is usually the only period seen in media systems comparisons and evaluations in Eastern Europe. This third time frame includes the period of post-socialist transition and the introduction and consolidation of democracy, further pluralization, and market and individual freedoms. The process of European integration also characterizes this period in terms of exerting an influence on media systems development. In Southeast Europe, this is the period of newfound independence and state building, which was complicated by war and different degrees of authoritarian rule. The manner in which these difficulties were overcome in different countries also plays a role in media systems development in this part of Europe.

In addition to the institutional analysis, the political culture is sometimes used to explain the post-socialist democratization trajectories. Gross thinks that in the "Eastern European societies . . . their pre-communist and communist eras having embedded cultural traits inimical to democracy that are 'durable and persistent'" (2004, p. 112). The inclusiveness of political and economic institutions (Acemoğlu and Robinson 2012), as variables describing the political institutional framework within media systems (Peruško et al. 2015), accounts for the differences in the field of politics. The differences in the party and electoral systems are also expected to be the conditions that figure in the explanations of media systems character.

In terms of the changes in media genres and media technologies, this period coincides with the development of the World Wide Web, the post-television age (Missika 2006) of multichannel abundance, as ushered in by technological innovations in the 1980s, the combination of satellite delivery and increased digitalization, and the spread of the Internet. Increasing globalization also marks this temporal frame due to the increased speed of communication and cultural exchange. Mediatization, datafication, and platform society are all the concepts describing the changes in the social fabric that we are able to observe in relation to communication and media (Couldry and Hepp 2017; Van Dijck et al. 2018; Couldry and Mejias 2019).

The communication juncture

The fourth juncture happens over and over in all the temporal frameworks and is related to a communication revolution (McChesney 2007a) rather than to a regime change. It could perhaps be more properly named a junction, that is, a place of convergence, not a critical point in time. While it may at first appear to be only technologically induced, in that the movable print, electric or electronic media, and digitalization have changed the communication ecology of the affected temporal frameworks, we can also see the challenges to the journalism profession (in present times the whole fake news controversy concerning the discrediting of journalism by "democratic" leaders, in the past the professionalization of journalism) and the shifts in the political field (development of democracy, the rise of populism, new social movements, and the crisis of representation) identified by McChesney (2007a) as the ingredients for a communication revolution.

The idea that the change in the communication ecology is interacting with broader society in such a way as to bring about a noticeable social change at the level of both social institutions and social practices is associated with the recently developed mediatization approach in communication studies

(Hjarvard 2008). The mediatization theory is not unanimous with regard to when the transformative role of communication actually begins (Lundby 2014). The cultural changes seen in the types of mediation include a shift from the mass media as the main institutional type of the public sphere during the 19th century to the social media as the new institutional form in the 21st century, alongside the legacy media. The consequences of the mixing of the two distinct institutional forms in contemporary media systems produce a hybridity (cf. Chadwick 2013) that has yet to be understood. Processes such as "continuities, overlaps, and modes of symbiosis" take place both in and between media and communication technologies (Morley 2009, p. 115), with no clear break between old and new media. Similarly, when studying the changes in the institutional makeup of media systems, the focus is not only on the breaks and disjunctions but also on the continuities and overlaps of institutional frameworks and audience practices across time or space.

It is not easy to pinpoint the exact time at which this juncture appears, and it is likely that it actually appears at different times in different countries. We might approximate the time of the latest junction to the past decade or to 20 years (Hjarvard 2008; Couldry and Hepp 2017), or 30 years as marked by technological changes including personal computers and the Internet that enabled the present datafication of society (Couldry and Mejias 2019). The technology of production, as the criterion for periodization, is well known in social theory (i.e., from hunting and gathering to industrial or post-industrial societies), although communication technology as the benchmark is more recent. While this juncture is different from the first three junctures, which are anchored in predominantly political ruptures, here the technological change and the related practice of media use turn the situation on its head. Now we see changes in the social and economic fields, as well as in the political field, which are primarily prompted by changes in communication practice (Mazzoleni and Schulz 1999; Hjarvard 2008; Strömbäck 2008) and which can speak of the communication revolution (McChesney 2007a).

Our analysis of the conditionalities related to the development of media systems is necessarily colored by the regular appearance and domestication/spread of new media technologies, institutions, and forms. The word "regular" is used here to highlight the predictability of the appearance of always new technological inventions which are able to fulfill a communication purpose and which, when domesticated, tend to influence changes in the social habits of the populations and institutions (Innis 1951; McLuhan 1964; Meyrowitz 1985; Krotz 2014; Hjarvard 2012). In the history of human communication, changes in the mode and predominant technology of communication have been linked to social change. For instance, *printing* (first of books, then of newspapers) is associated with growing urbanization, secularization, the de-monopolization of education, and increasing literacy rates and education levels among general populations. The development of printing technology and its subsequent institutionalization in the mass media of books and newspapers, together with the development of the main professions linked to the institutional forms, marks the first period we study. While our focus in that chapter will be on the "long 19th century," we must also take a look at the conditions and domestication of this technology from the end of the 15th century onwards in Southeast Europe. The *telegraph* was yet another 19th-century technology that revolutionized international communication. Its younger cousin, the wireless telegraph, aka the *radio*, developed a content-producing institutional form that we now associate with the mass media.

Television is definitely the main mass medium in relation to socialist modernization, although the mass development of the printed press will also feature in our second temporal period, as covered in Chapter 4 of this book. Within the *age of television*, the periodization of television cultures based on generic changes provides a useful theoretical stepping-stone for spatial comparisons of socialist/post-socialist spaces with those in Western Europe. During the time of paleo-television (public service), when, as Eco (1983, p. 12) writes, television was "subject to censorship and considered ideal for its obedient and catholic audiences," and when there were "few things to see," the division of genres into modes of fact and fiction was easier to maintain than following the advent of commercial neo-television in the 1980s, when the content changed not only in terms of its size but also its type. Missika (2006) identifies the paleo stage of television with the mass audience and few channels. Television is thus a sacral place that the audience does not enter. The full logic of television has not yet developed, and the information and entertainment genres transferred from other media to television do not include new formats and formulas. The same is true of fiction programs, which do not yet venture into the new topics and possibilities offered by television. With the end of the state monopoly and the advent of commercial television comes the fragmentation of the audiovisual landscape and the beginning of the time of neo-television. Post-television, as conceptualized by Missika (2006), denotes an age after neo-television, an age in which the reality genre takes television to new lengths in relation to the transformation of individuals in public view.

Harold Innis (1951) was the first to understand how historical media changes contribute to the "sudden extensions of communication [that] are reflected in cultural disturbances" (p. 31, quoted in Strate 2004, p. 9). Within the media ecology approach and the work of McLuhan (1964), the periodization of communication and media changes was first defined as three communication ages, namely the oral, the literate, and the electric ages (Logan 2002). Perhaps the best-known recent example of the periodization of media and social/political change is Blumler and Kavanagh's (1999) notion of the *ages of political communication*. Describing changes in "most democracies," these ages, or temporal frames, are defined by shifts in both the relation to the media and the relation to the changes in society. These

Explaining the transformations 31

social changes include modernization, individualization, secularization, economization, aestheticization, rationalization, and mediatization, with the "media moving toward the centre of the social process" (1999, p. 211). The first age of political communication starts in the post-war years, lasts for two decades, and is marked by the predominance of politics over the media (1945–1960). Here, the political message is still substantial and policy related, and it is not adapted to the media process. The second age is marked by the rise of television as the main medium of political communication, the first adaptations of the political field that include new practices aimed at providing the media with regular information, and the development of new media formats that report on them (the news) (1960–1990). The third age is marked by media abundance and ubiquity, as well as by the full professionalization of political communication (1990–2010). The third age media system is "like a hydra-headed beast, the many mouths of which are continually clamoring to be fed," and it is not marked by one dominant tendency or medium but rather by "conflicting cross-currents" (Blumler and Kavanagh 1999, p. 213). The third age exhibits several trends, some of which become intensified in the fourth age (2010–present) of political communication due to the unprecedented media abundance (Blumler 2013) – the intensified professionalization of political advocacy, increased competitive pressures, and anti-elitist popularization and populism change the shape of the public sphere, while the diversification of communication exerts centrifugal effects on the community (instead of the centripetal effects of the first and second ages) with a whole host of related consequences in terms of communicating identity and belonging. The audience reception of politics is changed, becoming more flexible and fragmented (Blumler and Kavanagh 1999).

The *digitally* based media – computers, the Internet, and the new institutional forms the media today take the guise of platforms, apps, and social media (Van Dijck et al. 2018) – all play a part in the post-1990 media systems. Both the media system and the media culture were historically linked to a certain predominant type of communication media as a technology that modulated the entry of citizens into the public sphere as well as into the character of the "symbolic forms . . . that are meaningful to the individuals who produce and receive them" (J.B. Thompson 1995, p. 11). In today's poly-media world (Madianou 2014), we no longer speak of one dominant medium but rather of ubiquitous communication and media, thereby again changing our social practices and institutions. Recent investigations of this long-term relationship are united under the banner of mediatization theory (Hjarvard 2008; Lundby 2014; Couldry and Hepp 2017).

In relation to media and social change, periodization is today perhaps most important in the mediatization approaches. Lundby (2014) shows how the three central approaches of mediatization theory differently perceive the beginning of the mediatization process as the process in which the relationship between the media and society began to show a transformation in social institutions or social practices. The longest temporal frame is set in relation to the cultural perspective, which sees the beginning of the process at the beginning of human history with the first modes of communication (Krotz 2009; Couldry and Hepp 2012). For the institutional perspective, mediatization is a social process linked to high modernity and to television, which started in the 1980s with broadcasting organizations gaining independence from politics (Hjarvard 2008). The material/technological perspective sees mediatization as a process in the recent digital decades and in relation to the new media platforms (Finnemann 2011). More recently, Couldry and Hepp (2017) develop McLuhan's (1964) periodization of the media epochs to include the latest temporal frame of deep mediatization (and datafication as an emerging fourth epoch), which follows electrification as the second epoch and mechanization as the first epoch of media development. Clearly, these periodizations are predominantly rooted in the understanding of changes in media technology or institutions, although the labels of the most recent epoch, as described by Couldry and Hepp (2017), point to communication- and media-related social processes as being predominant.

All the described periodizations of communication and media "ages" in the modern times have in mind the Western (post-)industrial world. In our study, we will attempt to keep track of these periods and to look for indications of similarity or difference in Central and Eastern Europe, particularly its southern part.

The problem of comparison

The key to any comparative analysis is the theoretical framework – what we need to look at and the data that describe it (Blumler and Gurevitch 1995). In the following section, we present those external and media system conditions that we use in subsequent chapters to examine each period following a critical juncture for the patterns of the relationships of media system development, with a view to developing a theoretical explication of the relationships between the combination of specific conditions and the present-day media system character.

We have defined our theoretical approach to understanding media system change as being related to social change, and social change as a series of transformations stemming from a combination of exogenous and endogenous influences following critical junctures, which allow for the change of the normative and institutional character of societies. We find the historical institutionalist approach to be particularly useful for the empirical analysis of media systems so conceived due to the ability to focus on both the moment of change (the critical juncture) and the period of path dependency or continuity. The theoretical logic of historical institutionalism is particularly well suited to the fsQCA method, which is the tool we will use to determine which combinations of conditions appear with particular media system outcomes.

A set theoretic research approach: fuzzy set qualitative comparative analysis (fsQCA)

The method used in a given comparative media systems analysis depends on the type of research questions or hypotheses, the nature of the data, and the number of cases being compared. If the nature of the research questions is descriptive, the research usually draws on descriptive statistics, multidimensional scaling, or cluster analysis (Vliegenthart 2012, p. 487). Cluster analysis is useful for building typologies of media systems, and it has been used to operationalize Hallin and Mancini's (2004) model with aggregate data for the construction of media system models, although it is less useful for explanatory purposes (Peruško et al. 2013; Brüggemann et al. 2014; Peruško 2016; Castro Herrero et al. 2017). Comparative researchers also use methods such as multilevel modeling and pooled time-series analysis if their aim is to perform a comparative explanatory analysis (Vliegenthart 2012, p. 487). This kind of analysis can help to explain whether effects, processes, or relationships between variables differ between different contexts. Comparative explanatory studies are used to explain how the contextual levels of media systems or media environments moderate or influence communication effects and processes at the individual level (Shehata 2010; Shehata and Strömbäck 2011; Aalberg et al. 2013; Peruško et al. 2015, 2017). This kind of analysis is possible if there are larger quantitative datasets available, for example, from comparative surveys.

Recently, the qualitative comparative analysis (QCA) and its fuzzy set variant (fsQCA) has become more common in comparative research concerning media systems and political communication processes. This kind of analysis can be used for explanatory purposes without the need for larger quantitative datasets. The QCA approach offers several advantages for comparative analysis in the social sciences, including the political science and communication and media studies (as the areas of study with the largest and the smallest application of QCA, Roig-Tierno et al. 2017). First, QCA fills a hole in the comparative research, which is usually set to a small or large number of cases. QCA is also suitable for the analysis of a medium number of cases (Dolenec 2013b, p. 108) but works well also with a large number of cases. QCA focuses on causal explanations, although it is based on a logic that is different from that used in statistical analysis in relation to quantitative comparative research. Due to this, QCA can explain some causal mechanisms or outliers that are not explained by means of statistical analysis.

Since its inception, fsQCA theory has had many applications in various social sciences, including wide application in the fields of sociology and political science (Smithson and Verkuilen 2006), and more recently, in political communication. Downey and Stanyer (2010) propose the use of fsQCA in media systems and political communication research. They demonstrate the validity of this approach by analyzing the conditions necessary

34 *Explaining the transformations*

for personalized mediated political communication in 20 democracies. In their subsequent comparative analysis using fsQCA, Downey and Stanyer (2013) analyze the conditions that contribute to the frequency of political sex scandals in the media. Brüggemann and Königslöw (2013) explain the level of cosmopolitan coverage in 12 newspapers from six European countries through various structural and cultural conditions. Humprecht and Büchel (2013) analyze the diversity in reporting regarding the Occupy movement in online news from six countries. Although QCA is mostly used to identify the set relationship between conditions and outcomes, Büchel et al. (2016) demonstrate that it could also be used to establish empirical typologies of media systems.

Chapters 3 through 5 include comparative case studies of the three time periods in relation to the media systems in Slovenia, Croatia, Bosnia and Herzegovina, Montenegro, Serbia, and Macedonia. They provide the arguments that link the identified contextual institutional conditions to the media system outcomes so as to determine what is driving the path inertia that is blocking media reform efforts in some parts of the region, and conversely, what conditions contribute to positive outcomes of media freedom and media market development. These three chapters also provide the basis for calibrating the sets of conditions and outcomes for the final analysis presented in Chapter 6, where fsQCA is used to uncover the causal configurations (Ragin 2008) and explain what combinations of remote and proximate conditions and actions produce present-day media systems. While some of the main relationships between media and politics might endure the interruptions of regime change, others could become reversed.

The theoretical narrative used in our study to structure the critical junctures and path-dependent analysis of media systems change in Southeast Europe builds on the mainstream model of media systems (Blumler and Gurevitch 1995; Hallin and Mancini 2004), successful new adaptations (Peruško et al. 2013, 2015; Castro Herrero et al. 2017), and digital media system extensions (Mattoni and Ceccobelli 2018).

Conditions shaping outcomes in media systems

A media system is the outcome of the character and variation of the social conditions influencing the media field as well as the types of relationships between the political field, the economic field, and the different institutions within the field of cultural/symbolic power, within which the media themselves are established. Our goal is not, as is common in comparative media systems research, to create typologies of post-socialist media systems but rather to explain present-day media systems by identifying the combination of conditions and relationships that have contributed to their characteristics. Similarities in media system "types" might be identified in relation to those sharing the same combinations of conditions and outcomes. It is also possible that similar outcomes will result from different combinations of conditions and characteristics. This is our main theoretical and substantive question: can similar media systems be a consequence of dissimilar development paths? While our original aim was to understand how socialism has influenced the subsequent media systems in the third-wave democracies of Central and Eastern Europe, the model evolved to extend the comparison to the earlier past (i.e., the period of original modernization in Europe). In looking to identify the most important conditions for media systems change, we also need to account for the shape of media systems in the present temporal frame of high modernity, starting from the period of post-socialist democratic transformations in the 1990s.

To structure our analyses during the three identified temporal frameworks, we will now identify the conditions that shape and characterize media systems. These categories of conditions appear in all our temporal frameworks, but they will sometimes appear in altered manifestations and with distinctive indicators that define them. The distinctions will be analyzed in the respective chapters dealing with each specific temporal framework, and the adaptations to the concepts that we had to make will be reviewed in the final chapter. This completes our model for understanding media systems change, and it will enable us to identify and apply the indicators required for the empirical analysis, as per Blumler and Gurevitch's (1995, p. 59) well-known instruction regarding the prerequisites for comparative research concerning media and communication systems.

The political field

While the importance of the existing political framework has been strongly highlighted from the first normative theories of the press (Siebert et al. 1956), as well as in the most relevant contemporary studies (Blumler and Gurewitch 1995; Hallin and Mancini 2004, 2012), in contemporary media system studies the political system is generally assumed to fall within a certain Western democratic framework. We could even say that the media systems approach has a democratic bias, which needs to be unpacked if we hope to understand how media systems develop in non-democratic political conditions.

The underlying character of the political and economic fields may be related to the basic institutional type of the society or state in which the media operate. Acemoğlu and Robinson (2012) define two types of institutions that determine the political and economic development of nations: inclusive and extractive institutions. Inclusive institutions are supportive of private property, an unbiased system of law, and the provision of public services that provide a level playing field in which people can exchange and contract. Inclusive institutions also need to ensure the entry of new businesses and to allow people to choose their careers (Acemoğlu and Robinson 2012, p. 74). As the opposite type of institution, extractive institutions are coercive. Within this type of institutional structure, the elites extract economic and political benefits to the detriment of the population. Acemoğlu and Robinson (2012) show how differences in the institutional makeup between countries lead to different outcomes in similar historical circumstances. While inclusive institutions ultimately enable and support both democracy and economic prosperity, extractive institutions limit political and economic pluralism and also block economic progress by removing incentives for individual action.

Extractive institutions seek to control the channels of public communication as well as the participation of the public in general and individual citizens, which means that media are necessarily constrained. Inclusive institutions allow for technological innovation to the point of allowing for disruptive properties, for example, the disruption caused by the Internet in relation to newspapers. Inclusive institutions support media freedom, and the free media in turn support the further inclusiveness of institutions (Acemoğlu and Robinson 2012). At certain critical junctures, states may have an opening to introduce inclusive institutional structures in the place of the prior extractive ones. We will explore how this plays out in our six cases. The institutional dimension will consequently be operationalized with different variables in different temporal frameworks. For example, we will use the quality of democracy as the proxy for inclusive political institutions in the last temporal frame.

We will also expand the view of the political field beyond party relationships and government to the level of the political regime. This move is necessary to be able to work with regimes that have issues with democracy, or that are not democratic. In our different temporal frameworks, before we start to encounter democratic forms, we will encounter political regimes that are empires, sultanates, authoritarian dictatorships, and socialist authoritarian regimes.

The character of the democratic regime is one of the key points in Hallin and Mancini's (2004) models of media systems, and the names of the three models are derived from the predominant characteristics of the political field. The dimensions describing the political fields need to relate to the changes in the field in the periods before democracy, during socialism, and during post-socialist democratization.

The socio-economic field

Socio-economic conditions play a significant role in all modernization processes. Higher education levels (originally literacy) found in more economically developed (wealthier) societies. Economic development is also related to the development of the first media institutions – by the time the movable printing press was invented, capitalism was sufficiently developed to support the development of printing as a commercial enterprise. The different temporal frameworks in our study are marked by different economic regimes and their changes/transformations – from feudalism to capitalism, to socialist self-management, to market capitalism. Not all capitalisms are created equal, and in many locales crony capitalism prevented a fresh start and indicated the persistence of extractive institutional structures.

The institutional frameworks also influence the scope for technological innovation as well as the development of education, that is, the "two other engines of prosperity" (Acemoğlu and Robinson 2012, p. 77). Inclusive institutions allow for technological development, whereas extractive institutions block it due to a fear of change in the form of creative destruction that would bring the existing balance of power to an end.

The cultural and symbolic field

Media organizations have developed within the broader field of culture, alongside other institutions that deal in symbolic power, for example, religion and education. While in modern times the media itself is our main focus, the early modern period of media development includes other powerful symbolic institutions that we need to take into account. Building on the accounts of mainstream media systems theories (Hallin and Mancini 2004; Blumler and Gurevitch 1995) but also on the insights of Siebert et al. (1956), the following dimensions will be used in this study to describe and understand media systems: the relationship of the state to the media, journalism culture and professional autonomy, political parallelism, the media market and infrastructure, and globalization of communication. Changing social values also play a role as indicators of the ongoing cultural change. Different temporal frameworks might well be described by varied indicators, as the composition of the dimensions changes.

State and the media. Blumler and Gurevitch (1995, pp. 20–23) define the manner of state control of the media system through three areas of direct influence: legal constraints, normative constraints, and structural constraints. The fourth area, economic constraints, is the area of indirect state influence through the regulation of the market. The legal framework may serve either the independence of the media or the greater potential of control by the state, and it always relates to the definition of the boundaries of the freedom of the media (particularly the freedom of expression) in places where it may come into conflict with other freedoms (the right of individuals to privacy, the protection of individuals from libel) or the interests of the state (national security). In this field, Chalaby (1996, p. 177) also includes the possibility of the arbitrariness of the executive government in relation to the media, that is, the use of the administrative or bureaucratic apparatus for the supervision or control of the media, as well as the use of various covert forms of coercion, such as biased court rulings against opposition newspapers or a complicated process of media registration, or outright violence.

The policy and treatment of the public service media, as well as its position within the media system in terms of audiences, funding, and autonomy, represents another area where we know the CEE countries to differ among each other (Castro Herrero et al. 2017). This dimension obviously only appears with the advent of television, during the socialist temporal framework. The transformation of public service broadcasting (PSB) is, to date, one of the most difficult and complex transformations in all the post-socialist media systems, not only in Southeast Europe.

Journalism culture and professional autonomy. Thomas Hanitzsch and Wolfgang Donsbach (2012) define journalism culture as including a set of ideas (values, attitudes, and beliefs), practices (such as reporting and editing), and artifacts (news content) (p. 262). Comparative research on journalism culture has expanded following the launch of the Worlds of Journalism Study (WJS) (Hanitzsch et al. 2011). While studies show how journalism practices change with transnational similarities, national media systems and culture still influence the specific shape of these common transnational change patterns (Menke et al. 2016). Journalism culture can also be understood with regard to the professional autonomy or closeness to the political field as one of the dimensions that describe a media system focused on political journalism (Hallin and Mancini 2004). In this respect, the more the profession is based on its own internal rules, the more autonomy it exhibits. Clearly, in different temporal frameworks journalism is shaped by different predominant forces. Today, we see technology as the driving force behind change in journalistic practices and audience practices. In the past, the changing role of the state might have exerted the dominant influence on the patterns of journalists' practices as well as on the normative values attributed to the performance of journalism.

Political parallelism. The structural relationships between the field of politics and the media are particularly interesting in post-socialist countries, and they have been found to explain the differences between the media systems of such countries (Castro Herrero et al. 2017). Given the history of these countries, where the party has historically influenced what the media should be like, the unpacking of the differences or similarities between the role of the state and the role of the party, as well as the possible consequences of these entanglements in the present day, will prove challenging. The relationship between the political field of power and the related fields, including the media, can be expected to change with every historical process of change.

The media market and infrastructure. In the Hallin and Mancini (2004) typology, the shape of the newspaper market and the reading habits of the audiences is one of the key variables distinguishing media systems. Media technology innovations have, from the beginning, been responsible for the increase in media channels and for their availability. The media systems of today are composed of a comprehensive media matrix, that is, a set of available media together with their different institutionalizations and usages, which vary across media systems according to the political, economic, and cultural contexts (Finnemann 2014, p. 299). In the digital age, emerging media systems are affected by changes in media technologies, institutions, and practices: digitization, mobility, media abundance, network architecture, mass self-communication, and the hybridization of old and new media logics in media institutions and formats (Castells 2009; Couldry 2012; Chadwick 2013). The first media in early modern times were also based on technology innovations, and in this respect they were the result of inclusive institutions. But what happened in those states that had extractive institutions at this time?

While the spread of the media and communication infrastructure provides the structure of the media system/field, understanding how everyday media practices are meshed with the media environment contributes to understanding media cultures. In Northern European countries, the much larger newspaper audiences produce a different pattern of media use than in Southern European countries (Hallin and Mancini 2004). Geographical distinctions are found also in relation to the use of digital media. What changes are exhibited in media consumption patterns in Southeast Europe with the changes of temporal frameworks?

Media culture and global communication. Media systems, media cultures, and audience practices are all increasingly difficult to conceive of solely in relation to nation states, without paying attention to the increasingly global flows of media products and services, as well as to the corresponding consumption practices. Media and communication technologies are seen as the drivers of globalizations, and globalization of media markets is expected to promote the convergence of media systems (Hallin and Mancini 2004; Voltmer 2012; Flew and Waisbord 2015). Although important critiques of the media systems approach come from those who challenge the primacy of the nation state as an analytical unit (e.g., the methodological nationalism critique of Ulrich Beck 2003), the national media system retains importance as the place of media use and regulation. In cross-country comparisons of the Internet, Flew and Waisbord (2015) show that states also maintain legal control of the boundaries in the digitized media system. Without a doubt, contemporary media systems are affected, and can be differentiated, by their participation in global flows, where technological, institutional, and cultural (artifact/content) conditions have a role to play.

In the following chapters we will apply the theoretical framework from this chapter and look at the specifics of the conditions in the six states in Southeast Europe during the three distinct temporal frames initiated by specific critical junctures. The comparative analyses in Chapters 3 through 5, through their detailed and rounded analysis of the historical progression in the studied cases, will provide us with the substance necessary for calibrating the conditions for the fsQCA in Chapter 6, where we will show what combinations of conditions produce what kind of media system.

Note

1 The following section is based on Sztompka (1993).

3 Prelude to modernity

In this chapter, we face the first challenge associated with comparing postsocialist media systems, namely the temporal displacement of media systems analysis to a time in European history prior and leading up to the formation of the modern state. As our research objective is to understand the change in media systems in Southeast Europe from a comparative perspective, we now need to portray the development of media systems in temporal and spatial locales that did not share, or else only partly shared, in the early modern and modern Western European political or economic change. Most of the categories/dimensions that we identified in the previous chapter as describing a media system are, during this period, only just starting to form within the process of the social transformation of traditional into modern societies in Western Europe.

The beginning of modern society is associated with the mid-19th century (although this is not uncontested – different authors place the beginning between the 16th and the 19th century; Sztompka 1993). Sociologist Anthony Giddens (2012) argues that the exact date upon which modernity started was May 24, 1844, the day when Samuel Morse sent the first message by telegraph from Washington to Baltimore. The invention of the telegraph, which Giddens considers to be the founding moment of modernity, enabled the extension of communication across both time and space, and for the first time, it enabled the sending of messages to people in geographically distant places without the need for any physical movement.

The Industrial Revolution, as represented here by the invention of the telegraph, was a result of previous transformations. The transformation of the economic conditions of feudalism brought about the capitalist mode of production. The main actors in the commercialization of agriculture shaped the type of modern society that resulted (Moore 1966), and therefore, enabled the beginning of industrial civilization. Transformations of the political field gave rise to the nation state during the 19th century, which was enabled by the concentration of both capital and coercion (Tilly 1992). Modernization transformation is a "syndrome of parallel changes – industrialization, professionalization, specialization, bureaucratization, centralization, higher education levels of the population, development of the mass media, secularization, and entrepreneurship" (Inglehart 1995, pp. 68–69). Talcott Parsons (1971) frames the process as functional differentiation, a process in which different social systems achieve growing autonomy from politics, the political system achieves autonomy from civil society, social norms achieve autonomy from religious values (Merkel 2011, p. 56), and the professionalization of journalism is differentiated from political or literary practices (Hallin and Mancini 2004).

This great process of social change, which has been termed modernization, manifested in the institutional transformations of the main fields of social power – economic and political – as well as in the field of culture, where media institutions and practices gradually displaced both religion and education from the central position of symbolic power (J.B. Thompson 1995). Transformations in the cultural field relate to changes in the values that predominate in society (Inglehart and Welzel 2005) as well as to changes related to the rise of the media institution and its role in the development of modern societies (cf. J.B. Thompson 1995, pp. 44–80). This *mediatization* of culture arises from the development of the media institution during the late 15th century and from the cultural transformations that followed in relation to the new products and practices of production and consumption (J.B. Thompson 1995, p. 46).[1] Media histories usually begin at the time Johannes Gutenberg designed the printing press, as the first technological invention and the first media institution, which enabled the later development of the newspaper, as the main content-producing media institution linked to the prelude to modernity (Eisenstein 1993/1979; J.B. Thompson 1995; Briggs and Burke 2005; Chapman 2005).

To establish whether, at which point in history, and in relation to which social, political, and/or economic conditions the media systems in Southeast Europe diverge from the Western European type of media institutions and media systems, we will begin from the same starting point. This first media invention created a critical juncture at which different political and economic contexts reacted differently. The patterns of institutional adoption or adaptation of the media/communication innovation in Southeast Europe also play a role in the study of changes in the institutional conditions of media development in the following temporal frameworks.

In the subsequent section, we will map the differences or similarities in the processes of modernization transformation of the political, economic, and symbolic/cultural fields in Southeast Europe during the period leading up to and including the turn of the 20th century and the first half of the 20th century. We will end with the start of World War II as our next critical juncture.

This long temporal framework is divided into two distinct periods. The first is the (much longer, spanning centuries) late medieval/early modern period, in which the countries in question experienced divergent political, economic, social, and cultural conditions as members of two different, and opposing, empires: the Habsburg and the Ottoman. The second is the modern period, which starts in the mid-19th century with industrialization and political pluralization. This period includes the final decades of the two empires and their diverse modernizing developments, as well as the interwar period of (one would expect) convergence of the countries to a common political and economic framework within one common state: the Kingdom of Serbs, Croats, and Slovenes (SHS)/Yugoslavia.

The first contours of the emergent modern media systems during this "long 19th century" appear for some countries toward the end of the early modern period, while for others they appear only after the start of the modern era. There are marked differences between the countries with regard to the time of the establishment of the first media institutions and how the state regarded the media in question. At the turn of the 20th century, the familiar dimensions of (mass) media systems – political parallelism, autonomy and professionalization of journalism, media markets, and the globalization of communication – start to make sense in media system explanations in the countries of interest.

The following brief historical account will reveal how, by the first early modern period (15th to 18th centuries), some parts of Southeast Europe had experienced similar transformations to those seen in Western Europe, albeit with less intensity due to their peripheral position, while others remained in the traditional grip of the Ottoman Empire, with a significantly different type of government and institutional framework (Tracy 2016). While Western European states were developing modern institutions during the 18th and 19th centuries – building cities and developing transport infrastructure, industry, state bureaucracy, and capitalist economy – their eastern neighbors were often still struggling with mainly agricultural extractive economies and extractive political institutions according to the divergent path of institutional development that began in the 14th century (Acemoğlu and Robinson 2012).

The remainder of this chapter unfolds as follows. First, we present a brief political history of Southeast Europe through the stories of two empires and one state in order to explain the broader geopolitical setting of the historical contexts of the six countries under investigation.[2] Through this context-setting process, we examine the modernizing (or not) transformations in the political and economic fields in the respective political entities with regard to the comparative country cases before proceeding to explore the transformations in the cultural field. Here, the subsequent development of media institutions will take place alongside the development of media systems. We start with the differences in the media markets, which here involves a focus on the spread of printing, the appearance of newspapers, and the political public spheres, through to the appearance of the telegraph and radio during the first decades of the 20th century. Then, with two aims, we apply the well-known dimensions of media systems. First, to test how they can be applied within this historical displacement, and second, to use familiar concepts to understand the social change contained within the transformation of the symbolic field during times of emerging modernity.

Transformations of the political field

Habsburg and Ottoman Empires

At the time when Johannes Gutenberg invented the printing press, circa 1439, the majority of Europe was subject to imperial rule: the Holy Roman Empire to the west, the Habsburg Empire in the center, the Russian Empire to the northeast, and the Ottoman Empire to the southeast. Europe was fragmented into a multitude of state-like units with overlapping territories, many of them with semi-autonomous governments within large empires that straddled the continent. Most technical inventions still originated in China. Dante had recently written his *Divine Comedy* and Francesco Petrarca had discovered Cicero's speeches – thereby, in accordance with the received history, opening up the path of the Renaissance. The western expansion of the Ottoman Empire was preceded by an epidemic of plague in Europe that reduced the continent's population by 60%. Acemoğlu and Robinson (2012) argue that the arrival of the plague, as well as the states' different responses to it, created the first critical juncture, which generated the divergence of Eastern Europe from Western Europe. This primarily influenced the character of the economic field, which would, due to being challenged by diminished human resources, continue in the East on the path of feudalism and the further entrenchment of coercive institutions, while in the West it would bring about reforms and the gradual improvement of the position of peasants. The second divergence was brought about by the Ottoman conquest.

In Southeast Europe, the Ottoman Empire occupied the Balkans, including today's North Macedonia, Serbia, Montenegro, and Bosnia and Herzegovina (as well as Albania, Greece, and Bulgaria). The territories to the west were under the rule of the Habsburg Empire, including today's Croatia and Slovenia (Tilly 1992, p. 31). The empires that ruled these lands replaced the independent medieval kingdoms of Croatia, Bosnia, Serbia, and Montenegro. The history of these lands and their peoples is complicated by their shifting territories over the centuries (Banac 1984). To simplify matters, we will keep in mind the present-day borders of the six countries, even if, for instance, the name of Slovenia was first mentioned during the 19th century, while today's North Macedonia was previously known as the southern region of Serbia. Macedonia was the first (among the six countries we are studying) to come under Ottoman rule following the Battle of Maritsa in 1371. It was followed by Serbia and Montenegro in 1389, following their defeat in the Battle of Kosovo, a legendary mythologized defeat that resulted in the loss of statehood and remains a point of identity for Serbs to this day. The Islamic conversion of Kosovo and neighboring Albania occurred during the 17th century. The Kingdom of Bosnia was conquered by the Ottomans in 1463, and it was unusual due to the massive early conversion of its Catholic population to Islam. Indeed, by the turn of the 16th century, 46%

of households had converted (up from 1% prior to the conquest). Finally, Herzegovina became an Ottoman province in 1481 (Tracy 2016, pp. 8–22).

Tracy (2016) describes the political institutions in the territories under Venetian, Habsburg, and Ottoman rule. While the first two regimes in Southeast Europe developed traditional Western/Latin political institutions characterized by power sharing at different levels of authority, no such power sharing was known within the Ottoman Empire, as there were no subsidiary powers for towns or provinces. In the occupied territories, the governing institutions were primarily geared toward the military, and they ruled over the civilian population by extension. The non-Islamic populations had no legal standing and could not approach the Ottoman authorities with grievances, as the Ottomans differentiated populations according to religion. Some religious communities had the right to be ruled by their religious leaders with regard to civilian matters, which reflects the status of Islam in the government of the Ottoman Empire. This strengthened the role of the Orthodox Church in Serbs' national identity and the perpetuation of the memory of their lost state. As the Catholic Church was international in character, subordinated to the pope, and not linked to any state, the Catholic populations – in this case principally the Croats – were mostly left without protection or standing (which probably contributed to the unusually high Islamic conversion seen in Bosnia-Herzegovina) (Banac 1984).

From the end of the 15th century, a hundred years of wars with the Ottoman Empire unfolded in the lands of present-day Croatia (and the south/easternmost parts of Slovenia), which warded off attacks from the already conquered Bosnia and Herzegovina. Parts of Croatia's easternmost lands fell to the Ottomans at the end of the 16th century and were held for over a hundred years. A military border (Vojna Krajina) was established by the Habsburgs in Croatia, and settlers from Ottoman-occupied Bosnia and Herzegovina or Serbia were obliged to serve in the Habsburg military. The rule here was also military. Croatia proper remained a kingdom within the Habsburg Empire, while most of the Adriatic coastal regions of Dalmatia and Istria were ruled by Venice. The merchant city of Dubrovnik remained independent, although it paid tribute to the Ottoman Empire, before being integrated into Dalmatia as a consequence of the Napoleonic conquest at the turn of the 19th century (Karaman 2000, p. 274). After the Turks were pushed back into the Balkans at the end of the 17th century, the present-day Croatian lands were united within the Habsburg Empire but divided in terms of administrative governance between Hungary and Austria, which hindered indigenous modernization processes. The peoples of today's Slovenia lived in three Austrian provinces within the Habsburg Empire from the 15th century onwards: Carniola, Crain, and Steiermark. Venice ruled over several coastal cities in Dalmatia during the first half of the 15th century, as well as over the coastal towns of today's Montenegro, while Croatia controlled two coastal ports. The Dalmatian cities were also sites of global cultural flow during the Renaissance, although Venice mainly used the Croatian coastal region and islands for their natural resources (wood and stone).

State consolidation processes transformed the political field between the 15th and 18th centuries, leading to a tremendous reduction in the number of political entities – from some 500 to around 30 at the beginning of the post-socialist transitions (Tilly 1992). Following the dissolution of the federal socialist states (USSR, SFRY, and Czechoslovakia) during the post-socialist democratic transformations of the 1990s, the number of states in Europe is today around 40. Throughout the centuries, the conditions for the development of modern society advanced in Europe at different paces. In the west, urbanization took hold in the 16th century. During the 17th and 18th centuries, small-scale manufacturing experienced a boom around the capital centers in the most developed parts of Europe, and it spread to other large cities over the next century. The population growth linked to modernization in Europe only occurred in the mid-18th century. In Western Europe, consolidated nation states predominated from the 18th century onwards, introducing common language, educational, and cultural practices, and expecting loyalty from "connected and coherent populations" (Tilly 1995, p. 35). The late 18th century was the period of initial modernization in Central Europe under the "enlightened" absolutism and reforms instigated by the Habsburg rulers Maria Theresa and Joseph II (Karaman 2000, pp. 46–88). This reform epoch marked the transition from a late agrarian-feudal to a bourgeois capitalist society, and educational reforms further contributed to increased literacy in their lands.

The year of the European revolutions, 1848, was also significant in the Southeast European region. The Croatian national revival began in the 1830s, with cultural and political motives. The Slovene national movement in the latter part of the 19th century had the predominantly cultural agenda of highlighting the Slovene language as the seat of national identity (Scuteri 2016). The "spring of nations" in 1848–1849 (Banac 1984) brought neither independence nor a bourgeois revolution to Croatia and Slovenia. Instead, it strengthened absolutism and the development of neo-absolutism (Gross 1985).

The Croatian national revival contributed to a lively party-political scene, especially after 1860, which marked a new constitutional phase of the monarchy when civil and political rights were granted in all parts of the Habsburg Empire. The expansion of political ideas as reflected in the parties was echoed among the increasingly interested populations, in the midst of the continued repression of national expectations by Austria and Hungary. In Slovenia, political parties were established during the last decade of the 19th century.[3] This political phase will also have repercussions in relation to newspaper publishing (discussed further below).

Despite the existence of the Croatian assembly (Sabor),[4] which indicated a degree of self-rule from the 13th century onwards, both economic and monetary policies were outside of its jurisdiction, and were therefore decided in Vienna or in Budapest after the Habsburg Empire became the dual Austro-Hungarian monarchy in 1867. Croatia became part of the Hungarian part of the monarchy following the Croat-Hungarian Nagodba (Agreement).

While retaining a semblance of state power (i.e., the Sabor [assembly], as headed by the Ban [prorex or viceroy]), this ushered in a time of diminished power for Croatia. Increased pressure from the awakened Magyar nationalism and attempts at assimilation were met by Croatian resistance.

For some of the Southeast European Balkan states, independence from the Turkish Empire came before its downfall at the end of World War I, although this did not necessarily produce conditions conducive to modernization. In Serbia, the earliest signs of any kind of democratic traditions are linked to the local Orthodox Christian elders who were Ottoman tax collectors during the 18th century (Lampe 1989). After the Serbian uprisings in 1804 and 1815, autonomy was granted to the country in 1830 by the Ottomans. The Serbian landed elites were annihilated by the Ottomans during the early 19th century, and the peasants became the free owners of private holdings, producing a kind of classless system of peasants as the only social class (Stokes 1989, p. 235). The state then took the place of the other, previously dominant class. Serbia started to develop state institutions from the 1840s onwards under the leadership of Prince Alexander, a staunch supporter of the constitution introduced by the Ottomans. State institutions were developed, schools were established, and a period of general development began. These institutions were, however, still established within an Ottoman state context (Banac 1992a). Two Balkan wars (Serbia, Montenegro, Greece, and Bulgaria pushed back the Turks in the first, while the second was fought against Bulgaria over the control of North Macedonia and other territories liberated from the Ottomans) took place in the Balkan Peninsula during the early 20th century. Austria-Hungary and the South Slav lands of Slovenia and Croatia were not participants in these wars, although they were influenced by the consequences. The country's success in the wars left the much stronger Serbia with territorial aspirations regarding its neighbors to the west, including Bosnia and Herzegovina and parts of Croatia, in accordance with the radical nationalist policies that emerged during the 19th century and called for the integration of all Serbs into one state.

Serbia and Montenegro were constitutional monarchies following the turn of the 20th century, although liberal democracies were not allowed to develop. In North Macedonia, the first of our countries to be occupied by the Ottoman Empire, the peasants revolted in 1903 and formed the short-lived Kruševo Republic, which is a matter of national pride to this day. It took almost another decade for the country to be free of Ottoman occupation in 1912, and Macedonia remained part of Serbia until it became a federal republic within the socialist Yugoslavia after World War II.

Kingdom of Serbs, Croats, and Slovenes/Kingdom of Yugoslavia

After their divergent experiences under the Habsburg and Ottoman Empires, the breakup of the two empires during World War I enabled the 1918 unification of the South Slav nations into a common state, namely Yugoslavia.

The Croatian Sabor pronounced independence from the Habsburg Empire and, in a process that involved negotiations concerning the future status of Slovenes and Croats in the country, formed the Kingdom of SHS by uniting with the Kingdom of Serbia, including the already annexed Montenegro and today's North Macedonia. The new country was ruled by the Serbian Karađorđević dynasty, and it was renamed the Kingdom of Yugoslavia in 1929. In the future, Yugoslav monarchism will be followed by Axis occupation and the dissolution of the state, the establishment of a second Yugoslav socialist state in 1945, and its final dissolution in 1990–1992.

For the different nations, different motives propelled this unification. The Croats were primarily looking to achieve the long desired unification of their lands. In the case of the Slovenes, they were hoping for a South Slavic unification of a reciprocal character, with equal status in the new country being granted all the South Slav nations/peoples. The Serbs were more interested in expanding the Serbian state, which was already independent and confident following its successful rebellion against the Ottoman Empire (Banac 1984). Some saw the first Yugoslavia as a "state glued together from the remnants of the Ottoman and Austro-Hungarian Empires . . . in a deliberate attempt to contain Serbian expansion" (Tilly 1995, pp. 235–236). In fact, with unification, Serbian oriental-influenced patrimonial institutions were spread to the western lands of Croatia, Bosnia and Herzegovina (which came under Austro-Hungarian occupation in 1878),[5] and Slovenia (Banac 1992a). Different government styles conflicted in the new state: the Habsburg legally based bureaucracy collided with a Serbian bureaucracy based on clientelism and corruption (Horvat 2003, p. 339). Banac (1984) argues that the key reason for the failure of this Yugoslav project was the general disinclination to ensure a consociational system of government with equal representation and status for all the constituent nations. The constant conflicts about the desired type of government, the legitimacy of the state's institutions, and the fall into an outright dictatorship indicate this new country to be highly polarized and to rely on coercive measures.

While a multi-party political system already existed at the time of the establishment of the Kingdom of SHS/Yugoslavia (parties were first established in Croatia in the 1840s; see the section below on political parallelism), the state was far from being a liberal democracy. Military occupation and repression were ongoing in Croatia (Horvat 2003), which had lost its independent assembly (Sabor), as well as in the southern parts of the kingdom, that is, today's North Macedonia and Kosovo (Lampe 2014). The country was divided into administrative units that separated historical lands. A policy of Serb domination was introduced into all cultural and educational activities – schools that taught in the Macedonian and Albanian languages were closed. The fully fledged royal dictatorship of King Alexander was proclaimed on January 6, 1929, which aimed to enforce a Serb-based "Yugoslav" identity onto the resistant Slovenes and Croats. The country was at this time renamed the Kingdom of Yugoslavia. The parliament in Belgrade was dismantled, political parties were banned, and many newspapers were closed. Political pluralism returned after King Alexander was assassinated in Marseilles in 1934. Further, elections for the national assembly were held in 1935. During the last period, Croatia succeeded in negotiating the union of its lands internally in the Croatian Banovina established in 1939. The new Yugoslav government made many liberal promises, which were not kept (Bjelica 1968). In summary, both multi-party politics and democracy in this region saw many reversals and setbacks. Moreover, at all times they developed in a context of contested state legitimacy, a unitarist/royalist versus federalist/republican divide, and state suppression of opposition ideas. We present more details regarding the political parties and their goals in relation to their media-related activities in the section on political parallelism.

Yugoslavia disintegrated during World War II as a result of German and Italian occupation and separate administration – Slovenia was annexed to the Reich; in Croatia, the Independent State of Croatia (Nezavisna država Hrvatska [NDH], extending into Bosnia and Herzegovina, but giving away Croatian Istria and Dalmatia to Italy, which also occupied Montenegro) was installed by Hitler and implemented racial laws; while Serbia also had a Nazi collaborationist regime. The anti-fascist resistance in Yugoslavia was the largest in Europe.[6] In 1943, the liberated territories of Yugoslavia – Istria, parts of Dalmatia, Lika (Croatia), large parts of Bosnia and Herzegovina, and small parts of North Macedonia – were, apart from the UK, the USSR, Sicily, and small parts of southern Italy, the only free territories in occupied Europe (Lampe 2014). We will discuss the aftermath of this second critical juncture in the next chapter.

Transformations of the economic field

The transformations of economic institutions from the 11th to the 15th century in Europe resulted in a capitalist economic system, which developed alongside the enduring traditional feudal economy, while trade and commodity production in and around the growing cities complemented the peasant-based feudal production. J. B. Thompson (1995) argues that by the time the Gutenberg printing press was invented and printing houses started to appear in Europe, the economic conditions necessary for the development of media institutions as commercial organizations were already present (cf. also Eisenstein 1993/1979). We now focus on the economic conditions evolving in the six analyzed countries during those times.

The whole of Eastern Europe was economically underdeveloped long before the Industrial Revolution. While the indigenous dynamic development of Western Europe was enabled by the political stalemate between towns, lords, monarchs, and the Catholic Church, which created an intellectual atmosphere in which parliamentary systems developed, such a power balance never developed in Eastern Europe (Chirot 1989, p. 3), primarily because urban development in Eastern Europe was much less pronounced in the predominantly coercive states with low capital concentrations (Tilly 1992). Instead of early capitalist development, Eastern Europe experienced a "second serfdom" when the landed elites and aristocracy attempted to profit from the world economic market for agricultural produce, although rather than introducing advanced industrialized modes of agricultural production in order to increase production, they pressed more peasants into increased serfdom. Poland and Hungary represent the main examples of these backwards economic practices (Lampe 2014). In the Ottoman-occupied lands, the peasants escaped this deterioration in conditions due to Ottoman feudalism being of a different type, although their economic situation was even worse and agricultural production even less productive. In the mid-18th century, the Balkans "remained uncommercialized, fragmented in sovereignty, blessed or cursed with powerful landlords and subject to a tribute taking empire" (Tilly 1995, p. 177). The fact of the economic backwardness of Eastern Europe, especially its least developed southeastern parts, is also seen by modernization theorists to be significant in terms of explaining the delay in the region's political evolution (Norris and Inglehart 2009; Huntington 1991; Inglehart and Welzel 2005; Lampe 2014).

The Habsburg Empire was, overall, essentially less progressive than Western European countries such as France and England (Lampe 1989), and it was more successful in delaying modernization in both political and economic terms. Moore's (1966) proposition regarding the relationship between the type of the transformation of feudalism and the outcome regime includes three main cases. The first case is exemplified by the French and British revolutions. It comes about when the transforming force is the bourgeoisie and the outcome is democratic and industrial revolution. The second case dealing with modernization or the transformation of feudalism concerns the agency of the aristocracy and the landed classes, as in the case of Germany, and the result is fascism. The third case is a peasant revolution resulting in communism: the case of Russia and China. Stokes (1989) argues for the similarity between the situation in Southeast Europe and the second scenario of revolution from above by the landed aristocracy, which controlled politics in Austria, Hungary, and Croatia (Serbia could also be included, as the leading class was the state itself) – all these countries experienced fascist/Nazi episodes before or during World War II.

While the lands of the Habsburg Empire had some kind of advantage, at least in terms of having a similar culture, similar political institutions, and a common religion, over those lands under Ottoman control, their position within the empire was equally peripheral as that of the South Slav lands within the Ottoman Empire. The main interest of the Habsburgs was maintaining the military border with the Ottomans and extracting a constant supply of soldiers for the defense of the empire. The southeast borderlands of the Habsburg Empire did not share in the integration into the world economy during the 19th century to the same degree as the central countries of the empire – Austria and Bohemia-Czechoslovakia. When industrialization began, the main goal of the Habsburgs was to develop their capital cities and their international reach, with the support of resources extracted from their peripheral lands (Karaman 1991). Some transportation infrastructure built at that time to connect Vienna and Budapest with the Adriatic ports of Rijeka (Croatia) and Kopar (Slovenia) brought collateral benefits. Literacy, however, increased significantly in Slovenia and Croatia, rising to some three-quarters of the empire's average.

The Ottoman Empire did not benefit from the industrialization-related transformations happening in Western Europe, and its decline since the 16th century is linked to this negative effect (Adanir 1989). This also rendered the transition to the capitalist mode of production more difficult for the occupied territories in the Balkan part of Southeast Europe. Chirot (1989) advances the case of Western European exceptionalism in which the dynamic Western European development was unique, a consequence of a set of unparalleled conditions that created the potentials for the development of modern societies. The capital-intensive regions of Southeast Europe lay along the Adriatic coast, including Dubrovnik, which was part of the global cultural and economic flows, while the South Slav lands of the Habsburg Empire, as well as the Balkans, are examples of the coercion-intensive type of state formation (Tilly 1995). The Balkan economic backwardness was a result of a complex mix of ecological (mountainous terrain unfit for developed agricultural production), political (constant instability due to long-term wars), and cultural forces, which were exacerbated by the long-term Ottoman occupation. Bursts of growth and prosperity were followed by decline, in a similar manner to that seen in other Mediterranean European countries (Chirot 1989). Chirot (1989) argues that their peripheral position within the Ottoman Empire and their lack of contact with the West are the primary reasons for the continued lagging behind of these countries, which largely did not participate in the currents of global trade or cultural exchange either within or between their respective borders.

A similar peripheral position was held by the Slovene and Croatian lands within the Habsburg Empire. Industrialization was reserved for Austria during the Theresian reforms (Stokes 1989, pp. 220–221), which favored Slovenia, while indigenous industrialization in Croatia was not supported by state policies or funding and was discouraged by both Budapest and Vienna (Karaman 1991). Industry in the periphery was primarily related to the exploration and exploitation of natural resources (Gross 1985). In Croatia, this included coal mining, the lumber industry, grain mills, and agriculture, while in Istria and Dalmatia, it also included the shipbuilding industry. The major industry included the paper-mill industry and the oil refineries established in Rijeka. Oil was found in Croatia in the 18th century, although excavation only began in the 19th century. The number of larger industrial companies (with between 21 and 100 workers) experienced an increase of 2.5 times between 1890 and 1910 (reaching 207), while the number of large industrial companies (with more than 100 workers) increased to 64 companies during the same period. In 1910, there were more than 23,000 industrial workers in Croatia (Mirković 1958, as quoted in Karaman 1991, pp. 188–240).

In the Kingdom of SHS/Yugoslavia, the two westernmost lands became the most developed parts of the new South Slav state. Indeed, Slovenian and Croatian manufacturing was responsible for the majority of the 19% of the Kingdom of SHS/Yugoslavia's GDP attributed to the industrial sector. Mirković (1958, p. 7), in his *Economic History of Yugoslavia*, highlights the differences and similarities between the economies – trade was especially important for Dubrovnik, and at one time, for Serbia; industry was important for Croatia (especially Zagreb and Rijeka), Slovenia (Ljubljana and Kranj), and Vojvodina; and agriculture was important in all parts of the new country. Industrialization was very uneven. For example, in today's North Macedonia, the beginnings of industrialization were only seen at the start of World War I, when there were fewer than 300 industrial workers in the country. The country's two electric power plants only produced electricity for illumination because there was no industry in need of supply (Mirković 1958).

Transformations of the cultural field

We now turn to the notion of a media system and its journey back in time. We first focus on the broader field of culture within which the media institution will eventually develop. In this way, we turn to the functional equivalent of the present-day media that existed in the premodern temporal framework characterized by an early state of political and economic differentiation. Before the capitalist mode of production separated the fields of economy and politics in Europe, both these fields of power were much more conflated – those with political power also had economic power (monarchs and the aristocracy), while religious institutions held supreme symbolic power. In some places, the supreme religious authority also enjoyed political and coercive power, as embodied by monarchs. This separation of politics from private enterprise and profit making was a characteristic of Western modernity. In the Ottoman Empire, the granting of economic privilege was the prerogative of the sultan.

The media field, as part of the cultural field, in Western Europe was, since the beginning, based on the capitalist market economy (J. B. Thompson 1995). Before the capitalist economy was developed and the media institution first appeared in the form of the printing press, other institutions were in charge of disbursing power in the cultural field. The transformations in the field of symbolic power thus include interrelated changes in the field of education and knowledge control, the power of religious institutions, and the development of the media institution.

From the 11th century onwards, the development of universities not under the control of the Catholic Church slowly eroded its monopoly on knowledge production and dissemination, and it also led to a demand for secular books by the time printing presses appeared. In the West, the previously strong role of the Catholic Church was gradually eroded as states grew in both capital and coercive power (Tilly 1992), while the Protestant Reformation during the 16th century ended the church's monopoly, bringing about a pluralism of religious world views (J.B. Thompson 1995, pp. 51–52). In parts of Europe, the pushback by the Catholic Church kept the Reformation at bay over the following hundred years – this also happened in Slovenia and Croatia, as the Habsburg Empire joined in with the church's efforts in this regard, which contributed to its own self-preservation.

No such transformations occurred in the Ottoman Empire, where the symbolic power and monopoly of Islam and its institutional hold over both education and religious values, as well as over the judiciary, remained in place until the 20th century and Atatürk's secular modernization reforms. In the Russian Empire, the state Orthodox religion was the only one permitted until the beginning of the 20th century. The Austro-Hungarian Empire included religious freedom in its constitution in 1867, although some religions were already tolerated from the late 18th century onwards (Islam was officially included in 1912).

States' evolving relationships with the media

Habsburg and Ottoman Empires

The attention paid by the state to any type of organized public communication precedes modern times. In the Habsburg Empire, printing was always subject to government scrutiny, and from the introduction of printing, the existing centers of symbolic power, namely the Catholic Church, did what they could to interfere with the printing or distribution of independent books or pamphlets. Censorship was officially introduced in 1787, and it was executed by both the church and the military (Horvat 2003, p. 43). Books were also censored, with some titles being banned. For example, a list of censored books found in the records of the Zagreb censorship office includes works such as Goethe's *Werther*, Mirabeau's *Système des nations*, and *The Memoirs of Casanova* (Horvat 2003, p. 60). Although everything political was the main target of censorship, the underground publication of politically motivated pamphlets and brochures flourished.

The freedom of the press was proclaimed within the Habsburg Empire in 1812, but it was not long lasting. Before the revolution of 1848, only two papers were published in Croatia – *Agramer Zeitung* and Gaj's *Novine dalmatinsko-horvatsko-slavonske*. In 1848, complete freedom of the press was proclaimed within the empire, including in Slovenia and Croatia (Markus 1998). The new Press Law abolished the royal privilege in terms of establishing newspapers and introduced a deposit in silver, with the price varying in regard to the weekly or daily type of the paper. In the same year, the freedom of the press was proclaimed in Croatia. The Croatian Ban,

Josip Jelačić, was appointed by Vienna and also elected in the Sabor as the champion of the Croatian national program (territorial unification and independence within the empire), a role for which he is still praised in that country. The freedom of the press was also included in the proclamation of the modern liberal democratic program within the "Peoples' requirements" adopted by the Croatian Sabor in 1848, together with equality in law for all nations, religions, and classes; the unification of Croatian lands; the right to the national Croatian language; and other matters (Zahtevanje naroda 1848, as quoted in Macan 1995). Most of these remained only wishes, as the conservative monarchy was reasserted. During the war with Hungary, in 1849, Croatian Ban Jelačić introduced a controversial Temporary Law on the Press (Privremeni zakon o tisku) primarily aimed at controlling the opposition press. While the required deposit remained the only restriction in relation to starting a newspaper, the penalties for insulting the ruler or instigating rebellion included up to ten years' imprisonment for the editor, as well as the possibility of being banned from working in journalism, in addition to fines for the publisher (Bjelica 1968). The improvement over the previous situation was that any such allegations had to be adjudicated in a trial. Interestingly, the law also forbade hate speech against any "nationalities and faiths," introduced the right of reply, forbid the publication of material offending public decency, and introduced the offense of libel (Markus 1998). The law was condemned by the liberal political opinion and opposition dailies *Slavenski Jug* and *Sudslavische Zeitung*, which Jelačić banned in 1850 (Švoger 2013). The emperor then proclaimed an even stricter Press Law in 1852. The first press laws were adopted by the Sabor in Croatia in 1874–1875 under Ban Ivan Mažuranić, and they continued to form the basis of the press legislature until 1918 (Čepulo 2000). Čepulo (2000) finds that the normative basis for even this new, more liberal press law was the general consensus that the freedom of the press and freedom of expression are something granted by the state, not rights that the government should protect. Government repression of the press and censorship were such that most newspapers had to agree to toe the government line in order to exist. The degree of self-rule that Croatia retained even under the Croatian-Hungarian Settlement was not helpful in relation to the freedom of the press. The Hungarian Ban, Károly Khuen-Hedervary, who was appointed in 1883, cracked down on press freedom as part of his absolutist rule aimed at the Magyarization of Croatia, and he especially harassed the opposition papers (the Party of Rights' paper *Sloboda* and the *Obzor* of the People's Party were confiscated countless times). The degrees of press freedom differed in the different lands within the empire – by the beginning of the 20th century, when police oversight of the press was prohibited in Croatia and Slovenia, together with the previously obligatory deposits for publishing and the ban on street selling being lifted, in Bosnia-Herzegovina (which had recently been occupied by the Habsburg Empire) such constraints were still implemented.

Meanwhile, under the Ottomans, the publishing of newspapers was not allowed until the late 19th century. The Ottoman Empire allowed printing presses in Serbia from 1830 within the scope of the internal autonomy granted to the country. Schools were also established as a consequence of the newfound autonomy, and the Serbian government policies were geared toward developing education and culture. The ruler, Knez Miloš, passed a decree in 1832 that set out what it was forbidden to publish: "blasphemy, ideas against Christian religion, scandalous thoughts against public morale, thoughts against the government of Serbia and all foreign government and its members" (Radenić 1969, p. 68). In 1848, under the rule of Aleksandar Karađorđević, Serbia launched a renewed censorship regime that forbade any political content as well as the distribution of any books or newspapers without prior approval by the censor. The pressure of censorship regarding book and newspaper publishing remained in place until 1870 and the adoption of the first Serbian Law on the press, when the most difficult restrictions were lifted. The first Press Law in 1870, and the new constitution, gave rise to a friendlier environment for press development and for political life. The new law included the right of freedom of expression for "every Serb," although it retained the censorship clause (Bjelica 1968, p. 53). In 1881 a new, more liberal press law was issued that did not require police permission to publish and stated that a ban on publication could only be ordered by a court (Bjelica 1968, p. 58). This law was reminiscent of the Austrian law from the mid-19th century.

Kingdom of SHS/Yugoslavia

Bjelica (1968, p. 129) offers a periodization of the state and press relationship in the Kingdom of SHS/Yugoslavia, which is divided into four periods: the first concerns the initial two years of state consolidation (1918–1920); the second, the following years of parliamentary monarchy when the theoretical parliamentarism ended following the announcement of the dictatorship on January 6, 1929; the third period lasts until the assassination of King Alexander in 1934; and the fourth period ends in 1941. Ademović (1998, p. 28) similarly highlights three main milestones in relation to the position of the press in the Kingdom of SHS/Yugoslavia: the first was the government Obznana (Proclamation) in 1920, which was endorsed in the *Law on the protection of the state* in 1921; the second was the *Law on the press* in 1925; and the third was the cue that introduced the dictatorship of King Alexander on January 6, 1929.

The Obznana (Proclamation) banned the Communist party and the communist and workers' press. In the subsequent law, certain communications were treated as a crime in terms of the penal code: "writing, publication, printing, distribution of books, newspapers, posters, or proclamations. . . . This relates to any oral or written communist or anarchist propaganda or persuasion of others that the political or economic system in the state should be changed" (Article 1, *Law on the protection of the state*, as quoted in Ademović 1998, p. 30). These offences were punishable by death or 20 years' imprisonment.

The Kingdom of SHS only replaced the 1907 Press Law of the Dual Monarchy in 1925. The new law was promoted as being liberal, and it was modeled on the previous Habsburg law, albeit with important reversals that reduced the freedom of the press. It was now possible to start a newspaper without government approval or a financial deposit, and the publishers could now appeal the decision of the police to ban an issue of a newspaper. The law criminalized acts against the "interest of the state, army and social order, acts against honor" which had to be adjudicated. Five copies of every paper had to be delivered to the public prosecutor prior to publication; in practice, this meant that state officials could ban any issue, or any part of the paper, for defamation of the state and the king. Censorship was evident in the printed papers where blank spots were left, which were sometimes signed by the journalists, and the "red pen" of the censor was protested by intellectuals (Ademović 1998). Due to the huge fines and the banning of individual censored issues of newspapers, even if the court later resolved the issue in favor of the publisher, the economic damage was already done and many papers were financially ruined (Ademović 1998, pp. 31–33). The law also created the Central Press Bureau, which was charged with monitoring the work of foreign correspondents and censoring or banning any publications, whether domestic or foreign, that "express hatred of the state" (Lampe 2014, p. 110).

After the royal dictatorship was established in 1929, newspapers were forbidden from publishing any comments regarding the political situation in Yugoslavia, and opposition party papers were banned.

Although one might expect that a common state framework would unify the legal and economic conditions for press (as well as radio) developments and also create the impetus for a convergence toward a common media system, the Kingdom of SHS/Yugoslavia presented a mixed picture of conditions and state treatment of the press. Serbia, whose dynasty ruled the new country, saw for the first time a flow to urban populations of Western high and popular culture. At the same time, in Croatia, the military occupation was intended to support the economic pillage and to contain the "enemy territory" (even though the lands were united in a diplomatic agreement and were not conquered militarily). The military censorship of the press lasted there for the first two years of the joint state. In Macedonia and Montenegro, state repression was also present, while in Bosnia and Herzegovina, frequent revolts by the population were quelled by the military. Slovenia, the furthest country from the new center, was the least harassed. The press did not enjoy the same economic position either: state taxes were much higher in all the territories aside from Serbia. Despite these adverse conditions, a host of new newspapers were established during the interwar period. After 1934, censorship was somewhat relaxed, and the growing number of publications, books, and magazines made it more difficult for the state to monitor everything closely.

Development of media markets

During the very long temporal framework analyzed in this chapter, four key media institutions were created. J.B. Thompson (1995) argues that printing represents the first major institutional transformation within the symbolic field that subsequently stimulated the development of the media industries enduring the second part of the 15th century. This was followed by the development of the newspaper, including the institutions of news and journalism. The next most important technological innovation is the telegraph, which, according to Giddens (2012), introduced modernity when it enabled only the messages to be transported to another person, without the sender of the message going to the place where the person who received it was. Radio followed this first wireless technology, and the rest, as the saying goes, is history.

We are familiar with the Western European and American developments regarding these inventions and their appropriation (Eisenstein 1993/1979; Briggs and Burke 2005; Chapman 2005). In the next section of this chapter, we will observe how different, or similar, the spread and appropriation of these four media technologies and institutions was in the six analyzed Southeast European countries.

Differences in the spread of printing

The conditions of institutional transformation differed in the field of cultural symbolic power, as well as in the fields of economy and politics, between the different empires in Europe. The development of printing and the media industries also developed at different paces. In our countries of interest, the conditions for modernization transformation were linked to the empire that ruled them.

The familiar early modern institutional transformations in the cultural field were present, if sometimes to a diminished degree, thanks to their peripheral position in the territories included in the Austro-Hungarian Empire (Slovenia, Croatia, and some parts of Vojvodina [the northern part of today's Serbia]) or those under Venetian rule (the cities along the Croatian Adriatic and Dubrovnik). In the territories under the Ottoman rule (Bosnia and Herzegovina, Serbia, Montenegro, and what is today North Macedonia), these transformations were significantly delayed, in some places until the 19th century and in others until the 20th century.

The Protestant Reformation during the 16th century is linked to our understanding of the cultural field within the pre-modern or late medieval period. In Southeast Europe, it was felt in Croatia and especially Slovenia, where it contributed to the first books being published in its national language. However, the Catholic Church re-established its dominance in both countries after some 150 years, aided by the strong Habsburg support for the Counter-Reformation, which aimed to block the claims for political and religious autonomy in its peripheral provinces and therefore maintained its power with the support of the Catholic Church. Protestantism remains a minority faith in both countries to the present day. In the Orthodox states (Serbia and Montenegro), the church promoted state power (Tilly 1995, p. 47), and no similar transformations occurred.

The first book printed in a Slavic language was the Croatian *Glagolitic Missal* (Missale Romanum Slavonico Idiomate), which was printed in 1483 (Dimnik 1984) in the vernacular and in Glagolitic script. It is not quite clear whether it was also printed in Kosinj, which was the first publishing house established in Croatia by the magnate Frankopan family (the second was established in Senj in 1494). The first book in the Slovene language is linked to the Protestant priest Primož Trubar, and it was published in 1550 in Tübingen (Županić 1911), some 25 years before the first printing press was established in Ljubljana (Dimnik 1984). The earliest libraries available in Slovenian and Croatian monasteries show a predominance of books produced in Italy and Germany, on both religious and secular topics, thereby indicating participation in the cultural flows of that time (Dimnik 1984). In Cetinje (Montenegro), printing was established in a state-owned press in 1493, and it went on to publish some of the first books in the Cyrillic script, mainly Orthodox religious texts, although this did not last long due to the Turkish occupation. In the town of Goražde in Bosnia and Herzegovina, a printing press was briefly established in 1529, although the Turkish occupation stopped the development of printing for the next 300 years (Papić 1969). Serbia and Macedonia had to wait until their liberation from the Ottoman Empire during the 19th century before such developments were possible. Both books and journals by Serbian writers were published abroad (in Venice, Vienna, and St. Petersburg) from the 18th century onwards, reaching very small audiences of 100 or 200 (Bjelica 1968).

In Slovenia and Croatia, where printing was first introduced by the clergy and magnate families soon after its invention and appropriation in Western Europe, the role of printing in the promotion and development of standard national languages is linked to its role in nation building. Benedict Anderson considers the virtual community of fellow readers to precede the imagined community of a nation (as quoted in J.B. Thompson 1995, p. 62). In both Slovenia and Croatia, from the time of the Reformation in the 16th century onwards, the development of their respective national languages was an important issue as well as a constant effort to preserve them from the attempts at Germanization, Italianization, or Hungarization. The community of readers was initially small and limited to the elite, but it began to broaden with the introduction of the periodical press.

Meanwhile, in the Ottoman Empire, printing was forbidden. The fear that the introduction of printing would challenge the legitimacy of the Ottoman ruler, as supported by the Islamic religious authority, did not allow for the possibility of such a cultural transformation. If the authoritarian model of the media system was the original model in Croatia and Slovenia, as in Western Europe (Siebert et al. 1956), it was not the case in the countries of Southeast Europe that were under the Ottoman rule, as the sultanistic dictatorial regime imposed a set of power relationships of a different kind.

The Ottoman Empire did not allow printing in Arabic before 1729, when secular sources of legitimacy started to appear alongside the traditional religious ones, which had a strict monopoly on knowledge (Coşgel et al. 2012). The military, as one of the sources of such secular authority, had more authority in the Balkans in general, as a smaller percentage (some 20%) of households there had converted to Islam (a much higher percentage converted in Bosnia and Herzegovina, as already mentioned). Yet, printing in Arabic script was officially banned very soon after the technology was invented by Gutenberg, and "occupying oneself with the science of printing was punishable by death," according to a widely cited but disputed edict, although printing was permitted in Istanbul for some non-Islamic religious communities in their own languages and scripts as early as the 15th century (Coşgel et al. 2012, p. 14). The literacy rates were, overall, much lower in the Ottoman Empire than in Europe. When books were allowed, it was only as a result of a strictly regulated government-granted monopoly (Acemoğlu and Robinson 2012; Coşgel et al. 2012).

The principal weakness of the Ottoman regime concerned the rigidity of the sultan's bureaucracy and the hostility of the Muslim clergy to modern technology. Only in the early 20th century, before the beginning of World War I, did a class-like struggle develop between the ruling and the religious institutions (Lampe 1989, p. 190), which weakened the hold of religion over the state and eventually allowed for a secular Turkish modernization under Atatürk.

Printing was consequently introduced in the Ottoman-occupied lands in Southeast Europe during 19th century. In Serbia, the first state-owned printing press allowed by the Ottoman regime was imported into Belgrade in 1831 and later moved to Kragujevac in 1834, and it enabled the publication of the first newspaper (Radenić 1969). The production of religious books started in the Orthodox monasteries during the 16th century, although they were not produced using the new movable-type printing press. Attempts to establish printing once again in Bosnia and Herzegovina were only successful in 1866, when a municipal/state-controlled printing house was established in Sarajevo (Vilajetska štamparija) and two printers opened in Mostar, one of them private. The printing press was re-established in Montenegro in 1834 during the reign of King Petar II Petrović-Njegoš (Martinović 1965).

Literacy rates rose during the early 20th century. In Serbia, this was primarily the case in the cities (data for Belgrade, as quoted in Lampe 2014, mention 60% literacy as opposed to the 20% average in Serbia, with largely illiterate peasants). In Croatia, in 1910, 68% of the population was literate, and illiterates were only found among the older peasant populations (Horvat 2003). Slovenia had still higher shares of literate populations. The establishment of universities also contributed to the modernizing ferment in these states. Universities were established in Zagreb in 1669/1874 (Yugoslav Academy of Science and Art was established in 1866, as quoted in Macan 1995), in Belgrade in 1905, and in Ljubljana in 1919.

Newspapers and the political public sphere

The early newspapers were another type of media institution, appearing in Western European cities, especially those already on the main trading routes, during the early 17th century. In mid-17th century England, the press was already relatively free and printing was mainly uncontrolled. In continental Europe, different degrees of censorship of the press existed in the different absolutist monarchies and in relation to different topics. National political news was generally more controlled than international news. Despite the fact that continental European countries exercised different levels of press censorship, most often related to their domestic political news, private efforts to share news and ideas, as well as to make a profit, were impossible to stop altogether – similar to how efforts to censor or stop the publication of books were circumvented by printing them in other cities (Eisenstein 1993/1979; J. B. Thompson 1995). Over the next hundred years, at the end of the 18th century and after the French Revolution, the freedom of the press was enshrined in the French Constitution, similar to the situation in the United States. In the introduction of newspapers,[7] we see a divergence similar to that concerning book publishing between the countries in the Habsburg Empire and those under Ottoman rule.

HABSBURG AND OTTOMAN EMPIRES

In Slovenia, the first newspaper, the *Leibacher Zeitung* (the Ljubljana daily, which closed in 1918; Županić [1911] puts the year of its first publication as 1778), appeared in 1707, and in 1797 the *Ljubljanske novice*, the initial albeit short-lived paper in Slovenian language, was introduced. Its editor was Valentin Vodnik, writer and member of the Slovenian revival movement (Bjelica 1968). Županić (1911) argues that the *Kmetijske in rokodelske novice*, published in 1843 by Janez Bleiwais, was the first Slovene newspaper with a political and cultural role similar to that of *Novine horvatske*, which was published in 1834 by Ljudevit Gaj in Croatia. Periodical publications, in the form of calendars or "practical publications," date from the 16th century, with the first such calendar, *Ta slovenski kolendar*, having been published in the Slovene language in 1557 by Primož Trubar. This practice was continued by others, and the calendar became the most important vehicle for national peasant education, literacy promotion, and cultural and political consciousness among Slovenes. It was arguably more important than later newspapers (Vatovec 1969). In the mid-19th century, according to Vatovec (1969), one calendar was published for every ten inhabitants of Slovenia. The first calendar appeared in Croatia in 1694. It was published by the poet Pavao Ritter Vitezović, who was awarded the right to operate the printing press by the Croatian Sabor. The calendar included summaries of the meetings of the Sabor held in Zagreb, was written in the phonetic alphabet of the Croatian language, and included advertisements for books, as well as an occasional news poem, in addition to the usual content of calendars relating to the phases of the moon or yearly events. Horvat (2003, p. 29) describes how Vitezović and others published news in the form of poems as it was the form most easily understood by the uneducated population. The first actual newspaper in Croatia, the *Ephemerides Zagrebienses*, only came out in 1771. The first Croatian-language newspaper was published in 1806 (*Kraglski Dalmatin*, Zadar, published in both Italian and Croatian). In the early 19th century, the press in Croatia developed as a political platform for the national revival movement, which included strong cultural overtones, thereby contributing to the recognition of the national language in public and cultural affairs. The first newspaper, the *Novine Horvatske*, with its cultural and political supplement the *Danica horvatsko-slavonsko-dalmatinska*, was published and edited by Ljudevit Gaj, who played a prominent political and cultural role in the Ilyrianist movement. In addition to its political importance, the paper, which later changed its name to the *Narodne novine* (National Gazette), was the first to standardize modern Croatian orthography based on Czech-language diacritics (Gaj had studied law in Prague), which became the Croatian language's literary standard (cf. Balčytiene [2009] on the similar role of the press in the development of the national language in the Baltic states). The publishers and journalists of the time were members of the intelligentsia – poets and writers who invariably became politicians – although their readership was small and mainly comprised the elite. The *Novi list* (established in 1902) and *Obzor* were the first mass-audience general-information dailies in Croatia (Novak 2005, pp. 70–116), but their print runs were never very large. The role of print was important in Europe as a whole in terms of promoting and fixing the natural language and as a precondition for the development of a national identity (J. B. Thompson 1995, p. 62).

The first calendar aimed at a Serbian audience was published (probably in Venice) in 1765, a few years before the only issue of *Slaveno-serbskij magazin*, a paper aimed at Serbian emigrants. The first paper in the territory of today's Serbia was published in Belgrade from 1835: *Novine srbske*, which was published by Dimitrije Davidovič, the editor of the journal of the same name in Vienna in 1818 (until 1820). The paper had a circulation of a few hundred copies, and it was mainly aimed at the Serbs in Vienna and Vojvodina. The population in Serbia proper was largely illiterate. Bjelica (1968, p. 32) notes that only five copies of *Novine srbske* were sent from Vienna to Serbia and only one to Montenegro – to King Petar I Petrović-Njegoš. Other Serbian journals and newspapers were published in Budapest over the subsequent decades. To expand the circulation of the paper, in 1835, the king made it obligatory for all government offices, churches, cafes, and even wealthier priests to take out a subscription. In the meantime, only two new papers were published, and even then only irregularly, during the 1850s. The liberal opposition was related to several short-lived papers over the following decade. Conservative ideas were also promoted in several papers. A degree of press freedom was present throughout the early 20th century in independent Serbia, while there was more limited press freedom in Montenegro (Lampe 2014).

In Montenegro, schools started to be established after the 1830s, although newspapers were still not feasible due to the largely illiterate population. The first newspaper, the *Crnogorac*, was published in 1871, a decade after the political field started to awaken to the concept of political struggle.

In Macedonia, the first schools were opened during the first half of the 19th century, and the first books in the Macedonian language were published around the same time (Bjelica 1968). The first newspapers were established in 1908 by the Serb National Association, with the aim of promoting the idea of a Serb identity for North Macedonia. The first paper published by Macedonian emigrants, with a view to supporting the independence of the country, was the *Makedonskij glas*, which was published in Sophia in 1885 (Mokrov 1969). A few years later, the first magazine, *Loza*, was also published in Sophia by a recently formed group, namely the Young Macedonian Literary Society. Both these publications contributed to the Macedonian national revival movement, which was completed by the establishment in 1893 of the political organization the VMRO (Vnatrešna Makedonska Revolucionerna Organizacija [Internal Macedonian Revolutionary Organization]) with the aim of freeing Macedonia from Turkish occupation (Mokrov 1969).

The first paper for Ottoman-controlled Bosnia and Herzegovina, the *Bosanski prijatelj*, was published in 1850 in Zagreb by Ljudevit Gaj, who aimed to spread the ideas of enlightenment and national awareness. The Franciscan order, as the main proponent of attempts at press development among the Bosnian population, was also involved in this effort. Printing was allowed by the Ottomans in 1856, although the first newspaper was not published until a decade later. The *Bosna* paper was established in the same year as the official paper of the Ottoman government, while in Herzegovina the *Neretva* paper was established with a similar status. All three papers published under the auspices of the Turkish occupation were published in the Serbian language and in Cyrillic script (*Bosna* was also published in the Turkish language and script), and they all had the status of a semi-official paper. After Bosnia and Herzegovina came under the control of Austria-Hungary in 1878, 50 new papers and magazines were established (Bjelica 1968). Before World War I, press development again increased, and 140 new papers were launched, including five dailies in Sarajevo. Pejanović (1961) explains how, in spite of low subscription rates and low overall literacy, the audiences for newspapers in Bosnia and Herzegovina were more numerous because the stories were retold, which represents another confirmation of the spread of the early oral culture. Here again, we are uncertain as to the accuracy of the data. The Bosnian government published data concerning circulation that suggest, in 1905, that 19 papers had a total circulation of 20,292 copies and 16,269 subscribers, although some 40% were foreign subscriptions (Pejanović 1961, p. 11). In addition to the political papers, there was a high readership for religious and professional papers.

Printing presses were established by the Ottomans starting from around 1860 in all six centers of the newly defined administrative units (*vilajet* [*departman*, province]) in the territories of our countries of interest: in Prizren (Prizren vilajet), Priština, and later Skopje (the Kosovo vilajet); in Bitolj (the Bitolj vilajet); and in Mostar for the Herzegovinian vilajet (Kaleši 1969). The *Prizren* paper, established by the Turkish authorities in 1871, was the first paper published in Kosovo and Macedonia. The *Kosovo* paper was later published as the official paper of the vilajet (Kaleši 1969). It was published in Turkish and, for a few years, also in Serbian. The diffusion of printing by the Ottomans in these provinces is explained by Kaleši (1969) as being related to the planned reforms of the administration of those European provinces under Ottoman rule, which never happened.

Following the turn of the century, positive social and economic developments (increased urbanization, industrial development, and literacy levels) and changes in the political field (where the new democratic middle-class gained influence) in most of the analyzed countries brought about increased press growth and the development of both general informative newspapers and party political papers. This was accompanied by growth in the circulation of newspapers, which were becoming more focused on the news, including increasingly sensationalist topics. Political debate or partisanship remained, although the largest newspapers declared themselves to be independent of all political parties (Bjelica 1968). The largest numbers of newspapers were published in Zagreb (121), Belgrade (89), and Ljubljana (58) (Bjelica 1968). Several daily papers that still exist today were established during the first years of the 20th century, including *Novi list* (Rijeka, Croatia) and *Politika* (Belgrade, Serbia).

KINGDOM OF SHS/YUGOSLAVIA

The development of the public sphere in modern Europe resulted from institutional transformations in the fields of political power and the mercantile economy, as described by Habermas (1962, 1989), and the new media institution of print became the key instrument for the critique of government. A mutually reinforcing relationship between the freedom of critique, religious pluralism, the freedom of economic enterprise, developing democracy, and the growing literacy levels of increasingly urban populations presents a picture of the indigenous modernization of Western Europe. In the Kingdom of Yugoslavia, however, the public was still largely more of the listening kind than of the reading kind. Oral coffeehouse storytelling traditions were still present in some parts of Yugoslavia in the 1930s (Briggs and Burke 2005), and the development of a media-centered public sphere was delayed until the mid-20th century in most of the country.

The high level of illiteracy influenced the character of the public sphere in these countries in a way that privileged inter-elite political discussion in the newspapers, and the development of the mass press only occurred during the 20th century. The literacy level was higher in Slovenia and Croatia than in the other lands due to having been slowly improving since Ottoman times. In the early 20th century, literacy improved as a prerequisite for the growth of the mass press ("everyday literature" according to Rački, as quoted in Gross 1985, p. 401) and mass culture. The Kingdom of Yugoslavia had a very low newspaper readership – in 1929, only 35 newspaper copies were sold per 1,000 inhabitants, with the figure much lower in Bosnia and Herzegovina and other less developed parts of the country (e.g., ten copies of newspapers were published per 1,000 inhabitants in Bosnia and Herzegovina at the beginning of the 20th century; Ademović 1998).

Interest in the news grew following the Balkan Wars and World War I, and this spurred on the development of the press, increasing print runs to an unprecedented 10,000 and 20,000 copies (Horvat 2003). In the period before World War I, dozens of new papers emerged, including party political, entertainment, satirical, and educational papers. Immediately after the formation of the new country, a number of opposition newspapers were banned. In spite of this, new papers were established after a while, with the readership expanding to include women, and the print runs for the Sunday editions of some Croatian papers rose to 60,000 copies (Horvat 2003).

The data concerning the numbers and types of publications are sketchy and incomplete. Bjelica (1968, p. 165) offers the following data: the number of magazines between 1920s and 1937 rose from 430 to 803, while the number of newspapers rose from 218 to 322. In 1927, 35 daily papers were published in cities across the Kingdom of SHS of which "16 were independent, 2 were official government papers, and 12 were affiliated with various political parties" (Bjelica 1968, p. 140) (see Table 3.1). In 1941, as a consequence of the dictatorship and the increased repression of the press, there were only 23 daily papers left: four published in today's Serbia, ten in Croatia, six in Slovenia, two in Bosnia and Herzegovina, and one in Macedonia. At that time, there were five radio stations operating in the Kingdom of Yugoslavia, with one radio receiver for every 100 inhabitants.

Technological and economic development played an important part in the professionalization of the press. The invention and implementation of telegraph services in Slovenia, Croatia, and Serbia improved the placement of international news in terms of front-page coverage (Bjelica 1968). Market-based press and publishing developed more strongly after the turn of the century. Larger publishing companies were first established in Zagreb – Tipografija and Jugoštampa (publishers of *Večer* and *Obzor* and of *Novosti*

Table 3.1 Newspapers and journalists (19th & early 20th century)

	Bosnia and Herzegovina	Croatia	Macedonia	Montenegro	Serbia	Slovenia
Year of the first newspaper in the territory	1866 *Bosna*	1771 *Ephemerides Zagrebienses* *Novine horvatske* 1834	1908 *Vardar*	1871 *Crnogorac*	1835 *Novine srbske*	1707 (1778) *Leibacher Zeitung* *Kmetijske in rokodelske novice* 1843
1900–1914	140 (5 dailies in Sarajevo)	240 (17 dailies + 51 weeklies in Zagreb)		6 dailies	89 (13 dailies) (all in Belgrade)	180
1927*	42	232 + 29 (Zagreb 10 dailies, Rijeka 1)		8	151 + 110 (Belgrade 8 dailies, Novi Sad 3)	131 (3 dailies)
1941	14	119	4	4	179	35
Main general information newspapers 1900–1914	*Sarajevski list*	*Novi list, Novosti*		*Dnevni list*	*Politika*	*Jutro*
Main dailies 1918–1941	*Jugoslavenski list* *Večernja pošta*	*Novosti, Jutarnji list, Obzor* *Večer* *Novi list*		*Novo doba*	*Politika, Pravda* *Večernje novosti* *Epoha*	*Jutro* *Dom* *Jugoslavija*

Dailies & circulation 1941				
Jugoslovenska pošta 15,000	Novosti 23,400	Vardar 5000	Politika 145,700	Večernik (Maribor) 20,000
Jugoslavenski list 7000	Jutarnji list 21,000		Vreme 65,000	Jutro 18,000
	Hrvatski dnevnik 16,000		Pravda 45,000	Slovenec 17,500
	Hrvatski list (Osijek) 7000		Dan (Novi Sad)	Slovenski narod 10,000
	Hrvatska straža 3500			Slovenski dom 8000
	Novo doba (Split) 3200			Mariborer Zeitung (Maribor) 6000
	Morganblatt 3000			
	Obzor 2500			
	Jugoslavenski Loyd 2100			
	Jugoslavenska zastava (Osijek) 2000			

Members of the journalist associations

1919	20	96	84	40
1940	22	132	226	83
Year of establishment	1911	1910	1881	1905

Sources: Adapted from Bjelica (1968), Pejanović (1961), Ademović (1998), and Županić (1911).

and *Riječ*, respectively) – while separate publishing consortia published dailies in Ljubljana (*Jutro*) and Belgrade (*Politika* and *Vreme*).

Radio

The first receiving radio stations were established in Montenegro in 1905 (primarily for navigation) and in Zagreb in 1918 (primarily for receiving foreign news). Radio, as a broadcasting medium, was introduced during the time of the Kingdom of SHS. Zagreb had the first emission radio station in the region, which was established in 1926. Ljubljana followed the next year, and Belgrade followed in 1929. These developments were the results of actions by enthusiasts from radio clubs in Zagreb and Ljubljana. Radio Zagreb and Radio Belgrade were established as private shareholder companies, while Radio Ljubljana was state owned (Mučalo 2010). The audience of Radio Zagreb grew from 700 subscribers to 11,000 in 1936, three years before the remaining two private radio stations were confiscated by the government in the face of World War II. The radio stations continued as state-owned and state-operated enterprises in 1940. The honor of being the first radio station cost Zagreb the strength of its emitter, which was only 700 W, when compared to the 2.7 kW emitters of Radio Belgrade and Radio Ljubljana. This limited its audience reach and economic success in subsequent years. The radio program was geared toward culture, education, and entertainment, and it steered clear of news that had not previously been published in the (censored) newspapers.

The new technology and its potential were met with significant fear and distrust on the part of the government, which passed a very restrictive ordinance concerning the ownership of radio receivers in 1924 – one had to ask permission to have a receiver, receivers could be confiscated by the government at will and must not be moved from the approved location, and listeners should not "divulge secrets they might inadvertently hear" (*Ordinance on private radiotelegraph-telephone receiving equipment*, as quoted in Mučalo 2010, p. 132). As there was no special law dealing with radio diffusion, the content was regulated for each radio station as part of their concession agreement with the Ministry of Post and Telegraph. The broadcasting of any propaganda or any program not to the liking of the ministry could lead to the confiscation of the radio station. One radio station broadcast only foreign-language programs (from 1936, in Batajnica, Serbia), and another was established in Skopje in 1941 to relay the programs of Radio Belgrade (Bjelica 1968).

By the end of the final period in the relationship between the media and the state in the Kingdom of Yugoslavia, only the economically viable news and information-oriented press remained. As an adaptation to the context of repression in which the party political press was increasingly harassed, the informative press increasingly published foreign news while the previously critical *feuilletons* ceased publication. The increasing commercialization also brought about an expansion of entertainment news and the use of photographs, while comments and political news were relegated to the second and other internal pages. Bjelica (1968) further argues that before World War II, the Southeast European press had attained a state of development (in terms of technology, genre, and content) similar to that of their Western European counterparts. Also similar was the degree of journalism professionalism, which now included journalist specializations – reporters, commentators, sports reporters, and documentarists.

Political parallelism

Habsburg and Ottoman Empires

By the 19th century, the concept of political parallelism starts to make sense as a dimension for understanding media systems, and it can also explain developments in the analyzed countries. A high degree of exchange between the journalism and political professions was seen in the first newspapers of the 19th century, echoing well-known patterns of press development in the West, although in some cases with a significant delay. Political parties were first established in the mid-19th century. In the second half of the 19th century, new political papers were established in Croatia, Serbia, Slovenia, Bosnia and Herzegovina, and Montenegro, while such papers were established in Macedonia toward the end of that century (Table 3.2).

Political parties were first established in Croatia in the 1840s, accompanied by the establishment of newspapers that promoted their causes. The *Novine Horvatske*, which was published from 1834 by Ljudevit Gaj with the aim of promoting the Croatian national revival (Ilirski preporod), was the main organ of the pro-Illyrianist movement. The editor and the main journalists/contributors were all intellectuals who had studied in Prague or Vienna. Bogoslav Šulek was the first to introduce the *feuilleton* form, and social and political critique later appeared in the newspapers.

The Croatian Peasant Party published the *Dom* (Home) paper, which was the most read newspaper at that time in Croatia. The political battle was reflected in the newspapers, with the *Dom* soaring to circulations of 80,000 (Bjelica 1968).

Papers with a political agenda, including the *Slavenski jug*, which was published between 1848 and 1850 and which promoted the idea of democracy and federalism in Austria as well as the national identity rights of Croats and other Slavs within the empire, were short-lived. After 1860, the political press advanced in Croatia due to the changed and more open atmosphere coming from Vienna. The Croatian language was introduced in schools and in government. Due to their role in the general promotion of national political development and democracy, newspapers only gradually acquired party affiliations. The main cleavage in politics as well as in the party-associated newspapers was related to the national question, that is, the desire for the unification of Croat lands and the independence of Croatia within the empire, or attempts at Croatia's subjugation due to rising

Table 3.2 Parties and their newspapers (19th & early 20th century)

	Bosnia and Herzegovina	Croatia	Macedonia	Montenegro	Serbia	Slovenia
1843*/1890–1914	Srpska nacionalna grupacija – *Srpska riječ, Narod, Otadžbina* Muslim movement – Bosansko-Hercegovački glasnik, Vrijeme – Vakat, Pravda Croatian (Archbishop Stadler) Hrvatski dnevnik; Hrvatska zajednica; Jugoslavija	Hrvatska* stranka prava – *Hrvatsko pravo, Obzor* Hrvatska napredna stranka – *Pokret* Hrvatska seljačka stranka – *Dom, Narodna volja* (Mađaronska) Narodna stranka – *Dnevni list*	Serbian national organization – *Vardar, Srpski jug, Bitoljske novine*	Narodna stranka – *Narodna misao* Prava narodna stranka – *Glas Crnogorca, Cetinjski vjesnik, Ustavnost, Slobodna riječ* Unitarist supporters – *Ujedinjenje* Serbian radical party – *Crna Gora*	Radikalna stranka – *Samouprava, Zastava* (Vojvodina), *Vreme* Demokratska stranka – *Demokratija*	Konzervativni tabor (later formed as a party) – *Kmetijske i rokodelske novice* Liberal leanings – *Slovenija*, Celjske novine** Katolička narodna stranka – *Slovenec* Jugoslavenska socijaldemokratska stranka – *Rdeči prapor*
1918–1941	Demokrati – *Glas naroda* Zemljoradnička stranka – *Težački pokret* Croatian peasant party – *Slobodni dom*	Demokratska stranka – *Riječ* Čista stranka prava – *Novo vreme* Komunistička partija – *Borba*		Samostalna demokratska stranka – *Narodna riječ* Zemljoradnička stranka – *Slobodna misao*	Zemljoradnička stranka – *Novosti* Samostalna demokratska stranka – *Reč*	Samostalna seljačka stranka – *Kmetijski list* Narodno socijalistička stranka – *Nova Pravda; Republikanec* Radikalna stranka – *Radikalski glasnik*

Source: Adapted from Bjelica (1968).

Note:

* Party newspapers appear in Croatia in 1848 with the establishment of political parties, and in Slovenia newspapers established in 1843 will only become formally affiliated to their political parties when these are established at the end of the 19th century.

Hungarian nationalist tendencies. Many new papers and journals were established during this period, contributing to increasing political parallelism and the development of the public sphere. After the fall of the ill-famed Khuen-Hedervary regime in 1903, the renewed development of the political press began. Dozens of party political papers at both the national and regional levels were born during the ensuing period. However, censorship was again increased in Croatia after a new law was passed in 1912. It was "the most reactionary press law in Europe, except the one in Tsarist Russia," and it allowed for exorbitant fines (Horvat 2003, p. 324). *Novi list*, due to being published in Rijeka, which was directly ruled by Hungary and thus escaped the reach of the restrictive law implemented in Croatia, was for a while the only free voice. The party political scene is particularly responsible for a number of new publications that contributed to the development of the public sphere.

In Slovenia, the poet France Prešern published in the short-lived paper *Kranjska bčelica*, which was established in 1830 by the democratic and pan-Slavic forces. The conservative forces published *Kmetijske in rokodelske novice* (Peasant and Artisanal Paper) from 1843, which was at that time the only paper in the Slovene language, with a circulation of some 1,800 (Bjelica 1968). Political papers appeared in Slovenia in 1848, first *Slovenija*, then *Celjske novine*, which had a clear radical and liberal political program (Vatovec 1964, as quoted in Bjelica 1968). Yet, only the two conservative papers survived the revival of absolutism under the Austrian Minister of the Interior Alexander von Bach. The liberal press was first established in 1863 with the publication of the short-lived *Naprej* paper. Political parties were established in the 1890s: the conservative Catholic Party Slovenska ljudska stranka (SLS), the Yugoslav Social Democratic Party, and the liberal Slovenian Peoples Party.

In other countries in the region, the establishment of papers with political ideas and causes preceded the establishment of political parties. In Serbia, the *Napredak* paper, associated with the Serb national movement in Vojvodina, was published in 1848 in Sremski Karlovci, and it used the new Serbian orthography developed by Vuk Karadžić for the first time. The first political parties were established in 1881. The party press was born. The Napredna radikalna stranka published the *Samouprava* paper, Liberalna stranka published the *Srpska nezavisnost*, and Naprednjačka stranka published the *Videlo*. The first commercial and non-party-affiliated paper in Serbia with significant print runs (30,000 copies) was *Male novine*.

In Bosnia and Herzegovina, the press was produced and consumed along national lines. The most popular political papers had print runs of around 2,000, and newspapers were sold in kiosks and shops in addition to via subscription (colportage was not allowed). In the new country, the most popular papers were those published by the cultural societies. However, less than 5% of the population were newspaper subscribers.

In Montenegro, the first paper, the *Cernogorac*, was published in 1871, and it followed a distinctly pro-Serbian program promoted by the United Serbian Youth organization, for which it was banned by the Austro-Hungarian Empire and by the Ottomans. The first two political parties were formed in 1905, after a new constitution was passed, each with a newspaper in tow. The government party had several supporting newspapers while the opposition party had one. Six dailies were published in Montenegro at the time of World War I (Martinović 1965).

Although the Macedonian national revival started in the mid-19th century, with the aim of promoting a separate Macedonian language and campaigning against the domination of the Greek Orthodox Church, the first paper, the *Makedonac*, was only published in 1880. It was actually published in Bulgaria, where the intellectuals had emigrated after Bulgaria was freed from Turkish occupation. Several other papers were published in Bulgaria and Greece during the last decade of the 19th century. In 1908, the first paper was published in Skopje by the Serb minority.

Kingdom of SHS/Yugoslavia

Most parties and papers continued their life in the new country. Many socialist and workers' papers were published in the territories of the six countries during the first decades of the 20th century, although all of them were quickly banned in the Kingdom of SHS. In December 1920, the *Law on the protection of the state* was adopted, which outlawed the Communist party and all the leftist papers. The workers' papers in Croatia and Slovenia (founded in 1874 in Zagreb and in 1889 in Ljubljana) did not have a predominantly political content as they were primarily educational and practical, being linked to the workers' clubs and aiming to give advice to the workers. The socialist press in Serbia toward the end of the century was promoted by young intellectuals despite the lack of industry or industrial workers to form their audience. The *Borba* in Zagreb would later become the paper of the Communist party of Yugoslavia (the party was not yet established), and it would continue during the times of socialist Yugoslavia (Bjelica 1968, pp. 58–75).

After a parliamentary monarchy was introduced in the Kingdom of SHS by the new constitution in 1921, political polarization continued to escalate, mainly along the dividing line between the unitarist/royalist (Serb) parties and the federalist/republican (non-Serb, especially Croat and Slovenian) parties. The non-Serb parties did not accept the imposed constitution and therefore left the assembly in protest during its adoption. The election for the Constituent Assembly in 1920 had the following results: two Serbian government parties, namely the Democratic Party (Demokratska stranka [DS]) and the National Radical Party (Narodna radikalna stranka [NRS]) each had 22% of the representatives; the Communist party had 14%; the main opposition party, the Croatian Republican Peasant Party (HRSS), as the only party to gain more than 50% in its constituency, gained 12% but did not participate in the Constituent Assembly; the Agrarian Party (unitarist) gained 9%; the Slovenian People's Party (SLS) and the Croatian People's Party (HPS) both gained a little over 6%; the Yugoslav Muslim Organization (JMO) gained a little under 6%; and there were a host of other smaller parties (Banac 1984, pp. 394–395).

A certain parallelism between the economy (i.e., banks as the providers of capital), politics, and the press owners developed in the newly formed Kingdom of SHS. In Croatia, this was the first time that serious capital had been interested in the press, and banks were happy to fund the papers, which would in return report positively on the bank's political allies or on the bank itself (Horvat 2003, p. 346). This kind of business parallelism is something that we also find in the post-socialist transitions.

Journalistic professionalism and autonomy

A commercial, informative press with no specific political affiliations started to develop during the second part of the temporal framework of modernization. The development of the press market had also contributed to the development of journalism as a profession by the turn of the 20th century. Journalistic associations were established in most of the six countries of interest (Table 3.1). When the Kingdom of SHS was formed, the associations of journalists based in Zagreb, Ljubljana, Sarajevo, and Belgrade started to discuss uniting within one organization. These discussions took some time because the first two organizations employed the federal principle rather than the unitary one promoted by the other two organizations. The Slovenian association also proposed that a union of journalists be established.

The first congress of journalists in the Kingdom of SHS was held in Zagreb in 1919, and the last was held in Belgrade in 1940. The first congress was organized by Krešimir Kovačić from the Zagreb association, who was the first to propose the establishment of the Yugoslav Association of Journalists and who became its president in 1924 (after the provision that the president must live in Belgrade was removed). This first congress was attended by a wide selection of people of various profiles, including teachers, writers, politicians, artists, and apothecaries (Historija 1927), testifying to the early days with regard to journalism's professionalization. The fights over the definition of who was a journalist, as well as whether newspaper owners could also be members, continued. The freedom of the press was the main topic of interest during the next meeting in Sarajevo, especially as communist papers had been banned the preceding year, and journalists from those papers sought support. Party political fights also continued, and the planned discussion of the work- and status-related questions was only begun during later meetings. The Yugoslav Association of Journalists was established in Sarajevo in 1921. The association played a part in securing the inclusion of the possibility of providing social security for journalists in the 1925 Press Law, which was again very restrictive. It also demanded, albeit unsuccessfully, that the police be left out of the business of journalism. The association joined the International Journalists Association and established a monthly journal, *Novinar (Journalist)*, published in Zagreb since 1924. The journal published texts about the profession in the country and abroad, informed readers about journalists' congresses in other European countries, and published the texts of proposed or adopted laws. Regular reports of the meetings of the national associations in Slovenia, Croatia, Bosnia and Herzegovina, and Serbia were published, including changes in the number of members. The journal was published in the Latin and Cyrillic scripts, depending on each author's origin, and in addition to Serbian and Croatian it was also published in the Slovene language.

The profession was clearly developing during those early years in an atmosphere characterized by government pressure and by political divisions between journalists and between various sections in Ljubljana, Zagreb, Belgrade, and Sarajevo, while opinions as to who constitutes a journalist and who should be included in the association remained the subject of contention.

The autonomy of the journalism profession was not the same in all parts of the country: due to military censorship, repression, and higher taxes outside of Serbia, much higher pressure was placed on independent journalism. While the situation in Serbia involved less pressure by the government, strife within the association during the first decade of the Kingdom of SHS rendered the role of the Belgrade section almost insignificant. The number of journalists in the Yugoslav Association of Journalists more than doubled within 20 years, rising from 249 to 620 (Table 3.1).

Journalism was a predominantly male profession in these countries. The one notable exception, Marija Jurić Zagorka, was the first female journalist in Croatia and in Yugoslavia, and she also became the first woman member of the Yugoslav Association of Journalists when she joined in 1927. She worked, during the first decade of the 20th century, as the correspondent for the Zagreb journal *Obzor* based at the joint parliament of Croatia and Hungary in Budapest, while between the two wars she was the editor of the first female magazine, *Ženski list* (Female Paper, which was published in Zagreb) (Vujnović 2008)

In the interwar period, the commercialization of newspapers and the profit motives of their owners contributed to the development of a general information press, with the resultant publications no longer being invested in exclusively promoting the political aims of their founders (Horvat 2003).

Globalization and communication flows

An organized postal service started in the Habsburg Empire during the 16th century, and the first routes to the analyzed countries included Klagenfurt-Kranj-Ljubljana; Bihać-Senj-Ogulin-Istria-Ljubljana (Lučić 1962); Graz

(Austria), Maribor, and Celje (Slovenia) to Jastrebarsko (Croatia); and shortly after that, Vienna to Zagreb (Povijest ND). While specific families had monopolies over the courier and postal services in the beginning, postal offices became state organized during the 18th century. The first national postal authority was established in Croatia in 1848. The first telegraph became operational in 1850 in Bosnia and Herzegovina (Mostar). Lučić (1962) recounts the research published in the *PTT Arhiva* journal by Velimir Sokol regarding the first postal historian in Southeast Europe, Johan Weichard Valvasor, who lived in the 17th century Duchy of Carniola and who analyzed the history of the post as a vehicle for the spread of ideas within both the duchy and neighboring territories. The first international postal route, running from Krakow in Poland through Vienna and Ljubljana to Venice, was established during the second part of the 16th century, a decade before a regular postal service was established in Slovenia and Croatia. The Austrian post passed through Serbia to Turkey until 1868. The first postal offices were established in Serbia in 1840, although a postal service existed from the beginning of the 19th century. A regular postal service was established in Montenegro in 1873, while the first telegraph was established in 1913. Venice and Dubrovnik organized a courier service to distribute news during the 16th century in the Balkans between Europe and Turkey, with Dubrovnik, Kotor, and Belgrade playing prominent roles.

The Avala press agency was established in Belgrade in 1919, and it quickly established a monopoly over all foreign news received from foreign agencies – Havas, Reuters, and the Swiss Telegraphic Agency. In 1926, the agency was nationalized, while in 1929, it became a shareholder company with the state as the majority shareholder and several newspapers as minority shareholders.

Systematic data concerning international cultural flows are hard to come by, and therefore, we are left with anecdotal evidence, such as information about books on the censors' index, which show that books were imported in the westernmost lands, or the fact that international news was published in newspapers. All these data give us an idea of the different levels of participation in global cultural and communication flows.

Conclusion

In this chapter, we have covered a lot of ground and many centuries in order to show how the six countries in Southeast Europe compare in terms of the preconditions for, and the process of, media development during early modern and modern times. What we find is an early divergence in terms of the political and economic conditions, in addition to institutional state development linked to the establishment of the predominant media technology and institutions of that era, first with regard to book publishing and later newspapers. Delayed modernizations and late press development are evident in all the countries when compared to the Western leaders. We also find a disparity between the six countries. Westernmost Slovenia and Croatia had the advantage over the states occupied by the Ottoman Empire, especially in relation to early modernization indicators such as literacy, urbanization, and industrialization. The development of book publishing and a book culture was not possible in the analyzed Balkan countries. This divergence is also visible in other cultural areas, such as architecture, where Renaissance artifacts are not present, while baroque churches and buildings can only be found in Vojvodina.

The 20th century brought these south Slavic countries to a common state for the first time during a process of brief convergence of the political frameworks of these historically different countries, albeit similar with regard to their shared peripheral position in regard to their respective centers of empires. While important differences in the political and economic traditions distinguish these lands, which were part of the more developed Habsburg Empire, from those under the control of Ottoman oriental feudalism, like other CEE lands, all were less developed than the countries of Western Europe, and all experienced the more restricted development of political representation. The divergence between Yugoslavia and the rest of Southeast and East Europe will arrive after its breakup with Stalin in 1948.

Even though some countries started to form political parties quite early on with regard to the regional context (Croatia, for example, toward the middle of the first half of the 19th century), the majority of them only did so toward the end of the 19th century or in the early 20th century, although during the interwar period all the countries had both parties and party press. By the beginning of World War II, both newspapers and radio existed, and the genres and content of both were similar to those of their Western neighbors. The region certainly shows "a broad range of illiberal legacies" (Lampe 2014, p. 4), which need to be acknowledged and explored in relation to their participation in the outcome solutions of different contemporary media systems.

Notes

1 J.B. Thompson (1995) uses the term "mediazation" to mean the transformative social change related to the media of communication. This concept has subsequently been standardized under the term "mediatization" (Lundby 2014), which we use in the following text as well. A similar term – "mediation" – is used to denote any communication delivered or shared through technical communication media, albeit without a transformative effect on social relations or institutions.
2 For an authoritative political history of these lands and peoples from early modern times to the first Yugoslavia, see Banac (1984, chap. 1); for early modern times, see Tracy (2016); for the early modern period to World War I, see Lampe (1989); since the 1900s, see Calic (2019); and for after World War I, see Lampe (2014) and Ramet (2009). For a history of the region with a greater focus on Croatia, see Tanner (1997).
3 On political parties in the Austro-Hungarian Empire, see Cipek (2006).

4 The first Sabor (assembly) with legal power was held in Zagreb in 1273 (Congregatio Regni tocius Sclavonie generalis). The Sabor of the aristocracy that was held in 1527 in Cetina elected Ferdinand I to be the Croatian king, and the assembly was then transformed into a class assembly of the Kingdom of Croatia, Dalmatia and Slavonia. The first speech in the Croatian language was given in 1843 by Ivan Kukuljević Sakcinski, and in 1847 Croatian replaced Latin as the official language. After 1848, feudalism was abolished, parliament ceased to be class based, and political parties formed. The Sabor had a continuous bourgeois multiparty character for the next 70 years, albeit with only limited areas of influence under the dual monarchy. The Sabor was abolished following the formation of the first Yugoslavia. During World War II, the partisan resistance established the Zemaljsko antifašističko vijeće narodnog oslobođenja Hrvatske (ZAVNOH) as the legislative body, which was renamed the People's Sabor of Croatia in 1945, thereby providing an institutional continuity. The Croatian Sabor continued as the state's legislative body during the time of socialist Yugoslavia, but in the context of a one-party system the actual seat of power was the Central Committee of the Communist Party of Croatia and its presidency. Multiparty elections were again held in May 1990. www.sabor.hr/hr/o-saboru/povijest-saborovanja#no-back.
5 See Feldman 2017 on (unsuccessful) Habsburg attempts to create a common Bosnian identity.
6 While the official ideology of Yugoslavia celebrated the July 4, 1941, uprising organized by Tito in Serbia, the first organized resistance in Yugoslavia was actually the creation of the partisan brigade (the Sisak brigade or Sisački odred) on June 22, 1941, in Brezovica near Sisak in Croatia by 40 communist intellectuals. Croatia today celebrates this date as the Day of Antifascist Resistance. During World War II, the National Liberation Army of Yugoslavia (i.e., the partisan resistance) had a total of 96 brigades in 1943; of these Croatia supplied 38 brigades, Bosnia and Herzegovina 23, Slovenia 17, Montenegro 6, Serbia 5, Macedonia 1.5, and Kosovo 0.5 (Bilandžić 1999, p. 157).
7 With regard to press and publishing histories, in this chapter we relied on studies published in the Croatian, Serbian, and Slovenian languages, including the monographs by Ademović (1998), Bjelica (1968), Horvat (2003), Novak (2005), and Pejanović (1961), as well as the proceedings of two conferences on the beginnings of newspapers among the Yugoslav nations that included chapters on our studied countries – *Jugoslovenska štampa* (1911) and Popović (ed.) (1969). Bjelica (1969, pp. 245–248) lists the few early studies regarding the periodical press: the first one was included in the history of literature in 1833, the next was an article on the development of journalism in Yugoslavia published in 1861, several books on the subject in 1884, and so forth. The Yugoslav Journalism Institute was established in Belgrade in 1959, and it further focused on the study of journalism histories. The language question was historically contentious, as it was seen as the pivot of national identity for all the nations of Southeast Europe. These languages use two alphabets: the Latin script is used for Croatian and Slovenian, while Cyrillic is used for Serbian (which also uses the Latin script) and Macedonian. The historical development of the literary standards of Croatian, Serbian, Slovenian, and Macedonian languages is explained in Banac (1984).

4 Media systems in socialist modernity

The main challenge in this chapter concerns the application of our understanding of media systems to a socialist context. Our conceptual model, described in Chapter 2, proposes the inclusion of the whole gamut of media system dimensions in all temporal frameworks. The challenge of transposing our analytical framework to a political and economic regime without either pluralist democracy or a market economy appears to be even greater than the challenge of identifying the appropriate dimensions in the political and economic transformations during the first period of modernization (although on socialism see Sparks 2008, 2012). Another aspect is helpful, however: the historical period after World War II served as the temporal context for our main sources on comparative media systems (e.g., Siebert et al. 1956; Blumler and Gurevitch 1995; Hallin and Mancini 2004). Thus we have a strong comparative anchor. The question is, of course, how are the key dimensions and conditions reshaped through their implementation in the socialist/communist state?

World War II was the critical event, or exogenous circumstance, that precipitated the next critical juncture in the whole of Europe, while in Eastern Europe it enabled the introduction of socialism. The lands and peoples we are investigating are, during this temporal framework, part of a common state once again, namely the Socialist Federal Republic of Yugoslavia (SFRY). Koruška (Carinthia), Istria, and the Adriatic islands are again united with Slovenia and Croatia. The federal state, the SFRY, is composed of six republics (from the west): Slovenia, Croatia, Bosnia and Herzegovina, Serbia, Montenegro, and Macedonia, as well as two autonomous provinces within Serbia (Vojvodina and Kosovo) (Table 4.1 presents comparative data concerning the respective societies, politics, economics, and media). The socialist period of the common state lasted for 45 years, and it provided a much longer period of opportunity for media system convergence than did the previous 20 years within the Kingdom of Yugoslavia. This post–World War II period of socialism was, in our original conception, theorized as a time of convergence within a common socialist framework that would influence the previously divergent lands/republics in a common way, thereby enabling us to better understand the influence of socialism on media system formation

	Bosnia and Herzegovina	Croatia	Montenegro	Macedonia	Serbia	Slovenia	SFRY
Population size (in thousands)[1]	3,746	4,426	530	1,646	8,477	1,727	20,553
GNI per capita (USD)[6]	433	780	415	439	587	1,258	652
Illiteracy (%)[1]	23	9%	17	18	17	1	15
Households by agricultural source of income (%)[1]	28	22	24	27	31	10	26
Households by non-agricultural source of income (%)[1]	57	64	64	59	56	76	50
Urban population (%)[1]	28	41	34	48	38	48	39
Tertiary sector labor force (%)[1]	19	26	27	21	19	27	22
Population with university and higher education (%)[1]	1.4	2.8	2.2	2	2.5	2.5	2.3
Ethnic composition[2]	40	79	67	69	71	94	
Advertising development[3]	320	579	NA	130	475	181.5	1685.5
Members of the League of Communists (% of population)[4]	3.6	4.6	7.1	4	4.03	3.6	4.7
Number of newspapers and magazines[5]	188	560	27	112	1,061	317	2,265
Circulation newspapers and magazines (annual, in thousands)[5]	58,404	174,720	1,632	18,661	482,319	103,596	839,332
Newspaper sales per 1,000 adult citizens[5]	78	158	15	55	238	245	131
Radio stations in 1972[6]	29	67	1	25	47	16	185
Radio users in 1972 (in thousands)[6]	457	1,013	59	233	1,340	454	3,556
Television users in 1972 (in thousands)[6]	276	627	43	151	965	292	2,354
Ownership of TV sets in 1968 (% of households)[7]	15	32	12	34	28	40	
Ownership of radio sets in 1968 (% of households)[7]	53	75	50	65	67	89	
Establishment of university journalism programs[8]	1970	1970	Not established	1977	1968	1966	
Members of journalist associations in 1967[9]	424	817	70	310	2,100	485	4,206

Row groupings (left side): General, economic and social data; Political system; Media/press market; Journalism profession.

Sources:

1 The data refer to 1971 (The Population of Yugoslavia, 1974).
2 Share of the largest ethnic group in the population in 1971 (source: www.stat.si/publikacije/popisi/1971/1971_1-03.pdf).
3 Advertising development represents gross revenues of advertising agencies in millions of dinars in 1958 (Patterson 2011, p. 76).
4 Data refer to 1987 (Kalanj 1990).
5 Adult population is 19 years and older. Data on circulation refer to 1967 (Bjelica 1968).
6 Data refer to 1972 (Slovenian Statistical Yearbook 1974)
7 For ownership of consumer goods, TV and radio sets in 1968, see Patterson (2011, p. 40).
8 Source for Bosnia and Herzegovina, Croatia, Serbia and Slovenia is Peruško and Vozab 2016. Source for Macedonia is Terzis 2009. University education in journalism was not established in Montenegro in SFRY.
9 Bjelica 1968.

78 *Media systems in socialist modernity*

as well as its consequences for the institutional designs and practices during the period of democratic transition and consolidation. However – spoiler alert – not even socialism, as the major contextual condition, was the same, despite the existence of a common state.

We have two key aims in this chapter. We first seek to show how the media systems in the six countries of interest are shaped during socialism (when they are republics within a federal state) in order to contribute to our understanding of the dimensions and conditions that predominantly influence their present-day media systems. Our second aim is to review the common media system dimensions in relation to the socialist context so as to show what adaptations of the relationships between those dimensions are required if they are to be successfully applied to a socialist regime framework.

Transformations of the political and economic fields

Before proceeding to the analysis of the media systems in the SFRY and its constituent republics, we briefly review the nature of socialism in the European context, how Yugoslav socialism was similar or different to the socialisms seen in other European countries, and what kind of transformations it introduced into the social and cultural fabric of the SFRY. An important point must be made with regard to the periodization of the transformations. Discussion of socialism is often reduced to discussion of the first few years following its establishment. While these initial years clearly display the significant features of the unfolding socialist transformations in comparison to the previous regime(s), they are far from representative or informative in terms of the decades that follow. The Cold War view of the socialist media system, as presented by Siebert et al. (1956) and modeled on the Soviet Union, is somehow still influential in shaping our expectations regarding media ownership, the normative role of the press, and the type of state control of the media associated with socialism. In this chapter, we turn to the empirical domain to investigate the changing position of the media with the passage of time and with changes in the political and economic fields, focusing on the last two decades of the mature or decadent (Kolanović 2013) period of socialist Yugoslavia, after the major distinguishing political and economic reforms have set in but before the collapse of both the regime and the Yugoslav state.

As a system structured in such a way to be the opposite of capitalism and liberal democracy in every respect (Bunce 1999), socialism introduces purposeful transformations of the political, economic, and cultural fields. Contrary to a common bias, the socialist transformations seen in all the European socialist states were not identical. A recent example of this enduring misconception is the board game *Across the Iron Curtain*, which is described as having an educational purpose in that it deals with the European totalitarian socialist past. The game features different characters from various socialist Eastern European countries who are trying to flee to the West (Milošević 2019). The game also includes characters from Yugoslavia, even though Yugoslavia was not behind the Iron Curtain, nor did it have a totalitarian regime. In fact, if Yugoslav citizens wanted to travel to the West, they simply needed to take their passports and go. This kind of historical revisionism and false narratives concerning the past are often used for political purposes in contemporary post-Yugoslav states, although it should be noted that the politicization of the socialist past is far from unknown in other parts of post-socialist Europe. In this chapter, we navigate between the more authoritarian and liberal periods in the relationship between the media, the state, and its socialist citizens in order to paint a balanced picture of what socialism in Yugoslavia, as well as in its various republics, meant for both the media and public communication.

The oversimplified lumping together of all post-socialist European countries, which neglects important differences in their socialist experiences, changes in their socialist frameworks and practices over time, and their different post-socialist developments, is also not unusual in the field of communication studies. For a long time, scholarship regarding the Eastern part of Europe was focused on the democratic transformations of the post-socialist period beginning in 1990, and it is only recently that interest has emerged in analyzing the history of the media and communication during the socialist period.[1] At the opposite end of the spectrum, some scholars see socialist Yugoslavia as a unique case among the European socialist states (Denitch 1990; Lampe 2000), differing from other socialist countries in all respects. If this was the case, however, then the analysis of Yugoslavia would be useless as a theoretical exercise because it would not afford any explanations based on comparisons with other countries or situations (Bunce 1999; Malešević 2002). We will show that while some institutional designs in Yugoslavia were original, others were only radical or early in comparison to most types of real existing socialism in the countries of the Soviet Bloc (Bunce 1999). Let us first briefly examine the nature of the socialist project in theory, in its original Soviet and Eastern European matrix, and then look at the subsequent Yugoslav transformation. As there is no comprehensive social scientific theory of socialist society (although there are many theoretical/utopian ideas/ideals), we will provide a combination of theoretical ideas and empirical accounts of Yugoslavia and its republics.

The idea of socialism

Although socialist ideas existed before Karl Marx developed his critique of capitalism, its exploitation of labor, and the inherent inequality of the distribution of wealth and power, in his writings we find some of the key ideas concerning what socialism,[2] as a political and economic system, was envisaged to be. In *The Communist Manifesto*, Marx and Engels explain that "Communists may be summed up in the single sentence: Abolition of private property" (Marx and Engels (2005/1888). Schumpeter (1976/1942), writing his theoretical account of the transitions that occurred during the 1930s, defines socialism in purely economic terms:

> By socialist society we shall designate an institutional pattern in which the control over means of production and over production itself is vested with a central authority . . . in which . . . economic affairs belong to the public and not to the private sphere.
>
> (p. 167)

This means that the production of goods and the means of production are managed by a centralized government. Bottomore (1976), in his introduction to Schumpeter's classic text, extends the definition of socialism to include "the preoccupation with social equality and individual autonomy and self-determination" (p. xi). In his view,

> If socialism is to be characterized in a single phrase it would be more appropriate to describe it as a movement of human liberation, in which the transformation of the economic system is only one element, and itself gives rise to the diverse choices in the construction of a different type of system.
>
> (Bottomore 1976, p. xi)

According to Marx and Engels (2005/1888) communism develops in phases, with the first phase being the dictatorship of the proletariat, as described in *The Communist Manifesto*:

> The proletariat will use its political supremacy to wrest, by degrees, all capital from the bourgeoisie, to centralize all instruments of production in the hands of the State, i.e., of the proletariat organized as the ruling class; and to increase the total of productive forces as rapidly as possible.
>
> (Marx and Engels 2005/1888)

This also includes the abolition of property in land, progressive taxation, the extension of state-owned factories, the industrialization of agriculture and urbanization, and the centralization of the means of communication and transport in the hands of the state (Marx and Engels 2005/1888). Of course, the expectation was that the proletarian revolution would occur in the form of an international revolution in the most developed industrial capitalist countries.

In fact, Barrington Moore (1966) shows that rather than being the result of a workers' revolt against capitalism, the communist revolutions were belated modernization revolutions in peasant societies. "Real existing socialism" is a one-party political system in which the Communist Party, as the "proxy" for the working class, holds the only political power. Marx and Engels's expectation was also that the state would vanish following the development of socialism and a classless society (in their view, the state is the institutional embodiment of ruling class interests), and they wondered what kind of transformations would occur in the functions that states fulfilled in capitalism (see Jović 2009 for a discussion regarding Yugoslav socialism). What rights will the newly freed workers have within the political realm? What are the consequences for democracy? These questions have been discussed at length (e.g., Schumpeter 1976; Poulantzas 2000/1978), although we mention them here to make the point that the type of socialism that evolved in different European or non-European countries was not inevitable. Rather, concrete and contingent historical circumstances influenced the specific shape of each iteration of socialism. For instance, Bottomore (1976) points to the positive example of the self-management socialism seen in Yugoslavia, which, unlike centralized command socialism, allowed for a degree of citizens'/workers' participation in decision-making regarding matters related to production and distribution. Another case in point is contemporary China, which is developing a hybrid economic system with many capitalistic characteristics while still maintaining (or intensifying, through the use of digital data) its control over citizens in a one-party communist state.

Kitchelt (1995) shows that three types of socialism existed in Europe, as differentiated on the basis of the character of the previous political system, toleration of dissent within the elite and in relation to citizens, as well as in the rule of law versus corruption/clientelism. Bureaucratic-authoritarian communism is, in relation to political pluralism, the closest to a totalitarian, rule-governed technocracy, with no significant accommodation of opposition groups but with high rational-legal authority. Kitchelt (1995) recognizes this type of communism in Czechoslovakia and the German Democratic Republic (GDR). National accommodative communism exhibits the partial separation of state and party and the opposition groups, and it provides the largest space for non-communist ideas and civic development. In the accommodative type, dissent both within the elite (dissent is one aspect of democracy that is highlighted in the otherwise restrictive view Schumpeter [1976/1942] holds regarding democracy; Bottomore 1976) and within the public sphere was more pronounced. The countries that are representative of this type, prone to reforms, include Hungary, Poland, Slovenia, and Croatia. The patrimonial type of communism "relies on vertical chains of personal dependence between leaders in the state and party apparatus and their entourage, buttressed by extensive patronage and clientelist networks" (Kitschelt et al. 1999, p. 23). Most socialist states (and all the Soviet republics) exhibited the patrimonial type of socialism, extending the personal hierarchies and clientelist networks of the ruling classes. Over the following pages, we will analyze in more detail how this accommodative form of socialism worked in Yugoslavia with (or against) the patrimonial socialism of other republics with regard to the media system.

Economic transformations: real existing socialism versus self-management socialism

It is impossible to divorce the economic transformations from the political transformations, especially in a socialist context, which favors the causality of the economic relations. We have previously noted that Yugoslavia was among the poorest countries in Europe between the two world wars. Over the next 20 years, its economic indicators became comparable to the lower or average Western European indicators. If we consider only two consumer goods indicators, Yugoslavia had nine radio sets per 1,000 inhabitants during the pre-World War II period, while it had 160 sets by the end of the 1960s (Western Europe had between 110 and 200 sets at that time), and the number of cars per 1,000 inhabitants rose from 1 to 20 (in Western Europe, from 17 to 50) during the same period (Horvat 1971).

At the start of the rapid industrialization and mass education of the mostly agrarian country, Yugoslavia had only rudimentary industry and high illiteracy rates (Ramet 2009; Erdei 2012). The share of illiterates among the population was reduced from 40% before World War II to 25% by the end of the 1960s, although great disparities continued to exist between the republics (see Table 4.1). At first, the economy was organized according to the Soviet model, including state ownership and central planning. Some 80% of the industry, transport, banking, mining, and trade sectors were nationalized, while the agrarian reforms redistributed the nationalized land to those who worked it and the size of privately owned land was limited. After Yugoslavia was expelled from the Cominform alliance in 1948, an economic blockade by member states (the USSR and its Eastern European satellites) ensued. This allowed for the introduction of economic reforms. Indeed, the "New Economic System" that established Workers Councils was introduced in 1950, thereby kick-starting a decade of significant economic growth (Horvat 1971). Some authors consider that Yugoslav socialism was very much Fordist in terms of its inspiration due to "its productivist ethos and tendency to organize social life around work" (Cvek 2017, p. 103). Further, Yugoslav socialism was a "unique combination of controls and concessions, characterized by a party monopoly of political power but much less orthodox arrangements in the economic and cultural domain" (Arnason 2000, p. 89 n. 5).

The collectivization of agriculture was abandoned during this period after it proved to have little positive economic impact. The particular political position of the peasants, as the main force within the partisan resistance, also rendered their challenge to collectivization more successful (Horvat 1971). In economic terms, the differences between the initial administrative phase of government and the decentralization phase of the new self-government, as it was called at the time, are summarized by the renowned pre-war economist Rudolf Bičanić in his study from 1962 (as quoted in Horvat 1971) as

> state ownership vs. social ownership; central planning vs. social planning; administrative allocation of goods vs. market; administrative rules

vs. financial instruments; administratively fixed wages vs. free disposition of the income of the working collectives; all-embracing state budget vs. the budget of the state administration decentralized and separated from the economic operations; consumption as a residual vs. consumption as an independent factor of development; collectivization vs. business cooperation of peasants and large agricultural estates.

(as quoted in Horvat 1971, p. 80)

Unlike the Soviet model, the role of the state was to provide a general framework for the economy and to encourage growth through indirect incentives, letting enterprises set their own production goals and prices. Such liberalization resulted in remarkable economic growth as well as an increase in the standard of living (Robinson 1977). The economic reforms subsequently led to a change in the political position of the party and of the workers, who were also granted more political power following the establishment of the Council of Producers by the Federal Assembly. The third stage of the economic reforms took place in 1961 when market socialism was introduced: it opened up the country to international influences (Yugoslavia became an associate member of the General Agreement on Tariffs and Trade [GATT]), reformed the monetary system, and delimited workers' wages. The constitution was changed in 1963 to accommodate the increasing decentralization of the economy and of the federal state.

Economic reforms and the introduction of self-management during the 1960s caused an increase in intensive, rational, and profitable production due to the enhanced motivation of workers when compared to the situation of production under state control (Popović et al. 1977, pp. 10–11). Following the successful growth of the economy during the 1950s and early 1960s, the new changes to the institutional structure of the socialist economy implemented during the 1970s seem to have brought about greater confusion and caused a drop in production rates, thereby contributing to the growing crisis that was to become a hallmark of the 1980s.

In his examination of the crisis during the 1970s and early 1980s, Josip Županov (1983, p. 16), one of the leading Yugoslav and Croatian sociologists at that time and subsequently, follows the analysis of Ivan Prpić, who points to the institutional discrepancies and contradictions behind the social crisis. The problems within the political system stem from two simultaneously existing normative ideals – socialist democracy is opposed to the dictatorship of the proletariat, as the former favors decentralization and the latter etatization, and these opposing institutional designs clash. The economic system includes three types of institutions: self-managed companies (market economy), workers' associations (the self-management participation of workers), and central state planning (command economy). Županov (1983) argues that a variant of the command economy was applied in practice in opposition to the normative institutional design of self-management, and this clash was the reason behind the economic problems and inefficiencies.

Socialism has a distinct class structure, whereby the social differentiation/stratification promoted by the position within the market (i.e., working class, middle class, upper class) is supplemented by the stratification promoted by political patrimonialism, which allows for promotion to the elite position, or the political class, of individuals with working-class status (Berger 1986). This "party channel," as it was informally called, started to close in Yugoslavia during the 1980s, although we will see it resurrected in the next temporal framework. Berger (1986) points to the regressive character of this conflation of the economic and political hierarchies, which were separated by the development of capitalism. In the case of Yugoslav self-management, the separate political class was never as pronounced as it was in the Soviet Bloc (consequently there is no separate name for this class in Yugoslavia, while, for instance, "nomenklatura" is used in Romania, Albania, and the GDR).

Transformations of the state and the political field

Socialism worked because of the existence of a social contract between the citizens/workers and the party elite, which was based on a set of values and ideologies known as the egalitarian syndrome (Županov 1987, 1996). The party/state provided job security, health insurance, and adequate consumption, while the workers provided legitimacy to the ruling elite, and all this hinged on everyone having the same level of economic prosperity. The breakdown of this social contract could also serve to explain the collapse of socialism – the loss of workers' support for the legitimacy of the Communist Party was perhaps first visible in Poland (Županov 1987).

The state is, in the case of socialism, clearly a paternalistic state led by a communist party with a mission. We would expect the government to be a majoritarian one, as only one party is allowed and makes all the decisions, while management positions are predominantly allocated to party members. Yugoslavia represents a contradiction in which both majoritarian and consensual institutional designs coexisted. We would also expect this kind of state not to allow any type of pluralism, either individual or segmented, although this issue proves to be more complex, too. While the expression of divergent political views was not organized through political parties, political polarization proceeded around cleavages relating to the national question as well as around the centralization and decentralization of government. Organized religion was allowed and played an important cultural role, but it did not play a manifest political role throughout most of this temporal framework.

In Yugoslavia, two types of socialism existed: the accommodative type in Slovenia and Croatia; the patrimonial type in Bosnia and Herzegovina, Montenegro, and Macedonia; and a mix of the two types in Serbia (Kitschelt et al. [1999] reclassify it as a mix of patrimonial and accommodative regimes). The accommodative type was more open to dissenting views, allowed pluralism in most areas of society as well as within the communist elite, and showed less clientelism in government. The patrimonial type (which was also found in all the Soviet republics) represents the framework from which the usual presumptions regarding socialism stem, as it suggests a state arbitrarily ruled by a party oligarchy without accountability and with dire limitations on free public expression. The differences between the types of political regimes within a single common state were also reflected in differences in the media systems in the republics.

The SFRY introduced a federal structure to accommodate its multinational composition. While this was an important improvement on the previous unitarist Yugoslavia (some nations were recognized for the first time – Macedonian and Muslim/Bosniak), the national question would remain unsolved until its demise (Ivo Banac 1984/1991). The complex multinational, multicultural, and multi-confessional composition of the country, together with its geographic diversity and economic disparities, also shaped communication and the media system during socialism. Regular constitutional changes reflected the increasingly decentralized and regionalized political development,[3] economy, and media system (Robinson 1977; Denitch 1990), which produced a de facto confederal state following the constitutional reforms in 1974 (Bunce 1999; Malešević 2002).

The original Soviet template of socialism featured mass children's and youth organizations, which persisted in Yugoslavia until its demise, although with a much looser role (The Association of Pioneers [Savez pionira], the Association of Communist Youth of Yugoslavia [Savez komunističke omladine Jugoslavije, or SKOJ] later transformed into the Association of Socialist Youth of Yugoslavia [Savez socijalističke omladine, or SSOJ]) (Ramet 2009, p. 41). The central role of the Communist Party was a particular characteristic of socialist regimes, as was the conflation of the state and the party. The final ideological break with the Soviet Union included the decision by the Communist Party of Yugoslavia (Komunistička partija Jugoslavije, or KPJ) changed its name in 1952 into the League of Communists of Yugoslavia (Savez komunista Jugoslavije, or SKJ) so as to better reflect the primary role of its members and their cooperation (in the following text, the acronym KPJ is used for the party before 1952, and SKJ for the later period). The party congress in 1952 decided that it should not be a "direct operative manager and commander in economic, State, and social life" (Mihelj 2011, p. 526), but should instead rule "through the power of persuasion and example" (Burg 1983, p. 25). SKJ was to be the "vanguard of the working people," playing a guiding political role and having constitutional responsibility for the development of the socialist project (Radojković 1994, p. 137). Unlike the communist parties in the Soviet Union or Czechoslovakia (the other two multinational socialist states), SKJ also included republic's party organizations (Bunce 1999).

Pluralism, polarization, and cleavages of the political field

Yugoslavia exhibited a greater degree of political pluralism and more visible cleavages of the political field than is to be expected of a socialist society (although recent research shows greater diversity than anticipated in even Soviet societies; Roth-Ey and Zakharova 2019) due to its structural makeup including federalism and self-management. There are two separate chains of events related to dissent and dispute within the political elite and the public sphere in Yugoslavia. The first is related to the reform movements in Croatia and Serbia toward the end of the 1960s, which were led by their respective communist elites. The second wave of popular dissent and the more rapid diversification of the public sphere is linked to the transformations in society and youth popular culture that occurred during the 1980s, as well as to the pluralization of the Party, most notably in Slovenia, and the public discourse in Croatia and Serbia, in the mid-1980s.

The economic crisis and the abeyance of repression during the 1960s, and again in the 1980s, allowed for public expression of dissatisfaction. Political cleavages became clearly visible in the 1960s, particularly the liberalization of the political field and the unmistakable reform movements organized by the sitting political elites in Croatia and Serbia (Klasić 2012; Mihaljević 2015), intertwined with the students' movements, which resembled those seen in the West. The decade culminated with students' demonstrations, which were increasingly intended to support political reforms in the two largest republics. The reform movements in the two largest republics – the Croatian Spring reform movement (1967–1971), which was focused on economic reforms and securing more power for the republics, as well as the Serbian reform movement, although supported at the beginning, were finally both framed as ideologically hostile to the socialist project, and therefore, met with the disapproval of Tito and the Central Committee of the Alliance of the Communists of Yugoslavia (Centralni komitet Saveza komunista Jugoslavije or CK SKJ). The removal from the political scene of the reform-oriented elites in both Zagreb and Belgrade followed in 1971 and 1972, respectively. A number of politically prominent leaders connected to the national movements in each republic were purged (lost their jobs or were otherwise marginalized), while a number of student leaders and intellectuals were also jailed. Some of them would emerge in the 1990s as the leaders of new political parties. The purge also affected the heads of media organizations as well as prominent editors and journalists in Croatia and Serbia, where the main newspapers and republic's television stations supported the proposals of their respective parties and helped to secure popular support within the republic. The subsequent period saw a tightening of control from the federal center, especially in relation to the media, in the affected republics (Robinson 1977).

Despite the ousting of its leaders, some of the ideas of the reform movement were adopted. The new constitution adopted in 1974 *de facto* introduced a confederal regime and awarded increased power to the republics. The constitution now included the famous self-determination clause for the republics, which formed the legal basis for the Badinter Committee's declaration in 1992 that the referenda for independence in Slovenia and Croatia were legal and that Yugoslavia had ceased to exist.

Tito's death in 1980 seems to have prompted the increasing recognition of the growing lack of consensus and legitimacy on the part of the Yugoslav project. The following decade saw the resurgence of radical nationalist policies in Serbia and protests by Albanians in Kosovo. Key political cleavages from the previous temporal framework continued against the backdrop of socialism, and they were related to preferences for either decentralization or unitarism. The conservative centralist parts of the Communist Party (in Serbia, Bosnia and Herzegovina, and Montenegro) promoted unitarism and opposed those who sought the continuation of decentralization and the liberalization of the system (Slovenia and Croatia, with Macedonia and Bosnia and Herzegovina joining at the end). The growing tensions between these two camps and their incompatible views appeared in the context of economic crisis and disputes regarding nationalism, which added to the instability of the political system and its diminishing legitimacy.

The system was faced with workers' strikes and open public critique by intellectuals, students, and the media (Ramet 2009; Klasić 2012). The legacy of the growing liberalization of the public sphere and citizens' demands for greater responsiveness on the part of the political system resulted in a critical civil society. Discontent and dissent in Yugoslavia during this period were linked to the rampant economic and political crises, as well as to the influence of liberalization movements in the Eastern Bloc, such as the Polish Solidarity movement and Gorbachev's "perestroika" and "glasnost" (Križan 1989). The parties in Vojvodina, Serbia, and Slovenia liberalized their policies concerning culture, media, and religion, while the existence of critical and investigative journalism was particularly noticeable in Croatia (Ramet 2002). The "spontaneous protest actions by the workers have become a common and generally accepted phenomenon" (Križan 1989, p. 288).

The long-term decentralization process in Yugoslavia eventually resulted in rather different political systems and visions of the future in the country, which was becoming increasingly conflicted and unsustainable toward the end of the 1980s. The liberal camp in Slovenia and Croatia advocated "democratic pluralism" with a greater emphasis on minority rights and dissent, while the "democratic centralist" approach advocated centralized majority decision-making (Robinson 1977, p. 124). In the latter part of the 1980s, the ascension of Slobodan Milošević to the leadership of the Serbian party, coupled with the rise in nationalist ideology among Serbian intellectuals and the more pronounced centralization ideal, resulted in a change in the Serbian constitution in 1989, which abolished the status of Vojvodina and Kosovo as autonomous provinces. Nationalism and ethnocentrism also became more widespread among ordinary citizens, supported by the

Serbian Orthodox Church, and increasingly reflected in popular culture and the media (Ramet 2002, pp. 38–39). This triggered a similar response in the media and polities of the other republics (M. Thompson 1995). The political cleavages were also reflected in the type and speed of the democratic trends in the federal state toward the end of the 1980s. The Slovene Communist Party was the first to liberalize. The Communist Party in Croatia was passive and silent during the 1980s, and the first initiatives concerning democratization developed from civil society. In 1989, 12 political parties and alliances (at that time still illegal and unregistered) signed a formal public petition to the Communist Alliance of Croatia (Savez komunista Hrvatske or SKH) calling for free democratic elections in Croatia, which was accepted (Spehnjak and Cipek 2007; Dunatov 2010). The new leadership of the SKH legalized the political parties together with the reformed communists, and 33 were registered for the first multi-party elections held in the country. Slovenia and Croatia were the first to hold multi-party elections in the spring of 1990, with the other republics following their example. Ultimately, the fall of socialism also brought about the end of the Yugoslav state.

Transformations of the cultural field

The ultimate end of social realism in Yugoslavia is linked to the famous speech given by the prominent Croatian essayist, novelist, poet, and playwright Miroslav Krleža at the Third Congress of the Association of Writers of Yugoslavia in Ljubljana in 1952, which was originally published in the literary and political journal *Republika* in 1952. This marked the end of the long polemic with the theory of social realism in art promoted by Stalin and Ždanov (Krležijana 2012). After this, a new period of free and non-ideological autonomous development of art and literature began. This enabled the development of abstract art and modern architecture (MOMA organized an exhibition, *Toward a Concrete Utopia: Architecture in Yugoslavia 1948–1980*, New York, 2019), and also influenced the development of popular culture in directions not possible in other communist countries. Yet despite this freedom of artistic and scientific expression, all the repressive institutional and legal tools and measures remained at the disposal of the authorities, and the party was attentive to the more politically influential genres, such as film (Arnautović 2012). The most common reasons for prohibiting the distribution of films were ideological, although quality issues were also put forward (Nikolić et al. 2010). However, the inherent ambivalences and inconsistences of the Yugoslav system made possible the publication of oppositional, dissenting, or controversial cultural works. The liberalization of culture started again after the period of state repression following the reform movements of the 1960s. Although cultural and media production was more rigorously regulated in the 1970s, the cracks in the system's legitimacy were captured in the so-called Black Wave films (1960–1970; especially prominent were Serbian directors), which critically examined the discrepancies between the promises of the socialist project and the social reality, often portraying topics such as poverty or unemployment (Levi 2009). Many of the Black Wave films were banned, and several directors left the country to work as dissidents abroad.

The debates regarding jazz in the early 1950s signified the end of social realism in popular culture. Popular music developed freely from the 1950s onwards, although it was not totally outside the scope of ideological scrutiny by the party and its committees for *šund* (i.e., lowbrow commercialized culture). Traditional folk music and domestic light pop music were considered to be politically harmless and in keeping with the official ideology. The market potential of very popular domestic and commercial "folk" music was recognized from the beginning. The production and promotion of pop and commercial folk music was based on the principles of industrial mass production and market logic[4] (Dragičević-Šešić 1994; Arnautović 2012).

The New Wave movement in rock music (1970s and 1980s), as well as punk, represented a trend of cultural development in Yugoslavia that was in line with Western sensibilities. While at its beginning in the 1960s, some political debates took place within the party regarding the desirability of the Western style of music, it was soon accepted and even promoted. The punk and new wave music popular in Yugoslavia during the late 1970s and 1980s held the ambiguous position of being both accepted and suspected due to its role in simultaneously pacifying and subverting the system, including the aesthetics of Western new wave music. As there was no non-institutionalized alternative culture (Martić et al. 2011), even the official prizes for achievements in relation to socialist culture were awarded to such alternative and "subversive" music. Even the subversive Neue Slowenische Kunst (New Slovene Art) movement was given an opportunity to design posters for the official celebration of Tito's birthday, which then proceeded to call out the state as repressive by designing posters that resembled Third Reich propaganda posters (Martić et al. 2011).

Socialist values and modernization

Before we turn to mass media artifacts, structures, and communication practices to show the extent of the cultural change or transformation, as is customary in media and communication studies, we will first explain the changes, or continuity, of values, as per the sociological view of cultural transformations, where the change in values is related to the modernization of society (Swindler 1986; Inglehart and Welzel 2005). While communism is seen by some as "an extreme case of modernity" (Blokker 2005, p. 506), the opposing totalitarianism theory sees it as a pathology and denies that it has any modernist aspects. The shared premise of the transitology approach is that "the Soviet model is seen as having failed in competition with the West, and its legacy is reducible to after-effects: dysfunctional patterns of development and mentalities un-adapted to the market continue to obstruct the progress of transformation" (Arnason 2000, as quoted in Blokker 2005, p. 506). The thesis of deficient socialist modernity mainly centers on the idea that the material aspects of modernity were attained, such as "urbanization, new division of labor, growth of education, industrial stratification, [and] growth of living standards" (Županov 1995, p. 168, as quoted in Dolenec 2014, p. 55), though without the development of a democratic political culture or modern individual value orientations (Dolenec 2014. p. 56).

Did a specific set of socialist values exist, and consequently, was there a socialist culture? Were these values different than those seen in modern Western societies? We will briefly examine the answer to this question because a cultural explanation invoking socialist values is not infrequently used to explain the lag in media developments in CEE countries. While we have, in Chapter 2, explained our position as being a predominantly institutionalist one, we do not discount the importance of values, which can be seen as the results of experiences of the practice of life (either adaptation or socialization) in certain institutional settings (Schwartz and Bardi 1997).

In his critique of socialism's economic inefficiency, Josip Županov (1983, 1995) developed a theory of socialist values in his theory of the egalitarian syndrome (TES) seen as a set of social values composed of radical egalitarianism in relation to wages, which was promoted by the socialist economy through low salaries and the absence or a significant reduction of competitive mechanisms. This was linked to a dislike of personal initiative within the public sphere, while individualist and utilitarian values existed in the private sphere and stimulated the development of the gray economy, corruption, and crime (Županov 1996, p. 430; see also Županov 1983, 1995).[5] The egalitarian syndrome develops in conditions of economic scarcity, and it also includes a moral reproof regarding non-material achievements beyond the average. Although he does not rely on modernization theory for his theoretical framework, Županov's (1987) radical egalitarianism is somewhat similar in type and cause to the attitudes associated with survival values in traditional societies (World Value Survey, WVS).[6] In the following, we present some empirical results from different studies conducted in Yugoslavia during the 1970s and 1980s, which give an idea of the values and their variations in the republics and therefore enable some comparison.

Popović et al. (1977) find that values[7] such as modernism, collectivism, non-egalitarianism, openness toward the world, a positive view of self-management, a non-material orientation, humanitarianism, and non-religiousness are related to social status; that is, they are more prevalent among managers, intellectuals, and bureaucrats than among workers, peasants, and craftsmen/artisans. Craftsmen/artisans scored highly in terms of having a positive regard for private property and relatively highly in relation to non-egalitarianism and openness toward the world. Županov (1983) also finds a certain weakening of values such as authoritarianism, non-participation, and conservatism (which he frames in terms of being supportive of self-management socialism) as well as a strengthening of utilitarian individualism at the individual level.[8]

With regard to orientations toward general human values – happiness, freedom, equality, solidarity, justice, and relations with others – two contrasting value orientations have been identified. The first is an orientation toward the social and the collective, and it is compatible with the ideology of self-management socialism in addition to being uncritical and secular (Radin 1986b, pp. 144–145). Similar to the findings of Popović et al. (1977), this orientation is more common among members and functionaries of the SK and the SSO, white-collar workers, workers with higher education, atheists, and older workers. The second orientation is toward the individual and the private, contrary or ambivalent toward the socialist system, as well as critical and religious.

The acceptance of the official ideology was less than perfect. Indeed, a pan-Yugoslav study of employed citizens conducted in 1985 finds that only 10% of respondents believed that decision-making power rested with the "working people and the citizens," as per the ruling ideology (Goati et al. 1989). Instead, the respondents answered overwhelmingly (51%) that decisions are made by the executive in the "socio-political communities," that is, territorial-administrative governing units such as the municipalities, cities, the republic, or the federal government, while 14% thought that the SKJ was the main decision maker and 11% chose business leaders (Goati et al. 1989). Gregor Tomc argued already in 1988 that the Communist Party, as the dominant sub-culture, failed after 50 years to establish the socialist character of the state, and thus the socialist project never became the "dominant culture" throughout all of Yugoslavia (as quoted in Tomić-Koludrović 1993, p. 851).

A comparative study of youth values conducted in the mid-1980s in all the republics and provinces shows that the least developed republics and provinces (Kosovo, Montenegro, and Macedonia) were in the process of developing modern values, while the most developed republics (Slovenia and Croatia) were developing post-materialist values. Slovenian and Croatian young people were the most autonomous in terms of their assessment of society, politics, and culture as well as being the least traditional (Ule 1988, as quoted in Tomić-Koludrović 1993, p. 848 fn. 13). The strong differences in the values of the young population were related to both the republic and nationality. Those from more developed republics exhibited a higher degree of modern values, less approval of the political system, and less of a desire to join the SK, and they were the most dissatisfied with the educational opportunities available to them (Aleksić et al. 1986, p. 91).[9] In a longitudinal study of value transformation in Croatia, Sekulić (2011) finds that the most accepted set of values in Croatia in 1985 were gender conservativism, political authoritarianism, and national exclusivism (all of which are related to traditional society). Economic and political liberalism and the intensity of religious feeling were at that time in the zone of non-acceptance (below

3 on a scale of 1 to 5; these values are related to modern society). By 1989, national exclusivism and political authoritarianism had fallen below the acceptance threshold, while economic and political liberalism had risen into the acceptance zone. Sekulić (2011) explains this as anticipation of changes to come. In one study (Schwartz and Bardi 1997) where comparisons exist between Eastern and Western Europe for this temporal framework, Slovenia, as the only country included from among the six countries under investigation, was found to have more or less similar authoritarian and conservative values to other Central European countries (Hungary, Czechia, Slovakia, and Poland, while Eastern European values were found to diverge even more sharply from Western ones). Slovenia was also found to have higher personal autonomy values (these values are related to post-materialism, that is, to the next transformation of modernity) than many Western European countries.

The existence of post-materialist values in Slovenia and Croatia is also indicated by the development of alternative and popular culture initiatives during the last two decades of Yugoslav socialism, which showed similarities to the new social movements developing at the same time in Western democracies. These activities included similar topics – feminism and gender equality, sexual practices, human rights, and ecology – but the organizational structure was different, as in the case of socialism these alternative cultural practices were developed within the framework of socialist institutions (Tomić-Koludrović 1993). Punk and rock concerts and the Neue Slowenische Kunst art and theatre initiative grew from the socialist youth alliances in Slovenia. Croatian feminist groups worked within the Socialist Alliance of the Working People, and within the professional academic Sociological Association of Croatia. Feminist and homosexual topics were (briefly, before being banned) explored in "The Frigid Socket"[10] radio show on *Omladinski radio* (Youth radio, later Radio 101, Zagreb). During the 1980s, the feminist, environmental, and cultural civil society emerged in larger urban centers, mostly in Ljubljana, Zagreb, and Belgrade (Ramet 2002, p. 45). The extent to which the system tolerated these alternative cultural practices depended on the degree of their perceived challenge to the system; countercultural practices were seen as more acceptable than initiatives related to traditional national or religious organizations or practices, which were actively restricted in the case of nationally motivated initiatives (Tomić-Koludrović 1993).

The role of the state: making the socialist media

Marko Zubak (2018) shows that three dimensions differentiate the Yugoslav media from their counterparts in other socialist CEE countries and the Soviet Union: self-management socialism introduced the idea of free access to information for working people, the economic reforms introduced by self-management, and federalization. At the same time, the media were subject to the framework of a one-party state and expected to function as creative professional enterprises, thereby continuing the paradox of conflicting institutional designs and expectations identified by Ivan Prpić (as quoted in Županov 1983, p. 16).

As socialism in Yugoslavia transformed, so did its expectations of the media. We can distinguish several periods characterized by different normative media roles, as well as evolving media legislation and the changing position of media institutions *vis-á-vis* the state and the party.

The administrative period: 1945–1952

At the start, media growth in Yugoslavia was sustained by the Communist Party, which mobilized the media for the purposes of socialist development (Robinson 1977). Even during the partisan resistance, journalists were tasked with making news, and the Telegraph Agency of the New Yugoslavia (Telegrafska agencija nove Jugoslavije or TANJUG) news agency was established in 1943 (Polojac 2011, p. 229). The media were originally supported through subsidies given to media organizations, journalism training programs, and the ideological favoring of particular media. Further, the media were expected to promote economic development, ethnic diversity, and the political culture of socialism, as well as to provide regime legitimacy and to contribute to the country's international status. Although the socialist government invested in media growth, the lack of economic development, technical infrastructure, and trained journalists stalled such growth during certain periods, while development was also uneven among the republics, which continued the imbalance seen during the previous period. The development of a broad variety of media at the regional level was motivated by the national and language diversity of the population (Robinson 1977, pp. 34–35).

During the administrative period, the media were the least autonomous, while the role of the state was the most pronounced. The revolution represented a radical break with the past, and the new state sought to ensure the strict control of the elements of cultural memory, including media outlets. Consequently, some high-quality pre-socialist presses were discontinued (Kramberger et al. 2004). The mass media in the immediate post–World War II Yugoslavia were defined by the expectation of being the means of achieving the goals of the Communist Party, in alignment with Lenin's ideas on the role of the press. Modern culture was perceived as a tool for socialist progress and the emancipation of the working class (Mihelj 2011). The political re-education of the predominantly peasant populations of Yugoslavia was seen as the main responsibility of the party and of the developing media (Robinson 1977, p. 18). The media were expected to assist in the promotion and legitimization of the economic and social modernization and the socialist political project, and they were seen as an aspect of public communication rather than of the propaganda process (Zubak 2018).

The Yugoslav press was seen as a tool for education and development, not as art or entertainment, and it was understood in opposition to the bourgeois culture of the West (Mihelj 2011). Newspaper articles encouraged by the Communist Party emphasized this normative role in the education of the workers, which was expected to bring about faster industrialization and the establishment of the socialist state. Newspaper genres usually intended for entertainment, such as comics and cartoons, were used during this period to depict Yugoslav workers and peasants in the revolutionary struggle (Mihelj 2011).

The press was modeled on the Soviet system – horizontally across republics and vertically across various segments of society (Robinson 1977; Zubak 2018, pp. 24–26). Restrictive policies and measures were found at all possible levels of state intervention. The press was nationalized. The freedom of expression was affected by laws that effectively limited the freedom of the media and subjected them to strict party control through the newly established Office of Agitprop (the term coined by G. V. Plekhanov to refer to the Department of Agitation and Propaganda, which was a mechanism of communist propaganda, as quoted in Lilly 1994, p. 396), which was in charge of censorship. "Cadre" policy was introduced, whereby the party directly appointed the top editorial and executive personnel, and political parallelism was very high due to the overlap of journalist and political/government roles.

As in most countries worldwide, the press in the SFRY was declared to be free. The first socialist Press Law, adopted in 1945, formally guaranteed the freedom of the press, although it only allowed officially sanctioned organizations to publish (Zubak 2018, p. 26). Josip Broz Tito addressed journalists as workers engaged in the development of socialism who created content to inform the popular masses: "You provide the material necessary to serve our propaganda. You, comrades, contribute with your labor to socialist education of all our broad masses of workers" (Broz 1949, as quoted in Senjković 2008, p. 51). The Agitprop department was established at the federal level, while ministries of information and Agitprop were established in all six republics (Zubak 2018, p. 26). The central Agitprop department within the Central Committee of the KPJ was headed by Milovan Đilas, the third most influential member of the politburo in charge of ideology, and its goal was "to concentrate, directly or indirectly, all political, cultural, educational and scientific life in the hands of the Party" (Lilly 1994, p. 396). The Agitprop department regularly sent instructions to party, state, and other organizations, held meetings with the directors of relevant institutions, and sent instructions regarding content deemed appropriate for publication. Newspaper articles were prepared in advance by the Agitprop department, which also placed party members in leading positions in newspapers, radio stations, film production companies, and state publishing agencies and made recommendations concerning the cadre to be included in editorial boards (Knezović 1992). Zlata Knezović (1992) also shows how the cultural politics of the early years promoted Soviet mass media, especially film, which amounted to more than 90% of films shown in cinemas still in 1949.

Another important normative role of culture and the press concerned its contribution to state building. This was symbolized by the slogan "Brotherhood and Unity" (*bratstvo i jedinstvo*), which contributed to the narrative of the "people's liberation struggle" during World War II and to the struggle of the proletariat, and it was intended to overcome the national and ethnic differences between the peoples of the socialist Yugoslavia.

Self-management of the socialist media market: 1950s and 1960s

After its expulsion from the Cominform alliance in 1948, Yugoslavia sought to establish its own means of cultural development, thereby completely breaking with the Soviet cultural politics of social realism and instead turning to the West in terms of economic, educational, and cultural exchanges. Yugoslavia's President Josip Broz Tito, along with Jawaharlal Nehru, the prime minister of India, and Abdel Nasser, the president of Egypt, launched the Non-aligned Movement as an organization of developing countries that were not part of NATO or the Warsaw Pact.

Organized censorship was abolished when the Agitprop department was terminated in 1952, and Yugoslavia then opened its borders to imports of cultural products from the West. Other forms of control remained, however, primarily in terms of self-censorship regarding taboo topics (such as the socialist/communist utopia itself and the "Brotherhood and Unity" idea; according to Županov [1987], the egalitarian syndrome also held the status of a taboo because it was never questioned in the media or public discourse), which was aided by party-supervised employment in the field of journalism. The control of the media was also achieved through publishing and program councils, which oversaw the proposed programs, goals, content, and economic performance of media organizations (Leković and Bjelica 1976; Robinson 1977). The directors of media institutions were appointed by the party until the 1960s, when the right to elect them was given to the workers' councils, which resulted in prominent journalists becoming the directors of media institutions (i.e., Slobodan Glumać in the case of *Borba* and Božidar Novak in *Vjesnik*; Robinson 1977, p. 45).

Media production was transformed not only ideologically, but also economically and organizationally. Trends in the diffusion of the media during the Yugoslav modernization process changed from the initial rapid diffusion of the print media and the slow development of radio to the drop in newspaper circulation figures and more rapid diffusion of radio (Robinson 1977, p. 34), which was followed by the introduction and growth of television as the first mass medium established during socialism, together with the establishment of a socialist consumer society (Duda 2010). Although cooperation with the Soviet Union was re-established following Stalin's death, Yugoslav

Table 4.2 Media legislation timeline (SFRY federal level)

1945	Press Law (Zakon o štampi)
1947	Law on publishing and distribution of children's and youth literature and press (Zakon o izdavanju i raspačavanju omladinske i dječje književnosti i štampe)
1955	Law on publishing (Osnovni zakon o izdavačkim poduzećima i izdavačkim ustanovama)
1956	Law on radio broadcasting institutions (Zakon o radiodifuznim službama)
1956	Newspaper Publishing Act (Zakon o novinskim poduzećima i ustanovama)
1960	Law of the press and other media of information (Zakon o štampi i drugim oblicima informacija)
1971	Law on the taxation of books, magazines and other publications (Zakon o oporezivanju knjiga, novina i drugih publikacija).
1973	Law on the prevention of misuses of the freedom of the press and other forms of information (Zakon o sprečavanju zloupotrebe slobode tiska i drugih oblika informiranja)
1974	Law on the importing and distribution of foreign mass media and on foreign information activities in Yugoslavia (Zakon o unošenju i raspačavanju inozemnih sredstava masovnog komuniciranja i o inozemnoj informativnoj djelatnosti u Jugoslaviji)

Source: Authors.

socialism further developed in terms of increased economic, political, and cultural pluralism to a degree not experienced in any other European socialist states. During this period, more information and other media and cultural content came from the West, and the Soviet Union was depicted as a bureaucratized, centralized, and repressive political regime (Mihelj 2011).

The cultural policy now aimed at facilitating greater ideological pluralism. The discourse of the political elite on popular culture changed, and media products belonging to popular or "lowbrow" culture started to be produced in large quantities (Mihelj 2011). The word *šund* (trash, pulp fiction) was used to designate lowbrow media formats and genres. While this kind of content was allowed, a special tax was levied on *šund* media, with the genre determination made by state committees within the republics' ministries of culture (Sekretarijat za kulturu). Indirect economic measures of media control were thus instigated. By the end of the 1950s, following the birth of consumer society in Yugoslavia, the popular entertainment press was widespread, with the content including popular culture and celebrity news (Duda 2010, p. 19). The popular and entertainment media were also less scrutinized, meaning that politically liberal or critical ideas could be buried within entertainment pages or television programs (Senjković 2008; Žikić 2010; Zubak 2012).

Leković and Bjelica (1976) explain the communications policy of Yugoslavia from the perspective of its creators (see Table 4.2. for a media legislation timeline). The constitution envisioned a steering and harmonizing role for the republic and provincial media laws, which were the primary regulators of the federal units' media and communication systems. The areas of regulation included licensing media, freedom of information, freedom of public activity, social self-management of mass communication, and the right of reply and correction, among others. The federal-level institutions were mostly responsible for the regulation of foreign press distribution and information activities within Yugoslavia, as well as for the regulation of the radio communication system.

The 1963 constitutional changes resulted in the abolition of a number of federal ministries, including the Ministry of Information. The new constitution liberalized media access to news sources. Further, it introduced the citizen's right to know, the right to be informed about the government and political and economic development as well as the right of expression. It also reinterpreted the role of the journalist as that of interpreter and critic, and it decided that all debates by the federal bodies should be open to the press. Even before the constitutional changes were instituted in 1963, the 1956 *Newspaper Publishing Act* awarded publishing enterprises the right to organize and control their own affairs. After the 1960 *Law of the press and other media* was passed, followed by the constitutional reforms of 1963 and 1974, each republic regulated its own media based on guidelines found in the federal laws and the constitution, often in a more liberal fashion (Robinson 1977, pp. 45–60).

As a consequence of "the abolishing of administrative management and transition to social self-management, [the media] have become autonomous social institutions, freed from the private, state and other monopoly" (Osolnik 1960, p. 4). For the first time, the Press Law (1960) and the constitution (1963) guaranteed the freedom of expression by ruling out censorship, providing for rectification and compensation for libel, introducing the right of reply, guaranteeing the accessibility of information sources, permitting the import of foreign press, and also defining which topics are "taboo" (Robinson 1977, pp. 41–42).[11]

Publications could not be financed by foreign sources (except from sales, advertising, the UN or other international or foreign organizations, which had signed cooperation agreements with Yugoslavia). Imports of foreign publications were allowed (although regulated). In effect, most well-known weekly and monthly magazines, such as *Time, Newsweek, National Geographic*, and *Playboy*, and the most important dailies from Western countries (e.g., *Le Monde, New York Times, Frankfurter Allgemeine Zeitung*) were available to the population in specialized bookshops or kiosks in the larger cities across the country. Individual issues were sometimes banned when the content was critical of the SFRY.

The *Law on radio broadcasting institutions* (1956) guaranteed the autonomy in terms of management and financing of broadcasting organizations (based on a mandatory license fee that was collected autonomously), defined their role in informing the public about all spheres of life in both Yugoslavia

98 *Media systems in socialist modernity*

and abroad, gave permission to increase advertising, and awarded tax relief (Robinson 1977, p. 44). Radio and television broadcasting was organized in a very similar manner to Western European public service broadcasting with a public service mission, socialist style.

The federal *Law of the press and other media of information* and the *Penal Code* were there to prevent unwanted content from finding its way into the public sphere, or if it had already been made public, to punish the authors. The *Penal Code* included the infamous article 133 or "the verbal delict," which prohibited any communication in any form that advocates a change in government; advocates against the socialist constitutional order, brotherhood, and unity; advocates for the demise of socialism; or untruthfully or maliciously represents the situation in the country.[12] Many intellectuals were jailed or otherwise harassed for this offense. Émigré publications were formally forbidden but distributed by private channels.

The mature period of decadent socialism: 1970s and 1980s

The 1974 constitution[13] treated information as a social right and added certain elements of liberal theory to the approach to the media and communication system. Journalists and the media played a certain kind of "watchdog" role according to the constitution, whereby they were expected to assist in the social control of the functionaries and self-management institutions (Leković and Bjelica 1976). Article 168 of the constitution asserted the right of citizens to be informed through truthful and objective reporting by the media, guaranteed their freedom of speech and freedom of association, and also guaranteed the right of citizens to publish their opinions in the media (Leković and Bjelica 1976). As socialist Yugoslavia perceived democracy to be at work within the economic domain, whereby workers would manage the firms in the self-management system, the communication system was expected to inform workers of political and economic system issues so that they would be able to make informed decisions in relation to their work organizations. The right to information was only viewed in the context of supporting the functioning of the self-management system. The implementation of the self-management logic in terms of media enterprises in Yugoslavia added another significant difference to the communication system. The theory of self-management assumed a well-informed[14] worker who was better able to contribute to the decision-making processes taking place within self-managed enterprises, so the "free access to information" became an indispensable tool in relation to the functioning of the socialist media system in Yugoslavia (Zubak 2018, p. 28). The transfer of power from the executive to the legislative branch of government during the reforms of the 1960s also contributed to the pluralization of society (Rudi Supek 1970, as quoted in Robinson 1977, p. 123).

During the 1970s, the liberalization of the media system was tempered by a set of new laws that more strictly controlled the growing commercial enterprise. In 1971, the *Law on the taxation of books, magazines and other publications* was adopted, bringing about the harsher taxation of the *šund* media, which it defined as media exhibiting the "tendencies of commercialization and corruption of the socialistic value system" (Popović et al. 1975, as quoted in Žikić 2010, p. 56). The *Law on the prevention of misuses of the freedom of the press and other forms of information* was adopted in 1973, followed by the *Law on the importing and distribution of foreign mass communication and on foreign information activities in Yugoslavia* (Hebrang Grgić 2000).

While the 1980s proved to be a decade of increased diversity in the cultural field and in public discourse, the attention of the party was still very much focused on the content of publications, with a view to prohibiting those deemed to be ideologically suspect. The infamous *White Book* (*Bijela knjiga*) was produced in the mid-1980s by a committee in the CK SKH (Central Committee of the Communist Alliance of Croatia); it listed books, media articles, and other cultural content in all the republics considered to be ideologically problematic, mostly in terms of nationalistic ideas. This provoked a furor, especially in Serbia (Nikolić et al. 2010). As most of the authors highlighted for their supposed nationalist writings came from Serbia, although authors from Slovenia and Croatia were also cited, this was interpreted as an attack on the republic within an atmosphere of growing discord and confrontation. The media and the public sphere in Bosnia and Herzegovina, Montenegro, and Macedonia were less open to dissent than those in the other three republics.

During the last decade of declining socialism, the media field was increasingly open and diverse, and the public sphere was increasingly critical. The decreasingly legitimate state and the socialist project still remained dangerous to those who dared to challenge their taboos.

Journalistic professionalism and autonomy

One would expect, based on the four theories of the press (Siebert et al. 1956), that media autonomy would not exist in a media system controlled by the politicized state. Yet from the first years of journalism as propaganda for the socialist modernization, the normative position of the media and the practice of journalism in Yugoslavia changed with time, alongside changes in the political and economic fields. The situation was highly nuanced, and different types of media enjoyed different degrees and types of autonomy. The professionalization of journalism would also not be expected in a socialist media system in which the media are expected to only perform the propaganda role. However, greater diversity in terms of journalism roles is found than would generally be expected (Stępińska and Ossowski 2012; Roudakova 2017; Vozab and Majstorović 2017).

Gertrude Robinson (1977) likens the normative foundation of the Yugoslav media system to the social responsibility theory codified by Siebert et al.

(1956), and not to the Soviet media theory described by the same authors. If gradually liberalized media and information laws are interpreted as normative assumptions regarding the profession of journalism in Yugoslavia, then it can be said that journalism had three primary roles: to supply objective information from a variety of sources to citizens and self-governing units, to provide a public forum capable of criticizing negative trends in society, and to educate the audience with regard to the social and political system and process (Osolnik 1966, as quoted in Robinson 1977, p. 119). The preamble to the *Press Law* (Osolnik 1960, p. 8) highlights the principles of social responsibility and professional ethics in journalism, as set down in the Code of Journalism Ethics of the Federation of Journalists of Yugoslavia. Following the liberalization of the Yugoslav media system, the normative expectations regarding journalism also changed: in addition to interpreting party views, journalists were now also expected to criticize the system and to promote public debate by using various sources in reporting (Zubak 2018, p. 29).

The development of journalistic professionalism and ideas regarding the normative functions of journalism during the Yugoslav socialist period stemmed not only from the ideological foundations of the state but also from various influences that were in place during the establishment of the media institutions, which created a specific combination of sometimes contradictory norms. For example, the financial independence of media organizations and their reliance on advertising and sales fostered a commercial orientation and style. As some media institutions were part of, or cooperated with, international institutions, the transfer of knowledge and ideas concerning the profession of journalism occurred through this cooperation. The Yugoslav Radio and Television (Jugoslavenska radio televizija or JRT) organization was, from the beginning, included in various working groups and managing bodies due to being a member of the European Broadcasting Union (EBU), while television professionals and journalists visited European and American media and regulators (e.g., the US Federal Communications Commission [FCC]). In terms of technological education and necessary equipment, the television system was established through professional contacts with Western European companies such as the French Compagnie Française Thomson-Houston (CFTH) or the Italian Marelli. Certain institutions inherited liberal norms from previous periods, especially in Slovenia, Croatia, and Serbia. According to Vukasovich and Boyd-Barrett (2012, p. 701), the TANJUG press agency adhered to the Western journalism norms of objectivity, mainly thanks to its liberal first director, Moša Pijade.

The journalism sector in Yugoslavia had a greater gender imbalance when compared to the situation in some Western European countries due to the greater difficulty of entrance of women into the (at the time) still prestigious profession (Robinson 1977, p. 97) (this is consistent with the still rather traditional social values in the country). Journalists from the national majority in the respective republics dominated the newsrooms. A significant share of journalists (41%) had a university or professional degree (Robinson 1977, p. 99) – a much higher percentage than that seen in the general population. As an indicator of the high political parallelism, a position of a journalist or editor was easily exchanged for a government or diplomatic position, much more so than a media position in profit-making areas such as advertising or public relations (Robinson 1977, p. 102).

The hybrid position on the part of Yugoslav journalists resulted in two main modes of practice: apologetic and critical (Robinson 1977, p. 124). Criticism and debate were "allowed" in the discussion concerning cultural and economic themes, while the apologetic style was expected when reporting on political matters (Robinson 1977, p. 124). Robinson (1977, p. 125) reports on a study by the Association of Journalists of Yugoslavia (Savez novinara Jugoslavije) from 1969, which demonstrated that a large majority of journalists adhered to the apologetic rather than the critical style of reporting. A survey from 1965 found that 65% of journalists belonging to the Association of Journalists of Yugoslavia were also members of the party (Carter 1982, p. 187).

Several types of normative journalistic roles can be identified in academic articles from the time (Vozab and Majstorović 2017). The most prominent role was that of journalists as socio-political workers, the term used to describe the role played by journalists in sustaining the socialist political system. Journalists, as socio-political workers, were tasked with informing the public, being engaged, being socially and politically accountable, and respecting the ethics of the profession in order to contribute to the development of socialist self-management (Vozab and Majstorović 2017). However, the next most desirable role was that of the journalist as a neutral observer of events. Moreover, other "Western" journalistic roles also appeared in socialism, including the role whereby journalists are expected to support the public sphere, the standard gatekeeper role, and the responsiveness of journalists to the interests of the audience.

At first, journalists were expected to prove their loyalty to the party before entering the profession, and only later were they to develop their professional skills (Robinson 1977, p. 99). Although during the early days of the establishment of the Yugoslav media system it suffered from a lack of resources and trained journalists (the first journalists in socialist Yugoslavia were, as in the 19th century, intellectuals), the institutional framework supporting journalism education and training gradually developed. As the Yugoslav government recognized the dire need for the expansion and improvement of the journalism profession, the first non-university-based journalism schools and training programs were founded during the late 1940s and early 1950s (Bjelica 1968, p. 206). By 1947, TANJUG had launched a one-year journalism program for training correspondents (Vukasovich and Boyd-Barrett 2012, p. 702). Further, university-based journalism programs in Yugoslavia began developing in the 1960s, first at the universities of Ljubljana (1966), Belgrade (1968), and Zagreb (1970), and all connected to the schools of political science (Peruško and Vozab 2016). Due to the late introduction and recognition of journalism as a university program, the majority of journalists had degrees in the liberal arts or law, while a smaller share had degrees in the social sciences or journalism (Robinson 1977, p. 100). The Yugoslav Institute of Journalism in Belgrade was established in 1959 by the Federation of Yugoslav Journalists (Zubak 2018, p. 22), and it played an important role in journalists' education and training (Leković and Bjelica 1976, p. 57).

Journalism associations were established in the federal republics and provinces, and they were all affiliated with the Association of Journalists of Yugoslavia, which was part of the Socialist Alliance of the Working People of Yugoslavia (Socijalistički savez radnog naroda Jugoslavije or SSRNJ). Its role was to coordinate the republic and provincial associations and to encourage the "ideological-political and professional specialization of journalists" (Leković and Bjelica 1976, p. 53). Membership in federal and republic or province-level journalists' associations was voluntary. The federal association was not a member of either the International Federation of Journalists (based in Brussels) or the International Organization of Journalists (based in Prague), although it had links to several Western European journalism institutions and associations (Leković and Bjelica 1976, p. 54).

Political parallelism in a one-party system

Despite being a one-party state, a degree of both internal and external pluralism existed in the Yugoslav media and in the polity. With regard to the exchangeability of the positions of the journalist and the politician, the parallelism was again high. The journalist was considered to be a "sociopolitical worker," and since the party largely controlled entry into the profession (if only informally after the end of the first period), journalists were considered to be members of the ruling elite. Several prominent journalists became politicians (although the reverse was not common). This started to change with the increased commercialization of the media and the toleration of the increasingly critical positions of the press (especially in political weeklies such as *Start* and *Danas* in Croatia, *Vreme* and *NIN* in Serbia, and the youth *Mladina* in Slovenia).

Political parallelism is more noticeable in relation to the higher circulation press, which had a greater connection to the party and acted as the promotors of the official culture, than in the smaller, alternative cultural, intellectual, and youth press (Carter 1982, p. 190). At the federal level, *Borba* was initially established as the paper of the Communist Party (see Chapter 3 for its origins), but during the time of the SFRY, formal establishment rights were transferred to the SSRNJ, a much broader organization that encompassed all sorts of initiatives. A degree of political parallelism was retained, although it was somewhat diluted due to the broad character of the SSRNJ, which had the mandate to include a plurality of socialist ideas and interests. After self-management socialism was introduced, big media companies became the "social property" of their workers, and they were not directly owned by the state or by the party (Table 4.3 presents a list of the main media and their publishers in the respective republics). The Communist Party published the paper *Komunist*, but while it had a large circulation because all Communist Party organizations were required to subscribe to it, it did not have a large audience. The political pluralism reflected the political cleavages developing between the camps within the Communist Party, between the parties of the republics, and between the various elements of Yugoslav civil society.

Golubović (1988, p. 136) shows how Yugoslavia exhibited actual, albeit not formal, institutionalized pluralism. In socialist Yugoslavia, large organizations intended to enable citizen cooperation were state sponsored, for example, Socialist youth alliances and workers' unions, and the government was backed by the Communist Party. The existence of non-state-organized civil society attests to a degree of pluralism within the civil society, for example, in religious organizations in all the republics (Catholic, Orthodox, Muslim, Jewish) as well as in various organizations such as the scouts, sports groups, music and other cultural organizations, and different hobby groups. Workers' unions were associated with their corresponding media as well. There were also some isolated cases of alternative civil society media, such as the Croatian rock magazine *Pop Express* (Zubak 2018), although most alternative and oppositional voices appeared within the institutions of the system (Tomić-Koludrović 1993), meaning that we can define them as "gray zones" that simultaneously legitimize and subvert the official culture.[15]

The socialist public sphere

The decentralization of the media in Yugoslavia created distinct public spheres, mostly along republic lines, which led to a low degree of knowledge concerning other republics (Kramberger et al. 2004). Ramet (2002, p. 40) shows that readers' preferences for newspapers in the 1980s were strongly divided along national lines. In the multi-ethnic Bosnia and Herzegovina, this was maybe less pronounced, but Serbs tended to read Serbian papers and Croats Croatian papers, while Bosniaks tended to read the Sarajevo-based *Oslobodenje* (Ramet 2002, p. 41). Indeed, a study from 1970 (RTV Zagreb 1970, p. 9) found that only about 2% of citizens in Croatia read weekly papers from Serbia (*Čik and NIN*). Daily morning papers were "elite" and had smaller audiences, while the more popular were the evening papers and weeklies. Slovene audiences as well judged that the JRT-shared main evening television news program included too little information about Slovenia and too much about Yugoslavia, and did not appreciate that it was not broadcast in the Slovene language (Obradović and Stupan 1968). Aside from the common public sphere that was attempted by television news on the Yugoslav level, the media during the socialist period were addressing the

104 *Media systems in socialist modernity*

Table 4.3 Media in SFR Yugoslavia

	Daily newspapers (year of establishment)	Political and information weeklies and magazines	Sport, economy, entertainment and lifestyle press (daily and weekly)	Provincial, local and minority press	Religious press	Alternative and youth press	Delegate system press	Development of radio and television (chronologically by the year of establishment)***
SR Bosnia and Herzegovina	Oslobođenje (1943)* Večernje novine	Svijet	Male novine Vesela sveska		Preporod	Naši dani Valter	Bilten za delegacije i delegate	Radio Sarajevo (1945) RTV Sarajevo (1969) Radio Sarajevo 202 (1971)
SR Croatia	Vjesnik (1940)* Večernji list (1959) Novi list (1902)	Vjesnik u srijedu Telegram Plavi vjesnik Informator Izbor Danas	Sportske novosti Studio Arena Moto magazin Oko Privredni vjesnik Vikend Fokus Kviz Sam Start Svijet Tina	Novi list Slobodna Dalmacija Glas Slavonije Glas Istre La voce del popolo Jednota	Glas koncila Mali koncil	Studentski list Omladinski tjednik Tlo Polet	Delegatski Vjesnik	Radio Zagreb (1926) RTV Zagreb (1956) Radio Zagreb Channels 2 and 3 (1964) Radio Pula, Split, Rijeka, Radio Sljeme (1966) TV Zagreb Channel 2 (1966)**** TV center Osijek (1977) TV center Split (1979) TV Zagreb Channel 3-TVZ3 (1988)
SR Macedonia	Nova Makedonija (1944)* Večer	Naš svet	Ekryan	Birlik Flaka e vellazerimit		Mlad borec Studentski zbor	Delegatski informator	Radio Skopje (1941) RTV Skopje (1964)
SR Montenegro	Pobjeda (1944)*	Privredni život			Pravoslavlje	Omladinski pokret Univerzitetska riječ	Delegatske novine	Radio Cetinje/Titograd (1944) RTV Titograd (1971)

SR Serbia (including AP Vojvodina and Kosovo)	Politika (1904)* Večernje novosti (1953) Politika ekspres (1963)	NIN Dnevnik* Međunarodna politika	Sport Privredni pregled Politikin Zabavnik TV Novosti Ilustrovana politika Svet Ekonomska politika Kekec Filmske novosti Bazar Tempo Jež Radio TV revija Duga Nada Praktična žena Vojvodina: Poljoprivrednik Lovačke novine Veseli svet Zanatlijske novine	Dnevnik Rilindija* Narodne novine Magyar Szo Bratstvo Hlas Ludu Ruske Slovo Libertatea Tan	Student Susret Omladinske novine Glas omladine Indeks Zani i rinisë Novi svet	Skupštinski pregled Gazeta e Delegateve Delegatske novine Delegatski glasnik Küldöttek Hiradója	Radio Belgrade (1944) Radio Priština (1944) Radio Novi Sad (1949) Radio Belgrade Channel 2 (1957) TV Belgrade (1958) Radio Belgrade Channel 3 (1965) Radio Belgrade 202 (1969) TV Belgrade Channel 2 (1971) RTV Priština (1975) RTV Novi Sad (1975) TV Belgrade Channel 3 (1989)
SR Slovenia	Delo (1959)* Dnevnik Ljudska pravica	TT Tovariš Tovarišev NN	Avto Zvitorepec Antena Jana Pavliha STOP	Večer	Mladina Tribuna	Družina Ognjišče	Poročevalec	Radio Ljubljana (1928) Radio Maribor (1945) Radia Koper-Capodistria (1949) Radio Ljubljana Channel 2 (1951) RTV Ljubljana (1958) Radio Ljubljana Channel 3 (1969) Television Koper (1971) Radio Val 202 (1972)

(Continued)

Table 4.3 (Continued)

	Daily newspapers (year of establishment)	Political and information weeklies and magazines	Sport, economy, entertainment and lifestyle press (daily and weekly)	Provincial, local and minority press	Religious press	Alternative and youth press	Delegate system press	Development of radio and television (chronologically by the year of establishment)***
Federal level	Borba (1922)*	Komunist** 4. jul Front Narodna armija Rad				Mladost Ideje		Radio Yugoslavia (1951)*****

Sources: Adapted from Biškup 1981; Bjelica 1969; Leković and Bjelica 1976; Milutinović 2014; Galić 2016; Ramet 2002; Spasovska 2017; Zubak 2018.

* Papers of the SSRN in the respected republic, autonomous province, or the federation.
** *Komunist* was the organ of the League of Communists in Yugoslavia, which had editorial offices in all republican and provincial centers.
*** RTV Belgrade, Ljubljana, and Zagreb broadcasted in two or three channels. Certain radio-television centers mirrored ethnic and linguistic diversity: RTV Skopje broadcasted in Macedonian and Turkish; RTV Priština in Albanian, Serbo-Croat and Turkish; RTV Novi Sad in Serbo-Croat, Hungarian, and other minority languages; and Television Koper in Slovenian and Italian.
**** In the beginning (1966), TV Zagreb's second channel broadcasted only program produced by Italian RAI, while it started broadcasting its own program in 1972.
***** Radio "Free Yugoslavia" was broadcasting between 1941 and 1945, serving partisan movement. It was reestablished as Radio Yugoslavia in the post-war period to produce program for audiences abroad (Milutinović 2014).

public spheres in the republics and nurturing national identities rather than focusing on the official ideology of "Brotherhood and Unity" (Mihelj 2011). Political cleavages were regularly seen in the media and popular culture. The media were simultaneously seen as "mediator and an independent factor in generating democratic discussions . . . participate independently in the crystallization of decisions" (Miodrag Avramović 1968, as quoted in Robinson 1977, p. 58). Liberalization and greater openness toward ideological pluralism influenced greater freedom in terms of expressing national interests, which was additionally boosted by media systems organized around the centers of federal republics that primarily addressed national audiences. In the latter part of the 1980s, the cleavages would fully open along republic and national lines.

The right to publish opinion became a constitutional right in Yugoslavia in 1963, although it was only enforced by law in the 1980s in Slovenia. This right, together with the right of reply and the right of correction, was widely used by citizens in other republics as well, for example in the letters columns in the daily press. In 1985, the Supreme Court of Slovenia ordered the newspaper *Delo* to publish an article by a citizen that criticized a political functionary (Splichal 2001).

Newspaper readership was low in Yugoslavia. In fact, in some of the republics it was much lower than in even the least developed Southern European press markets (see Table 4.1). According to one study from the mid-1960s, 66% of citizens read a daily paper regularly (75% regularly watched television and 69% listened to radio). Some 36% of daily news audiences read hard news, 24% read entertainment content such as comics, 18% were interested in true crime and disasters, 14% were interested in sports, and 10% were interested in culture and art (Jugoslovenski institut za novinarstvo 1965, pp. 25, 96, as quoted in Robinson 1977, p. 211). Political engagement was shown to correlate highly with interest in political news (including press, radio, and television), even in the context of socialism, as members or functionaries of the SK reported higher news use than non-members (Ilišin 1986). As self-management socialism was institutionally structured in such a way as to allow for a "pluralism of self-management interests" through its various organizations (SK, SSO, workers' unions), non-institutional actions were rare. Nonetheless, 53% of young workers reported their willingness to participate in informal, non-institutional, collective action if doing so could solve a problem or help someone (Ilišin 1986, p. 54). A higher level of interest in political news in the daily and weekly press also correlated with a higher age, a higher level of education, an urban living context, and atheism.[16] Young people were dissatisfied with the freedom of expression: 32% in Slovenia, 22% in Croatia, 20% in Vojvodina, 16% in Serbia and Bosnia and Herzegovina, 13% in Macedonia, 24% in Montenegro, and 11% in Kosovo (Aleksić et al. 1986).

Public opinion as we understand it today emerged in Yugoslavia during the 1980s (Golubović 1988). Critical and oppositional voices reached massive audiences when compared to the narrow critical public sphere around cultural and scientific magazines, as well as student and youth media, during the 1960s and 1970s. In the 1980s, openly critical voices appeared in daily newspapers, party press, and political magazines and on state television and radio. Despite being highly critical and liberalized, Yugoslav public opinion was still surveyed or watched over by the Communist Party (Golubović 1988, p. 128). The 1980s was characterized by a proliferation of commercially and often youth-oriented media published by the respective republic SSO organizations, including print media; radio stations in Belgrade, Zagreb, and Ljubljana (*Program 202, Omladinski radio, Radio Sljeme, Radio Student, Mladina, Radio študent*); and television shows. Freedom of expression was still limited by both the influence of the SK and internal self-censorship. The most liberal public opinion was found in Slovenia.

One specific area where alternative or even dissenting ideas could emerge was the youth press, and a variety of media were published by various student and youth organizations with the aim of mobilizing socialist youth (Zubak 2012, p. 24). According to the self-management paradigm, socialist youth and student organizations should be less "bureaucratized" and more autonomous from the SK, and addressing the interests of socialist youth should be their primary activity (Zubak 2012, p. 24). Although Zubak (2012) holds that the success of such efforts was dubious, the result was the proliferation of youth magazines such as *Studentski list* (1946), *Polet* (1976), *Omladinski tjednik* (1967), and *Tlo* and *Pop-Express* (1969) in Croatia. Youth press were established in all the republics. This demonstrated the ambiguous relationship between the political regime and rock and alternative youth culture: if it remained within the aesthetic and commercial realm then it was tolerated, but it became problematic and subversive if it challenged the dominant political ideology or values. The development of youth culture through socialist organizations occurred in a way that pacified and legitimized the political regime, although it had clear subversive and oppositional potential. The weekly paper *Mladina* (Youth) was notable for its dissenting views and in the democratization process in Slovenia during the 1980s.

The cultural journals with lower circulation were those in which views not favored by the political elite were more likely to be expressed. For example, more favorable views regarding the national program were expressed in smaller intellectual publications in Slovenia such as *Naša Sodobnost* (Our Contemporary Times), *Perspektive* (Perspectives), and *Problemi* (Problems) (Kramberger et al. 2004), and *Hrvatski tjednik, Kritika*, and *Telegram* in Croatia. A similar role is seen here for the cultural press as seen during the 19th century, when they were the mouthpieces of national independence movements. In 1952, the Slovenian Catholic Church started publishing a newspaper, *Družina* (Family), considered to be the most important Slovenian religious newspaper (Kramberger et al. 2004). *Nova revija* was another Slovene magazine in which the Slovene national program was openly expressed in the 1980s (Magaš 1993, as quoted in Patterson 2000, p. 417). In Croatia, the Catholic press (*Glas Koncila*) remained independent of party interference in editorial matters and did not take an overt part in political discussions during the 1980s. More radical left social critique was published in the academic journal *Praxis* (Zagreb).

The newspaper content analysis (conducted in the course of research conducted for this book) also supported the division of the various public spheres along republic lines. Conversations mainly occurred within the federal units rather than across them or at the common, federal level. The dominant themes in the Yugoslav press were foreign policy (18.7%) and international (16.8%) and domestic politics (16.5%), followed by economy and business (13.9%) and law, security, and crime (11.1%). The least present themes were "lighter" content such as lifestyle, popular culture, and entertainment (0.2%) and human interest stories (0.9%) as well as social institutions that played a marginal role, such as religion (0.2%) or civil society (0.5%). The front-page articles focused the most on stories that covered issues from Yugoslavia (33.8%), followed by those that focused exclusively on stories and issues regarding the republic in which the relevant newspaper is based (30.7%). Sabina Mihelj (2011) notes the media in Yugoslavia nurtured the national identity much more than the "brotherhood and unity idea." The results of our analysis suggest that the Yugoslav press addressed both the common "Yugoslav" public sphere and the republics' public spheres, although the inside content was more oriented to the domestic republic news. In addition, the press also covered a larger share of stories from countries and regions outside Europe or the United States (19.6%), which is explained by Yugoslavia's role in the Non-aligned Movement. As Yugoslavia was located between West and East, and because it tried to escape its peripheral status through engagement with the Non-aligned Movement (Mihelj and Huxtable 2018), the media did, however, place more emphasis on issues coming from the West (9.5% from Western Europe and 4% from the United States) than on issues from the East (only 1.9% of articles). Most of the articles originated from news agencies (39.5%), followed by those with original authors (36.9%). For a rather large share of the articles, it was impossible to determine authorship (23.2%), which also made it more difficult to address the issue of gender equality among journalists at the time. However, of the articles that clearly stated the name of the author, male journalists stand out (87% were male authors, while 13% were female authors). The majority of articles on the front page were small in size (less than a quarter of the page; 78.3%) and presented only in textual form (72.6%), while 27.2% of the textual articles included photos or figures as well.

These patterns differ somewhat across the Yugoslav republics. What is noticeable is the difference between the "media-richer" republics (Croatia, Slovenia, and Serbia), which lead in terms of original production, and the "media-poorer" republics (Bosnia and Herzegovina, Macedonia, and

Montenegro), which in a way function as a periphery inside the SFRY. For example, original authors publish the most in Serbia (60.5%), Croatia (59.3%), and Slovenia (42.2%). In the other republics, less than 30% of articles have original authors, as they are more commonly taken from news agencies – 63.1% in Macedonia, 59.7% in Bosnia and Herzegovina, and 44.6% in Montenegro. The press of media-rich countries also focus on issues from the republics in which they originate to a larger extent. For example, *Večernje novosti* dedicates 39.5% of articles to issues from Serbia, 39% of articles in *Večernji list* are dedicated to issues from Croatia, and 37.5% of articles from *Delo* are dedicated to issues from Slovenia. The newspapers with the largest share of original authors (Serbia and Croatia) are the least diverse in terms of the geographical focus of their articles: *Večernje novosti* dedicates only 10.5% of articles to stories from outside Serbia and the SFRY, while *Večernji list* dedicates 25.5% of articles to stories from outside Croatia and the SFRY. The most "outward" looking newspapers are *Pobjeda* (57.1%) and *Delo* (42.3%). The diversity of the geographic focus is the widest in Montenegro and Slovenia, followed by Macedonia, Croatia, Bosnia and Herzegovina, and Serbia as the least diverse.

The newspapers differ with regard to the dominant topic, which is law, security, and crime in *Delo* (18%), economy and business in both *Večernje novosti* (37%) and *Večernji list* (19%), domestic politics in *Oslobođenje* (27%), international politics in *Pobjeda* (39%), and foreign policy in *Nova Makedonija* (32%). Those newspapers that rely more on news agencies publish more about politics, while those that have a larger share of original authors cover or place an emphasis more on stories from outside the political sphere. The diversity of themes is the widest in Slovenia and Croatia, followed by Bosnia and Herzegovina, and then Serbia, Macedonia, and Montenegro as the least diverse. Television had a greater influence on the creation of a common public sphere, with inter-republic discussion being achieved to some degree through TV news, which rotated between studios on some days of the week. Shared television programs began at the end of 1958 following the establishment of the JRT (Vončina 1999). Daily news and informational programs were exclusively transmitted by TV Belgrade between 1959 and 1968. TV Zagreb, TV Ljubljana, and later other republic TV centers sent their material to Belgrade, where it was edited for inclusion in the common news program (Vončina 1999, 2001). According to Vončina (2001, p. 170), audiences complained about the programs being in other languages and about other republics, which led to changes in shared programming. The constitutional reforms of 1963 led to further changes in the production and distribution of shared informational programs, which were still transmitted from Belgrade but now included more minutes from republic TV centers (Vončina 2001, pp. 221–223), until the daily evening news started to be broadcast from the various republics' studios (from 1968) and shared news was only broadcast on Sundays.

Self-management of the media market in a socialist society

The media were predominantly produced at the level of the federal republics or provinces, and they largely aimed to reach their local national audiences, as political decentralization was coupled with market segmentation. Broadcasting was organized within the individual republics, while newspapers were often available outside the original republic in which they were published (although those in the Macedonian and Slovene languages were less likely to attract outside audiences) and some, such as teen magazines and cartoons, had pan-Yugoslav audiences. The Western republics benefited from a wider selection of television programs delivered via transborder signals from Austria and Italy, and this was also the case for the neighboring television signal regions within the country. The differences between the media sub-systems of the republics were visible with regard to the media infrastructure and the spread of media technologies, while citizens in those republics with less developed infrastructure adopted the media later and at a slower pace. The influence of the market and self-regulation made a difference in terms of media development, which went further than in other socialist countries.

There were only a few media outlets at the federal level: the daily newspaper *Borba* (Struggle)[17] and the TANJUG news agency. TANJUG held a pivotal position among the non-aligned countries during the Cold War period due to being a coordinating agency for the Non-aligned News Agency Pool (NANAP) (Vukasovich and Boyd-Barrett 2012). The JRT had no broadcasting channel of its own, although it was a coordinating network of republic broadcasters. It played a primary role as the exchange network for programs produced at the levels of the republics, and it coordinated certain programing decisions (Radojković 1994, p. 138).

The press: profit, advertising, and audiences

The press in Yugoslavia largely functioned in accordance with the market logic present within the specific Yugoslav type of market socialism. Thanks to economic reforms designed to replace state socialism with a self-management socialism model, the economic models of media organizations substantially differed from those of state-owned organizations and capitalist market organizations. Nixon and Bryan (1966, p. 291) suggest that the distinctive type of the Yugoslav media system stems from its different ownership, as defined in the 1956 law, which stated that the press industry is owned not by the state but by "society," that it is managed by its employees, who share the profits, and that the firms must compete with other media firms for both readership and revenue. The media were the "social property" of those who worked in them, and they were "legally independent and compete with each other in a relatively free market," with the only requirement being that they should operate for a profit (Robinson 1977, p. 27).

The self-management reforms introduced the institution of workers' councils into all business organizations, including the media. They were responsible for broad questions regarding planning, determining economic policy (e.g., salary and investment), establishing productivity norms, setting disciplinary rules, and prescribing working conditions (Robinson 1977). The managing board of each council, headed by the director general, and the editorial board, headed by the editor-in-chief, made daily editorial and production decisions (Sokolović et al. 1967). The media were also subject to a publishing council, which "performs much like a board of trustees in the American system, or advisory board and keeps away from day-to-day management" being "entitled to examine the general policy of the enterprise from the social standpoint, to approve plans, or general policy," although it did not take part in daily management (Robinson 1977, pp. 28–29).

Publishing houses, which were largely financed through advertising, competed for readership, attracting readers by printing materials in popular "Western" media genres (Nixon and Bryan 1966, p. 292). They had control over a significant part of their profits (Robinson 1977; Mihelj 2011). Additionally, the publishing houses had strong market research departments that tracked the tastes and preferences of their audiences (Mance 1976, 1985; Lamza and Rihtar 2003; Senjković 2008; Šrot 2008). Nixon and Bryan (1966, p. 292) offer the example of the Communist Party paper *Borba*, which was unable to compete with the self-managed and more commercially oriented *Politika*, which attracted much larger audiences (see Table 4.1 for comparative circulation data). From the 1960s onwards, the various media institutions had diverse sources of income: subscriptions for newspapers and license fees for radio and television broadcasting, sales to audiences, advertising, and state financing. Data regarding the broadcasting budget for 1971 show that license fees accounted for 73% of the budget, advertising for 19%, and government funding for only 8% (Robinson 1977). Due to the greater dependence of media organizations on advertising, the tendency toward the maximization of profit was growing and media production was becoming reoriented toward entertainment content and specialized media products aimed at specific market niches (Mihelj 2011).

The financial autonomy of the media grew alongside the development of both the advertising industry and consumer society (Duda 2010). Patterson (2003) describes the growth of the advertising industry, whose personnel learned and transferred advertising practices, organization, ideas, and styles through their close connection with Western colleagues and organizations. Some republics' centers had a more developed advertising industry than others, especially Croatia. The Zagreb-based agency Advertising Institute of Croatia (Oglasni Zavod Hrvatske or OZEHA) became prominent during the 1950s and later opened offices in other cities in Croatia as well as in Belgrade, Sarajevo, Banja Luka, and Skopje. Another prominent advertising agency was *Ekonomska propaganda* in Belgrade. Large media publishing companies such as *Politika, Borba*, and *Vjesnik* also had their own in-house advertising agencies (Hanson 1974).

Audience research began in the 1970s (Lamza and Rihtar 2003). A significant role was played by the most successful newspaper publisher in Yugoslavia, Vjesnik, whose audience research unit conducted several extensive studies on the reading habits of media consumers. Vjesnik was continuously engaged in audience research from 1973 onwards, which "opened certain unstandardized channels of readers' feedback to the press and the possibility for audiences to influence this publisher's production" (Mance 1985, p. 1). Newspaper and magazine audiences were profiled according to their sociodemographic characteristics, lifestyles, and consumption and media use habits. Similar studies were conducted in Serbia by the publisher *Politika*, which used audience research to improve its market competitiveness (Todorović 1987). During this period, an important role in audience research was also played by media broadcasters. RTV Zagreb and RTV Belgrade became the first broadcasters in Yugoslavia to establish their own audience research units in the 1960s, and RTV Ljubljana followed in the 1970s (Šrot 2008).

The growth in the number of published newspapers and magazines, as well as in the number of established radio stations, was rapid. This growth in production eventually brought about the diversification of media formats and genres. For example, the evening press introduced in the 1950s brought about a different, more commercialized style of journalism, with shorter information and illustrations, and tried to attract readers through the use of more interesting presentation styles (Bjelica 1968, p. 210).

Another cultural form that was important to the socialist working culture was the factory newspaper (Cvek 2017), which according to some sources was read by 77% of young workers in 1986 (Ilišin 1986, Table 4.4). Workers' newspapers could be evaluated from the standpoint of political parallelism as a venue for Communist Party influence (this might be suggested by the findings of Ilišin [1986], which show that members and functionaries of the Communist Party read the factory papers more than other groups), although

Table 4.4 Young workers as audiences for the printed press (regular use, personal or family)

Daily newspapers (morning and evening)	72%
Reviews and magazines	51%
Women's interest magazines	20%
Radio and TV magazines	18%
Information weeklies	7%
Specialized magazines	6%
Entertainment magazines	3%
Youth press	3%
Papers of "socio-political organizations" (*Komunist, Radničke novine*)	1%

Source: Adapted from Ilišin et al. (1986).

114 *Media systems in socialist modernity*

they were officially presented as a platform for all "social forces shaping the life of the socialist enterprise" (Cvek 2017, p. 106). These newspapers were not limited to information concerning the workplace, as their content varied and also included cultural, political, and entertainment topics.

The disparities in the economic development and cultural traditions of the Yugoslav republics influenced the concentration of media outlets in the large cities in the less developed republics (Robinson 1977, p. 96). Due to the linguistic diversity and complex decentralized media system, the media market was highly segmented, while the circulation figures were (especially in the less developed republics) far lower than the European average (Radojković 1994, p. 138). The circulation of 2,265 newspapers and magazines stood at 839 million in 1967 (Bjelica 1968, p. 219). Newspaper sales in Yugoslavia averaged 133 copies per 1,000 of the adult population by the end of the 1960s, albeit with very large differences between the republics – Slovenia sold 245 copies per 1,000, while Macedonia sold only 54 (see Table 4.1 for the other republics).

The largest press market was that of the largest federal republic, namely Serbia, whose capital Belgrade was also the capital of the SFRY, where the central communist paper *Borba* was published and distributed throughout the country, together with the Serbian daily paper *Politika* (Robinson 1977), to all business and companies.[18] Consequently, almost half of all press in Yugoslavia were published in Serbia, which also accounted for 57.5% of the total circulation. Among the other republics, large discrepancies can be seen between the more developed Croatia and Slovenia and the less developed Bosnia and Herzegovina, Montenegro, and Macedonia, which had weak press markets.

Developing television in self-management socialism

The socialist temporal framework in the six countries overlaps with the age of television. While the press, radio, and telegraph were all introduced during the previous temporal framework, television was first introduced into the socialist context. Other media also took off during this period – the press only truly became a mass medium in the 1960s, at the time of the liberal socialist era. The television was introduced in Yugoslavia at similar time as in other Mediterranean countries. Television began regular broadcasts in Italy in 1954, in Spain, Portugal, and Croatia in 1956, and in Greece in 1966. All these countries were late adopters when compared to France and the UK, which started regular television broadcasts almost immediately following the end of World War II. The context in which the television system was introduced in Yugoslavia was, however, different from the contexts of the Southern European countries as well as from the state-directed systems of Eastern European socialist countries. The development of television went hand in hand with the establishment of the self-management socialist system in Yugoslavia, which enabled a degree of market influence, freedom of speech, and pluralism.

Radio and television broadcasting were not institutionally centralized at the federal level, and despite some centrally and politically driven trends toward unification, the republic radio and television systems remained institutionally independent and, therefore, diverse in terms of their technological equipment and financial and human resources. The federal umbrella organization, the JRT, was established in 1954. It was neither a television channel nor a broadcast organization, but rather an association of republic radio and television centers amenable to the coordination of common program broadcasting, program exchange, and co-production. The JRT was governed by a board of directors whose members were the general directors of the republic radio-television centers. The organization of the broadcasting of radio and television in the republics was also linked to the organization of the frequency spectrum, and broadcasts from one republic could not, as a rule, be received in other republics. Therefore, there was no national channel for either radio or television (e.g., in the USSR; Mihelj and Huxtable 2018).[19]

After a period of experimentation, regular television broadcasting in Yugoslavia began in 1956 (in Croatia), although the establishment of a regular daily flow took much longer. In Croatia, Slovenia, and Serbia, television was established in the 1950s, in Bosnia and Herzegovina and Macedonia in the 1960s, and in Montenegro in the 1970s. During the 1970s, all the Yugoslav television services introduced a second channel, as well as color programming, following a significant increase in broadcasting time over the previous decade (in Croatia, the increase was almost tenfold, comparable to the increase seen at the time of the introduction of digital terrestrial television in 2011; Peruško and Čuvalo 2014). Throughout the socialist period, Croatia, Serbia, and Slovenia remained at the forefront of television development due to being the most technologically, professionally, and financially well-equipped TV centers.

The republic TV stations had significant autonomy in terms of their broadcasting policies and schedules. The exact distribution of shared versus domestic programs was not fixed and so varied across the republics over the decades. Due to differences between the republics with regard to their wealth, socio-demographic characteristics, and market conditions, the party leaders' orientation toward more liberal and pluralist or more centrist and unitary values, technological resources, and the professional skills and values of journalists and other media professionals, television audiences in different republics were not confronted with an identical TV culture.

Cultural history of European television has been fruitfully discussed on the basis of changes and differences in genres (Bourdon 2011). The periodization of television ages on the basis of the dominant genres and their relationship with audiences (Eco 1983; Missika 2006) is useful for our comparison between the Southeast European region and Western Europe. How similar or different were these cultures, in terms of the character of their television flows, to those seen in Western Europe at the time?

116 *Media systems in socialist modernity*

Television was in Yugoslavia seen by its audience as a form of entertainment (51% of all audiences in 1965), while only 20% saw it as a means by which to be informed. Entertainment programs, including popular music and dancing shows, were the most popular programs among Croatian audiences, which were already familiar with their Italian and Austrian counterparts, as well as with imported American entertainment series and soap operas (Vončina 1999). Comic television series and stand-up comedians represent the genre most often used as the conduit for a more direct social critique (Mihelj 2013, 2014). Light entertainment combining music with humor was, along with sport and fiction, especially comedy drama (Vončina 2003, 2005; Mihelj 2013, 2014; Mihelj and Huxtable 2018), the most popular television genre. Among the programs found to appeal to audiences, educational programs that combined entertainment with education and that were aimed at children gained cult status (Smogovci by TV Zagreb; Kocka, kocka, kockica by TV Belgrade; Nedjeljni zabavnik by TV Sarajevo). Audiences' preferences initially settled on quiz shows, film, entertainment, and drama programs (RTV Zagreb 1970). In other socialist countries television was also able to attract large audiences, also primarily for entertainment (Imre et al. 2012).

The generic composition of the three main program modes (information, entertainment, and fiction) across the six republics during the era of socialism is presented below, with a view to situating these flows within the known cultural map of television development in Western Europe.

The flows of television differed across the republics, reflecting differences in their respective television cultures (Figure 4.1). Slovenia had the lowest

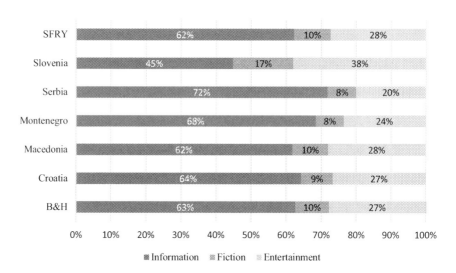

Figure 4.1 Main types of programs on republican TV channels (1979) (% of daily minutes, one-week composite sample)

Source: Authors.

share of informational programs (a composite category that included cultural and educational programs, current affairs, documentaries, and news), which could be interpreted as an indication of neo-television in which the traditional "high culture" role gives way to the second commercial phase (Eco 1983; Missika 2006). In 1979, fiction was the least well-represented program group on Yugoslav television (this category included comedy and drama series and films). TV Ljubljana (Slovenia) had the highest share of fiction programs (17%), while other TV centers broadcast between 8% and 10% of fiction. The relatively high share of informational programs on TV Belgrade (72%) when compared to the other TV centers, especially Slovenia (45%), might be interpreted as a lag in the television age, whereby Slovenia was entering the neo-television age while Serbia was still exhibiting the culture of the paleo-television age in which information/news and education represented the main purposes of television (Eco 1983). Paleo television predominated in Western Europe during the 1950s and 1960s, the time of strong public service broadcasting.

The informational/factual formats (including news and current affairs, art and highbrow culture, and documentary) also prevailed during prime time (19:30–23:00) in all the republics, followed by the fiction genres (most prevalent in Slovenia [30%], then Macedonia), while others were around 20%, and entertainment in the third place (Slovenia, Macedonia, and Serbia in the lead with 18%, with others between 13% and 15%). In our classification, the category of entertainment includes sports, chat and talk shows, children's programs, media and popular culture, music (other than classical or jazz), and quiz and game shows. During prime time (19:30–23:00), the diversity of the broadcast genres was lower than throughout the whole day, with much higher shares of the entertainment and fiction genres. All the Yugoslav television stations were more family oriented during prime time, while the morning and afternoon programs were oriented toward children and educational topics.

Table 4.5 shows the distribution of particular genres in the republic television cultures. Cultural programs (including education) were the most well-represented genre across all the television stations: the lowest share was found in Slovenia (20%, although with this percentage the cultural programs were the most represented single category also for this broadcaster) and the highest (38%) in Croatia. Slovenia had the most diverse program in terms of genres. Slovenia had the highest share of programs for children (16%), films (11%), and sports (10%). The smaller shares of cultural programs and current affairs and the highest shares of films and sports programs on Slovenian televisions indicate its greater commercial, or entertainment, orientation, even in the 1970s under socialism. TV Zagreb had the lowest share of news broadcasts, although this was somewhat compensated with current affairs programs.

The most commonly aired prime-time genres were news, cultural programs, and films. Cultural programs were prevalent in TV Sarajevo prime time (31%), and least represented in TV Ljubljana (17%), where films

118 Media systems in socialist modernity

Table 4.5 Genre distributions on republican TV stations (1979) (% of daily minutes, one-week composite sample)

Genre	Bosnia and Herzegovina	Croatia	Macedonia	Montenegro	Serbia	Slovenia	SFRY
Children's	9%	7%	7%	6%	6%	16%	9%
Comedy	0%	0%	0%	0%	0%	2%	0%
Cultural program	34%	38%	30%	33%	33%	20%	32%
Current affairs	6%	5%	2%	4%	4%	3%	4%
Documentary	9%	10%	13%	14%	14%	7%	11%
Drama	2%	1%	4%	1%	2%	4%	2%
Film	7%	7%	7%	6%	6%	11%	7%
Media and popular culture	8%	8%	7%	8%	5%	7%	7%
Music	3%	2%	5%	3%	5%	5%	4%
News	13%	11%	17%	18%	21%	14%	16%
Reality program	0%	1%	0%	0%	0%	1%	1%
Soap opera	1%	1%	0%	1%	0%	0%	0%
Sports	8%	9%	8%	6%	4%	10%	7%
TOTAL	7,246	7,046	7,005	7,705	6,380	6,905	42,287

Source: Authors.

prevailed (25%). The differences in the generic composition of prime-time programs and the orientation toward fiction or entertainment could be the result of differences in audience preferences but also of differences in financial, technological, and human resources between the republic TV centers.

Television content from other republics flowed through the republic broadcasting organizations in varied proportions. We analyzed the sources of broadcast programs so as to determine the shapes and directions of these flows. Serbia (58%), Croatia (48%), and Slovenia (42%) had the highest share of domestic production. The share of domestic programs was the smallest in Montenegro (7%), which also had the highest share of TV programs from TV Belgrade (49%). Bosnia and Herzegovina, Macedonia, and Montenegro had a lower share of domestic programs than of programs produced in Serbia. At the same time, in Serbia, programs from other republics had relatively low shares. Exceptions were programs from Croatia (17%) and Bosnia and Herzegovina (8%). Programs from Serbia, Croatia, and Bosnia and Herzegovina were most frequently aired on Yugoslav television, probably due to the fact that their languages could be understood in all three republics. The Macedonian and Slovenian languages were not readily understood by other citizens, which might explain their smaller presence in the shared flow. Programs from the EU, the United States, and other countries had similar shares in most republics television systems. Thanks to the policy of subtitling of foreign productions, films could be shared more easily.

Table 4.6 Origins of prime-time TV (1979) (% of daily minutes, one-week composite sample)[20]

Origin of prime-time	SFRY republic television						SFRY
	Bosnia and Herzegovina	Croatia	Macedonia	Montenegro	Serbia	Slovenia	
Bosnia and Herzegovina	30%	9%	0%	6%	13%	8%	12%
Croatia	21%	45%	14%	23%	20%	14%	23%
Macedonia	1%	1%	38%	2%	2%	4%	8%
Montenegro	0%	0%	1%	10%	1%	0%	2%
Serbia	19%	21%	22%	29%	37%	17%	24%
Slovenia	1%	4%	7%	3%	6%	29%	8%
EU	12%	9%	14%	11%	11%	14%	12%
US	6%	7%	4%	7%	7%	0%	5%
Other	4%	4%	0%	2%	3%	7%	3%
YU unspecified	6%	0%	0%	7%	0%	7%	3%
TOTAL	3,315	2,975	2,755	3,060	2,610	2,825	17,540

Source: The authors.

The less developed republics (Macedonia and Montenegro), which had small markets, faced difficulties providing original programs, although their prime time was more oriented toward domestic programs than programs from other TV centers (Table 4.6). When we look at the production origins of the different genres broadcast across the SFRY, Serbian production dominates in all genres (especially in light entertainment shows), except in relation to drama, films, and fiction for children, which were mostly produced in the EU.

Republics with more developed and/or relatively bigger media markets (i.e., Serbia and Croatia) could muster more original programing. In 1968, TV Zagreb broadcast 29.9% of the JRT program, TV Belgrade 28.3%, TV Ljubljana 24.3%, TV Skopje 14.8%, TV Sarajevo 2.5%, and TV Titograd 0.2% (YRT Yearbook 1971/1972). Macedonia and Slovenia, the countries with languages not spoken outside of their republics, had more leeway in terms of constructing their television flows. The television culture was the most distinct in Slovenia, and it was also the most similar to the contemporaneous developments seen in the television genre composition in Western European countries (cf. Bourdon 2010), although it still lacked some genres already present on Western Europe television at that time. The other five republics shared more of the television flow, and their television schedules had a more similar composition. The shared culture was mainly oriented toward schoolchildren through educational programing, while current affairs programs and the news were more nationally oriented. Television audiences preferred to receive news about their own republics and were less interested in developments in other parts of Yugoslavia (Obradović and Stupan 1968). For illustration in the differences and similarities of the TV flows, Table 4.7 provides an example of one day of TV schedules in all the republics.

Table 4.7 A day in the life of socialist TV broadcasting (1979)

Friday, May 11, 1979	TV Sarajevo (Bosnia and Herzegovina)	TV Zagreb (Croatia)	TV Skopje (Macedonia)	TV Titograd (Montenegro)	TV Belgrade (Serbia)	TV Ljubljana (Slovenia)
Morning	9:00–11:20 School/education program for children and teenagers, produced by TV Zagreb and TV Belgrade					
Afternoon	14:00–17:25 Reruns of the morning educational program	15:00–17:10 Reruns of the morning educational program	15:05 News (TV Skopje) 15:15–16:45 Reruns of the morning educational program	15:10–16:40 Reruns of the morning educational program	14:10–16:40 Reruns of the morning educational program	15:00–16:00 Reruns of the morning educational program
	17:25 News (TV Sarajevo)	17:15 Regional news (Rijeka)	16:45 News in Albanian (TV Skopje) 17:10 News (TV Skopje) 17:25 Documentary on British museums	17:30 News (TV Titograd)	16:40 News (TV Novi Sad) 17:40 News (TV Belgrade)	
	17:45 Educational program produced by TV Sarajevo			17:45 Educational program produced by TV Sarajevo		17:25–18:45 TV series (TV Zagreb); youth series (TV Ljubljana); rock concert News (TV Ljubljana)
	18:45 Classical music concert produced by TV Zagreb					18:45 Social self-defense (TV Ljubljana)

Media systems in socialist modernity 121

Evening	19:15 Cartoon (TV Sarajevo)	19:15 Cartoon (TV Zagreb)	19:15 Cartoon (TV Skopje)	19:15 Cartoon (TV Titograd)	19:15 Cartoon (TV Belgrade)	19:15 Cartoon (TV Ljubljana) TV Ljubljana transmitted 10 minutes of popular health and science before the cartoon
	19:30 Daily news (TV Sarajevo)	19:30 Daily news (TV Zagreb)	19:30 Daily news (TV Skopje)	19:30 Daily news (TV Titograd)	19:30 Daily news (TV Belgrade)	19:30 Daily news (TV Ljubljana)
	20:00 Seven plus seven, pop-music show (TV Belgrade)	20:00 Seven plus seven, pop-music show	20:00 Petročeli, series (TV Skopje)	20:00 Concert in honor of Security Day	20:00 Seven plus seven, pop-music show (TV Belgrade)	
	21:00 Series *Hod po mukama* (TV Belgrade)		21:55 News (TV Skopje)		21:00 Series *Hod po mukama* (TV Belgrade)	21:00 "625" TV show
	22:15 In memoriam sculptor August Augustinčić (TV Zagreb)	22:15 News (TV Zagreb) 22:30 Documentary Latin America (TV Zagreb)	22:15 In memoriam sculptor August Augustinčić (TV Zagreb)			22:25 News (TV Ljubljana) 22:45 Film
	23:00 News (TV Sarajevo 23:15 Documentary Latin America (TV Zagreb)		23:00 Documentary Latin America (TV Zagreb)	23:00 News (TV Titograd)	23:00 News (TV Belgrade)	

122 *Media systems in socialist modernity*

Young (workers) audiences preferred fiction and entertainment programing on television over news and information (Table 4.8), as did other audiences (RTV Zagreb 1970). Newspapers retained at that time the primacy as the medium for information.

The afternoon program varied more from one republic to another. The genre diversity[21] (all day minutes) was the highest in Slovenia and Bosnia and Herzegovina, while the prime-time genre diversity was the same in all six republics. The diversity of content with regard to the place of production was the highest in the smaller republics (Slovenia and Macedonia), while the larger republics relied more on their own program-producing capacities.

Audiences' preferences in terms of radio programs also varied with their education, social status, and gender, with male manual workers (as in the case of the printed press) preferring sports topics and women preferring popular music (Ilišin et al. 1986). The main contents of radio stations in Yugoslavia were the news (41.5%), folk music (15.84%), and foreign and home affairs (15% and 7.59%, respectively) (YRT Yearbook 1971/1972). By the 1980s, the role of radio was predominantly related to entertainment, although the largest urban radio centers (Belgrade, Zagreb, Ljubljana, and Novi Sad) operated three channels of public service radio, where the first channel was oriented toward news and current affairs, the second toward music and entertainment, and the third toward culture, classical music, and science. The other republics' broadcasters only operated two public radio channels. Many local radio stations were operated by cities and municipalities, adding to the diversity of owners and content.

Media culture and global communication flows

During the Cold War era East/West divide, Yugoslavia clearly opted to be more connected to Western cultural flows and practices. From the beginning, television in Yugoslavia was involved in the transnational television system and therefore was under the influence of the West. The first television schedules were shaped by the practice of established Western television, which served as a role model for developing television in Yugoslavia (Vončina 1999). During the experimental phase, television stations broadcast Austrian and Italian programs, television staff were educated in Western

Table 4.8 Young workers as audiences for television

Film	74%
News	59%
Sports	51%
Entertainment and music shows	35%
Educational	21%
TV drama	11%

Source: Adapted from Ilišin et al. (1986).

Europe (France, BBC), and television companies received technical support and equipment (Vončina 1999). The JRT was a member of the EBU, had a PAL system for color TV broadcasting as in Western Europe, and was largely exposed to Western media.[22] TV Zagreb served as the focal point for the EBU news exchange. Yugoslavia's participation in the Eurovision Song Contest since 1961 enabled the participation of Yugoslav audiences in a symbolic ritual of Western European television flows. The JRT was also creating content for Yugoslav emigres abroad as well as for audiences in non-aligned countries in Africa, Asia, and South America (Leković and Bjelica 1976).

The international flow of television programs differentiated Yugoslav television stations from the stations of the federation's socialist neighbors. While most socialist countries imported the majority of their programs from other socialist countries (in Bulgaria, 40% of foreign programming was of Soviet origin in the early 1970s; in the GDR, two-thirds of programs came from the Soviet Union and the rest from other socialist countries; Hungary was more diverse and had more Western programing), on TV Belgrade during the early 1970s more than 80% of imported programs came from the West (Nordestreng and Varis 1974, p. 25), the majority from the United States (45% according to the YRT Yearbook 1971/1972). At the end of the 1970s, our sample shows a reduction in imports, although the same reliance on Western imported programs can be seen. At the time, Western European television broadcasts comprised, on average, one-third fictional programs (films and series, including comedies), while informational programs constituted about half of the total output, although there were some stark variations – 15% of Italian broadcasts were fictional programs, while two-thirds of Portuguese broadcasts were informational programs (Nordestreng and Varis 1974, p. 23).

Yugoslavia aspired to escape its peripheral position within the global flows by itself becoming an independent center, which was made possible by its strong position within the Non-aligned Movement (Mihelj and Huxtable 2018). The TANJUG agency (in Belgrade) was one of the news exchange centers for the NANAP. Yugoslavia was also very much involved in the United Nations, and it participated in many UNESCO initiatives and proposals. During the 1970s, together with other countries belonging to the Non-aligned Movement, Yugoslavia advocated a more equal transnational communication flow through the New World Information and Communication Order (NWICO) movement, which preceded the famous MacBride Report (MacBride 1984).

From the 1960s onwards, Yugoslav record companies began buying licenses from the largest foreign (usually Western) record companies. The biggest record companies were Jugoton (Zagreb, Croatia) and PGP RTB (part of RTV Belgrade).[23] Student and youth press and organizations played a key role in the promotion of rock in Yugoslavia, as did smaller record companies (such as Suzy Records in Croatia) (Arnautović 2012; Zubak 2018).

Youth music audiences varied by republic, urban or rural life environment, education level, and social status. However, a socio-cultural homogenization of tastes was under way (Ilišin et al. 1986). Rock was primarily an urban phenomenon (Ramet 2003), and the most vivid rock scenes were found in the big cities (Ljubljana, Zagreb, Belgrade, Sarajevo). The Yugoslav cultural space was also divided by music genre preferences. In Serbia, commercial folk (*novokomponirana narodna glazba*) remained the most popular genre (Ramet 2003), while in Croatia the most popular genre was domestic light pop (*zabavna glazba*). Rock music was more popular (and more commercial) in Croatia and Slovenia than in Serbia.

Similar to the approach of Yugoslav record companies, Yugoslav publishing companies began buying licenses for Western materials in the 1960s (Nikolić et al. 2010). The Croatian Jadran film company was famous for film co-production with Western companies, and it was one of the largest studios in Central and Eastern Europe.

The openness to international communication flows is evidenced also in the programs of other republics and foreign television services in the daily press. For example, the Slovenian newspaper *Delo* published the daily schedules of Croatian TV Zagreb and TV Koper (the entertainment-oriented Slovenian regional TV channel). The Montenegrin daily *Pobjeda* published the TV schedule for the Italian RAI. The Serbian *Večernje novosti* published a selection of television schedules from other republics (Bosnia and Herzegovina, Croatia, Macedonia, and Montenegro) as well as regional television schedules for TV Novi Sad and TV Priština. The Croatian daily *Večernji list* published the television programs of TV Ljubljana, TV Sarajevo, TV Belgrade, Austrian ORF1 and ORF2, and Italian RAI1. The Bosnian and Herzegovinian and Macedonian dailies only published the television programs of their own republic. In Croatia, 20% of the audience listened to foreign radio programs at least once a week, and 10% watched foreign television at least once a week (RTV Zagreb 1970, p. 12). In Slovenia, 26% of the audience watched foreign television news (Obradović and Stupan 1968).

The dissimilar media histories, traditions, and professional standards associated with journalism in the various republics contributed to the centrifugal tendencies of the media system (Zubak 2018). Differences remained among the republics in terms of receiving transnational flows, and media-saturated Croatia and Slovenia received more Western broadcasts (Vončina 1999; Pušnik and Starc 2008). A longitudinal analysis of socialist Croatian television genres points to the continuous increase in the European and American fiction and entertainment genres from the 1950s onwards (Peruško and Čuvalo 2014). Yugoslav citizens were exposed to Western values through the translation of contemporary and classic Western literature, performative art exchanges, rock concerts (Robinson 1977; Vončina 1999), and imports of films and music as well as through the development of the tourism sector and the migration of Yugoslav guest workers to Western Europe.

Conclusion

Our study shows that dichotomies such as East/West, market/state, media freedom/propaganda, entertainment/state information (Mihelj 2014), and the contrast between two powers – the Soviet Union, from which the blueprints for journalistic practice are taken, and Western Europe and the United States, which had influence on the Eastern Europe entertainment media (Imre 2014, p. 124) – are not appropriate for the study of the Yugoslav self-management socialist media system. In terms of the political character of the state, while majoritarian government is naturally linked to a one-party state, in Yugoslavia this was tempered by the country's federal structure and decentralization, meaning that cooperation and sometimes even consensus were necessary in relation to government decision-making. Political polarization occurred between the territorial organizations of the SK in different republics as well as within the organizations along the lines of nationalism/universalism and decentralization with democratization versus unitarism. The rule of law, as a differentiating dimension, is also usefully applied (Kitchelt et al. 1999) to differentiate socialist regimes.

With regard to the transformations of the cultural field, evidence of the existence of the specific socialist value code associated with the egalitarian syndrome (Županov 1983, p. 87) was reviewed, although this did not show as a prevalent value. We show the existence of a value transformation from traditional to modern and then to post-modern in the least developed to the most developed republics, respectively.

The relationship between the media and the state fluctuated between liberalization and control, which followed when political democratization and liberalization were blocked during the early 1970s, while the liberalization of practices followed the growing commercialization of the media market. The introduction of media legislation that enabled a great degree of autonomy on the part of the media within the ideological boundaries of the taboo topics – the main one being the socialist project itself – meant that the judiciary now played an important role in addition to the executive branch.

The introduction of self-management into the media system completely changed its matrix, and Yugoslavia abandoned the Soviet model of journalism and media in favor of a more pluralistic and open system. The openness to foreign content in television, film, and other media as well as to new cultural practices differentiated Yugoslavia from the other socialist countries. In this chapter we show that it is possible to find political parallelism and autonomy in a one-party political system, and that we can really talk about the market when there is no private ownership (but there is a profit motive) within the media sector in the context of self-management socialism.

Political parallelism was filtered through several layers of indirect controls and organizations, not centered only on the party, and gradually decreased. The main press and broadcasting organizations stuck closely to the ideas of their own republic parties, and this provided for the pluralism of the media at the federal level. Smaller and alternative media were more autonomous. Yugoslavia had multiple public spheres at different levels of national and territorial organizations, including the federal and the republic/province levels, and most of the media aimed to reach their local, national audiences. While the media systems in the different republics were based on similar laws, which stemmed from the common federal laws pertaining to the media, at the level of media practice a comparison of different media cultures in terms of both the press and television shows distinctions between the types of content available to citizens within the different republics.

Journalism also played different roles. In addition to the role of the "socio-political worker" (i.e., the apologetic role; Robinson 1977), it played the critical role, which increased with the commercialization of the media market and the development of self-management. Disparities between the republics were noticeable in terms of the level of professionalism of the press, thereby continuing historical disparities between the countries.

In comparison to the media cultures of several other European socialist countries, Yugoslavia was consistently found to exhibit the most "liberal" type of socialism (Mihelj and Huxtable 2018). Less centralization of the economy and more inclusion within transnational media/cultural flows produced a more varied media culture (Mihelj and Huxtable 2018). A longitudinal study of television culture since the 1950s, which was based on the patterns of changes in television flows between the socialist and post-socialist media cultures in Croatia, primarily showed the diversification of genres of television programs and unearthed patterns of transnational thickenings (Peruško and Čuvalo 2014). In this study, a similar finding concerning cultural similarities can be taken forward. Of the Yugoslav republics, Slovenia enjoyed the most diverse content in relation to both television and newspapers, alongside the most international content and the most advanced alternative cultural practices. As the most developed republic, Slovenia also exhibited more modern and post-modern values, followed by Croatia, which also exhibited liberalized openings up of the political and public spheres as well as alternative culture and the most advanced advertising market in Yugoslavia. While the media content in Serbia and Montenegro showed a degree of traditionalism in terms of the cultural content and taste, the development of the Serbian media market was strong during socialism, partly due to its continuing position at the center as the Serbian capital Belgrade was also the capital of the SFRY. This quantity is not reflected in the opening up of news and television programs, although we do see alternative developments in both rock music (the New Wave) and film (the Black Wave). The other three republics lagged behind in terms of both the quality and quantity of their media production.

Ambivalences within the system, frequent political changes, exchanges between periods of liberalization and repression, poorly prepared and inconsistently implemented liberalization and decentralization reforms, and the discrepancy between the normative idea and the practice of self-management socialism all rendered the system prone to crisis, especially when faced with the negative trend of the global economy. Elements of decentralization and liberalization (the autonomy of enterprises) and *statisms* (central planning) coexisted and conflicted, and this instability resulted in an opening for public debate (Županov 1983; Klasić 2012). These factors are also considered by some authors to be the reason for the more human and liberal face of Yugoslav socialism (Nikolić et al. 2010).

Notes

1 Bajomi-Lázár et al. (2020) overview the media history of four CEE countries; Splichal (1989) and Peruško and Vozab (2016) analyze the history of the communication and media studies in Yugoslavia and Croatia, respectively; television culture and programing during socialism is the topic of the majority of new historical studies; see Pušnik and Starc 2008; Luthar and Pušnik 2010; Imre et al. 2012; Mihelj 2012; Gorsuch and Koenker 2013; Peruško and Čuvalo 2014; Mihelj and Huxtable 2018.
2 A word about terminology: in the literatures dealing with this historical period both the concepts socialism and communism are used to describe the same empirical regimes/societies/politics. The term communism is often used pejoratively and is linked to the past Cold War western (American) discourse. In the original Marxist ideology, communism was a classless utopian society which was the aim of the communist revolution. We will primarily use the term socialist when referring to the Eastern European countries during this temporal framework, and communist if the previous studies that we build on have used the concept, predominantly in relation to the political regime.
3 Each republic and autonomous province had its own parliament and constitution. The Federal Assembly (Skupština) had two houses: the Federal Council, which included delegates from the self-managed work, political, and cultural organizations of the different republics and provinces; and the Council of the Republics and Provinces, which was composed of members of the republic and provincial parliaments, although the number and composition of the houses changed. Following Tito's death in 1980, the country had a collective presidency, whereby one member was elected by each of the republic and provincial parliaments with a five-year mandate. The collective presidency then elected one of its members to serve as president of the presidency for one year.
4 Record companies used all the familiar means for the mass market promotion of albums and stars (radio, concerts, festivals, cult of the singer, etc.) (Arnautović 2012).
5 Županov's (1983, 1995) original TES does have some empirical confirmation, with manual workers in several non-probabilistic surveys of employed citizens in Croatia reporting their support for the radical egalitarianism of income, although white-collar workers, experts, and managers rejected it. Dolenec (2014) challenged the TES primarily on the basis of the lack of empirical evidence. A debate ensued that seemingly confirmed the validity of Županov's TES and its persistence in post-socialist Croatia (especially in traditional, rural areas) (Štulhofer and Burić 2015; Šonje 2016; Vuković et al. 2017; Burić 2017; Rimac et al. 2017). Dolenec and Širinić's (2018) critique of recent empirical homages to the TES points to its failure to integrate Županov's theory within the classic and contemporary modernization theory. Dolenec and Širinić (2018) analysis suggests an average egalitarian orientation of Croatia within the EU.

128 *Media systems in socialist modernity*

 6 The World Values Survey project is available online at www.worldvaluessurvey. org/WVSContents.jsp.
 7 The data concerning the transformations of values in socialist Yugoslavia are patchy and not always systematic or inclusive of all the republics. Scientific research was predominantly undertaken within specific republic(s), and studies that include samples from all the republics and provinces and interpret those samples in a comparative fashion are rare. We also note a tendency to extend the generalization to the whole of Yugoslavia on the basis of one republican sample. In this study, we predominantly rely on the following empirical studies. Popović et al. (1977) conducted a survey of working people in Serbia in 1972 and 1974. Ilišin et al. (1986) reported on an anonymous survey of young industrial workers conducted in Croatia in 1982, which included a quota and stratified sample of 1,017 manual workers as well as a control group of 281 non-manual workers from the same companies. The respondents filled in the written questionnaire privately. Aleksić et al.'s (1986) work was the first representative survey (with a stratified sample) of youth (aged 14–29 years) in all the republics and autonomous provinces of Yugoslavia. Their study was conducted in 1985 and 1986 using the face-to-face method. It is important here to consider the soundness of survey results that were obtained in a face-to-face manner in the home of each respondent. Although the survey was intended to be anonymous, the respondents could have been reluctant to voice an opinion contrary to the official ideology. Županov (1996) discussed this in terms of explaining the very high proportion of "don't know" or "can't evaluate" answers in the study conducted by Ilišin et al. (1986) as actually being negative answers that the respondents were reluctant to give, even in the context of a private, self-report questionnaire survey. Goati et al. (1989) conducted an anonymous survey of working people in all the republics and autonomous provinces of Yugoslavia. Their study included a quota and a stratified sample, whereby half the respondents were members of the SK (n = 4,543), and it took the form of an anonymous pen-and-paper standard questionnaire. All these studies were published in Yugoslavia at the time.
 8 Yet another difference with regard to Yugoslavia in relation to socialist Eastern Europe was its development of the social sciences, including the quantitative methodology (Splichal 1989; Batina 2006; Štulhofer et al. 2010; Peruško and Vozab 2016). While sociology and empirical research were not allowed in the rest of Eastern Europe (Poland was an exception here due to the existence of strong sociology of an interpretive kind), in Yugoslavia sociology was developed, empirical (some, such as Splichal [1989], remain critical of the extent and quality of the empirical communication research), and exhibited paradigmatic ties to the West. The social sciences and humanities had links with US and European (especially German) universities.
 9 Some 51% and 41% of young people in Slovenia and Croatia, respectively, were dissatisfied with their educational opportunities, as compared to 12% in Kosovo (Aleksić et al. 1986). Young people's membership in the SK in 1985/1986 amounted to 5% in Slovenia, 12% in Croatia, 21% in Vojvodina, 24% in Serbia, 25% in Bosnia and Herzegovina, 18% in Macedonia, 33% in Montenegro, and 22% Kosovo. Further, 70% of Slovene non-members did not wish to be members, while the same was true of 46% in Croatia, 31% in Vojvodina, 12% in Montenegro, and 20% elsewhere (Radin 1986a, pp. 51–52). Religious traditionalism among young people (a woman should be a virgin at marriage) was quantified at 75% in Kosovo, 59% in Montenegro, 46% in Macedonia, 35% in both Bosnia and Herzegovina and Serbia, 26% in Croatia, and 20% in Slovenia (Radin 1986a, p. 73).
10 "The Frigid Socket" radio talk show was cancelled after four weeks of broadcasts due to being too controversial. One of its hosts was reportedly then invited

by the Party Central Committee in Zagreb to establish a homosexual association within the SSOH similar to the one that already existed in Slovenia: http://culturalopposition.eu/registry/?uri=http://courage.btk.mta.hu/courage/individual/n108962. Parts of one broadcast can be accessed via this link: www.portaloko.hr/clanak/-poslusajte-ovdje-kultnu-emisiju-frigidna-uticnica-iz1984/0/6484/. Homosexuality was decriminalized in 1977 (Šonje and Polšek 2019).

11 In the Constitution of the SFRY (1963), Article 34 is devoted to the right of all citizens to self-government, which, in addition to the rights to participate in management, to stand for elections, to make decisions in meetings, to petition and propose to government bodies, and to initiate a referendum, includes in para. 5 and 6 the right to be informed:

> The right to be informed about the work of the representative bodies and their organs, the organs of social self-government, and organizations carrying on affairs of public concern, and in particular, in the working organization in which he works and in other organizations in which he realizes his interests, the right to be informed about material and financial conditions, the fulfillment of plans, and business, with the obligation that he keep business and other secrets; The right to examine the work of the state organs, the organs of social self-government and the organizations that discharge affairs of public concern, and to express his opinions on their work.

In full, Article 40 states:

> Freedom of the press and other media of information, freedom of association, freedom of speech and public expression, freedom of meeting and other public assemblage shall be guaranteed.
>
> The citizens shall have the right to express and publish their opinions through the media of information, to inform themselves through the media of information, to publish newspapers and other publications, and to disseminate information by other media of communication. These freedoms and rights shall not be used by anyone to overthrow the foundations of the socialist democratic order determined by the Constitution: to endanger the peace, international cooperation on terms of equality, or the independence of the country; to disseminate national, racial, or religious hatred or intolerance; or to incite to crime; [nor shall they be used] in any manner that offends public decency. The cases and conditions in which the utilization of these freedoms and rights in a manner contrary to the Constitution shall entail restriction or prohibition shall be determined by federal law. The press, radio and television shall truthfully and objectively inform the public and publish and broadcast [those] opinions and information of organs, organizations, and citizens which are of interest to public information. The right to correction of information that has violated the rights or interests of man or organization shall be guaranteed. In order to assure the widest possible information of the public, the social community shall promote conditions conducive to the development of appropriate activities.

12 Article 133 of the Penal code of the SFRY:

> Hostile propaganda; Article 133. (1) Whoever in an article, leaflet, drawing, speech or in some other way calls on or incites the overthrow of the government of working class and working people, the unconstitutional change of the socialist self-management social system, breaking-up of the brotherhood and unity and equality of nations and nationalities, overthrow of the organs of social self-management and authorities and their executive organs, resistance to decisions of competent organs of authorities and of self-management

which are significant for the protection and development of socialist self-management relations, the security or defense of the country; or whoever maliciously and untruthfully represents the social and political situation in the country, shall be punished by imprisonment for a term exceeding one year but not exceeding 10 years. (2) Whoever commits an act referred to in paragraph 1 of this article with a help or under influence from abroad, shall be punished by imprisonment for not less than three years. (3) Whoever dispatches or transfers agitators or propaganda material into the territory of the SFRY for the purpose of carrying out activities referred to in paragraph 1 of this article, shall be punished by imprisonment for not less than one year. (4) Whoever, with the intention of distributing, manufactures or copies enemy propaganda material, or who holds this material despite knowing that it is intended for the distribution, shall be punished by imprisonment for a term exceeding six months but not exceeding five years.

Yugoslavia: Criminal Code of the Socialist Federal Republic of Yugoslavia, July 1, 1977, available from: www.refworld.org/docid/3ae6b5fe0.html [accessed 26 December 2019].

13 The articles of the 1974 Constitution related to the media and to the freedom of expression (available from: www.worldstatesmen.org/Yugoslavia-Constitution1974.pdf) include:

On the right to be informed: "keeping the working people informed on all questions significant for the realization of their socioeconomic status and for the fullest and most competent possible decision-making in the performance of functions of power and management of other social affairs" (Basic principles, IV, p. 64).

On the role of the SSRNJ and the SKJ: "make sure that the working people and citizens are kept informed, and ensure their influence on the social system of information and the realization of the role of the press and other media of public information and communication" (Basic principles, VIII, p. 75).

Chapter III: The freedoms, rights, and duties of man and the citizens.

Article 166: "Freedom of thought and option shall be guaranteed."

Article 167: "Freedom of the press and other media of information and public expression, freedom of association, freedom of speech and public expression, freedom of gathering and public assembly, shall be guaranteed. Citizens shall have rights to express and publish their opinions through the media of information. Citizens, organizations and citizens' associations may, under conditions specified by the statute, publish newspapers and other publications and disseminate information through other media of information."

Article 168: "Citizens shall be guaranteed the right to be kept informed of developments in the country and in the world which are of concern of their life and work, and of questions of concern to the community. The press, radio and television and other media of information shall be bound to inform the public truthfully and objectively, and to make public the opinions and information of bodies, organizations and citizens which are of concern to the public. The right shall be guaranteed to cause correction of published information that has violated the rights and interests of an individual, organization or body."

14 Information flows within the socialist workers' "delegate system" were also a topic of interest for academic research at the time, for example, Novosel (1976).

15 An ongoing COST (European Cooperation in Science and Technology, https://www.cost.eu) project, namely "New exploratory phase in research in East European cultures of dissent," is investigating the gray cultural zones in socialism. See https://nep4dissent.eu/working-groups/group-2/.

Media systems in socialist modernity 131

16 Religion was a mediating factor in many attitudes and value orientations exhibited during socialism (Radin 1986a).
17 *Borba* was established in 1922 in Zagreb as the newspaper of the Communist Party, and it later became the KPJ's central newspaper. In 1954, it became the official newspaper of the SSRNJ, published in Belgrade, the capital of the SFRY and of the Federal Republic of Serbia, but had editorial offices in all the republics.
18 The average newspaper sales figures for Serbia are thus much higher than the actual readership/sales of individual papers. This was also true, albeit to a lesser degree, in other republics, as businesses were obliged to subscribe to the main daily paper in the republic as well as to *Borba*.
19 Western observers sometimes misunderstood the national diversity of the country and its media system and, drawing an analogy with their US or Canadian origins, thought that the media produced in the federal capital, that is, Belgrade, were "national" media (Robinson 1977, p. 208), when no such thing was the case.
20 The *Other* category refers to programs produced outside Europe and the United States, together with programs for which the coders were not able to identify the country of origin. Within this category, we have a film from Canada, a drama from Ukraine, and a war drama from the USSR.
21 Republic's TV genre diversity indexes are based on the Herfindahl-Hirschman index (HHI; Hillve et al. 1997; Napoli 1999; Van Cuilenburg 2007; Van Cuilenburg and van der Wurff 2007) and were calculated as the sum of the squared proportions of the 12 identified genre categories. Lower index value indicates higher diversity. The same procedure was used to determine the diversity of newspapers.

Slovenia had the highest total time genre diversity (HHI = 0.12), followed by Macedonia (0.16), Bosnia and Herzegovina (0.17), Montenegro (0.18), Serbia (0.19), and Croatia (0.20). Results for prime time genre diversity were less variable. The most diverse prime time was on Macedonian and Serbian televisions (HHI = 0.15), followed by Croatia (0.16), Slovenia and Montenegro (both 0.17), and the least diverse prime time was in Bosnia and Herzegovina (0.18). Origin diversity in total broadcast time was the highest in Bosnia and Herzegovina (0.20), followed by Slovenia (0.24), Macedonia (0.26), Montenegro and Serbia (both 0.28), and Croatia (0.31). Slovenia had the most diverse prime time in terms of the origin of the TV production, followed by Montenegro, Bosnia and Herzegovina, Serbia, Macedonia, and Croatia. These data speak also to the strength of the local television production, where the studios with more local strength imported less foreign programs (compare Nordenstreng and Varis 1974).
22 Countries in the Soviet Bloc were members of the OIRT broadcasters' union and the SECAM standard of color television, and they were, with some exceptions, less exposed to Western programs (Mihelj and Huxtable 2018, p. 86).
23 Apart from the big two (Jugoton and PGP RTB), there were also several smaller record companies, including Diskos (Aleksandrovac, Serbia, 1962), Helidon (Ljubljana), ZKP RTLJ (Ljubljana, 1971), Suzy Records (Zagreb, 1972), Diskoton (Sarajevo, 1973), and Jugodisk (Beograd, 1974).

5 Toward democracy
Post-socialist media systems in digital modernity

During the second decade of the third millennium, the geopolitical space of the six countries of interest in this book has been reshaped as part of the broader transformations influencing Europe toward the end of the 20th century. The collapse of communism in Central and Eastern Europe was marked by the highly recognizable visual of masses of people crossing into West Germany following the fall of the Berlin Wall, a concrete symbol of the Cold War era division of Europe into democratic and communist parts. The events that led up to November 9, 1989, had been unfolding in some countries for more than a decade, however. The pluralization and liberalization of the political life, political culture, public discussion, and the media were already taking place in the Yugoslav republics in the 1970s and 1980s, as described in the previous chapter. Political liberalization, including the establishment of political parties and the holding of free multi-party elections, occurred in all the republics from 1989 to the end of 1990. The media had also started to change during this period, leading up to the breakthrough seen in 1989/1990. Further transitions toward democracy and regime consolidation continued to unfold in the republics, which were soon to be independent states, where pluralization and liberalization had begun. This seemingly easy first step in the transition was then complicated to the point of violence. The regime change that occurred in Yugoslavia, where multi-party elections were never held at the federal level, was accompanied by the collapse of the multinational federal state, which was unable, in conditions characterized by growing liberalization, to find a peaceful means of overcoming the deep-seated cleavage between the approaches of centralization and decentralization. Thus the collapse of communism also represented the collapse of Yugoslavia (Banac 1992b).

While the temporal framework of modernization was marked by the development of the press, and the post-war socialist period witnessed the rise of television, the post-1990 years were additionally shaped by the digital communication revolution (McChesney 2007a), which not only changed the way individuals communicate or receive information and entertainment but also shaped the social, political, and economic fields and institutions. The third wave of democratic revolutions in the socialist countries that began in 1989 refocused analytical and theoretical interest on the relationship between the media and democracy for those interested in the transition of media systems. The communication and political revolutions both renewed academic interest in the media-democracy nexus. The role of the media in a democracy (Keane 1991; Christians et al. 2009) was especially explored in relation to the new democracies in Central and Eastern Europe (Czepek et al. 2009; Dobek-Ostrowska et al. 2010; Voltmer 2013; Zielonka 2015). The latest body of work investigating changes to democracy and politics in the modern media-saturated environment makes use of the mediatization paradigm (Mazzoleni and Schulz 1999; Esser and Strömback 2014). The consequences for democracy in both the West and the East of the recent shift in the mediatization process toward the datafication of society (Couldry and Hepp 2017; Couldry and Mejias 2019) are yet to be fully understood.

The digital communication revolution was influencing the media systems of the newly democratizing CEE countries at the same time as they were being disentangled from the structures of the state. During the early 1990s, the process of media transition in post-socialist Europe was expected to be completed quickly following the implementation of regulatory reforms that were seen as the key step toward the introduction of capitalism and democracy. This specific understanding of media transition as a process of media reform, framed almost exclusively in terms of the establishment of democracy, was unique to the region, which underwent a post-socialist transformation. The analysis is different when undertaken with the benefit of 30 years' hindsight. While the media policy plays an important part in our study, since it served to focus the normative media theories (McQuail 2007; Christians et al. 2009) of the respective societies, the analysis necessarily includes the gamut of media system dimensions. The challenge for this chapter is to move forward with the media systems approach so as to embrace the digital media landscape, and we extend the regular dimensions of the media market, journalistic professionalism and autonomy, political parallelism, and the global communication flow with indicators and concepts pertinent to the digital mediascape.

The temporal framework investigated in this chapter is the shortest of the three that bound our *longue durée* inquiry as it comprises only three decades, although the changes occurred very rapidly and the amount of change included is greater than that seen in relation to the much slower progressing first and second temporal frameworks. During this volatile period, several mini-junctures altered the directions of the post-socialist transformations of the media systems in several countries. As discussed in previous chapters, the transformations seen in the fields of politics and the economy are inextricably linked with, and reflected in, the media system, and in order to understand the democratic transition of socialist media systems into democratic media systems, we need to briefly engage with these adjacent fields and the processes of their transformation from socialism to democracy in the six countries under study.

Transformations of the political field

Two main strands of literature and approaches provide us with insights into the political aspects of the post-socialist democratic transitions in the CEE countries. One is the comparative political science approach, which studies the CEE countries within a broader comparative analysis of post-autocratic democratic transitions. Within this approach, the CEE transition is analyzed as part of the third wave of democratic transitions (Huntington 1991), starting with the South European transitions of Portugal and Spain during the 1970s (Schmitter and Karl 1994, pp. 178–179; Linz and Stepan 1996). Katrin Voltmer (2013) applied this approach to compare the media transitions during third-wave democratic transitions from military dictatorships, authoritarian regimes, and socialism. This approach is sometimes criticized for its (modernization) expectation of linear progress toward liberal democracy and market economy without accounting for the nuances and alternative paths of development of non-European polities with different cultural traditions (Sparks 1994, quoted in Kokushkin 2011, p. 1045). The second approach focuses on specific country cases or geographic areas, and it argues that the nature of democratization is linked to historical legacies, socio-economic development, and the choices and agency of political actors in building institutions (Dolenec 2013a). Karl and Schmitter (1995) convincingly argue for the value of combining both approaches when studying post-authoritarian transformations, where large-N comparisons provide insights not available through case study analysis (and vice versa), which resonates with the recent rise in popularity of mixed method approaches in both political science and media and communication studies. In focused case studies or small-N comparisons, the dimensions/variables used to evaluate the process of transformations include the nature of the former authoritarian regimes, the type of change of political systems, the power relations between the new political actors, the nature of the social and political cleavages, the type of state building, the level of internal conflict or heterogeneity, the influence of the international environment (in this case, the EU accession prospects), the historical democratic legacies, the economic disparities, the type of party formation, and the political culture (Parrott 1997; Kitschelt et al. 1999; Ekiert and Hanson 2003; Boduszyński 2010).

In this context, transition is simply the "interval between one political regime and another" (O'Donnell and Schmitter 1986, p. 6, as quoted in Stradiotto and Guo 2010, p. 9). Carothers (2002, pp. 6–8) summarizes five assumptions said to define the transition paradigm that informed early expectations regarding post-socialist transitions: any country moving away from a dictatorial regime is assumed to be moving toward democracy; democratization unfolds in stages from the opening/liberalization, through the breakthrough of the collapse of the old regime, to democratic consolidation; elections are of key importance; structural features are not considered vital for the successful start of a transition; and transition happens in a functioning state. Thirty years after the start of the post-socialist transitions, we now know that some of these assumptions were not validated by the reality in a number of countries, where the de-democratization or consolidation of new autocratic regimes occurred rather than the development of democracy. In some countries, however, the expectations were initially validated. In their comparative study, Schneider and Schmitter (2004) show that the transition and consolidation of democracy in (certain) Central European countries progressed much faster than in the Southern European countries that were previously considered to be the most successful cases. The CEE countries averaged eight years from the start of the transition to the achievement of satisfactory democratic consolidation, while the Southern European countries took approximately 14 years. The recent trends of illiberal backsliding seen in some of these more successful new democracies of the third wave (Hungary and Poland) represent an unanticipated challenge.

All the phases of post-autocratic transition include a media-related aspect. The first component of the liberalization-transition-consolidation processes of democratization (Schneider and Schmitter 2004) unfolds before the actual visible breakdown or change of the regime. During the liberalization phase in all the CEE countries, access to media and communication channels was the easiest to attain (in comparison to transitions from military or authoritarian rule, where this was more problematic), while during the consolidation phase, agreement concerning the rules of access to, and ownership of, the media was one of the hardest things to achieve. Slovenia (the only one of the countries we analyze to be included in the study by Schneider and Schmitter [2004]) performed even better than most of the other included countries, indicating that it was not damaged by the very brief war it experienced during the dissolution of Yugoslavia. In Schneider and Schmitter's (2004) international comparison, the individual CEE countries cluster with regard to the success of the transition in groups with countries from other regions of the world according to their success in relation to liberalization and the consolidation of democracy (similar to how they cluster in terms of their media systems; Peruško et al. 2015).

Most studies of the transition and consolidation of the CEE countries ignore the Southeast European countries, as do the majority of studies of socialism (Boduszyński 2010). Studies focusing on the issue of transition in Yugoslavia rarely employ the comparative concepts used to analyze the transitions seen in other CEE states (Linz and Stepan [1996] recognize their focus on only those countries in the Soviet zone of influence and the members of the Council for Mutual Economic Assistance [COMECON] and the Warsaw Pact; this focus, which is often present in other studies, necessarily excludes those countries that did not participate in the named associations). When the Southeast European countries are included in comparative studies of democratization or media system transformation, the negative impact of war is commonly ignored (with regard to democratization, the exceptions include the work of Dolenec [2013a], while with respect to the media, the exceptions include the study by Irion and Jusić [2018]). The delay in the democratization of the media in some of these countries is, therefore, not placed in a proper explanatory context. What follows is a brief account of the transition and consolidation of the regimes in Slovenia, Croatia, Bosnia and Herzegovina, Serbia, Montenegro, and North Macedonia, that is, the six post-Yugoslav countries included in our study. As previously noted, the seventh country in the post-Yugoslav space, namely Kosovo, was not included in our comparison.

First transition: exiting socialism

Stradiotto and Guo (2010, pp. 17–19) classify the CEE countries according to different types of transitions: Hungary and Bulgaria underwent transition by conversion, where the incumbent elites arrange the transition without input from opposition groups (this type of transition is labeled transformation by Huntington, *reforma* by Linz, pact by Karl and Schmitter, and revolution from above by Munck and Leff). Czechoslovakia, Poland, and Slovenia are classified as having undergone cooperative transitions through negotiation between the incumbent and opposition elites, usually in a peaceful way due to the balance of power and pro-democratic moderates in both camps (this type of transition is labeled transplacement by Huntington, pact by Karl and Schmitter, and reform from below by Munck and Leff). Romania and East Germany are said to have undergone the collapse type of transition, which takes place when the opposition is stronger than the incumbent elite and the authoritarian regime is overthrown or collapses (this is labeled replacement by Huntington, rupture by Linz, revolution/imposition by Karl and Schmitter, and reform through rupture by Munck and Leff). In the post-socialist transitions, the breakthrough phase of the regime change, often a combination of pacts and mass protest, is considered to have been most successful in terms of democratization when the break with the communist elites was the most thorough (Bunce 2010).

Following Stradiotto and Guo's (2010) typology, in the post-Yugoslav space, the type of transition depends on the level of analysis: the federal-level transition can be viewed as state collapse, while at the level of the republics/new states, different types of transitions occurred in different countries as well as at different times in the same countries. In addition to Slovenia, a cooperative transition occurred in Croatia, while in Bosnia and Herzegovina, Macedonia, Serbia, and Montenegro, incumbent groups arranged the elections during regime conversions. Although all the communist elites expected to remain in power after the elections, they only retained power in Serbia and Montenegro. During its second transition in 1999/2000, Serbia experienced a combination of collapse and foreign intervention, the final type of transition described by Stradiotto and Guo (2010), in which the incumbent authoritarian regime is not willing to negotiate its demise (this is labeled intervention by Huntington and imposition by Karl and Schmitter).

Due also to the different types of transitions, socialist Yugoslavia's successor regimes during the 1990s displayed a divergence ranging from substantive democracies (Slovenia) to populist authoritarian regimes (Serbia), although some of them converged toward semi-consolidated democracies in the 2000s (Boduszyński 2010), only to diverge again in the last decade.

The first multi-party elections in Yugoslavia took place in 1990, as was the case in the majority of the other CEE countries: in Slovenia and Croatia the elections took place in April/May, in Macedonia and Bosnia and Herzegovina they took place in November, and in Serbia and Montenegro they took place in December. As previously noted, elections were held for the parliaments and governments in the republics, while federal-level elections were never called. In four republics, new parties came to power. In Slovenia, Croatia, Bosnia and Herzegovina, and Macedonia, the citizens elected those new parties or coalitions that had the strongest national independence programs. In Serbia and Montenegro, the old communist elites retained power and opposed the democratization and nation-building programs of the other parties while continuing to build up the Serbian nationalist policy begun in the mid-1980s (Daskalovski 1999; Ramet 2009; Berglund et al. 2013). The old decentralization/unitarist cleavage opened up once again.

War and the collapse of Yugoslavia

All the CEE countries had to manage a triple transition: in relation to the territorial issue of borders and nations, in relation to democracy, and in relation to the economic and property order (Offe 1991, pp. 872–873). Most countries attempted a simultaneous transition, although those involved in the Wars of Yugoslav Legacy (necessarily) focused on the issue of the contested state.

A peaceful or violent mode of transition also differentiates the breakthrough phase of democratic transformation (Schneider and Schmitter 2004). The transition in Yugoslavia was marred by war, rendering it the only case of democratic transition during the third wave in Central Europe in which the incumbent elite used the army to resist change. After Slovenia and Croatia declared independence based on popular referenda in 1990 and 1991, respectively, followed by Macedonia (in 1991) and Bosnia and Herzegovina (in 1992), the Badinter Commission pronounced the dissolution of Yugoslavia to be completed in 1992, and further, declared that the SFRY no longer existed. For the four new independent states, this concluded the first phase of the transition, and the consolidation of democracy was then played out in the new context. However, the existence of complications was violently announced.

Slovenia clashed with the Yugoslav army during the brief Ten-Day War in 1991. Next was Croatia, where the conflicts first started in 1991 and ended in 1992 following a negotiated ceasefire with the Serb-controlled Yugoslav People's Army (JNA), which agreed to pull out of a part of Croatia, and local Serb insurgents. Yet this left a third of the Croatian territory occupied by Serbian (mostly) paramilitary units. Croatia regained most of its territory through military actions in 1995, thereby ending its Homeland War, with the final part of its occupied territory in Eastern Slavonia being peacefully reintegrated in 1998. Then came conflict involving Bosnia and Herzegovina, with the JNA armies that pulled out of Croatia stationed principally around its capital Sarajevo, which they laid siege to for 1,425 days (1992–1996). While Serb forces and the JNA were again the main adversaries in Bosnia and Herzegovina, conflicts also erupted between Muslim Bosniak and Croat Bosnian and Herzegovinian forces in 1993, although a joint defense agreement was eventually signed. Montenegrin forces participated in attacks on Croatia and Bosnia and Herzegovina as part of the Serb and JNA forces (Montenegro only became an independent state in 2006). No battles were fought in Serbia and Montenegro, although they waged war first in Slovenia, then in Croatia and Bosnia and Herzegovina, and after 1998, in Kosovo. Kosovo's status as an autonomous province was revoked by Serbia in 1990, while Kosovo pronounced itself a republic in the face of increased repression by Belgrade. Tensions continued, and the conflict and humanitarian crisis in Kosovo increased to the point that NATO intervened by bombing Serbia in 1999, thereby finally bringing the wars to an end (for a chronology of the events surrounding the dissolution of Yugoslavia, see Bethlehem and Weller [1997]). In 2000, Milošević attempted to rig the presidential election, but when massive fraud was discovered and the mass protests known in Serbia as the Revolution of the 5th October went on for several weeks, he finally resigned. The new president was elected, supported by an 18-party coalition DOS (Democratic Opposition of Serbia), which also won the parliamentary election. Milošević was indicted by the Hague Tribunal for the Former Yugoslavia in 2001, and he died in prison in 2006. As Todosijević (2013, p. 527) succinctly puts it, "Kosovo and the break-up of Yugoslavia are both linked to the Serbian national question." Kosovo proclaimed its independence in 2008, which was recognized by most Western countries including Slovenia, Croatia, Macedonia, and Montenegro. Serbia is still resisting this development (while the recognition by Bosnia and Herzegovina is similarly blocked by the stance of the Republika Srpska), and the two countries remain locked in the situation of contested states. Macedonia had escaped attack by Serbia and the JNA and so enjoyed a peaceful first decade after transition, although it experienced an insurgency in 2001 following the attack by the NLA (Albanian National Liberation Army) on government forces. The disputes were resolved but resurgences reoccurred during 2014 and 2015.

As in all other wars, the media played a role in the wars in the former Yugoslavia (see M. Thompson [1995] for an analysis of the different roles of the media in the various republics). While the domestic media predominantly took the side of their own state and elite and so framed the narrative in terms of how each country saw the conflicts, the international media and dominant narrative framed the conflicts as "ancient tribal hatreds"

(Carruthers 2011, p. 163), although the thesis regarding ethnic hatred as the cause of the wars in the former Yugoslavia was later disputed by Sekulić et al. (2006)[1] in a longitudinal study of value change, which shows no significant pre-war ethnic intolerance. Following the introduction of television, the graphic visual depiction of suffering and the horror of war added an additional element of government control, censorship, or "management" of the war narrative in Western democracies (Carruthers 2011; see also Kamalipour and Snow 2004; Tumber and Palmer 2004). There is no reason to doubt that the unified elite also produced a unified media narrative (Hallin 1984) in the respective states, and when the elite narrative started to split, so did the media accounts. While in this book we do not investigate how the media and governments shaped the stories of war, which even decades later remains a matter of conflicting interpretation by the involved states and their polities despite the adjudication of some of the events by the Hague Tribunal for the Former Yugoslavia,[2] it is important to not overlook the fact that war never contributes to the democratization of the media and media freedom (Kenny 2019). The war also delayed the public focus on issues related to media freedom and the more thorough reforms of the media system.

Conflict and war have detrimental effects on democracy building and the establishment of the rule of law. As wartime institutions are authoritarian, demand stricter control and hierarchies, and suppress civil and political rights, war challenges the stability and coherence of the political community, which is vital for the establishment of democracy (Zakošek 2008, p. 589). Dolenec (2013a) shows that the war was the key condition that inhibited the development of the rule of law during the post-communist transformation in the countries that experienced it. While these legacies of war should be taken into account, European history demonstrates that democracy and media autonomy can be introduced or rebuilt after even the most dreadful of conflicts.

State building and institutions

State building was part of the transition processes in all the multinational post-socialist states: Slovakia and Czechia separated, the Baltic republics gained independence together with the other republics of the collapsed Soviet Union, while the Soviet satellite states also had to overcome their previously limited state autonomy and accomplish a degree of state building, albeit without violence. Linz and Stepan (1996) link the lack of violence to the change in Soviet policy regarding military intervention in its satellites, and later, in respect of the Soviet republics.

Stateness and the existence of a political community are understood by many authors to be a prerequisite for democracy, as the political community demands territorial integrity and consensus concerning its common political identity (Merkel 2011, p. 311). The stateness issue is especially salient in post-socialist democracies, where the contestation of borders and nationhood could render the democratic path more difficult (Bunce 2000). Prior statehood is seen as a helpful condition for sustaining democracy, while public consensus regarding the nation and its state borders is a necessary condition. Bunce (2000, p. 713) further argues for the positive general role of nationalism (unless in its negative manifestation, which also showed in Southeast Europe), which "provided the political resources necessary for a powerful and sustained challenge to authoritarian rule, it was nationalism that constructed citizenship, and it was nationalism that set the standard that government was to be responsive and responsible to its citizenry."

After the Wars of Yugoslav Legacy ended, the stateness issues were settled for most countries. Serbia and Kosovo still have unsolved stateness issues, although the conflict in Macedonia now seems to have been concluded. Bosnia and Herzegovina's continuing status as a protectorate of the international community through the Office of the High Representative, as well as the growing divisions between the Republika Srpska and the Federation (the two main territorial entities of Bosnia and Herzegovina, as created by the Dayton Agreement in 1995), clearly indicate that the stateness crisis is still relevant for this country, too (Donais 2013).

Since 2000, all six analyzed countries have multi-party parliamentary systems, and save for Bosnia and Herzegovina with its complex, power-sharing consociational regime, they all have proportional representation with thresholds that privilege larger parties or coalitions, thereby supporting the stability of their political systems. Nevertheless, in most countries governments rule by majority, and minority governments or substantive coalitions with important role of the junior partners are rare. With regard to the rule of law, Bosnia and Herzegovina, Montenegro, North Macedonia, and Serbia belong to the set of countries with high perceptions of clientelism and corruption. Croatia exhibits similar scores to the other CEE countries, while Slovenia is closer to the EU average (see data in Table 5.1).

What divides the polities?

After the collapse of socialism, the political systems were discovering certain old cleavages while some new ones were forming. In most of the CEE countries, the historical cleavages include ethnicity and nationalism, religion, fascist versus antifascist values, and communism versus anticommunism (Berglund et al. 2013, p. 32). In the six countries included in our study, the focus is still on different cleavages. In Bosnia and Herzegovina and Macedonia, the main party divisions still occur along national lines (Donais 2013; Hislope 2013). In Slovenia, the nation building versus centralization of the federation divided the polity, although a socio-economic cleavage (usually one of the key cleavages in developed democracies) is also present, in addition to the state versus church division (Zajec 2013). In Croatia, the center/periphery cleavage and the secular/religious cleavage are also present, as is

Table 5.1 Comparative overview of SEE social, economic, political and cultural/media statistical indicators

		Bosnia and Herzegovina	Croatia	Montenegro	North Macedonia	Serbia	Slovenia
Economic and social field	Population (in millions, 2018 estimate)[1]	3,849	4,27	0,614	2,118	7,078	2,102
	Urban population (in %, 2017)[2]	47,88	56,67	66,48	57,75	55,94	54,27
	GDP per capita (in $, in 000, 2018)[2]	6066	14910	8844	6084	7247	26124
	Exports of goods and services (as % of GDP)[2]	38,9	51,1	41,1	55,4	52,4	82,2
	GINI index, most recent available data[2]	33	31,1	39,5	35,6	28,5	25,4
	Unemployment (in %, most recent data)[2]	20,8	8,9	15,5	21,6	13,5	5,5
	Human development[3]	0,768	0,831	0,814	0,757	0,787	0,896
	Globalization[4]	69,19	81,42	72,05	70,79	78,98	81,14
Political field	Political rights[5]	19	36	23	22	24	39
	Civil liberties[5]	34	49	42	37	43	55
	Rule of law[6]	0,53	0,61	NA	0,54	0,5	0,67
	Year when EU offered Stabilization and Association Agreement/ Year of becoming a candidate/Year of entering EU)[7]	2005/ potential candidate, not a member	2000/2004/2013	2006/2010/ not a member	2000/2005/not a member	2005/2012/not a member	1995/1997/2004
	Year of becoming a Council of Europe member[8]	2002	1996	2007	1995	2003	1993
	Clientelism[9]	0,71	0,18	0,75	0,71	0,63	0,17

Toward democracy 141

(Continued)

142 Toward democracy

Table 5.1 (Continued)

		Bosnia and Herzegovina	Croatia	Montenegro	North Macedonia	Serbia	Slovenia
Cultural field	Number of daily newspapers [10]	9	11	4	5	NA	NA
	Number of radio stations [10]	141	151	NA	70	321	NA
	Number of television channels [11]	90	115	18	60	355	94
	Public service media television market share (%) [12]	19,6	27,4	22	4,3	23,6	22,1
	Public service media television youth market share [12]	Between 15% and 23%	Between 7% and 15%	NA	Less than 7%	Between 15% and 23%	Less than 7%
	Public service media television weekly reach [12]	Less than 47%	Between 62% and 77%	NA	NA	Between 62% and 77%	Between 47% and 62%
	Position of the main PSM television channel compared to its competitors [12]	1	2	NA	5	1	2
	Number of national PSM television channels [12]	1–2 channels	5–10 channels	1–2 channels	3–4 channels	More than 10 channels	3–4 channels
	Number of regional or local PSM television channels [12]	1 to 4 channels	None	None	None	None	1 to 4 channels
	Monthly cost of public service media per citizen (in €) [12]	0,28	3,28	1,5	0,72	0,8	3,9
	Annual advertising revenue in the media sector (in million $) [10]	23,2	320	11 to 12	39,2	191,8	NA
	Year of digital switchover implementation [13]	Ongoing	2010	2015	2013	2015	2011

Fixed-broadband subscriptions (2017, per 100 inhabitants)[13]	18,93	26,16	21,85	19,02	21,29	28,93
Internet access of households (in %, 2018)[14]	75	82	72	79	73	87
Facebook penetration (in %)[15]	42,8	43,3	50,8	47,9	38,9	43,7
Active social media users (in %)[16]	48	48	59	53	41	48
Active mobile social users (in %)[16]	43	41	49	47	34	42
Potential reach of daily newspapers (in %)[17]	32,58	59,38	41,15	NA	52,25	50,8
Media assistance from 1992 to 2006 (in million €)[18]	87,1	36,6	7,6	23,8	44,9	NA
Persons in cultural employment per million 2015[19]	23718	32761	NA	21551	24118	NA
Exports of cultural goods (in million $, 2017)[19]	28	64	3	10	75	119
Pressure on journalism autonomy (a)[20]	17	13	8	13	29	6
Pressure on journalism autonomy (b)[21]	155	50	35	56	215	NA

1 The World Factbook, https://www.cia.gov/library/publications/the-world-factbook/
2 World Bank, https://data.worldbank.org/
3 Composite Human Development Index, 2017, http://hdr.undp.org/en/composite/HDI
4 Globalization: Gygli, Savina, Florian Haelg, Niklas Potrafke and Jan-Egbert Sturm (2019): The KOF Globalisation Index – Revisited, Review of International Organizations, https://doi.org/10.1007/s11558-019-09344-2. Data refer to 2017.

(*Continued*)

Table 5.1 (Continued)

5. Freedom House, data for 2019: https://freedomhouse.org/report/freedom-world/freedom-world-2019. Maximum value for political rights is 40 and for civil liberties is 60.
6. World Justice Report: http://data.worldjusticeproject.org/
7. Year when the EU offered Europe or Stabilisation and Association Agreements (Schimmelfenning, 2008)
8. Council of Europe: https://www.coe.int/en/web/about-us/our-member-states
9. Clientelism index for 2018. Data is taken from V-dem project (https://www.v-dem.net/en/). Clientelism index refers to "clientelistic relationships include the targeted, contingent distribution of resources (goods, services, jobs, money, etc) in exchange for political support". The index is formed by taking the indicators for vote-buying, particularistic vs. public goods and whether party linkages are programmatic or clientelistic. Higher score means higher clientelism.
10. IREX Media Sustainability Index 2018, https://www.irex.org/sites/default/files/pdf/media-sustainability-index-europe-eurasia-2018-full.pdf. The data for annual advertising revenue in the media sector in North Macedonia are estimate by IREX.
11. Mavise Database, accessed 10.12.2019. http://mavise.obs.coe.int/
12. EBU PSM Barometer 2018. Data published with permission of EBU. Public television audience share for Montenegro is taken from Petković et al. (2016).
13. ITU Statistics
14. Eurostat, data refer to 2018. https://ec.europa.eu/eurostat/statistics-explained/index.php/Digital_economy_and_society_statistics_-_households_and_individuals. Internet penetration in Bosnia and Herzegovina is taken from We are social (https://www.slideshare.net/DataReportal/digital-2018-bosnia-herzegovina-january-2018).
15. Internet World Stats, latest available data (for the years 2017 and 2018)
16. We are Social. Data refer to 2018.
17. Ipsos Media. Data refer to 2018.
18. Irion and Jusić 2018.
19. UNESCO Institute for Statistics, http://uis.unesco.org/
20. Council of Europe, data refer to the period from 2015 to the end of 2019. Alerts on different kinds of pressures to journalists are calculated: attacks on physical safety and integrity of journalists, detention and imprisonment of journalists, harassment and intimidation of journalists and impunity.
21. Reports on attacks and threats to journalists and media, reported from 2010 until October 2019. Source: Western Balkan's Regional Platform for advocating media freedom and journalists' safety.

the historical fascist/antifascist cleavage (Henjak et al. 2013). The political cleavage in Montenegro was formed on pro-Belgrade and pro-reform lines (Boduszyński 2010, p. 202), while in Serbia, the cultural/value cleavage predominates with regard to conservatism versus modernism as well as sovereignty versus EU integration (Todosijević 2013). The polarization of all these political systems is historically high due to experiences of fascist and communist governments.

Consolidation of democracy or hybrid regimes

Both the transition and the consolidation were delayed in the six countries due to the Wars of Yugoslav Legacy. Slovenia quickly consolidated democracy, despite problems with inclusivity for non-Slovene born citizens, a large number of whom (some 25,000) were "erased" and lost their citizenship rights. A mini-juncture at around the year 2000 (also in some CEE countries, for example Slovakia; Fisher 2006) and the government shift to the new center-left party coalition enabled progress toward consolidation and European integration in Croatia, the start of the reform movement that would result in independence for Montenegro within a decade, while in Serbia a second post-authoritarian transition began. In Macedonia, following a time of instability, this period saw the beginning of international integration (World Trade Organization, WTO) and cooperation with the EU. By the end of the second decade of the 21st century, not all the countries have achieved a satisfactory democratic consolidation, while some have even experienced reversals.

Slovenia went through substantive democratization somewhat sooner and consolidated its democracy both in procedural terms and following liberal values (Boduszyński 2010), and with the highest level of democratization seen among the countries included in this study, it resembles the CEE countries more than Southeast European countries (Dolenec 2013a). It joined the EU in 2004. The other political systems that followed the dissolution of Yugoslavia were, in the 1990s, ruled by authoritarian "unreconstructed communists" (Serbia, Macedonia, and Montenegro; Dolenec 2013a, p. 107) or nationalists (Croatia), or they were mired in long-term war and instability (Bosnia and Herzegovina). Boduszyński (2010) summarizes the developments as follows: Croatia and Macedonia both had functioning procedural democracies, with Macedonia lacking a liberal basis, while Croatia had a mixture of liberal and nationalist values that supported the democratization process; and Serbia (and Montenegro during the period of common state) had both low liberal content and weak procedural democracy. The true democratization in Serbia started late in comparison to other post-socialist countries, only after the "liberal opposition backed by the West had driven the nationalist authoritarians from power" (Boduszyński 2010, p. 223).

Although we identified two (or three) different modes of post-socialist transition, national differences proved to be even greater during the phase of consolidation because all the structural conditions came to play a significant role (Schmitter and Karl 1994, n. 4, p. 176). The region underwent the process of democratization by way of divergent paths and the countries now differ significantly in terms of the democratization of their institutions, with high volatility visible in several of the countries.

The past 30 years show that the path toward democracy is neither linear nor irreversible, and further, that democracy is not the only type of regime to result from transitions from authoritarian regimes. Indeed, democratic backsliding is occurring in many contemporary democratic systems worldwide (Mechkova et al. 2017) as regimes fluctuate between more democratic forms and procedures and certain authoritarian practices, which drive them to become hybrid regimes (Bieber 2020). Moreover, the contemporary populist challenge is likely to have a negative impact for media systems, as research shows the negative influence of populist rule on media freedom (Kenny 2019).

Hybrid regimes are not democratic, nor are they fully authoritarian regimes; democratic institutions and procedures exist but are violated and pressured to the extent that "the regime fails to meet conventional minimum standards for democracy" (Levitsky and Way 2002, p. 52). Liberal democracy includes "solid protection of civil liberties under a strong rule of law," while hybrid regimes combine democratic and authoritarian elements to different degrees (Diamond 2002, p. 169). According to Levitsky and Way (2002, pp. 53–54), in competitive authoritarian regimes free elections are violated, sometimes by fraud, but more often by the abuse of state resources in favor of one party, and there are heavy pressures placed on the opposition, journalists, the media, and civil society through harassment, threats, jail, exile, or even murder. Furthermore, unlike fully authoritarian regimes, competitive authoritarianisms do not completely abolish democratic institutions and procedures, and they are more likely to apply more "subtle" and less visible pressures: economic control, bribery, the co-optation of opposition and civil society, and the use of different state institutions for legal harassment. The erosion of democratic institutions includes threats to the rule of law, which "skew the electoral process in its own favor; extend partisan control over state agencies, media and civil society; and develop a harshly anti-liberal ideology, which de-legitimizes left-wing and liberal competitors as foreign to the national community" (Herman 2016, as quoted in Cianetti et al. 2018, p. 244).

The trend of democratic backsliding to concentrate political and economic power by eliminating or weakening those institutions that back democracy has been particularly strong in Poland since 2015, Hungary since 2010, and (North) Macedonia since 2008 (Hanley and Vachudova 2018, p. 279). In Southeast Europe, democratic backsliding emerged soon after the short-lived period of democratic consolidation in certain countries during the 2000s. In Montenegro and Bosnia and Herzegovina, undemocratic procedures were never fully discontinued, as nationalist and clientelist elites have ruled these countries since their independence. Bieber (2020, p. 34) describes the patterns of democratization and de-democratization as follows: in Montenegro, "continuity and change from within," as changes were brought about by restructuring its only ruling party; "return to semi-authoritarianism" characterizes Serbia; "new semi-authoritarianism" characterizes North Macedonia after 2006 until the regime collapse in 2017; "ethnocratic authoritarianism" is seen in Bosnia and Herzegovina, where Milorad Dodik (SNS), the political leader of Republika Srpska, managed to achieve the strongest hegemony in his constituency; "authoritarianism under international tutelage" is characteristic of Kosovo; while Croatia established "conservatism without authoritarianism," thereby avoiding to backsliding. Slovenia has also avoided deconstruction.

Based on both the most recent Freedom House Index (2019) and Diamond's (2002) scale, Slovenia and Croatia continue to be classified as liberal democracies (scoring 1 and 1.5, respectively), while Serbia (3), Montenegro, North Macedonia, and Kosovo (3.5), and Bosnia and Herzegovina (4) remain ambiguous regimes, being classified somewhere between electoral democracies on the one end (scores between 2.5 and 3) of the Freedom House scale and hybrid regimes on the other (including electoral autocracies, competitive authoritarian regimes, and hegemonic authoritarian regimes, with scores between 4.5 and 7; authors' opinions vary as to the borders between the regime types and in respect of the country placement; see Mechkova et al. 2017). The decline or breakdown of democracy is always related to increased pressure on the independence of the media from increasingly authoritarian governments, as well as to a decrease in transparency and the rule of law (Diamond 2015). Such governments use state-run media to promote state views and narratives, they also marginalize the political or civil movement opposition (Walker and Orttung 2014), and increase political pressure on the print media (Hungary, Serbia) and television as the primary sources of news in most countries (Poland, Hungary, Serbia).

Schneider and Schmitter (2004) use two distinct media and communication criteria to assess the degree of liberalization of autocratic regimes and their consolidation as democracies. During the liberalization stage, "an independent press and access to alternative means of information that are tolerated by the government" are necessary (Schneider and Schmitter 2004, p. 6). In the consolidation phase, either a formal or an informal agreement as to the rules concerning the governance and ownership and access to the media needs to be reached (Schneider and Schmitter 2004, p. 10). This proved to be one of the more difficult tasks, and it remains problematic in some states. It is also the first aspect to show reversals when democratic backsliding or illiberal tendencies develop (Mechkova et al. 2017).

Economic transformation: (re)turn to market economy

Unlike transitions from military dictatorships or one-party statist regimes, the post-socialist transformations, in addition to the political dimension, also included an important economic dimension because state-owned or socially owned media and other enterprises had to be privatized. Changing the economic system was perhaps an even more difficult task than changing the political system. Béla Greskovits's (2015, p. 60; cf. Bohle and Greskovits 2012) analysis of post-socialist capitalism in the CEE countries identifies three types of capitalisms: "a neoliberal type in the Baltic States (Estonia, Latvia, and Lithuania), an embedded neoliberal type in the Visegrád countries (the Czech and Slovak republics, Hungary, and Poland), and a neo-corporatist type in Slovenia." While the consolidation of capitalism was as difficult as that of democracy for many other post-socialist countries, Croatia, in Greskovits's (2015) view, after 2000 also developed an embedded neo-liberal regime featuring more compromises between social cohesion and demands by unions and market transformations.

All the post-socialist countries experienced grave economic downturns during the years following the collapse of communism, but those countries in Southeast Europe that were unable to escape the wars of Yugoslav legacy entered a long period of isolation, which lasted for almost a decade. During the transition, they went through the process of heavy de-industrialization, instability, and poor economic performance, becoming a kind of European "super periphery" (Sokol 2001, in Bartlett 2009, p. 23). This fate only partially related to Croatia, while Slovenia was completely exempt, having quickly escaped after only a very brief conflict. The region was "re-peripheralized" or "de-developed" with regard to many economic and social aspects (Schierup 1992), with a higher share of practices being seen in the informal economy when compared to other regions in Europe (Williams and Horodnic 2015).

The disproportionate economic development (see Table 5.1) continues the divergent trends of development seen in previous periods. Slovenia, as one of the most economically successful countries in post-socialist Europe (Crowley and Stanojević 2011), is the state with the highest gross domestic product (GDP) per capita, the highest industrial production, and the lowest unemployment among the post-Yugoslav countries. Among the six countries of interest, Croatia is the second most developed (despite being among the least wealthy EU members, with a GDP per capita that was 63% of the EU average in 2017), while all the other countries lag substantially behind (see Table 5.1). The economic crisis that started in 2008 hit the region of the "super periphery" especially hard and resulted in various austerity policies (Bartlett 2014). It also negatively influenced journalists' autonomy and media systems development. The negative effects of the crisis were less pronounced in Slovenia, although it has also experienced waves of protests and citizen discontent over the past decade.

While the economic and political transformations of the analyzed countries do not show the desired progress, the position at the periphery can be reversed, as was shown by the Nordic countries after the 18th century. Closer to home, from the start of the third wave of democratization, the four Southern European countries – Italy, Greece, Portugal, and

Spain – had by the dawn of the new millennium left their position at the semi-periphery of the world system and became part of its center, exhibiting democratic persistence as well as economic growth and development (Diamandouros and Gunther 2001; although reversals are again possible, as shown by the example of Greece in the post-recession economic downturn of the world economy in 2008). In the political sphere, the legacy of right-wing authoritarianism was replaced over a period of 40 years by a modern democratic polity. After 30 years of post-socialist transition, Slovenia is approaching this position. Croatia, which followed a longer consolidation path due to war and incomplete statehood throughout a larger part of the 1990s but which is an EU member, has the chance to change its position during the next decades, while the outlook for the other countries seems to depend on their future EU integration paths. Greskovits (2015) believes that the most successful CEE media systems have reached the position of the semi-core, and further, that the term "periphery" characterizes the media further to the east and the south. More than a few of the media systems studied in the remainder of this chapter fit the description of the persisting periphery, while some could be characterized as having left that position.

Transformations of the cultural field

Before we proceed to study the media systems transformations, we will briefly look at what happened to social values during the course of the post-socialist transformations. The cultural explanation for the (failed) transitions/transformations of the post-socialist societies and their media systems is based on the notion that values from the socialist period persist and inhibit new developments (Gross 2002). There are two competing theories that explain why values persist. The first expects the state/party indoctrination to have changed the values of the population to conform to the required socialist ideology (in the previous chapter, we showed that this was not particularly successful). The second, and possibly more substantial, theory relates the value change to the process of rational adaptation/socialization of citizens to the conditions of social life, whereby the changes in values follow the practices observed to gain results (Schwartz and Bardi 1997). The socialization thesis is similar to the idea of path dependency in relation to institutional behavior, and it can help to explain why certain media-related practices persist at the individual and institutional levels. While there have been no systematic spatially and temporally comparative longitudinal studies that would prove this point, some post-1989 research shows that differences in values exist between the eastern and western parts of Europe. During the early years of the transition, the post-socialist countries exhibited a greater acceptance of conservative values and hierarchy and less acceptance of intellectual and affective autonomy, egalitarianism, and mastery values (Schwartz and Bardi 1997,[3] in Sekulić 2010).

The political culture in Southeast Europe is characterized by low interpersonal trust, low trust in institutions, and high polarization (Milosavljević and Poler 2018, p. 1157). The post-Yugoslav states exhibit higher authoritarian orientations and greater lifestyle intolerance when compared to Western and CEE countries, and they share similar attitudes toward gender equality with the CEE countries (Kirbiš 2013). The degree of support for a strong leader (a sign of authoritarian tendencies) ranges from 26.3% in Slovenia to 31.4% in Croatia, 41.9% in Bosnia and Herzegovina, 51.1% in Montenegro, 67.7% in Serbia, and 72% in Macedonia (2008 EVS). The latest European Value Survey (2017) enables us to compare post-materialist values: in Slovenia, 26.2% of citizens exhibit post-modern values associated with advanced social development; in Croatia 19.8%, and in Serbia 10.4%. Post-materialist values have doubled over the past ten years, indicating a positive trend in modernization and social development (although opposing trends are also evident in the simultaneous rise of authoritarianism in some instances, signifying a growing polarization in those societies).[4]

Acceptance of democracy is very high in the studied countries (82.6% in Bosnia and Herzegovina to 93.8% in North Macedonia [European Value Survey 2008] and over 90% in Croatia, Slovenia, and Serbia [EVS 2017]). Citizen engagement in the region is regularly translated into protest and social movements, often targeting media systems, attests to the growing attention to the value of freedom of expression. The political protests in Serbia known as the "One of Five Million," which started in late 2018 and targeted the conservative government of the SNS under the leadership of President Aleksandar Vučić, emphasize the role of the Serbian media, alleging political interference in the regulatory agency and public television. In Croatia, civic action in support of media autonomy marked a turning point in the democratization of both society and the media system in 1996, as more than 100,000 people took to the streets of Zagreb in support of Radio 101 (Peruško Čulek 1999a). However, in recent years neo-conservative groups have also attempted to exert pressure on the media regulatory bodies. A large protest was organized in 2019 by the Croatian Journalists' Association in support of media freedom and against political pressure on journalists. In Slovenia, citizens were on two occasions invited to directly decide on media-related laws (not only to propose changes to the process of public discussion, as required in all EU members states). Slovenia has thus far held two referenda regarding its media system, both concerning the status of public service television.[5] In Bosnia and Herzegovina and Macedonia, civil society is also important in terms of pushing for democratic reforms in the media sector, although as Mirna Buljugić[6] from the Balkan Investigative Network notes, such efforts very often hit a wall when presented to government bodies.

In the remainder of this chapter, we investigate the character and the success of states' interventions through media and economic policy means in order to create democratic media systems, in concert with the development of media markets, journalistic professionalism, and the influence of participation in global cultural flows. The six countries included in our comparative sample are very much under-researched when compared to the countries in the Visegrád group (Poland, Czechia, Hungary, and Slovakia), and they have seldom been included in comparative studies within the growing body of literature dealing with the democratization of media systems in CEE countries. Among a host of important recent studies focusing on media systems development in the wider CEE region, none includes a focus on, or even a country study of, the countries in Southeast Europe (sometimes with the exception of Slovenia).[7] Apart from the comparative monitoring projects (Television Across Europe, Mapping Digital Media; Open Society Institute 2005, 2012) and certain country-by-country monographs that also include some Southeast European countries (Terzis 2007), there are no previous monographs dealing specifically with this region's media or media systems post-1989 in a comparative context (although see the country chapters in the edited collections by Paletz and Jakubowicz [2003] and Irion and Jusić [2018]). A notable exception is the comparative study conducted by Boguslawa Dobek-Ostrowska (2015), who analyzes 21 CEE countries' media systems according to several macro level criteria. She also includes the non-EU Southeast European countries in her proposed four media system models for the CEE countries. The exceptions also include a number of quantitative comparative media systems studies involving the operationalization of Hallin and Mancini's (2004) typology in Central and Eastern as well as Western Europe (Peruško et al. 2013) and studies featuring a digital media systems framework (Peruško et al. 2015, 2017; Castro Herrero et al. 2017).

The role of the state: creating democratic media systems

In democracies, the nature of state intervention in the media field is evaluated by the role and strength of the public service media (funding, size, audience share) and other media that are owned by the state or by state-owned enterprises, including news agencies or newspapers, as well as by direct and indirect state subsidies for the media and state advertising. States also formulate legislation that might regulate libel, privacy, the right to reply, hate speech, the protection of the confidentiality of sources, access to information, the media ownership concentration, political campaigns and broadcasting licensing, and the pluralism of media content (Hallin and Mancini 2004, pp. 43–44). All these areas had to be tackled in the new media policies during the post-socialist democratic transformation, in addition to two other tasks: securing the freedom of expression and securing the economic freedom of establishment. The latter task also included the privatization of the media, or finding owners for what was previously the social property of self-managed media. The post-socialist transformation of the media was happening simultaneously with media policy making, pretending that the context was already democratic.

Post-socialist makeovers

Fabris (1995) imagines several scenarios concerning media transformation following socialism, some involving the domination of foreign media (westification and Germanification) and some in which the previous media cultures are continued, either as competition between old cultures and the newly developing post-socialist culture, or as what he terms the "post-perestroika" repoliticized media. Among the early theories, Splichal (1994) suggests the Italianization model (anticipating the later Mediterranean model in Hallin and Mancini's [2004] typology), in which the broadcast media are highly politicized and remain under state control, there is a strong degree of both media partisanship and integration of the media and political elites, and professional journalistic ethics have not yet been consolidated. Jakubowicz (2004) distinguishes three value orientations held by national political elites in terms of drafting media policies during the transitional period: idealistic, mimetic, and atavistic. The idealistic orientation was shared by the cultural opposition, and in line with the dissenting ideas of communicative democracy and media systems, built on the principles of equality, justice, and solidarity. This orientation was weaker than the other two. The mimetic orientation was supported by Western institutions, and it included the "full liberalization of the print media and creation of a balanced dual system of broadcasting" (Šmıd 1999, quoted in Jakubowicz 2004, p. 57). The atavistic orientation was characteristic of most post-socialist political elites, at least during the first decade of transition, when they were creating liberal media policies while still seeking to retain elements of tighter state or political control.

The dominant proposal regarding the democratic transformations of European post-communist media systems involves the imitation, or *mimesis*, thesis, which presumes that these media systems will develop in imitation of their Western counterparts, copying their regulatory solutions and adopting their media system values (Splichal 1994; Jakubowicz 1995). This mimesis theory later became recognized as the policy transfer theory in the political science literature, especially with regard to EU policy diffusion (Dolowitz and Marsh 2000; in relation to global media policy transfer, see Sarikakis and Ganter 2014).

We can identify three main phases in the post-socialist media policy of the CEE countries: (1) de-linking the media from the state; (2) media market development, including the privatization of media companies, the creation of new ones, and foreign investment in the media; and (3) EU harmonization. The same phases also apply in Southeast Europe, albeit with a shift in timing. In some countries in Southeast Europe, the first and second phases overlapped after 2000, with market developments leading even in cases of an unfinished first phase. The third phase only engaged the EU candidate countries, and it involved the transposition of the Television Without Frontiers Directive (TWFD) and later, the Audiovisual Media Services Directive

(AVMSD). The length of the EU harmonization was an influential dimension shaping the context of media development in the participating countries. All the CEE countries' media reforms were influenced by conditionalities stemming from the processes of EU accession, during which media freedom, pluralism, and independence were evaluated as part of the political criteria[8] (for an overview of media policy regulation and regulatory bodies, see Table 5.2). The Council of Europe and its standards were especially important in this regard.

While it is certainly true that the introduction of new media regulations was supervised for both the new EU members and candidate states by the Council of Europe and the European Commission, media systems are shaped by multiple influential factors that sometimes resist the implementation of borrowed regulations that have not been measured for a good fit; this was particularly unfortunate during the transformation of self-management broadcasting organizations into public service broadcasters, as we will discuss. The media systems of the CEE countries were, however, exceptionally influenced by policy and legislature, which was supposed to transform the media in just a short time, in comparison to those of Western European countries that developed over many decades. The media reforms hinged on the expectation that the new norms and values specified in the legislation would be quickly implemented, but even after 30 years, some practices from the previous normative framework persist (which again points to path dependency as an explanation for this cultural persistence).

The success of any policy is strongly constrained by the path dependency of the institutional values and cultures of the past. While in other CEE countries the differences in the position and values of the media sphere between socialism and democracy were rather significant, the socialist self-management media had already experienced market competition, pluralism and diversity, and a greater degree of freedom for the public sphere. We would thus expect that such media would have been much easier to democratize. This, however, did not prove to be the case. Instead of more rapid democratizations and the increase of the autonomy of the media from politics and the government, in several of the countries the political field exerted increased pressure. In the new democracies of Central and Eastern Europe, broadcasting in the 1990s was very much defined by political considerations and by the elites wish to preserve their control (Jakubowicz 1995). As we had already noted, this 30-year period was not homogeneous in terms of the democratic consolidation or in terms of the media system democratization. The developments were also not linear, and reversals sometimes occurred as increased and sometimes as decreased autonomy.

The transformations of the media systems in Southeast Europe supported by international financial and institutional assistance served different purposes (Irion and Jusić 2014, pp. 13–15, 2018), from promoting independent media to assistance in achieving democratic media reforms and institution building (e.g., establishing regulatory bodies, transition to public media,

Table 5.2 Comparative SEE media policy and regulation

	Bosnia and Herzegovina	Croatia	Montenegro	North Macedonia	Serbia	Slovenia
Media strategies and longer-term policies	Electronic Communications Sector Policy of Bosnia and Herzegovina for 2017–2021	Media in the Strategy of Cultural Development (2002) Media Strategy (2011–2015)			Strategy for the Development of the Public Information System in the Republic of Serbia (2011–2016)	The Strategy of Media Development, announced in 2015
Direct and indirect public subsidies for media	State advertising No subsidies for media in terms of promoting public interest, minorities etc. Direct subsidies for local media	Fund for pluralism Reduced VAT on daily press State subsidies for minority media	State advertising No subsidies for media in terms of promoting public interest. Financial support for minority media, but not in a sustainable way	Practice of state advertising stopped after 2017, but the practice of local government funds allocation persists No subsidies for media in terms of promoting public interest, minorities etc.	State advertising, non-transparent public funds allocation Funding scheme for promoting media in public interest and minority media, but problems with implementation, evaluation, non-transparent allocation	Fund for pluralism
The performance of regulatory agencies	Regulatory Agency of Bosnia and Herzegovina – CRA (2001) Members appointed by the Council of Ministers and Parliament	Council for Electronic Media/Agency for Electronic Media – VEM and AEM (2003) Members appointed by Parliament	Agency for Electronic Media of Montenegro – AEM (founded in 2003) Members appointed by Parliament	Agency for Audio and Audio-Visual Services – AAAVMS (2014) Members appointed by Parliament	Regulatory Authority for Electronic Media – REM (founded in 2014) Members appointed by Parliament	Agency for Communication Networks and Services –AKOS (founded in 2001) with Broadcasting Council (SRDF, established in 1994)

	Preceded by Independent Media Commission (founded in 1998)	Preceded by the Radio and Television Council (1995)	Preceded by Broadcasting Council (established in 1997)	Preceded by RRA Republic Broadcasting Agency, founded in 2003)	Members appointed by Parliament
Governance model of public service media	Single governing body, 4 members Appointed by Parliament CRA submits the list for BHRT; Members of the council from three constitutive peoples	Separate governing and advisory bodies: Program Council (advisory, 11 members) Supervisory board (governance and finance, 5 members) Appointed by Parliament PSM employees also have their representatives	Single governing body, 9 members Appointed by Parliament	Separate governing and advisory bodies: Program Council (13 members) Supervisory board (oversees finance, 7 members) Program Council appointed by Parliament, Finance supervisory by the Program Council	Single governing body, 9 members Appointment by the Council of the Regulatory Authority of Electronic Media	Separate governing and advisory bodies: Program Council (29 members) Supervisory board (oversees finance, 11 members) Appointed by Parliament PSM employees also have their representatives

Sources: Trpevska et al. 2018; Petković et al. 2016; Udovičić 2015; web pages of the regulatory agencies.

156 *Toward democracy*

professional and self-regulatory organizations). The period from the mid-2000s was marked by the withdrawal of international assistance and the gradual transition to other sources of support for democratic institutions, but often without coordination and a common strategy. Moreover, they frequently disregarded local specificities and stakeholders, and therefore were counterproductive with regard to the sustainable development of media systems.

The three main topics of post-socialist media policy in the CEE countries were the transformation of state broadcasters into public service broadcasters; the adoption of press laws enabling the free establishment of media institutions, including the codification of the rights of journalists and the freedom of expression; and the regulation of broadcasting frequency distribution (Peruško Čulek 1999b). Regulatory distinction was drawn between the print media, which were expected to be self-regulated, and the heavily regulated broadcast media. Dual systems were established for public service and commercial broadcasting, and the establishment of independent media regulatory authorities to oversee and implement media legislation was also an important task (Irion and Jusić 2014).

The drafting of media policies in post-socialist states in order to create liberal democratic media systems turned out to be a long-term process characterized by frequently unclear strategies, which vacillated between over-regulation and liberalization (Bašić Hrvatin and Petković 2004, pp. 13–14). The dynamics of policy introduction varied among the six countries. Slovenia and Croatia introduced key legislative changes during the 1990s. The first legislation drafted in Slovenia was in many ways progressive, inserting liberal democratic regulation while limiting ownership concentration (Bašić Hrvatin and Milosavljević 2001), and later, envisioning democratic practices in the newsroom and emphasizing community media (Bašić Hrvatin and Petković 2008). In 1990, the Croatian Parliament adopted a resolution of adherence to the Council of Europe's standards on human rights and its dedication to uphold the European standards of media freedom, pluralism, and independence.[9] The first media legislation in Croatia was also adopted during the 1990s, starting with public service broadcasting, the standards of journalist autonomy, the freedom of the press and other media, and the right to public information as well as the regulation of commercial broadcasting. However, the early policy limited foreign ownerhsip in the broadcast media. Round tables and discussions regarding the nature of media system regulation were high on the public agenda after 1996, thanks mostly to Forum 21, a civil society group of important Croatian journalists, advocating for media autonomy (Peruško 2011). Bosnia and Herzegovina's media policy development was stalled throughout most of the 1990s, first due to the war; later it developed in a specific manner in light of peacekeeping efforts led by the international community (Jusić 2005; Hozić 2008; Irion and Jusić 2013). The Macedonian media system first developed through a sort of regulatory vacuum, with the first media legislation shaped during the second part of the 1990s and in the 2000s, largely in accordance with international and European standards of media freedom and pluralism (Šopar and Latifi 2005). The public and political acceptance of liberal reforms and media freedom[10] was, however, not sufficient to halt the media capture by the political field. In Bosnia and Herzegovina, a more robust media reform took place during 1998–2002. This reform included the creation of a regulatory and legislative framework, the reform of the public service media, and the creation of the conditions for an independent commercial media sector (Irion and Jusić 2014, p. 24). Those states that remained authoritarian during the 1990s (e.g., Serbia and Montenegro) maintained firm control over their media systems, with more democratic media policy not following until after the new government came to power in 2000 (Milivojević et al. 2012).

The turn of the century was marked by democratic consolidation in Croatia and by the start of the democratic transition in Serbia, while the following decades brought about de-democratization in the media systems of some countries in Southeast Europe. The construction of media policy in Croatia moved away from the "state-building" paradigm of the 1990s, which was characterized by a populist, majoritarian vision of democracy, limitations to the individual ownership shares of commercial broadcasters (both domestic and foreign), a state-controlled public broadcaster, and commercial and judicial pressures on the media by the state, toward the "pluralist" paradigm, which emphasized the lifting of restrictions on media freedom, liberalization of ownership, and the establishment of public service broadcasting (Peruško Čulek 1999a, 2003, Peruško 2005). For Serbia, the true start of the democratic transition began after the fall of the Milošević regime and the arrival of the new liberal government in the 2000s, although the positive movement was short-lived. In the period that followed, Serbian media policy passed through three phases: a strong pro-European orientation with plans of the privatization of the media and attempts to establish independent regulatory bodies, self-regulation, and public service media;[11] marginalization the EU accession process and more restrictive media policy with derogation of prior legislation by the government following after the assassination of Đinđić in 2003; and the new commercial media development supported for those who favored the government, with most of the critical media outlets closed (Matić and Valić Nedeljković 2014, pp. 330–331). The media market remained oversaturated and troubled due to the non-transparent allocation of state funds.

Slovenia also updated its media legislation after 2000. Not all legislative changes were welcomed by civil society and the media, as during the time of the right-wing SDS government changes to the media legislation were perceived as facilitating political influence over the media (Petković and Bašić Hrvatin 2019, p. 176).

This section will now review the media policies in the six states in regard to the freedom of expression, the regulatory system in broadcasting, media pluralism policy, digital media policy, and governance of the public service media.[12] During the past 30 years these policies were modified or changed, and while focusing on the present day, the early policies will be mentioned when necessary.

Freedom of expression and its restrictions

In the post-socialist states, freedom of expression is one area of the relationship of the state with the media that needs to be especially scrutinized. Even though western democracies have issues with the redefinition of the freedom of expression as well, especially in relation to the new communication ecology (namely the contemporary debates about controlling or protecting against hate speech on the Internet), in the post-socialist states freedom of expression is sometimes still challenged by the political/state elites for the well-known traditional reasons of controlling the public narrative or blocking competing ideas from entering the public sphere. A more comprehensive analysis is needed regarding freedom of expression and censorship in the contemporary CEE countries, but this task is beyond the scope of this book. We present briefly the situation in the 1990s, the later legislative developments, and the present practices that still limit freedom of expression in some of the six countries.

All the states guaranteed the freedom of expression and the freedom of the press in their newly adopted constitutions.[13] As there was no institutional censorship after 1952 in Yugoslavia, there was no need to abolish censorship legislation and related institutions. Nevertheless, censorship was explicitly prohibited in the new constitutions of Croatia, Macedonia, Montenegro, and Serbia. At the dawn of the 2020s, the six analyzed countries share a high level of compliance with European best practices in their formal legislative framework, although there are strong discrepancies in terms of effective implementation and a persistence of different informal practices. In the four non-EU member countries, we find "a pluralistic media landscape, broadcast licensing ... regulation effectively condemns hate speech, and the media and journalists are no longer criminalized for alleged defamations" (Irion and Jusić 2018, p. 288). The institutions established to protect media freedom are still, in many cases, not sufficiently effective.

All six analyzed countries are members of the Council of Europe and have, therefore, ratified the European Convention on Human Rights and the European Convention on Transfrontier Television.[14] The freedom of expression is part of the Copenhagen criteria for EU membership, and it is thus a strategic goal of the European Commission, as set out within the European enlargement policy, which in addition to creating media freedom benchmarks related to EU accession offers political and financial support in its strategy for greater media freedom and integrity for the 2014–2020 period.[15] Hate speech is prohibited by the criminal codes of all the six examined countries, and it is also included in the general media legislation (Zubčevič et al. 2017). In Serbia, Slovenia, and Croatia, hate speech is additionally prohibited in the constitution (Peruško Čulek 2003; Milosavljević 2012; Zubčevič et al. 2017).

During the 1990s, in some countries political and governmental pressure was exerted through ownership, economic pressure, and legal pressure through libel suits or other means, including the abrogation of journalistic standards, privacy violations, and non-media legislation (M. Thompson 1995; Peruško Čulek 2003; Milivojević et al. 2012). The freedom of expression and the press, as well as support for the journalism profession and public media, were not of primary concern during the first phase of media policy in Bosnia and Herzegovina, which instead focused on maintaining peace and the pluralization of the media sector in order to prevent further nationalistic discourse and propaganda, as had been prevalent during the war[16] (Jusić 2005; Irion and Jusić 2014).

Under the authoritarian rule of Slobodan Milošević, the Penal Law was often used to prevent criticism of the government and state institutions, and the judicial system was also used to arbitrarily put pressure on the media and journalists. Aside from legal pressures, the government also used illegal means to put pressure on the media and journalists, including police violence (M. Thompson 1995, p. 58). The media and communication laws were often amended or suspended in order to serve the goals of the dominant parties (Milivojević et al. 2012). In Serbia, the progress achieved in the early 2000s in the protection of freedom of expression, the right to information, and the journalistic right to protect sources was weakened by (many believe unconstitutional) amendments to the Public Information Law in 2009 (Milivojević et al. 2012).

As Montenegro was part of the FRY, its media policy resembled that of Serbia. The first legislation was adopted by Montenegro in 1993 (Public Information Act), and later, the Law on Public Information Service (1998) gradually opened the path toward media privatization. Nevertheless, during the 1990s, the most important media outlets were state owned and under tight political control (Ružić 2017).

In North Macedonia, the rule of the right-wing VMRO-DPMNE posed a serious threat to media freedom, with the state taking control over the major media outlets through different mechanisms.[17] After 2017, the new government began deliberating changing the legislation so as to diminish political influence over the media system (Trpevska and Micevski 2018, p. 3).

Although freedom of expression legislation and journalists' standards of protection of sources were introduced in Slovenia and Croatia in the early 1990s in accordance with international standards (except in relation to issues relating to libel, which in Croatia were rather overprotective of government officials in the beginning), Croatia issued a wartime restriction on the publication of military information in 1991 (Peruško Čulek 1993). Pressure was also exerted on independent presses through excessive taxation, difficulties with printing and distribution, and excessive libel suits (Peruško 2005).

Reports by media monitoring organizations in the past decade warn of the large number of lawsuits filed against the media, often on the grounds of defamation and libel and often by civil servants or politicians, in Bosnia and Herzegovina, Croatia, Montenegro, North Macedonia, and Serbia (Trpevska et al. 2018).[18] In Bosnia and Herzegovina, uncharacteristically, a separate *Law on the protection from defamation* does not prevent misuse of the legislation, as there are still around 100 lawsuits filed annually against media outlets and journalists.[19] In Croatia, the current number stands around 1,000 active law suits.[20] In Slovenia, the right to reply and correction contained within the *Law on the media* is often used to apply political or economic pressure to the media, thereby compelling the media to publish replies or corrections even when their reporting was factual (Milosavljević 2012). In Macedonia, the courts often fail to comply with the practice of the European Court of Human Rights (Nikodinoska and Šopar 2012; Trpevska et al. 2018), and both misunderstanding and a lack of education with regard to the protection of the freedom of expression have been also noted at the lower court levels in Bosnia and Herzegovina and Serbia (Trpevska et al. 2018).[21] Defamation was decriminalized in Bosnia and Herzegovina, Montenegro, North Macedonia and Serbia in 2012, although certain restrictive provisions remained (OSCE 2017).[22] Slovenia and Croatia retain libel in their penal codes, but the envisaged penalty is only financial (OSCE 2017), as is the case in many other European countries.

New legislation intended to protect privacy is also misused against media freedom. For example, in Bosnia and Herzegovina, the *Law on the protection of personal data* conflicts with the *Law on access to public information* (Halilović and Nadaždin-Defterdarević 2012, p. 40), and it is often misused to prevent the public from receiving relevant information on the pretext of protecting privacy.[23] In Montenegro, government bodies often ignore the *Law on access to information* and use the newly established *Law on the protection of private information* to avoid giving out information to the public.[24] In North Macedonia, privacy and the freedom of communication were threatened when new legislation obliged telecommunications operators to store data and transfer it to state authorities upon request (Bogdanovski and Lembovska 2015). Freedom of expression is also threatened by police action based on non-media-related legislation, which produces chilling effects on journalists. This is a relatively new and troubling trend that is also evident in many old Western democracies alongside new antiterrorist legislation granting much broader powers to the police and security forces (e.g., the UK, France).

With the rise of the right-wing movements in the CEE, freedom of expression is threatened again also in the non-journalistic areas like satire (one recent example is a lawsuit against a satirical TV show in Croatia).[25] Although these pressures from radical conservatives are at the moment less serious than the organized pressure or threats from state officials (especially in Serbia and in Bosnia and Herzegovina), they nonetheless signify an illiberal trend (evident also in other CEE countries) in which the social critique in the public sphere is attempting to be blocked. This area of study must certainly be in the future focus of comparative communication research (cf. Surowiec and Štětka 2019).

Regulatory system for broadcasting

The first regulatory bodies (usually radio and television or telecommunication councils) for commercial broadcasting were established during the 1990s in Croatia, Macedonia, and Slovenia. More substantial and autonomous agencies were established usually during the second decade.

In Slovenia, the Agency for Communication Networks and Services (AKOS) is an integrated regulator, with media regulation taking a smaller share of the agency's time, which results in a passive approach rather than reacting to possible abuses and misconduct. Slovenia has the unique institution of "media inspector," which is responsible for regulating language, hate speech, and media content in electronic media. However, this institution comprises only one person and so it is perceived as weak because it is difficult to conduct the monitoring and regulation in practice.[26]

In Croatia, the Croatian Agency for Electronic Media (AEM) and its Council for Electronic Media regulates broadcast and non-linear media, and it also administers the Fund for the Promotion and Protection of Pluralism and Diversity. While its role is seen as passive and it is not thought to be sufficiently effective in terms of monitoring and market regulation,[27] the regulatory agency was under significant political pressure because of some of its decisions that protected against hate speech. In 2016 the AEM sanction of a local television station for (right-wing) hate speech met with protests and street demonstrations by uncivil society which tried (but failed) to put pressure on the regulator. The subsequent change in the composition of its council and leadership tends to support the claim about recent state capture of this body, but the conclusions will only be possible after new decisions are made.

The establishment of the Communications Regulatory Agency (CRA) in Bosnia and Herzegovina was for a long time perceived as one of the most successful results of international assistance for the media sector due to its established independence from political pressures (Jusić 2005; Hodžić 2014; Irion and Jusić 2018). The CRA regulates broadcasting, telecommunications, and frequency allocation. However, the independence of the CRA has been eroded since 2003 thanks to political pressure after it became answerable to the domestic government (Hodžić 2014). The development of Bosnia and Herzegovina's regulatory framework, as well as the establishment of new institutions within the media sector, are the result of mutual and sometimes conflicting intervention by international actors, mostly the OHR, OSCE, and European Commission (Hozić 2008; Jusić and Ahmetašević 2018; Irion and Jusić 2014). The Office of the Higher Representative of

Bosnia and Herzegovina established a Media Development Office, which played an important role in steering media reform. The Open Broadcasting Network (OBN) was established thanks to international assistance in a (largely unsuccessful) attempt to create cross-national media.

Macedonia's early regulatory body was tasked with protecting public interest in the media sector, but at the beginning had only a limited regulatory role when compared to the government (Šopar and Latifi 2005, pp. 1180–1181). The broadcasting market consolidated with increased competition and choice, media pluralism developed, and cable networks were also included in the regulatory framework (Šopar and Latifi 2005, p. 1174). The subsequently created AVMU (Agency for Audio and Audio-Visual Services) aimed to create a transparent means of electing members that would prevent political influence (Trpevska and Micevski 2014). It was, however, complicit in the further flooding of the market with analog licenses for radio and television broadcasting due to pressure from powerful media owners, when it could have eased the oversaturated market and allowed the development of digital media (Nikodinoska and Šopar 2012; Trpevska and Micevski 2014). Unusually, the agency received "authority to conduct the so-called administrative supervision over the work of the print media and online publications and to initiate misdemeanor procedures," raising fears about possible control over the independent media (Trpevska and Micevski 2014, p. 264).

The Serbian Regulatory Authority for Electronic Media (REM) is obliged to create strategies for the development of the media and audiovisual sector, issue licenses and allocate frequencies, hold a register of broadcast and on-demand media, oversee the protection of human dignity and personal rights by the media, and monitor the media market (Zubčevič et al. 2017). It is evaluated as being influenced by media owners and having only weak capacity of monitoring and control. The result is increased commercialization and low-quality content.[28]

In Montenegro, the AEM regulates broadcasting and on-demand services, allocates frequencies, keeps a register of all media, and receives complaints about media providers. Members of the AEM are elected by the parliament. Its regulatory power is evaluated as being weak, and media close to the government are not sanctioned for disregarding their legal obligations.[29]

The regulatory agencies of Bosnia and Herzegovina, Macedonia, Serbia, and Montenegro are all considered to be non-autonomous and subject to political maneuvering by their governments.

Media pluralism policy

Media pluralism and diversity represent one of the three normative aims of democratic media performance, in addition to media freedom and equality (McQuail 1995). In the media policy discourse, the concept of pluralism is multifaceted (cf. Klimkiewicz 2005; Czepek et al. 2009). Hoffmann-Riem

(1987, quoted in McQuail 1995, p. 144) defines four standard dimensions of diversity:

> Of formats and issues: essentially referring to differences of media function, such as entertainment, information, education, etc.; of contents: in relation to opinion and topics of information and news, of persons and groups: essentially access, but also representation; of geographical coverage and relevance.

Media pluralism is thus commonly analyzed in terms of both content and structure (cf. Klimkiewicz 2005). Pluralism is regulated through provisions governing the concentration and transparency of ownership as well as through various subsidies and other forms of support for media diversity, both in content and in structure. Media systems handle political and social diversity through external pluralism, whereby the media represent distinct political orientations, or internal pluralism, whereby the news media seek to report the news in a "balanced" way (Hallin and Mancini 2004, p. 14). External pluralism is further defined in the media policy discourse as media-system-level pluralism (in terms of both its structural and content aspects), and it corresponds to high political parallelism within media systems. The public service media are expected, as part of their mission, to promote internal pluralism. This is also usually the case with the mainstream media, which are not politically affiliated or partial.

Croatia, North Macedonia, and Slovenia regulate ownership transparency in relation to print, broadcast, and digital media. Montenegro and Serbia do not regulate print ownership transparency, while Bosnia and Herzegovina has no regulation of ownership transparency in relation to any media. All the countries except for Bosnia and Herzegovina regulate the concentration of ownership of both print and broadcast media (Bašić Hrvatin and Milosavljević 2001; Peruško 2005; Hećimović 2019).

Of the six countries, only in Croatia and Slovenia was a functional Fund for Pluralism established early on to promote electronic media content that contributes to diversity. The daily press in Slovenia and Croatia is subsidized by reduced VAT. While the main focus is on supporting diversity in local and regional commercial media, the alternative or community media were also particularly well supported in Croatia (2011–2015), although this was discontinued as soon as the right-wing conservative government came to power and such media now only receive support though the pluralism fund. National or ethnic minority media are additionally supported from the state budget and by the municipalities and local communities, while the HRT is mandated to also include programs for national minorities (Peruško 2013b). The Slovenian Fund for Pluralism allocates funds for local and community media, although commercial media programs that add to diversity can also be supported (Bašić Hrvatin and Petković 2008).[30]

In Southeast Europe, states sometimes intervene in the media through subsidies and advertising for political instrumentalization and harm media pluralism and autonomy. Slovenia does not have a significant problem with direct state advertising, although state influence is expressed indirectly through advertising by state-owned companies. The situation is similar in Croatia, which has specific legislation to ensure the transparency of state advertising, although funding of local media through direct subsidies and municipal government advertising persists as a problem.

In Bosnia and Herzegovina, state advertising has significant influence, but there are no subsidies for the media in terms of promoting the public interest or representing minorities (Trpevska et al. 2018). One of the two entities in Bosnia and Herzegovina, Republika Srpska, established a Fund for the Media, which awards state financial support to only those media loyal to the government, and the media are also funded through advertisements by state-owned companies (Tadić Mijović and Šajkaš 2016). Montenegro also faces big problems with regard to state advertising, which is implemented in a non-transparent way. Many private media exist solely thanks to state advertising, and local media are mostly financed from the local government budget.[31] There are no subsidies for the media in terms of promoting the public interest, although there is financial support available for minority media, albeit not in a sustainable way (Trpevska et al. 2018). In North Macedonia, the functioning of the market is to a large extent managed by state and public funding through various channels. The government is one of the biggest media advertisers (according to the regulatory agency, having a 35% advertising share in the media market; Nebiu et al. 2016, p. 18). Following the change of government in 2017, the practice of direct state advertising stopped, but the practice of local government funding allocation persists (OMR 2018; Trpevska et al. 2018). Serbia also has a problem with unregulated state advertising (the state is one of the largest advertisers; Tadić Mijović and Šajkaš 2016, p. 12) and non-transparent public funding allocation (Trpevska et al. 2018). A funding scheme for promoting media in the public interest and minority media was recently established, but not without problems in terms of implementation and non-transparent allocation (Trpevska et al. 2018).

Digital media policy

Mattoni and Ceccobelli (2018) argue that the dimension of state intervention in the media system should include two more indicators of relevance to the digital age: investment in digital infrastructures and policies concerning digital media actors and content. Key issues in relation to media policy during the digital era include the regulation of misinformation, the regulation of technology platforms, privacy, and media literacy. Very few of these topics are recognized within the media policy in most countries in Southeast Europe, which are slowly moving toward the digital era and still struggling with the implementation of liberal legislation in environments characterized by political instrumentalization.

In terms of digitalization policies, some countries are front-runners while others are laggards. Croatia and Slovenia were the first to complete the switchover to digital television (in 2010 and 2011, respectively; Peruško and Popović 2008), while the other countries took until 2015, except for Bosnia and Herzegovina, which has not yet introduced digital terrestrial television but has adopted the Electronic Communications Sector Policy for the period 2017–2021, which aims to provide grounds for the development of telecommunications infrastructure. The Croatian market profited the most from the digital television switchover, as it helped new television channels to be introduced. The other countries suffer from oversaturated markets and weak advertising revenue, and they were not inclined to introduce digital television due to fear of an even more shrunken advertising share and the negative effect on weaker markets, such as that of Bosnia and Herzegovina, which would be increasingly subjected to broadcasts from neighboring states (Milosavljević and Broughton Micova 2013).

The adoption of new strategic documents intended to address the digital transformation of the media has been sporadic. In Croatia, a media strategy highlighting support for the online community and non-profit media was formulated during its second center-left liberal government (2011–2015), but even though the supporting measures (subsidies for non-profit, increasingly founded online media and lower VAT for printed newspapers) were implemented, the document itself was never adopted. The conservative government that followed announced it was working on a new media strategy and accompanying media laws, including the regulation of hate speech in digital media and a digitally motivated update to the *Law on electronic media*, but to date no proposals have been formally released. In Slovenia, there have been discussions about developing a new media strategy that would serve as the basis for new media laws, but there have been no changes in the media legislation (Milosavljević et al. 2018).

Following the application for EU candidacy in 2009 by the new center-left pro-European government, Serbia tried to harmonize its laws with those of the EU and adopted a liberal strategy for the development of the media field. This strategy involved the final privatization and withdrawal of the state from media ownership, with the aim of guaranteeing the public interest. The strategy focused more on the issue of decoupling the media from state and political influence than on the digital challenges to the media sphere. However, the subsequent populist conservative government (since 2012) ensured that all such plans came to naught.

Media literacy is the only topic from the digital policy agenda that has achieved serious traction in Southeast Europe. The media regulatory agencies are involved in the promotion of media literacy programs and initiatives in Croatia, Macedonia, Montenegro, and Slovenia, although civil society is more active in this area (Kanižaj 2016; Kerševan Smokvina 2016; Petković et al. 2019). Elements of media literacy have been taught in the formal education systems of Croatia and Slovenia since the 1990s (Kerševan Smokvina 2016), and media literacy has now been introduced as an elective subject in Montenegro and Serbia (Petković et al. 2019).

Governance of public service media

The reforms to the PSB systems in Eastern Europe are probably the most disappointing outcome of the imitative media policies introduced in the CEE countries during the course of their democratic transformations. Only decades later are media researchers pointing to the fact that normative solutions from one type of media system will not work in another type without "domestication," that is, without being adapted to the shape of the media market, the relationship between politics and the media, the political culture, and the structures of power in the implementing country. This failure to understand that the context of the whole media and political system influences the possibility of imported models being successfully applied is the reason for the perception of failed reforms. The often mentioned imitative media policy approach proves particularly troubling and produces adverse results in those countries and media systems that exhibit completely different political and social structures to the policy "role model." The first of the two primary role models was the BBC, a broadcaster from a majoritarian democracy with a long public service tradition, the rule of law, and a high degree of journalistic autonomy, as well as low political parallelism. The BBC model was used as the template in Bosnia and Herzegovina, a deeply nationally divided state. A model that took into account these divisions, and the national social segments present, would probably have worked better, for instance, the Swiss model that accommodates these kinds of divisions and serves all the national segments equally. The second PSB role model exists in democratic corporatist countries, primarily in Germany, where the governing bodies are composed of the representatives of civil society and thus separated from political party influence. In the model countries, the representatives of civil society play a key role in ensuring social pluralism in the governance of PSB (as in the case of Germany and the Netherlands). Additionally, the model countries employ a consensual type of government that is not present in many of the CEE countries (Slovenia is partly a functional exception and Bosnia and Herzegovina a formal exception). In countries with no historical social segments to which the representatives would be accountable, it is easier for informal political powers to influence civil society representatives within the media governing bodies.

All four basic models of PSB governance (Hallin and Mancini 2004, p. 30) were tested in these six countries: the government model, as the closest to state broadcasting, whereby the public broadcaster is governed directly by the government or by the political majority, was the most prevalent (in Slovenia until 1994, in Macedonia until 1998, in Croatia until 2001, in Bosnia and Herzegovina and Montenegro until 2002, and in Serbia until 2003). According to the parliamentary model, governance is divided between parties on a proportional basis; in some countries, different channels of public media are "awarded" to different parties in the national parliament. In Slovenia and Croatia, there is now a mixture between a parliamentary and a civic model, and the members of the governing bodies are elected in the parliament in government/opposition parity. In the civic or corporatist model, governance over public media is divided between different relevant political, civil society, and other social groups on a proportional basis: political parties, trade unions, religious groups, business associations, and so forth (Hallin and Mancini 2004, p. 31). This was the model most strongly advocated by the Council of Europe experts (most notably the media scholar Karol Jakubowicz), but as explained earlier, it was the least appropriate model, which was replaced in Slovenia and which collapsed in Croatia, leading to the total disintegration of PSB governing bodies in 2011. The professional model was attempted in Croatia next, although it also proved ineffective (Peruško 2011). According to the professional model, rule over broadcasting is left to media and journalism professionals, thereby minimizing political control, although this presupposes the unassailable professional reputation of the CEO, which was not the case in this instance. All these models expect a democratic political context, and they exhibit the described anomalies in contexts of immature democracy. In Bosnia and Herzegovina and in Serbia, the media regulator appoints members of the governing body, but due to its weaker independence from political power (Ahmetašević and Hadžiristić 2017; Marko and Veljanovski 2018), the governing of the public service broadcaster is actually managed within the parliamentary type of model. Macedonia and Montenegro also currently follow the non-functioning civic model of public service broadcasting, in which civil society, academia, and professional organizations nominate members and parliament appoints them, with special provisions existing to avoid a conflict of interest on the part of members of governing body. However, due to anomalies in the democratic field and clientelism, as well as to the non-existence of historical social segments as described earlier, these procedures cannot ensure the independence of the governing body.

The establishment of public service media in Southeast Europe is mainly considered to have been a failure, its public mission having been overshadowed by political and commercial pressures (Milosavljević and Poler 2018, p. 1151). Public service broadcasting (PSB) is perceived to be "government friendly," and rather than fulfilling its public mission it is considered to be institutionally adapting to every change in the political power structure (Irion and Jusić 2018, p. 290). In some countries (Croatia and Slovenia), however, the PSB organizations are well funded and organized, and in several countries they retain a relatively strong position with audiences (see Table 5.1).

Several of the public service media systems have a problem when it comes to collecting license fees, especially in Bosnia and Herzegovina, North Macedonia, and Serbia (Milosavljević and Poler 2018). Aside from being the most complex and politically troubled public broadcasting system, Bosnia and Herzegovina's system is also the least well-funded when compared to the systems of the other post-Yugoslav states. In Bosnia and Herzegovina, both the complex representation system and the conflicting interests stemming from the public broadcaster's structure render it difficult to efficiently collect PSB fees. All efforts to establish a Croatian language channel within the publicly funded federation television service were frustrated. In 2019, the television station Herceg Bosna (TV HB) bought several local TV stations and began broadcasting on their allocated frequencies and via cable, satellite, and Internet distribution, funded by communities and municipalities with a Croatian majority across the country. Public discussions about abolishing public service fees have increasingly emerged in several countries in recent years (in Serbia, such a proposition has also come from high levels within the government; Petković et al. 2016, p. 9).

Political parallelism

The nature of the political and party system influences the nature of the parallelism of the media and political parties, the way media policies are formed, and the level of party colonization of the media (Bajomi-Lázár 2015). Political systems that feature less dominance by a single party tend to have a higher degree of media freedom (Bajomi-Lázár 2015). In the six countries analyzed in this book, center-left parties democratized and liberalized the media systems, while center-right and nationalist parties first introduced more barriers to foreign ownership of the media and later greater market liberalization, and they placed more pressure on the independence of the media reporting and media autonomy.

The strong political parallelism seen in the media of the CEE countries exists on many levels: the interchangeability of the journalism and political professions, the organizational connections between the media and political and other organizations, the type of management of PSB, the type of management of regulatory bodies, and in the media content. Moreover, it also manifests through the parallelism of business elites, wherein such business elites are also connected to political power. Party colonization "in addition to the management of information is the exploitation of media resources such as airtime, radio and television frequencies, senior positions in the media authority and public service broadcasters, funding allocated for program production and advertising, and newspaper subsidies" (Bajomi-Lázár 2015, p. 8). These findings also apply to several of the analyzed countries.

The pattern of influence of the political parties in power in the 1990s over certain media outlets continued after 2000. Although in most countries the ownership of the broadcast media by political parties was legally prohibited, parallelism in the form of party colonization was exhibited through state subsidies or advertising and political appointments to top public service media positions or to regulatory bodies, and in some cases hidden party ownership is suspected.

In addition to political parties, religious institutions became stronger political actors during the transition period, sometimes being tightly aligned with political power. In Croatia and Slovenia, the Catholic press played an influential role and already had a rather large audience during the socialist period, while prominent religious press existed in Bosnia and Herzegovina and Serbia too (Ramet 2002). Catholic radio in Croatia received a national license, the HRT includes religious programs, and the Catholic Church is also a large publisher of books and press (Peruško 2007, p. 238). Further, Laudato TV, a Catholic television network, received a national terrestrial license in Croatia.

The countries differ in terms of the degree of parallelism exhibited, especially in relation to the spread of various extreme practices of parallelism that speak to media capture. In some countries, parallelism existed with the party in government (and it is hence very hard to distinguish from parallelism with the state, which is reminiscent of the former regime[s]), while opposition parties did not have their own media or supporting media. In certain countries, the elites were united behind the same major policy. This was especially true of the Serbian media in the 1990s, with the political opposition also supporting Milošević's Greater Serb policy (Banac 1992b). The most prestigious media in Serbia supported the regime of Slobodan Milošević during the 1990s, while the popular independent media were supported by civil society and foreign donors (Milivojević 2005, p. 1324) and threatened with closure. Media diversity was external and only present in large urban centers, as B92's and Studio B's signals only reached Belgrade audiences (Boduszyński 2010, p. 177). Citizens living in provincial and rural areas mostly received content from the state-controlled RTS, which exhibited no internal pluralism. State television played an influential political role: 60% of the population used the RTS news program as their main source of information, while only 2% relied on a newspaper (Gordy 1999, as quoted in Boduszyński 2010, p. 178). After the end of the 1990s, the private media that first received licenses were those that were primarily entertainment oriented and supportive of the regime, including TV Pink and BK Telecom (Milivojević 2005, p. 1324). The Serbian case represents an example of state capture as an extreme form of parallelism, in which the greater part of the media system, including the commercial media, is controlled by the party currently in government. Any similarity with Orban's Hungary is probably not a coincidence.

The most widely read media in Serbia today are sensationalist tabloids, which have an openly pro-government stance and which also engage in slander toward opposition and critical media and civil society (*Informer* and *Kurir*). The newspapers with the highest circulation in Serbia express the highest political bias, and they are the least critically oriented toward the government (Milivojević 2018). Moreover, quality and investigative journalism has been marginalized and transferred to the online sphere, which is funded by international donations or by the EU and is because of this under government attack.[32] The privatization of B92, once a famous critical and investigative media outlet, turned it into a media outlet oriented toward light entertainment (Tadić Mijović and Šajkaš 2016).

In Croatia, the parallelism was high during the 1990s, when members of the ruling HDZ party and members of parliament occupied decision-making positions within the state-owned media HRT, and the largest print media company, Vjesnik, at that time still in state ownership. (Peruško 2007). Although the HRT was then the only television station with national coverage in Croatia, some 15 local television stations and over 80 radio stations contributed to the media pluralism. The independent private press, including the weeklies *Globus, Nacional*, and *Feral Tribune* (the last was discontinued after 2000), as well as the dailies *Novi list* and *Jutarnji list*, were often subjected to libel suits and economic pressure, including higher taxation or printing problems (Peruško 2007, p. 234). In present-day Croatia and Slovenia, the mainstream foreign-owned commercial media follow the norms of neutrality, and they are not subjected to the influence of national political elites. Quality journalism is more or less supported within the Slovenian mainstream media as well as in the leading quality press.[33] Media with a strong political bias have emerged on the fringes of the media system. The most blatant example of political parallelism in Slovenia is the newly established NovaTV24, a media group established by members of the SDS, consisting of around 30 media outlets. These outlets include the daily *Demokracija*, the tabloid *Skandal*, online outlets, and local media. The media outlets belonging to the group engage in anti-immigrant, anti-human-rights, and anti-gender-equality discourse, and they attack their political opponents.[34] These media outlets are also funded by Hungarian companies with links to the Fidesz political party (Mladina 2019). Similar strategies for supporting right-wing media have been discovered in Macedonia, in which new media outlets were funded by Hungarian crony capital (Stojanovski 2018).

In Croatia, most of the mainstream print and broadcast media with the highest audience shares, equally attract audiences with different political orientations in a "catch-all" manner (Peruško and Vozab 2017). Political parallelism in terms of audience preference has been noted in the PSB media audiences (their online portal attracts more right-oriented conservative audiences) and in the audiences of smaller or newer digital media outlets (Peruško and Vozab 2017). The digital media amplify already existing political polarization, enabling the establishment of new media that further polarize the media audience. Digital media outlets tend to express bias when reporting on contentious political and social issues (Bilić and Balabanić 2016). Paradoxically, the leading digital media outlet, Index.hr, has a lower level of audience trust and is perceived as being biased (left-leaning), but it also attracts large audiences and is considered to be independent (Vozab 2017).

Political and social cleavages are also reflected in the media systems of the six countries of interest. Macedonia is a highly segregated country in which Macedonians and Albanians do not share the same religion or language, and they mutually reinforce interethnic stereotypes and distance. The relationship between the two national groups is marked by stark inequality, with the Albanians being less educated and less affluent than the Macedonians (Boduszyński 2010). The media in Macedonia produce two distinct public spheres: one for Macedonians and the other for Albanians (Trpevska 2017). As this split is also reflected in the parties, it can further be viewed as party parallelism. The Macedonian public television and radio outlets offer programs in minority languages (Albanian, Turkish, Romani) (Šopar and Latifi 2005, p. 1175).

In Montenegro, North Macedonia, and Serbia, the mainstream media are highly politicized and basically pro-governmental, while the independent media are marginalized or have lower audience shares. In Montenegro, the public media are perceived as being politically controlled, having a low degree of professionalism, and serving as mouthpieces for the ruling party. Their independence is diminished through the appointment of personnel and management, especially at the director level, as appointees are usually close to the government.[35] Pink Montenegro, which is based in Belgrade, is the most popular television station in Montenegro. Although its programming mainly consists of light entertainment content, in terms of its news and information programs, it is very much politically aligned with the ruling party. It often engages in attacks against political opponents, the opposition, civil society, and other media.[36] The Serbian tabloid *Informer* also operates in Montenegro, where it serves a similar function as in Serbia. The non-transparent allocation of state funding in Montenegro further contributes to the media being loyal to the government. The daily *Pobjeda* (established during socialism) was owned by the state until 2014, in contravention of the law, after which it was privatized and taken over by a Greek businessman (Tadić Mijović and Šajkaš 2016, pp. 8–9). Media outlets that are perceived as critical of the government usually receive donations and funds from international sources, and they often face pressure and attack domestically (dailies *Vijesti* and *Dan*, *TV Vijesti* and *Monitor*; Tadić Mijović and Šajkaš 2016, p. 10).

Marko (2012) divides the media of Bosnia and Herzegovina into three main groups. The first group advocates intercultural exchange between different nations and combines it with criticism of the government. The magazine *Slobodna Bosna*, daily newspaper *Oslobodenje* (which was previously close to the SDP BIH and is now closer to the conservative SDA), and public broadcaster BHTV belong to this group (Marko 2012, pp. 5–6). The second group of media acknowledge the existence of a common state but interpret events in such a way as to promote the interests of specific national and political groups. *Dnevni avaz* (reporting from the Bosniak position), *Večernji list BIH* (representing BIH Croats), and *Nezavisne Novine* (representing BIH Serbs) belong to this group. The third group of media belong to Republika Srpska and so promote its distinctive identity and statehood as opposed to those of Bosnia and Herzegovina. The public broadcaster RTRS, daily newspaper *Glas Srpske*, magazine *Novi Reporter*, and local television TV BN are in this group (Marko 2012, p. 6). A recent report on misinformation in Bosnia and Herzegovina identified several websites producing for-profit false information, news websites publishing misinformation, and news websites connected to political parties and publishing political propaganda (Džebo 2019).

Political pressure is also exerted through marketing agencies, which are connected to political parties or the state through ownership. In Serbia, the marketing agency Direct Media, which dominated the advertising market, was owned by the mayor of Belgrade during the rule of the DS. Following the change in government, Mediapol took over the market, and it was connected to the SNS by its members (Tadić Mijović and Šajkaš 2016, p. 13). In Slovenia, marketing agencies are sometimes connected to the state and to political parties, and they channel advertising away from critical media. Due to the connections between a marketing agency and the SDS, the critical media outlet Mladina lost a large share of advertising from several companies.[37] The adverse influence of large advertisers and connected advertising agencies on the content of the news media can be seen in Croatia as well, which has not escaped this negative aspect of the commercialization of the media. Moreover, the advertising of large public companies was also contingent on the adoption of a positive slant toward the government (especially during the government of Ivo Sanader [2003–2009], who was later found guilty of corruption) (H-Alter 2015).

The political parallelism seen in the six countries does not actually exhibit the characteristics of traditional (historical) party – press parallelism, whereby different media organizations are related (structurally or in terms of their ideology/content/audiences) to political parties. In fact, we see here asymmetric parallelism, whereby a relationship of parallelism exists between certain parties – usually conservative right/nationalist parties – who are in government and certain media that they can influence, particularly PSB, but in some countries also commercial media, while the left/liberal political parties have no related media and so instead rely on the mainstream legacy, and increasingly, online media. This situation of asymmetric polarization is also seen in the contemporary United States, where the right-wing political parties have their own partisan media, while the left is not represented by the same kind of partisan politics and instead relies on the professional journalism of the mainstream media (Faris et al. 2017). In the six countries of interest, political parallelism in some extreme instances also transmutes into the state capture of the media, where we again see the conflation of the state and the party, as seen during the socialist period, albeit minus the socialist ideology.

Media market after self-management socialism

The states formed after the collapse of communism followed the logic of the withdrawal of state ownership of the media, privatization, and the opening up of the market to foreign investment. However, the various countries followed different patterns throughout these processes. In most of the post-socialist states, the media were created spontaneously while regulatory frameworks were only established after a host of new radio and television stations were already in existence (Bašić Hrvatin and Petković 2004, p. 17; Dragomir et al. 2005). The early regulatory vacuum was used by media companies in some countries to sell shares to their journalists and editors, as in the case of the Czech Republic, Estonia, and Lithuania, while in other countries, such as Poland, the state regulated the privatization path from the outset (Bašić Hrvatin and Petković 2004, p. 19). The countries of Southeast Europe also followed different privatization strategies, and the media followed the patterns of privatization templates used for the whole economy. In the six countries of interest, the privatization involved a more complex process than that seen in the CEE countries characterized by real existing socialism. Due to the self-management economy, the ownership of the media was social rather than state, and the state first re-nationalized the formerly socially owned companies. The process of privatization of the media in the CEE countries after socialism is an under-researched topic, and the consequences of different strategies for media autonomy and economic success have not yet been systematically evaluated.

Foreign investors started "conquering" the Eastern European media markets during the 1990s, albeit at different paces (Štetka 2012, p. 436). In Slovenia, foreign investment was taken in more slowly due to the stronger governmental regulation of the privatization process and the better functioning media market (Bašić Hrvatin and Kučić 2004, in Štetka 2012, p. 436), but Central European Media Enterprises (CME) established the first commercial TV channel (Kanal A) in 1991, among the first in the CEE (Peruško and Popović 2009). In Croatia, privatization was also regulated, and the share of individual ownership was restricted during the 1990s, which slowed foreign entry into the broadcasting market and allowed for the development of indigenous media companies. In both Montenegro and Serbia, foreign ownership was restricted by regulation during the 1990s, so foreign investors only came to these markets after 2000. The German Westdeutsche Allgemeine Zeitung (WAZ) company entered the print media markets in the region in the 1990s. Štetka (2012) notes the withdrawal of foreign ownership from the CEE markets during the late 2000s, with local business owners taking over the media companies.

As public service media compete with their private rivals, the visible trends in Southeast Europe include the rise of entertainment programs at the expense of news and information (Milosavljević and Poler 2018, p. 1152). The public television audience shares remain between 20% and 27% in most of the six countries, close to the European average of 23%, although the share is particularly low in North Macedonia, attracting only 4% of audiences (the most successful European PSB organizations draw between 36% of the audience share in Denmark and 58% in Iceland) (EBU 2018). In several of the six countries they fare well in competition with leading commercial channels – FTV in Bosnia and Herzegovina and RTS 1 in Serbia are the market leaders in terms of television audiences, while in Croatia and Slovenia PSB take the second place. The Croatian HRT is the only PSB organization in the region with a dedicated news channel (Hungary, Poland, and Chechia are the only other CEE countries to have a PBS news channel). The countries in the region broadcast less domestic and European programs than is typical in Europe – less than 80% in fact (most Western European countries broadcast over 90%, and in the CEE countries that figure is over 80%). Only the Croatian, Serbian, and Slovenian PSB organizations manage their own online news sites, which attract large audience shares (Marko 2017, p. 228; Gemius 2019).

In terms of funding, the more successful public service broadcasters in the region tend to have a cost per citizen of around the European average of €3.08, while others more closely resemble the Eastern European average of €1 or less (see Table 5.1). In most of the analyzed countries, the public service media funding comes from a combination of license fees and advertising. The public service media in North Macedonia and Serbia also receive funding from the state budget (EBU 2018). In Montenegro, the public service media are funded directly from the state budget, and they also receive a share of state advertising.

Media audiences, advertising, and digital media

A media market can be defined by the general reach of the media (such as press circulation or Internet penetration), the nature of media development (some markets are newspaper-centric while others are television-centric), gender differences in terms of news consumption, and the position of the quality and tabloid press (Hallin and Mancini 2004). During the digital era, the digital media market dimension has become increasingly important as the orientation of media markets has shifted from the print media to diversified digital and hybrid media (Peruško et al. 2015; Mattoni and Ceccobelli 2018). This is also the case in the digital media markets of Southeast Europe. There, Internet penetration has reached an average of 70% (with differences between countries), and at least 40% of audiences are social media users (see the comparative data in Table 5.1).

A specific common trait of all the media markets in the region is their small size due to the rather weak national economies. Small media markets (i.e., where the number of inhabitants is between 100,000 and 18 million; Pupis 2009, p. 9, as quoted in Jones 2014, p. 1) have shared difficulties, and they often also share a peripheral position in respect of global cultural flows. Although Slovenia has a respectable GDP per capita, the size of the country contributes to its very small market. The Croatian advertising market had reached 1% of GDP (the mark of a developed media market) by the mid-2000s, although the global economic crisis after 2008 reduced the entire economy, which also impacted the media. Research shows that even countries with high GDPs suffer from small markets, which very quickly become oversaturated and in which the most stable are the "catch-all media outlets such as generalist television channels with national reach, strong investments, and stable ownership" (Milosavljević and Poler 2018, p. 1155). The small media markets in the region are burdened by the lack of advertising revenue and the dependence on public subsidies and public advertising (Irion and Jusić 2014). Some authors find that small markets are also more prone to higher political parallelism (Broughton Micova 2013). The common problems of the overall cultural and creative industries in Southeast Europe are the problems of small markets, smaller production, the heavy influence of international cultural and creative industries, difficulties with the distribution of products, and the higher dependence on the state (Primorac 2004). Another common trait of the media markets in the region is the interference of the state in the media market, mainly through state advertising, as discussed earlier. In some countries (Slovenia and Croatia), the state modifies some of the small market difficulties through subsidies and support to pluralism of media content production.

Small languages (in terms of the native speaker group size) are among the characteristics that inhibit the development of stronger media companies with the potential to reach outside the economically underdeveloped region (Milosavljević and Poler 2018). In this region, however, audiences from several countries can understand each other's languages, and they can consume media from their neighboring countries. Some media markets exhibit a greater influence than others. Serbian media attracts audiences and advertising revenue from Montenegro and Bosnia and Herzegovina (Vesnić-Alujević and Bajić 2013). This obviously negatively influences the fragmented market of Bosnia and Herzegovina.[38] Global media platforms such as Google and Facebook also intervene in the region's markets and claim their advertising shares, as more audiences access news through these platforms. In Croatia, Google dominated the online advertising market in 2016 (43.4%), while Facebook captured 12.9% (Bilić and Primorac 2018, p. 69). Print media companies are increasingly drawing revenues from their online portals too.

The print media market is consistently contracting in terms of its audience reach, commensurate with worldwide trends of a 10% annual reduction, and the broadcast and digital media are now the primary sources of news. Print media audiences are rather low throughout the entire region (Džihana et al. 2012; Ranković 2019). Television still holds the top position in the

176 Toward democracy

market in Croatia (Peruško 2017), Serbia (Ranković 2019), Bosnia and Herzegovina and North Macedonia (Hodžić and Pajnik 2016), and Slovenia (Milosavljević and Kerševan Smokvina 2012). Television dominates in the clearly television-centric media markets of the examined countries. Television is also the source that citizens trust the most, while they place the least trust in social media (Eurobarometer 2014). However, there are notable differences in terms of the reach and use of print media: Slovenia, Croatia, and Serbia exhibit a higher reach and use of daily newspapers and magazines when compared to the weaker press markets in Bosnia and Herzegovina, Montenegro, and North Macedonia (Figure 5.1, Figure 5.2). This market orientation strongly resembles the one inherited from the socialist period.

The potential of the media to reach different segments of society defines the inclusiveness of the media market (Brüggemann et al. 2014). Media markets

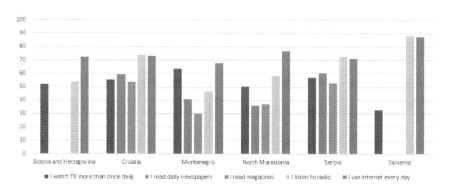

Figure 5.1 Audience use of different media platforms (%) (2018)
Sources: Authors' calculations; Ipsos Media Data 2018.

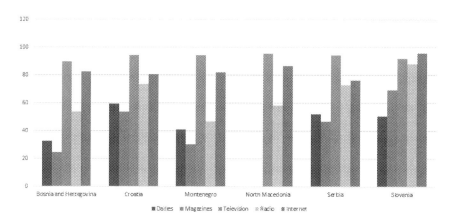

Figure 5.2 Maximum potential reach for different media platforms (2018)
Sources: Authors' calculation; Ipsos Media Data 2018.

Toward democracy 177

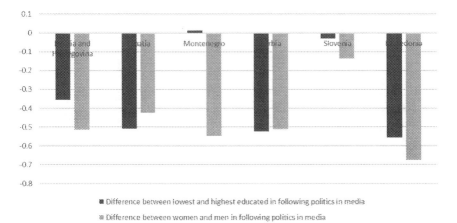

Figure 5.3 Media market inclusiveness toward education and gender segments (2018)

in which the media are more oriented toward the elite have a smaller share of newspaper and news audiences among those segments of society traditionally excluded from the public sphere. In the Mediterranean media systems, there is a large gap between male and female newspaper audiences (Hallin and Mancini 2004, pp. 23–24). Among the Southeast European countries, the Slovenian media market is the most inclusive of audiences in terms of gender and education level, while the largest inequality is found in North Macedonia (Figure 5.3). In Croatia, education creates a greater inequality in relation to media use than gender, while in Montenegro the newspaper market is inclusive in terms of the differences in education.

Another important characteristic of a media market is the position of the quality and tabloid media. In Slovenia, the quality press (*Delo, Večer,* and *Dnevnik*) have the highest circulation[39] while in Serbia, the situation is the complete opposite (see Table 5.3). There, the notoriously pro-government tabloid *Informer* has the highest circulation, followed by other sensationalist tabloids, namely *Kurir* and *Novosti* (Milivojević 2018). In Croatia, the semi-tabloid *24sata* has the highest circulation, although it is followed by the quality dailies *Večernji list* and *Jutarnji list*. In Bosnia and Herzegovina, the tabloids are not among the most widely read newspapers (the most popular dailies are *Dnevni Avaz* and *Oslobođenje*) (Hodžić 2014).

Journalistic autonomy

Journalistic autonomy is caught between political and economic interests, and it is often achieved through practices within a community of colleagues (Hallin and Mancini 2004). Inside such professional communities, journalists share distinct professional norms, for instance, ethical principles such as

Table 5.3 Main media outlets in Southeast Europe

	Bosnia and Herzegovina	Croatia	Montenegro	North Macedonia	Serbia	Slovenia
Public service media/type of funding	RTVFBiH (*Radio and Television of the Federation of BiH*, one television channel (FTV) and one radio channel (*Radio Federation BiH*) RTRS (*Radio and Television of Republika Srpska*, one television and radio channel) BHRT (*Radio and Television of Bosnia and Herzegovina*, with BHTV1 and BH Radio 1)/License fee and advertising (RTRS since 2013 has possibility of financing from the state budget)	HRT (*Croatian Radio and Television*, Television branch HTV, radio HR)/License fee and advertising	RTCG (*Radio Television Montenegro*, two television channels)/Financed directly from the state budget (no fees collected) receives great amount of state advertising	MRT (*Macedonian Radio Television*)/License fee, advertising and state funds	RTS (*Radio Television Serbia*) RTV (*Radio Television Vojvodina*)/License fee and advertising, considerable amount of state budget support	RTVS (*Radio Television Slovenia*) Three national television channels and two regional channels/License fee and advertising
Dailies/ownership	*Dnevni avaz*/Domestic owners *Euro Blic*/Foreign owners, Serbian *Blic*, owned by Ringier Axel Springer Ltd. *Oslobođenje* (5%)/Domestic owners *24 sata*/Foreign owners, Croatian, owned by the Austrian company Styria.	*24 sata*/Foreign owners, Styria Medien AG *Večernji list*/Foreign owners, Styria Medien AG *Jutarnji list*/Domestic owners, Hanza Media *Slobodna Dalmacija*/Domestic owners, Hanza Media *Novi list*	*Vijesti*/Mixed, Media Development Investment Fund, USA, Styria from Austria and local owners *Dan*/Domestic ownership *Dnevne novine*/Mixed, Greek foreign investment connected with local owners *Pobjeda*/Mixed, Greek foreign investment connected with local	*Utrinski vesnik*/Domestic and foreign (regional) owners *Dnevnik*/Domestic and foreign (regional) owners *Vest*/Domestic and foreign (regional) owners *Nova Makedonija*/Domestic owners *Večer*/Domestic owners	*Blic*/Foreign, Ringier Axel Springer *Alo*/Foreign, Ringier Axel Springer *Večernje Novosti*/Domestic, state and local owners*	*Slovenske novice*/Domestic, Delo d.o.o. *Delo*/Domestic, Delo d.o.o. *Dnevnik*/Mixed *Večer*

	BiH	Croatia	Montenegro	Macedonia	Serbia	Slovenia
broadcasters/ownership	Mitrović; OBN/Foreign, Ivan Ćaleta; BN TV/Domestic, Jela and Vladimir Trišić; HAYAT TV/Domestic, affiliation N/A; N1, Adria News Sarl, United Media (cable)	Broadband S.a r.l (KKR); RTL TV/Foreign owners, RTL Group Central and Eastern Europe GmbH; N1, Adria News Sarl, United Media (cable)	Željko Mitrović; TV Vijesti/Mixed, Media Development Investment Fund, USA and local owners shares; TV Prva/Foreign, Antenna Group	Kanal 5/Domestic; Alsat – M/Mixed; Telma/Domestic, marketing company; Alfa/Domestic, export company	Željko Mitrović; PRVA/Mixed; B92/Mixed; Happy/Domestic; N1, Adria News Sarl, United Media (cable)	Kanal A/Foreign; Planet TV/Domestic, Telekom Slovenija
Main private radio broadcasters/ownership	Radio Kalman/affiliations N/A; Radio Starigrad/affiliations N/A	Otvoreni radio/Domestic; Narodni radio/Domestic; Antena radio/Domestic		Macedonian radio; Antena 5; Kanal 77; Metropolis	Radio S/Domestic; TDI Radio/Domestic; Radio Beograd/Domestic	Radio 1; Radio City; Radio Center
Main digital media outlets/ownership	Klix.ba Doznajemo.com; Haber.ba; Café.ba; Magazin.ba; Tuzlanski.ba; Nezavisne.com	24 sata online/Foreign, Styria Medien AG; Index.hr/Domestic; Jutarnji online/Domestic, Hanza Media; Net.hr/Foreign, RTL Group Central and Eastern Europe GmbH	Vijesti.me/daily Vijesti digital edition/Foreign; Cafédel Montenegro-cdm.me/Mixed, Greek foreign investment connected with local owners; Portalanalitika.me/Mixed, Greek foreign investment connected with local owners	A1 ON/Domestic; Brief/Domestic; Kurir/Domestic; Mkd.mk/Domestic; Novatv/Domestic; Netpress/Foreign, USA	Blic.rs; Kurir.rs; Telegraf.rs; Espreso.rs; Alo.rs	24ur.com/Foreign, ProPlus; zurnal24.si/Foreign, Styria Media International Gmbh; siol.net/Domestic, Telekom Slovenija; slovenskenovice.si Domestic, Delo d.o.o.

Sources: Milosavljević and Keršеvan Smokvina (2012), Hodžić (2014), Matić and Nedeljković (2014), Trpevska and Micevski (2014), Brkić (2015), Udovičić (2015), Petković et al. (2016).

Internet sources: Raziskava Branosti i Bralcev Slovenia 2018 (https://rbb.si/, accessed December 10, 2019), Merenje obiskalnosti spletnih stran (www.moss-soz.si/rezultati/, accessed December 10, 2019), Gemius Audience (for Serbia, November 2019, https://rating.gemius.com/rs/tree/32, accessed December 10, 2019), Mavise database (http://mavise.obs.coe.int/, accessed December 10, 2019), Agencija za elektroničke medije (for Croatia, www.aem.hr/, accessed November 22, 2019).

* The overview of the newspaper market and ownership is from Matić and Valić Nedeljković (2014). However, they did not include popular tabloids *Kurir*, *Informer* and *Naše novine* in their overview because their circulation was not audited. The authors commented the ownership structure of these tabloids: "Their owners (an individual owner in *Kurir*, journalists in other cases) are widely believed to be only formal representatives of the interest groups behind them. Kurir and Informer are associated with the interests of the ruling Serbian Progressive Party, while Naše novine is ascribed a link with tycoons" (Matić and Valić Nedeljković 2014, p. 351).

the "obligation to protect confidential sources or to maintain a separation between advertising and editorial content, as well as practical routines – common standards of 'newsworthiness,' for example – and criteria for judging excellence in professional practice and allocating professional prestige" (Hallin and Mancini 2004, p. 35). Due to a lack of "esoteric knowledge," the journalism profession derives its legitimacy largely from a public service orientation, which Hallin and Mancini (2004) consider to be the third marker of the journalism profession.

In the studied countries, journalists fulfill various roles from among the normative possibilities described by Christians et al. (2009). In Serbia, the division over professional norms became more pronounced during the 2000s following the emergence of the "retrograde" line of journalism, which adopted a pro-government stance, and the "progressive" one, which emphasized the role of journalists in social change (Vobič and Milojević 2012, p. 473). This divide in professional positions was noticeable in different media (institutionally) as well as among the journalism profession, and it is partly linked to the ownership factor. In Croatia, too, we also find cooperative journalist roles, especially during the 1990s and in the HRT in the periods of conservative right governments (during center-left governments the PBS was much more critical of the government and its policies). The investigative type of journalism was consistently developed by the weekly press (*Globus, Nacional, Feral Tribune*), by the independent daily press (*Novi list, Jutarnji list*), as well as by some local radio stations (for instance, Radio 101 in Zagreb). The neutral watchdog role is today performed by the mainstream commercial television stations and press, as well as by online news portals that predominantly venture into investigative journalism. The opposition and advocacy role is now primarily seen in community online media.

A recent study on journalism roles and values among journalism students in Croatia and Serbia notes that the most valued role is the neutral role of "a detached observer, who reports facts and provides information that will help people make informed decisions" while the watchdog role is perceived as being more important than providing commentary and opinion (Pjesivac and Imre 2018, p. 13). The Worlds of Journalism Study also notes that "reporting things as they are" is the highest appreciated value in both Croatia and Serbia (Peruško et al. 2016; Seizova and Rupar 2016; Andresen et al. 2017).

In her analysis of the transformation of journalism in Macedonia, Spasovska (2011) finds that there is a noticeable discrepancy between what is perceived as "ideal" in terms of normative conceptions of the journalism profession and what is practiced in reality. Similar duality can be seen among online journalists in Serbia and Slovenia, who recognize their watchdog role as well as the basic principles of "journalism ideology," but who are caught between commercial and political pressures (Vobič and Milojević 2014). The clientelist relationship between media owners and political elites also contributes to the dual understanding of journalism roles and practices, ranging from cooperation to conflict with political elites (Camaj 2016).

In Serbia, the sense of the diminishing public role of journalism is related to a change in the perspective of the profession and in the professional roles of journalists: "The idea of passionate advocacy for professionalism, public interest . . . was far more pronounced in Milošević era . . ." while the present attitude toward the profession is much more pragmatic.[40] Quality journalism and investigative journalists have been marginalized by the major media, and independent and investigative journalism has transferred to the online sphere, funded by international donations or the EU, and for that reason it is under government attack.[41] The notion of the journalist as an author is fading – there is less context, more copy-paste, less quality, less investigative journalism, less analysis, and less debate.[42]

With increasing influence of the digital media landscape, there has been a shift from the neutral or "objective" roles of journalists to the roles of "*infotainers*, who reduce structural problems to individual motivations by blending news and entertainment, and who neglect the factual and reliable daily accounts of matters relevant to political life" and the further diversification of journalism roles (Vobič and Milojević 2012, p. 473). This is noticeable in Slovenia, Croatia, and Serbia.

Mattoni and Ceccobelli (2018) offer two additional indicators for studying the transition of the journalism profession into the hybrid form. The changes include an atypical workforce (because an increasing part of the work is performed outside the newsroom) and training in digital literacy, which encapsulates the broad range of ICT skills needed for professional practices. Journalism is changed under economic and technological pressures, and it is now being adapted to trends such as "new affordances of news websites (instantaneity, multimodality, interactivity, and hypertextuality), radical commercialization, increased audience participation in news production, and multiskilling," which renders it more dependent on audience attention (Kunelius and Reunanen 2016, p. 13).

Although the challenges of the digitalization of the media systems are equally evident in the CEE, the journalism profession in Southeast Europe is additionally burdened by the difficult economic position of the region as well as by declining job security and salaries (Car 2016, p. 164; Milojević and Krstić 2018; Trpevska and Micevski 2018). The low socio-economic position and precariousness associated with the profession have led to the prevalence of self-censorship practices (Trpevska and Micevski 2018). The socio-economic position of journalists is somewhat better in Slovenia (Lah and Žilič-Fišer 2012). As is the case with other professions that have lost their social and economic status, journalism in Southeast Europe is increasingly dominated by women (Lah and Žilič-Fišer 2012; Car 2016; Peruško et al. 2016; Seizova and Rupar 2016). The profession is becoming increasingly precarious and flexible, with more journalists working on temporary contracts or as freelancers. In Slovenia, almost a third of journalists work

182   Toward democracy

without a standard employment contract (Hrženjak 2019). Union membership is rather low in some countries: only a third of journalists are members of a union in Serbia (Milivojević et al. 2012), while less than half are in Slovenia (Lah and Žilič-Fišer 2012).

Political parallelism is also reflected in journalists' associations, and the political parties informally assist in creating new associations when they are unable to dominate the established autonomous ones. For example, in Serbia, there are three journalists' associations: UNS (Udruženje novinara Srbije), NUNS (Nezavisno udruženje novinara Srbije), and NDNV (Nezavisno društvo novinara Vojvodine). Both NUNS and NDNV are frequently attacked by the Serbian tabloid media (Ranković 2019). In North Macedonia, the main journalists' association has been revitalized and now tries to pressure the government through protests as well as cooperation with international associations and institutions. However, a parallel, progovernment association has been formed, which supports all government decisions. Such GONGOs[43] are formed by governments "to simulate civic sector and professional organizations," and in that way, to pacify or diminish the efforts of critical civil society.[44] In Slovenia, after its journalists' association (Društvo novinarjev Slovenije) led a movement campaigning for the freedom of the media in the late 2000s, a parallel institution (Association of Journalists and Writers [ZNP]) was formed in 2007, which adopted a pro-government stance. In Croatia, the long-standing journalists' association of which the majority of Croatian journalists are members is the Croatian Association of Journalists (Hrvatsko novinarsko društvo, HND), which was a very active leader of civil society groups in the 1990s in advocating media freedom, autonomy, and the standards of the profession. A new parallel institution (HNiP) was established in 2015, and it engages in public attacks on critical media and journalists. The number of members is kept secret, although it is rumored to be fewer than 20. HNiP members occupied most of the top editorial positions within the HRT and some within the AEM after the purge of independent editors conducted by the conservative government in 2015.

The self-regulation of the media is weak, although in some countries self-regulatory institutions serve an important role in the media system. In Slovenia, the *Novinarsko častno razsodišče* (Ethics Commission of Journalists) is a self-regulatory body shared between the Slovenian Journalism Association and the journalists' union. In Croatia, the *Novinarsko vijeće časti* (Ethics Council) is a self-regulatory body under the auspices of the Croatian Journalism Association. In Serbia, the *Savet za štampu* (Serbian Press Council) was established in 2009; however, it is not highly regarded by the public.[45] The *Vijeće za štampu* (Press Council) was established in Bosnia and Herzegovina in 2006, and the Ethics Council operates under the leadership of the Association of Journalists of Macedonia. In Montenegro, journalists' associations are not active in the area of self-regulation, so the Media Self-Regulation Council was set up by the government in 2012 to monitor print, broadcast, and online media with the aim of raising awareness of ethical standards within the media. On the ground, it is seen as an additional instrument for censoring media organizations that are more critical of the government.[46] While the ethics councils of independent journalists' associations play an important role in setting and maintaining journalists' professional standards, publishers are often not interested in their rulings. The success in achieving increased professional values, ethical reporting, and editorial autonomy will not come from government-established press councils whose opinions would be legally binding because, as in the contexts of flawed democracies or hybrid regimes, they would be a new path toward the practice of censorship.

Media culture and global communication flows

As the basis for television programming in all television systems and on all television channels, irrespective of their character (public, private, state, community) or of the political or cultural environment, genre (Berger 1992) figures as a common structural dimension for grouping countries with similar or dissimilar media cultures (Bourdon 2011; Peruško and Čuvalo 2014). A comparative content analysis of broadcast TV programs was conducted in order to gauge the differences or similarities in television cultures between the analyzed countries, where generic composition of broadcasting was seen as the key indicator of television cultures that relate also to the audience preferences (see the Methodological Appendix for technical details). Our findings present a comparative snapshot of the similarities and differences among the countries, based on the analysis of the selected commercial and PSB TV channels. Contemporary TV cultures were also compared in terms of transnational flows, which were analyzed through the origin of the program production.

Marked differences in genre distribution are visible in the analyzed television channels, but the major television channels in the six studied countries are, for the most part, dominated by the entertainment genres. The genres with the highest average shares in the region are film and reality programs (both at 11%), although with large variance between countries. The highest share of film is found in the Serbian TV market (18%), while the lowest is found in North Macedonia (1%) and Bosnia and Herzegovina (2%). North Macedonia is also low on drama (2%), as the average for the region is 8%. The TV program genres with the highest share in Bosnia and Herzegovina are (mostly Turkish) soap operas with 20% and reality programs with 17%, which are the highest shares in the entire region. At the same time, Northern Macedonian television broadcasts the most current affairs (18%) and cultural programs (7%).

Contemporary TV cultures are, expectedly, more versatile than during the socialist period. Aside from democratizing, these TV cultures also changed during the transition of television, as a medium, in concert with the increased commercialization (Eco 1983; Missika 2006), thereby reflecting (albeit with some delay) Western European developments.

184 *Toward democracy*

Table 5.4 Genre distribution on commercial and PSB TV channels 2016 (% of daily minutes, one-week consecutive sample)

	Bosnia and Herzegovina	Croatia	North Macedonia	Montenegro	Serbia	Slovenia	Average
Breakfast TV	0%	1%	8%	6%	2%	5%	3%
Chat and talk shows	2%	4%	6%	4%	2%	7%	4%
Children's	9%	7%	5%	6%	9%	8%	8%
Comedy	6%	11%	0%	2%	5%	3%	5%
Cultural programs	1%	1%	7%	4%	5%	2%	3%
Current affairs	4%	4%	18%	14%	11%	7%	9%
Documentary	5%	5%	4%	8%	6%	4%	5%
Drama	10%	10%	2%	6%	8%	7%	8%
Film	2%	14%	1%	9%	18%	12%	11%
Media and popular culture	10%	8%	9%	10%	3%	5%	7%
Music	3%	5%	7%	5%	2%	6%	5%
News	7%	9%	5%	7%	6%	9%	8%
Reality programs	17%	13%	7%	8%	14%	9%	11%
Religious	0%	1%	0%	0%	0%	1%	0%
Soap operas	20%	5%	12%	7%	3%	8%	8%
Sport	4%	2%	9%	4%	6%	7%	5%
TOTAL TIME (minutes)	26,157	39,183	19,408	25,577	38,100	35,562	183,987

Source: Authors.

The composition of the three program modes of information (a composite category that now included cultural and educational programs, current affairs, documentaries, news, and religious programs), entertainment (this category included breakfast TV, chat and talk shows, children's shows, media and popular culture, music [not classical or jazz], reality programs, and media and popular culture as light entertainment), and fiction (this category included comedy and drama series, films, and soap operas) is changed with regard to the comparative sample during the era of socialism. The first thing we notice is the appearance of certain genres not present in the first sample – most notably, religious programs, soap operas, breakfast TV, and reality TV (Table 5.4). In all the analyzed countries, entertainment programs are prevalent on the examined TV stations. The highest shares of entertainment are found in North Macedonia (51%), while the lowest are found in Serbia (38%). The information mode has the smallest shares in Bosnia and Herzegovina (16%) and the highest shares in Montenegro and North Macedonia (34% each). Croatia and Bosnia and Herzegovina (39% and 38%, respectively) have relatively high shares of fictional programs, while North Macedonia (16%) has the lowest share of fictional programs (see Figure 5.4).

Toward democracy 185

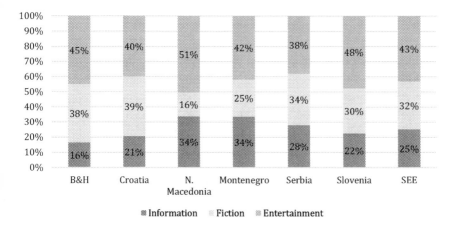

Figure 5.4 Distribution of information, fiction, and entertainment programming on commercial and PSB TV in 2016 (% daily minutes, one-week consecutive sample)

All the PSB channels broadcast more information programs than the top commercial channels. The difference between the shares of the information mode on PSB and commercial channels is the smallest in North Macedonia (9%), while it is the biggest in Montenegro, where the share of information programs on commercial channels is 2%, compared to 52% on PSB channels. This Macedonian finding could be explained by the fact that its top commercial channel was, at that time, oppositional and dedicated to the largest national minority (Albanians). The Northern Macedonian, Slovenian, and Croatian PSB channels broadcast more genres in the entertainment mode than the commercial channels, while the opposite is true in the other three states, where commercial channels are more entertainment oriented than PSB channels. The Slovenian and Croatian commercial broadcasters compete with the PSB channels through their strong orientation toward fictional programs (Slovenian 56%, Croatian 51%). In comparison, Montenegrin public television is high on information programs (52%) and low on fiction (18%) and entertainment, while its commercial channels are high on entertainment (63%) and low on information (2%). Bosnian and Herzegovinian PSB has the most evenly distributed program modes within the region. The Croatian public and commercial television stations are more oriented toward fictional programs than the television stations in neighboring countries. In North Macedonia, Serbia, and Croatia, the competition between PSB channels and commercial broadcasters is strongest in relation to entertainment programs, while in Bosnia and Herzegovina it is strongest with regard to fictional programs.

The Serbian Pink television station, with its distinctive aesthetics and discourse, is an example of a specific media culture, the "Pink culture," which mixes sexism and nationalism (Kronja 2016, in Volčić 2013, p. 336). Pink television is one of the pioneers of the reality genre in Serbia, and it is exported to several neighboring countries. Television in the successor Yugoslav states often provides reruns of entertainment and fiction television programs from the Yugoslav period, which attract older generations (Vesnić-Alujević and Bajić 2013). The cable channel Klasik TV specializes in content produced mostly during the time of socialism. However, nostalgia not only targets older audiences: the production of the series such as *Crno-bijeli svijet* by Croatian public television utilizes also the nostalgic narratives of the socialist past.

The national TV markets are dominated by programs of national origin, albeit not to the same degree. The largest amount of programs produced within the country is found in the case of Macedonia (88%), then in Serbia and Slovenia (66% each), followed by Montenegro (62%), Croatia (55%), and Bosnia and Herzegovina (46%). Bosnia and Herzegovina has the highest share (24%) of programs from countries outside of Europe and the United States, mostly from Turkey. Croatia has the highest share of programs from the EU (20%), while Serbia and Slovenia have the highest share from the United States (22% and 19%, respectively).

Program imports among the six countries in the region are limited (Table 5.5). The highest shares of regional programs are found in Bosnia and Herzegovina (16%) and Montenegro (7%), while other countries have relatively low shares of regionally produced programs (ranging from 0% in Macedonia to 3% in Slovenia). The commercial channels are more oriented toward regional flows than the public TV channels, with the exception of North Macedonia, where no regionally produced programs were found. While TV productions of the six countries seem to be more oriented toward the domestic market, some transnational regional flows were detected, revealing certain specialization on the part of countries in terms of cultural production. Music, comedies, reality programs, and soap operas are the genres that most easily cross the borders of the TV markets of the six countries. Croatia was the regional leader in the production and export of comedies and soap operas, while Serbia was the leader in the production and export of reality programs and comedy and drama series.

Although a significant amount of foreign programs are broadcast on the analyzed television stations, the impact of globalization on media content does not primarily occur through terrestrial television. Television cultures also changed in response to the altered digital media environment, which saw audiovisual content readily available not only thorough a multichannel television environment available via increasingly widespread cable delivery but also through new "television" platforms such as the international streaming channel Netflix, Disney, HBO, and YouTube. Similar to

Table 5.5 Origins of broadcasts on commercial and PSB TV in 2016 (% daily minutes, one-week consecutive sample)

	Bosnia and Herzegovina	Croatia	North Macedonia	Montenegro	Serbia	Slovenia
Bosnia and Herzegovina	46%	0%	0%	0%	1%	0%
Croatia	8%	55%	0%	2%	1%	2%
Macedonia	0%	0%	78%	0%	0%	0%
Montenegro	1%	0%	0%	62%	0%	0%
Serbia	7%	1%	0%	5%	66%	1%
Slovenia	0%	0%	0%	0%	0%	66%
EU	7%	20%	1%	15%	7%	8%
US	8%	14%	8%	5%	22%	19%
Other	24%	9%	9%	10%	2%	5%
TOTAL TIME	26,157	39,183	19,408	25,577	38,100	35,562

Source: Authors.

news cultures, which are increasingly composed of a repertoire of sources and choices that often remain stable for individuals with similar interests (Hasebrink and Domeyer 2012) the choice of entertainment repertoires also affects media cultures across different countries. It was beyond the scope of this study to investigate these newly conceptualized parameters of digital media cultures, and thus television cultures stand in for all the other missing data as elements of the national media system that are still visible and subject to policy and regulation. That said, we must be aware that however important television remains as a source of news (Reuters Digital News Report 2019) and entertainment, new conceptualizations followed by new research are needed to allow for the comparison of digital media cultures.

Among the Southeast European countries, Croatia, Serbia, and Slovenia are the most connected to globalization flows, and they are the most engaged in cultural trade (with Slovenia clearly having the strongest lead; see the data on globalization and cultural trade in Table 5.1). As small markets, the Croatian and Slovenian media markets are strongly influenced by non-domestic actors, mostly originating from the United States or Germany (Schneeberger 2019). Yet despite being peripheral in global cultural flows, Serbia is becoming a kind of regional center of cultural media production in the Balkans (Schneeberger 2019). As an illustration, Table 5.3 shows that US or German ownership of television media outlets is more prevalent in Croatia and Slovenia, while the other countries in the region are dominated by regional owners, mostly from Serbia.

Conclusion

One of the starting questions in this book concerned the legacy of socialism in the present-day media systems of the new European democracies. Obviously, we would not look for the influence of the communist legacy if all was well with the democratic transitions (Županov 1996). The difficulty of comparing, as defined in Chapter 2, was here exhibited in its original form when questioning the possibility of applying the media systems theoretical model to the analysis of media systems in societies that followed a different modernization path. The challenge we faced in this chapter was understanding whether the institutional changes (both formal and informal) after socialism reflect or represent a continuation of previous institutional designs and cultural practices, or perhaps even earlier solutions and values from the temporal framework that preceded socialism, or whether they are new solutions borrowed from the Western role models during the process of policy transfer.

The particularity of the post-Yugoslav democratic transformations concerned the fact that there was not only a regime change but also a collapse of the multinational state, which involved outright wars that seriously affected four of the six analyzed countries. This also influenced the transformations in that they were not only (or, perhaps, not primarily) liberal and democratic transformations, but rather transformations that primarily aimed to finish the process of national state formation (cf. Šonje and Polšek 2019). The contestation of the new states of Croatia and Bosnia and Herzegovina by Serbia and the JNA delayed the start of the liberal and democratic transitions in the affected countries. Croatia was, due to its better range of conditions, including the finalization of the statehood project with an overwhelming consensus, able to overcome this delay and join the EU. While Montenegro followed a similar path, Serbia and Kosovo remain locked in the statehood debate, which is blocking the liberalization and democratization of both polities. North Macedonia has made great strides in 2019 and is now expecting some positive news regarding its EU integration, while Bosnia and Herzegovina remains a foreign protectorate and so faces threats to its fragile statehood.

Although the economic transformation was considered the most difficult part for the countries formerly characterized by state socialism, the Yugoslavian self-management style of market socialism meant that the print media were already exposed to the market, while radio and television broadcasting had independent management bodies, albeit within the constraints of the socialist ideology and the Communist Party's oversight. The predispositions for the transformation of the media system into a market-based media system with public service broadcasting were thus much better than in the countries that were members of the Warsaw Pact. This expectation did not materialize, however, and the Southeast European countries continue to achieve less positive freedom of the media scores than the CEE countries.

With regard to the transformations of the cultural field, the social and political values continue the diversity seen during the previous period, in which Slovenia and Croatia exhibited more modern and post-materialist values than the other four countries. In terms of their media system transformations, the socialist temporal framework is continued as three countries – Slovenia, Croatia, and Serbia – continue to dominate in relation to market development, with the latter country having even expanded its leadership position as a regional exporter of television programs, especially to Montenegro and Bosnia and Herzegovina. In terms of the transformations of the political aspects impacting the autonomy and professionalization of the journalism profession, we find that transformations in the media field follow democratic consolidation. While both Slovenia and Croatia are considered to be liberal democracies, Croatia exhibits more problems caused by the (renewed) capture of the public service broadcaster by the conservative government and the misuse of libel protection to exert pressure on independent journalists. Both these countries sport pluralist and autonomous, professional mainstream media, while polarization appears in smaller, often Internet-based media.

The challenge in this chapter was to apply the dimensions and variables used thus far to analyze these media systems in a rapidly changing environment in which, for some countries, the rapid changes are still ongoing. While democratization was the expected outcome for both politics and media systems, alongside the accompanying privatization of the economy, we show that the media systems of Slovenia, Croatia, Bosnia and Herzegovina, Serbia, Montenegro, and Macedonia were transformed into diverse types of media systems, with the relationship between the media and the state, the character of political parallelism, the level of journalistic professionalism, the media market, and the participation in global cultural flows all taking different shapes.

When comparing these countries' media systems within this temporal framework in an attempt to apply or create media system typologies, different classification criteria have produced different results. In the first operationalization of Hallin and Mancini's (2004) typology, Peruško et al. (2013; Peruško 2016) found that all the countries except for Slovenia clustered in the Southeast European model together with Greece, Spain, Lithuania, Italy, Hungary, and Russia, while Slovenia clustered in the European mainstream model with Austria, Poland, Belgium, Ireland, and Portugal (see Table 1.1). That initial operationalization did not include the countries' political systems, which was identified as a flaw (Peruško 2016). In terms of the digital media systems that place more emphasis on digital media markets and global flows, all six countries clustered together with Greece and Portugal in the least affluent European cluster (Peruško et al. 2015). In a similar albeit more elaborate operationalization of the macro-level mediatization of the media system, Slovenia separated into the convergent cluster with more developed countries from east and west Europe, while Croatia, Serbia, and

North Macedonia clustered in the European peripheral cluster of countries with less affluent digital media markets together with Greece, Poland, and Czechia (Montenegro and Bosnia and Herzegovina were not included in this analysis due to a lack of data) (Peruško 2017; Peruško et al. 2017). Both these operationalizations included the quality of democracy. Castro Herrero et al. (2017), in an adaptation of Brüggemann et al.'s (2014) typology, as based on the work of Hallin and Mancini (2004), identifies three clusters of CEE countries, with Croatia and Slovenia clustering together in the central cluster with Poland and Czechia (the remaining four of our six countries of interest were not included in the analysis). Dobek-Ostrowska (2015) classifies the countries primarily in regard to the democracy index – Slovenia is classified in the hybrid liberal model (with the most advanced democracy rating) alongside Poland, Czechia, and Slovakia. Further, she places Croatia and Serbia in the politicized media model with Hungary, Romania, and Bulgaria, while the media in transition model includes Moldova, Macedonia, Montenegro, Albania, and Bosnia and Herzegovina. Clearly, the conceptualization of what defines a media system, as well as what dimensions or conditions describe such a system, critically influence both the placement of the countries and the typologies themselves. Perhaps the key question concerns not how the countries cluster in different groups, but rather why they do so. This is the topic of the final chapter.

Notes

1 These findings primarily pertain to Croatia, as ethnic intolerance between the Serbs and Albanians in Kosovo, as well as between the Albanians and Macedonians in Macedonia, preceded the conflicts.
2 As most academic books on Yugoslavia focus on conflict and war (some 300 were listed in WorldCat as of November 2019), we would like to direct readers interested in this topic to consult this extensive bibliography.
3 The basic social value orientations include conservatism vs. autonomy (intellectual and affective), hierarchy vs. egalitarianism, and harmony vs. mastery (Schwartz and Bardi 1997). The study was conducted on a sample of Western and Central and Eastern European countries in the aftermath of the 1989 revolutions. The sample (nonrepresentative, teachers and students) only included Slovenia from among the countries studied in this book.
4 In 2008, the European Value Survey showed the low prevalence of post-materialist values: 3.5% in Bosnia and Herzegovina, 8.2% in Croatia, 10.4% in Macedonia, 6.1% in Montenegro, 5.8% in Serbia, and the highest, 13.9% in Slovenia. Over the course of one decade, the share of post-materialist values doubled.
5 Slovenia held its first media referendum in 2005 to affirm the new *Law on public television*, which introduced the dominant role of parliament in electing members of the PSM management bodies, rather than the previous model involving direct election by civil society organizations. The second referendum was held in 2010 with the aim of changing the *Law on public television*, which was rejected by 72.33% of votes, albeit following a very low turnout (Referendum 2010).
6 Authors' interview with Mirna Buljugić, December 2016.
7 Important analyses of various CEE media systems, but not Southeast European media systems, include Sükösd and Bajomi-Lázár (2003); Dobek-Ostrowska

Toward democracy 191

et al. (2010); Downey and Mihelj (2012); Jebril et al. (2013); Bajomi-Lázár (2014); Dobek-Ostrowska and Głowacki (2014); Zielonka (2015); and Bajomi-Lázár (2017). In Chapter 4, we mentioned some monographs dealing with the media in socialist Yugoslavia (Robinson 1977; Mihelj and Huxtable 2018; Zubak 2018).

8 The EU regularly monitors the advance of the media and freedom of expression in its yearly country reports. https://ec.europa.eu/neighbourhood-enlargement/countries/package_en.
9 In 1990, the Croatian Parliament adopted the Council of Europe Resolution 428 on human rights (1970) with the *Declaration on the mass media and human rights*, Recommendation No. 834 (1978) relating to the dangers to the freedom of the press and television, Recommendation No. R(81)19 with the Annex (1981) on access to official information, and the *Declaration on the freedom of expression and information* (1982).
10 Authors' interview with Snežana Trpevska, December 2016.
11 The new laws adopted during this period are presented in Table 5.3. The regulatory agency known as the Broadcasting Agency of the Republic of Serbia was established, although it failed to function properly (Milivojević 2005, p. 1321). The transformation of the RTS from state to public broadcaster was slow and problematic, lacking a sufficiently developed regulatory framework and institutions (Milivojević 2005, p. 1322).
12 This section benefited from the concepts and models included in the UNESCO Media Development Indicators UNESCO 2008, UNESCO, Paris.
13 Croatia adopted its new constitution in 1990, Macedonia and Slovenia in 1991, the FRY (which included today's Kosovo, Montenegro, and Serbia) in 1992, and Bosnia and Herzegovina in 1995. The new Constitution of Serbia was adopted in 2006 and the Constitution of Montenegro in 2007, and Kosovo became the newest independent state in 2008. Macedonia amended its constitution in 2001 following the Ohrid Framework Agreement. In addition to the Constitution of Bosnia and Herzegovina, its federal units each have their own constitutions (Constitution of the Federation of Bosnia-Herzegovina and Constitution of the Republika Srpska). All these constitutional documents guarantee the freedom of expression.
14 Membership in the Council of Europe: Slovenia in 1993, North Macedonia in 1995, Croatia in 1996, Bosnia and Herzegovina in 2002, Serbia in 2003, Montenegro in 2007. The countries ratified the European Convention on Transfrontier Television in the following years: Slovenia in 1999, Croatia in 2001, North Macedonia in 2003, Bosnia and Herzegovina in 2005, Montenegro in 2008, and Serbia in 2009.
15 DG Enlargement Guidelines for EU support for media freedom and media integrity in enlargement countries, 2014–2020. https://ec.europa.eu/neighbourhood-enlargement/sites/near/files/pdf/press_corner/elarg-guidelinesfor-mediafreedom-and-integrity_210214.pdf.
16 Three provisions in the Dayton Peace Agreement relate to the media:

> First, the Constitution (Article III.1.h) provides that common State institutions should be in charge of creating and running common and international communication facilities. Another is the provision (in Annex 7, Article 1.3.b) which stipulates that the signatories of the DPA shall prevent any incitement of ethnic or religious hostility through the media. The third is the signatories' agreement to "ensure that conditions exist for the organization of free and fair elections, in particular a politically neutral environment [. . .] [and] freedom of expression and of the press" (Annex 3, Article 1.1).
>
> (Jusić 2005, pp. 263–264).

17 Authors' interview with Snežana Trpevska, December 2016.

192 *Toward democracy*

18 Concerns over the large number of lawsuits filed against the media were expressed in the interviews with Borka Rudić (Bosnia and Herzegovina), Paško Bilić and Hrvoje Zovko (Croatia), and Marijana Camović (Montenegro).
   More than 1,000 lawsuits were in process in Croatia at the time of the discussion with Hrvoje Zovko (March 2019).
19 Authors' interview with Borka Rudić, December 2016.
20 In Croatia, in 2011, the "shaming" clause was introduced into the Penal Code which allowed lawsuits against journalists even when they published true information. While this clause was modified by the subsequent center-left government (Peruško 2011) and was after this only moderately used as the basis for law-suits, it was completely dropped from the legislation only in 2019.
21 In Bosnia and Herzegovina, procedures concerning the media at the lower court levels often result in rulings diminishing media freedom, as judges are not sufficiently educated with regard to the practice of the European Court of Human Rights (assessment by Borka Rudić, who was interviewed by the authors in December 2016). In Montenegro, defamation is decriminalized, although there have been lawsuits against various media, with different rulings in different cases. The court ruled against the media when they were reporting the case of Milo Đukanović's sister, who was allegedly involved in a corruption scandal concerning the privatization of telecommunications. The court ruled against the media, which were alleged to have harmed her reputation (from the interview with Marijana Camović, December 2016). In North Macedonia, there was a prominent case of a lawsuit filed against a media outlet during the wiretapping scandal. The director of the surveillance agency, who was a relative of then Prime Minister Gruevski, sued a critical media outlet for defamation, with the court ruling against the media outlet, which had to pay a large fine for defamation (from the interview with Snežana Trpevska, December 2016).
22 In Montenegro, criminal defamation of the state could be penalized by a custodial sentence, while criminal defamation of foreign states and blasphemy/religious insult also remain as incriminations (OSCE 2017). In North Macedonia, some provisions within the *Law on civil liability for defamation and insult* and the Criminal Code are not harmonized with the case law of the European Court of Human Rights, which increases the risk of a "chilling effect" for journalists (Trpevska and Micevski 2018). Criminal defamation of the state, foreign states, and foreign heads of states is still retained (OSCE 2017). In Serbia, insult and the exposure of private and family life remains in the Criminal Code (Surčulija Milojević 2018).
23 Authors' interview with Borka Rudić, December 2016.
24 Authors' interview with Vladan Mićunović, December 2016.
25 The satirical comment in question was directed toward a notorious right-wing Croatian journalist and was ruled to be defamation. This kind of court ruling is to a great extent the result of a misinterpretation of existing laws protecting freedom of speech. This is also a regression in respect to the 1990s, when judges ruled in similar cases involving *Feral Tribune*, the satirical oppositional weekly, in protection of satirical expression and critique of politicians citing the relevant case law of the European convention on human rights.
26 Authors' interviews with Igor Vobič (June 2017) and Brankica Petković (May 2019).
27 Authors' interviews with Paško Bilić and Hrvoje Zovko, March 2019.
28 Authors' interviews with Dragan Janjić (December 2016) and Snježana Milivojević and Antonela Riha (November 2015).
29 Although the broadcasters in Montenegro are required to produce 10% of their own content, content can be imported from Serbian commercial television, such as Pink. Authors' interview with Marijana Camović, December 2016.

30 Authors' interviews with Brankica Petković (May 2019) and Igor Vobič (June 2017).
31 Authors' interviews with Marijana Camović and Vladan Mićunović, December 2016.
32 Authors' interview with Snježana Milivojević, November 2015.
33 Authors' interview with Brankica Petković, May 2019.
34 Authors' interview with Brankica Petković, May 2019.
35 Authors' interview with Marijana Camović and Vladan Mićunović, December 2016.
36 Authors' interview with Vladan Mićunović, December 2016. As he states, "Everyone brave enough to oppose the government can expect to be 'crucified' in this news program in the most horrifying way."
37 Authors' interview with Brankica Petković, May 2019.
38 Authors' interview with Borka Rudić, December 2016.
39 Authors' interview with Brankica Petković, May 2019.
40 Authors' interview with Dragan Janjić, December 2016.
41 Authors' interview with Snježana Milivojević, November 2015.
42 Authors' interview with Antonela Riha, November 2015.
43 Authors' interview with Besim Nebiu December 2016.
44 Authors' interview with Snežana Trpevska, December 2016.
45 Authors' interview with Dragan Janjić, December 2016.
46 Authors' interview with Marijana Camović, December 2016.

6 Why the media systems are the way they are

As Downey and Stanyer (2013) rightly point out, no previous study has actually explained "why media systems are the way they are" (Hallin and Mancini 2004, p. 14). Such an explanation can only be achieved through a research study designed to uncover the causal paths and solutions associated with media system development and transformation. While Hallin and Mancini (2004) provided the research community with a model describing the key dimensions that define media systems, which continues to maintain its status as mainstream science, their model lacks the power to explain what conditions (and what combinations of those conditions) lead to certain media system outcomes and types, especially outside the set of Western countries analyzed by the authors. After 30 years, we can see diverse developments and outcomes with regard to the media independence and autonomy of the emerging post-socialist democracies. What shaped these diverse developments? Why did some countries consolidate both democracy and independent media, while others developed hybrid or authoritarian regimes and media systems? The theoretical framework and research design that we employ in this book attempts to answer such questions.

We argue that the causal configurations that impact present-day media systems are influenced by the *longue durée*, and that these influences extend from the period of modernization and from the period of socialism. Our theoretical approach is grounded in the historical institutionalist comparative analysis (Mahoney 2000; Skocpol and Pierson 2002; Humphreys 2012; Peruško 2016), where the two historical temporal frameworks are examined as contextual conditions that set the stage for the next set of institutional and cultural conditions associated with media system transformations following the collapse of communism. Applying a set-theoretical research approach, the analysis employs the conditions from three temporal frameworks and three fields of power – the political field, the socio-economic field, and the cultural-symbolic field – alongside a number of dimensions that are familiar from the mainstream media systems theory introduced by Hallin and Mancini (2004), albeit with certain necessary adaptations and extensions. Using a fuzzy set qualitative comparative analysis (fsQCA) (Ragin 2008; Schneider and Wagemann 2012; Downey and Stanyer 2013; Büchel et al. 2016), this final chapter of the book presents the causal configurations of the conditions and paths leading to different outcomes in terms of media system transformations in Southeast Europe during the era of digital modernity that explain why the media systems are the way they are.

Calibrating the conditions within media systems across three temporal frameworks: the design of the fsQCA

The usual media system terminology was adapted to reflect the new set-theoretical methodological approach and research framework, meaning that instead of discussing variables we discuss conditions and outcomes. We started out with the idea of investigating a set of formerly socialist countries that were all parts of one state during the socialist temporal framework and then all independent countries afterwards. This approach was intended to ensure that the influence of socialism on the post-socialist media systems in question would be of the same type. In line with our theoretical understanding of social change from the *longue durée* perspective and in relation to the HI approach with the exchange of critical junctures and path dependency, we identified those causal conditions from the two previous temporal frameworks that contribute to different "solutions" of causal configurations, which differentiate among the media systems that were developed in the third-wave democracies of Southeast Europe.

Our final analysis builds on the steps that we undertook in the preceding chapters, including the three comparative case studies of the six media systems during the three temporal frameworks, following our theoretical idea that the *longue durée* of political, social, and cultural development plays a significant role in contemporary media systems, and further, that the actual influence of these historical conditions had the possibility of being altered – reversed or redirected – at each critical juncture that occurred through policy and/or political action. In Chapter 2 we discussed the reasons for choosing the set-theoretical approach to media systems analysis due to it being superior to the functionalistic approach of linear causal inference (Downey and Stanyer 2010). As Downey and Stanyer (2013) note, the difference between this approach and the more common approach of variable-based comparative research is that "rather than seeing variables as independent, it sees conditions as mutually reinforcing" (p. 498). Moreover, as Ragin (2008) summarizes:

> Set relations in social research (1) involve causal or other integral connections linking social phenomena (i.e., are not merely definitional), (2) are theory and knowledge dependent (i.e., require explication), (3) are central to social science theorizing (because theory is primarily verbal in nature, and verbal statements are often set theoretic), (4) are asymmetric (and thus should not be reformulated as correlational arguments), and (5) can be very strong despite relatively modest correlations.
> (p. 17)

The QCA approach acknowledges that two causal conditions may have different relationships in different contexts; therefore, a contextual analysis is important in terms of explaining causality (Dolenec 2013b, p. 110). A QCA also rests on the notion of equifinality, that is, the possibility that different conditions, or different combinations of conditions, can produce the same outcomes, or that similar conditions do not necessarily produce similar outcomes. For example, the success of the consolidation of democracy, or of media freedom, could be an outcome of different conditions or different combinations of conditions. Here we are clearly opting out of any kind of determinism when it comes to explaining media system developments. Asymmetry is the second important notion underpinning the QCA approach, as it allows for the fact that the existence of one type of relationship between certain conditions does not exclude the existence of other possible relationships. For example, if the relationship between development and democracy is established, it does not exclude the fact that undeveloped countries could also be democratic (Ragin 2008, p. 15). This is different from, for example, the notion of correlation, which presupposes a positive or negative linear relationship between development and democracy (Ragin 2008, p. 15).

The causal analysis associated with the QCA approach is also grounded in set theory and its logic of necessary and sufficient conditions. Necessary conditions are those whose absence makes the outcome impossible, but whose presence is not, on its own, a guarantee that the outcome will occur. Sufficient conditions can appear in different path configurations when they produce certain outcomes. While both these types of conditions play a role in the fsQCA analysis (Ragin 2008), Goertz and Mahoney (2005) highlight the role of the conjuncture of necessary conditions as the basis for the main level of a given social theory, while the secondary level of that theory is described by the configuration of sufficient conditions in the process of equifinality in which the desired (or predicted) outcome is arrived at via different paths.

A QCA can be based on either crisp sets (where the condition and the outcome variables are dichotomous or binary, that is, one is either a member of the set or not) or fuzzy sets (where the condition and the outcome variables feature more categories or are continuous). In fuzzy sets, the kind of analysis used in this book (i.e., the closest to the actual empirical world, which is more often fuzzy than crisp), the value of a case in a given category is determined by the researcher's calibration based on certain external standards (Ragin 2008). This calibration is performed by assigning "membership in sets using values in the interval between 0.0 (nonmembership) and 1.0 (full membership)" (Ragin 2008, p. 29). More specifically, the researcher can develop an ordinal scheme marking the scale, or degree, of membership of a certain category. For example, countries can be (1) full members of the democracy set (value 1), (2) fully not members of the democracy set (value 0), (3) to the same degree members and non-members of the democracy set (value 0.5), (4) more out of the democracy set than a member of that set (e.g., value 0.25), or (5) more a member of the democracy set than out of that set (e.g., value 0.75). The conditions that are calibrated (measured) in this way are subsequently analyzed using fsQCA software. In all the analyses that follow, we use the fsQCA software developed by Ragin et al. (2006), which is available for free download at www.socsci.uci.edu/~cragin/fsQCA/software.shtml.

Despite the calibrations/measurements and the use of quantitative data in some instances, the analysis must be understood as being predominantly interpretative and qualitative, even if a QCA is sometimes seen as being halfway between qualitative and quantitative research. The calibration decisions are made by the researchers on the basis of both substantive and theoretical knowledge, and the software only aids in sorting the different combinations of conditions and paths that are beyond the capacity of the human mind (the number of possible combinations is 2^n, where n is the number of conditions; in our study, the number of combinations for the original 38 conditions is greater than 274 billion). The primary instrument used to assess the causal relationship through a fuzzy set is the truth table, which enables the comparison of the different combinations of conditions that lead to an expected outcome (Ragin 2008, p. 23). A truth table is theoretically informed in that theoretical assumptions determine the selection of the conditions and the outcomes. All the relevant truth tables from the following analyses are provided in the Methodological Appendix.

We faced several challenges in relation to the chosen theoretical approach and research design. The design employed in our study is particularly novel, involving six comparative units across three different points in time. Chang et al. (2001, p. 418) found no similar (or even "two-by-two") comparative studies in their analysis of over 150 comparative studies in the field of mass communication. Over the 30-year period they surveyed, the studies mainly involved the spatial cross-cultural or cross-national comparison of two social units at one point in time. In recent years, multi-country comparative studies of communication phenomena have increased in frequency (cf. Esser and Hanitzsch 2012), although only a few such studies have employed a comparative design involving multiple countries and multiple time points or temporal frameworks (the exceptions are often found within the mediatization paradigm; recent two-country comparative longitudinal studies include Zeh and Hopmann [2013] and Magin [2015]). The historical comparative analysis approach is well developed in the HI tradition (cf. Mahoney 2001; Skocpol and Pierson 2002), but it does not usually include more than two temporal frameworks. The three temporal frameworks included in this study, as the contexts for the causal conditions, pose additional methodological challenges for the fsQCA approach, which was originally designed for cross-national rather than for longitudinal research. To show how the different temporal frameworks play a role in the present-day media systems and to show how the different fields of power play a role, we had to employ a combination of fsQCA approaches, including a two-step analysis, macro conditions, and contextual conditions. The specific solutions to these challenges are presented below.

One of the key theoretical challenges associated with our study was to identify how the causal conditions and outcomes of the different dimensions of media systems change and transform in diachronic transpositions and with synchronic relocations. We built on well-known and well-accepted notions regarding what media systems are within a new time-sensitive set-theoretical research framework, and we put them to the empirical test of time and space travel within a set-theoretical framework. Over the course of Chapters 3 through 5, we comparatively analyzed the media systems of the six country cases in Southeast Europe in three successive temporal frameworks: leading up to and including original modernization, socialism, and the post-socialist democratic transformation period of the historical present. In each of the three temporal settings, we analyzed the three fields of power and their transformations: the political field, the socio-economic field, and the cultural/symbolic field, including the media system. Each chapter can be viewed individually as a chronotope, wherein the configurations of the time and space of the analyzed media systems are presented. These detailed studies were necessary to form the qualitative comparative groundwork for the calibration of the conditions and outcomes in the fsQCA analysis. They also highlighted the kinds of concept adaptations that were necessary in order to describe our media system dimensions in their empirical surroundings in the various temporal frameworks shaped by the changing geopolitical locations of the six country cases.

The research approach and design employed in this book rely on a combination of aggregate data and case study research within a set-theoretical approach, which includes both internal and external factors and conditions when evaluating changes and comparing media systems across time and space. Therefore, Galton's problem, in which the source of similarities in practices or institutions in different countries is not clear, does not occur. Galton's problem results when the data and arguments concerning the internal characteristics of the states that are seen as the causes of the phenomena are not combined with the international context or with pressures that may affect the phenomena (Naroll 1961; Pfetsch and Esser 2008). In addition, contemporary research regarding media system transformations in the third-wave CEE democracies was originally framed in terms of mimesis or policy diffusion, meaning that external influences on media policy and system transformations are recognized (although it took time for it to be recognized that this was necessarily interacting with the internal conditions in the outcomes). Thus this study also represents a contribution to updating the methodological framework of communication studies with respect to "whether a phenomenon can be attributed to internal or external causes" (Esser and Pfetsch 2004, p. 402). The historical institutionalist approach combined with the fsQCA (cf. Schneider and Wagemann [2012] on the natural fit between these theoretical and methodological approaches) employed in this chapter provides us with some valuable insights into the combination of internal or external conditions and outcomes that have played a part in media system transformations from the time of the establishment of the first printing press to the present day.

As the calibration involved in an fsQCA takes the place of both the theoretical conceptualization of the research dimensions and their measurement, we will now present the temporal and spatial adaptations of the causal conditions and outcomes that had to be introduced so as to understand the media systems in a particular temporal framework in Southeast Europe, which resulted in the calibration of the specific conditions used in the fsQCA (Ragin 2008). As is the case in all analyses that employ systematic procedures in relation to variables, or conditions in this instance, the empirical world is necessarily simplified. Similarly, we were compelled to produce the smallest number of conditions in order to enable the fsQCA while still expecting those conditions to represent the broad reality.

Calibration is a process that relates concept formation to measurement by assigning scores to cases, and it is an integral and central part of any fsQCA (cf. Schneider and Wagemann 2012). As the calibration process critically influences the results of the analysis, we present the calibration justifications for all the causal conditions and outcomes used in the study. A conventional comparative case study analysis combines very well with the more formal fsQCA approach (Schneider and Wagemann 2010), which can be considered a bridge between the qualitative and quantitative methods of data analysis (Ragin 2008). Schneider and Wagemann (2010) further stress the importance of substantive knowledge of the cases being studied. During our process of calibration, we engaged in a qualitative assessment of membership of the sets for the chosen cases based on the comparative studies presented in the three temporal framework chapters, thereby relying on both theoretical and substantive knowledge in what is primarily an interpretive process (Ragin 2000, as quoted in Downey and Stanyer 2013, p. 502). Some conditions were calibrated based on aggregate/statistical data, in the fsQCA software, after first theoretically defining the necessary thresholds.

The conditions and outcomes for calibration were coded according to the temporal framework. Each condition or outcome code, which is later used with the fsQCA software to sort the paths to different outcomes, is preceded by a letter: the letter M refers to the modernization period, S to socialism, and D to the period of post-socialist democratization in digital modernity. The number of conditions differs within the three temporal frameworks, with the last temporal framework of present-day media systems including the largest number of conditions. The calibrated values that are used in the analysis are presented in Table 6.1, and the raw data for the calibration are included in the respective chapters and mentioned in the following calibration explanations. This allows for the replication and extension of our study to other cases or purposes (cf. the best practice list for conducting and publishing an fsQCA in Schneider and Wagemann [2010]).

Space-time transformations of media systems and the concepts that describe them

The equivalence of concepts is necessary for comparative research (Smelser 1976, as quoted in Chang et al. 2001), and a failure to understand the possible differences in the meanings of concepts in cross-cultural and cross-national research could lead to problems regarding external validity. Hallin and Mancini (2004, 2012) caution against the use of the media system dimensions featured in their model outside of their Western European context. Further, Voltmer (2013) questions how far the media system concepts can travel outside of this specific context. For these reasons, and because of the complex diachronic and cross-cultural design of our study, one of the key challenges concerned the examination of how the familiar concepts related to the media system dimensions change in different temporal or spatial locales. The adaptation of the media system dimensions for different temporal frameworks and the modifications that were found to be necessary also opened up the possibility of applying these dimensions in relation to other types of regimes or cultures, including those with non-European histories.

There is a lot of history packed into the 150 years that are of particular relevance for the six countries in Southeast Europe that we analyzed. Three major changes in the social (as well as the political and economic) systems of the analyzed countries occurred – changes that were revolutionary in character. Each of the changes introduced a new political order, which changed the scope of the concepts that are familiar to us from the second part of the 20th century in both Western Europe and North America. First came the fall of feudalism and the advent of modern industrial society, which brought about changes in the social structure as well as in political participation. This was accompanied by the fall of two antagonistic empires that had ruled for almost 500 years as well as the creation at the end of World War I of a common state in Southeast Europe from countries that had belonged to those opposing empires. The next upheaval was brought about by World War II, with the conditions on the ground and the actors involved in that particular context bringing about another revolution, this time a socialist one. The third revolution was brought about by the collapse of socialism, which allowed for the most recent democratic revolution to spread across the eastern part of Europe. Although these critical junctures also occurred in Western Europe, they did not result in revolutions. Western Europe only underwent one revolution during the same period, and the countries in the region proceeded to develop their democratic political and market economic institutions without (or with very brief albeit devastating) interruptions.

The main challenge associated with this study involved overcoming the democratic and capitalist bias of the mainstream media systems research, which was invisible before the attempt to comparatively use the mainstream model (Hallin and Mancini 2004) in times and spaces without (or before the introduction of) liberal democracy and capitalism. Although some of the media systems within the mainstream model (i.e., the Southern European countries that took part in the same third wave of democratization as the post-socialist countries featured in this book) had authoritarian or outright fascist political regimes in certain periods of their midterm histories (Portugal, Spain, Greece), all of them had capitalist economies with private ownership (even if the role of the state in the economy was rather large in some of the countries). The differences in terms of how the media systems developed in places with different political and economic regimes had to be taken into account in the analysis (cf. Voltmer 2008; Hallin and Mancini 2012). In the comparative chapters, we showed that there exist a number of prejudices regarding the socialist period in relation to all three fields of power. This temporal framework was, however, defined in our original research question as being critical to our understanding of the analyzed media systems. Also, the mainstream media systems model that is the "industry standard" today (i.e., Hallin and Mancini's [2004] model) is actually very much based on the shape of things in both the media and politics in Western European countries during exactly this time frame. The analysis of the dimensions of media systems during the period of modernization, that is, the period leading up to and including the 19th and early 20th centuries, was new, meaning that there were very few prior sources to draw from. Finally, the mainstream model also needed adaptations in order to work in the times of digital modernity and platform society (van Dijck et al. 2018), which constitute future times in relation to the mainstream model.

Each of the three fields of power – the political, the socio-economic, and the cultural-symbolic fields – included a number of adaptations to the classical concepts of what a media system is and what conditions describe it. We will now present these adaptations, together with a smaller number of conditions calibrated in respect of outside measures and with regard to the six analyzed countries, which we expect to play important roles in shaping the present-day media systems. The analyses will show that while some concepts from the mainstream model also explain developments in the six analyzed countries, the contextual differences render some of the dimensions/conditions largely irrelevant, while some of the old dimensions manifest in different ways.

The political field

The conception of the *political field* had to be expanded backwards in time to take into account the different empires that were present in Southeast

Europe during early modern times, as well as forward in time into the period of democratic reforms following the fall of socialism. The socialist period also added to the expansion of the concept of the political field in circumstances very different to those associated with liberal democracy. Obviously, the concept of the political field, or system, has different key descriptors (indicators) during these different times, all of which contribute to our expanded understanding of how different types of political arrangements interact differently with communication and media systems.

In the first temporal framework, we defined three conditions that influence the development of media systems. The first condition includes the countries characterized by the long-term rule of patrimonial regimes (*long-term patrimonial regime in the Ottoman Empire, m_ottemp*). The Ottoman Sultanate is an example of a fully blown patrimonial regime. A value of 0 signifies that there was no rule by a patrimonial regime at any point in time on any part of the present territory of the analyzed country. A value of 1 signifies that there was rule by a patrimonial regime on the entire territory and over a period of several centuries. Slovenia is completely out of this set (value of 0), Croatia is mostly out (value of 0.25), and the other four countries are fully in (value of 1).

The second set includes countries belonging to the Habsburg Empire (*long-term rule of an absolutist or constitutional monarchy – the Habsburg Empire, m_habemp*). A value of 0 signifies that there was no rule by the Habsburg Empire at any point in time on any part of the territory. A value of 1 signifies that there was rule by Habsburg Empire over the entire territory and for a period of several centuries. Slovenia and Croatia are fully in this set (value of 1), Bosnia and Herzegovina and Serbia are more out than in (value of 0.25), while the other countries are fully out (value of 0).

Due to the importance of statehood already being established at this early point, the third condition refers to the existence of autonomous self-government during the 19th century (*selfrule in the 19th century, m_selfrul*). A value of 1 signifies the existence of an autonomous state, while a value of 0 indicates the absence of autonomous self-governance. Serbia has a value of 1 because it had an autonomous state, while Croatia has a value of 0.7 because it had maintained its autonomy and self-rule within the Habsburg Empire. The other four countries are fully out of this set (value of 0).

In the socialist temporal framework, the political field is defined with the condition of *accommodative pluralism (s_accomplur)*. This condition aimed to establish a type of socialist rule based on the characteristics of the types of communist regimes defined by Kitschelt et al. (1999) combined with the level of political pluralism. According to Kitschelt et al. (1999), the cases included in the analysis belonged to either the national-accommodative type, such as Croatia and Slovenia, or patrimonial regimes. Serbia is defined as a case located somewhere between the national-accommodative type and the patrimonial type, while Bosnia and Herzegovina, Macedonia, and Montenegro belong to the patrimonial type (Kitschelt et al. 1999).

Aside from Kitschelt et al.'s (1999) distinction between regime types, we also evaluated the development of political pluralism as the development of civil society, the public sphere, or dissent. Croatia had a pronounced social movement at the end of the 1960s and beginning of the 1970s, Serbia at the end of the 1960s as well as a nationalist movement during the 1980s, while Slovenia had a vibrant civil society during the 1980s. Croatia and Slovenia have the value of 1, Serbia is more in than out of the set (value of 0.75), while Bosnia and Herzegovina, Macedonia, and Montenegro are fully out of the set (value of 0).

The political field also had to be adapted to the post-socialist period, especially in terms of accounting for aspects of the democratic transition. The third temporal framework includes the largest number of conditions that we expect to influence media system transformations. Here we include two sets of conditions: the first relate to the breakup of the SFRY and the transition to post-socialism, while the second address the character of the political regime described by Hallin and Mancini (2004).

The type of transition related to the success of democratic consolidation is the cooperative type of transition, which unfolded through negotiation between the incumbent and opposition elites. The set of countries with the *cooperative type of transition* (*d_cotran*) includes Slovenia and Croatia (value of 1), while in Bosnia and Herzegovina, Macedonia, Serbia, and Montenegro incumbent groups arranged the elections during the regime conversions (value of 0).

The transition from socialism is also defined by the absence or presence of violence or war. In our case, the level of conflict was operationalized as the length and intensity of the armed conflict in which the state participated (*intensity of war, d_war*). During the wars of Yugoslav legacy, which lasted from 1991 to 2000, the countries participated for various lengths of time with various intensities, numbers of casualties, and levels of damage. Bosnia and Herzegovina, Croatia, and Serbia were calibrated as having a value of 1. The Serbian participation in the wars lasted the longest (1991–2000), while in Croatia and Bosnia and Herzegovina the wars lasted for five years but were led on the territory of these states and were highly detrimental in terms of both casualties and damage. Montenegro participated in the wars for a longer period while it was part of the FRY with Serbia, although it did not experience conflict on its own territory (value of 0.8). Macedonia had a shorter interethnic conflict and was categorized as more out than in the set (value of 0.2). Slovenia engaged in the brief Ten-Day War in 1991 and is thus almost completely out of the set (value of 0.1).

Political science links the success of the democratic consolidation of the CEE countries to the (non)existence of authoritarian regimes during the 1990s. The condition of countries belonging to the set of *authoritarian regime in the 1990s* (*d_authorit*) was calibrated according to Kitschelt et al.'s (1999) analysis, where Slovenia belonged to full substantive democracies (value of 0), Macedonia to formal democracies (value of 0.4), Croatia was between formal democracies and authoritarianism (value of 0.6), Bosnia and Herzegovina belonged to a semi-authoritarian regime (value of 0.8), and the FRY (Serbia and Montenegro) belonged to an authoritarian regime (value of 1).

The aspects important to democratic consolidation, and thus to the development of a democratic media system, also include the following conditions. The issue of stateness has been highlighted as being important for democratic consolidation. The countries are calibrated as fully in the set of the condition of *resolved stateness issues* (*d_state*) if the stateness issue was resolved during the post-socialist period (Croatia, Montenegro, and Slovenia; value of 1). Bosnia and Herzegovina (as an international protectorate and due to the state contestation issue with Republika Srpska) and Serbia (due to the dispute over stateness with Kosovo) are more out than in the condition (value of 0.4). North Macedonia has almost resolved its stateness issue (controversy with Greece as well as the conflict with the Albanian minority) and is so more in than out of the set (value of 0.6).

European integration also plays an important role in both democratic consolidation and the degree to which a country participates in international flows (*European [EU] integration, d_euint*). EU member states are fully in the set (Croatia and Slovenia; value of 1). Accession negotiations and chapters have been opened with official candidates Montenegro and Serbia (value of 0.75), while North Macedonia is still waiting for negotiations to be opened (value of 0.25). Bosnia and Herzegovina is a potential candidate (value of 0).

While the political and media systems in Europe are, some 30 years after the collapse of socialism, perfectly able to be analyzed using the comparative concepts (as evidenced by a host of such projects in the field political science and somewhat fewer in the communication field), the volatile and sometimes unsuccessful consolidations followed by authoritarian backsliding also necessitate the expansion of the concept to include the quality of the consolidation of democracy. The set of *consolidated liberal democracies* (*d_libdem*) was calibrated quantitatively, based on both the latest Freedom House values of political and civic rights (Table 5.1) and Diamond's (2002) scale. Countries are ranked as liberal democracies if their rating is between 1 and 2, with scores of 2.5 to 3 indicating countries to be electoral democracies (Serbia; value of 3) and scores between 4.5 and 7 indicating hybrid and authoritarian regimes (including electoral autocracies, competitive authoritarian regimes, and hegemonic authoritarian regimes). Montenegro, North Macedonia, and Kosovo (value of 3.5), and Bosnia and Herzegovina (value of 4) remain ambiguous regimes (Freedom House 2019). The thresholds for calibration are set accordingly, and Freedom House values of 2 and below mean full inclusion in the set of liberal democracies (calibrated as a value of 1), 5.5 and above as full exclusion from the liberal democracy set (value of 0; these would be authoritarian regimes), and a value of 3 as a crossover point.

Clientelism is another dimension related to the quality of consolidated democracy. The set of countries with *high clientelism* (*d_clien*) was operationalized through the V-Dem clientelism index (see Table 5.1). The clientelism index ranges from 0 (no clientelism) to 1 (full clientelism). In Europe, the most clientelist countries are in the Balkans (with value 0.42 and higher clientelism), while the least clientelist countries are the Nordic countries (value 0.12 and lower). These values are taken as the thresholds for full inclusion and exclusion in relation to the set. Somewhere in between are the Southern European countries, with 0.31 as the highest value in the region, which is set as a crossover point. Direct calibration was made based on the defined thresholds using the fsQCA software. Slovenia and Croatia are almost fully out of the set, while the other four countries are fully in the set.

The type of government is, in Hallin and Mancini's (2004) typology, linked to the character of the media system. Belonging to the set of countries with *majoritarian government* (d_mgov) after 2000 was calibrated as a value of 1, while the countries with the consensus type of government were calibrated as a value of 0. The average of the shares of posts in government of the largest party during the period from 2000 to 2013 was calculated based on the work of Berglund et al. (2013). If the largest party had on average 80% (or more) of posts in government, it was categorized as being fully in the set (value of 1), while if it had from 60% to 79%, it was categorized as more in than out (value of 0.75). If the largest party had between 49% and 30% of posts in government, it was categorized as more out than in (value of 0.25), while it was defined as fully out if it had 29% (or less) of posts in government (value of 0). In Bosnia and Herzegovina and Slovenia, the largest party had on average 30% and 40% of posts in government, respectively (value of 0.25). In Serbia, the largest party occupied on average 60% of posts in government, while in Croatia and Montenegro it had 70% of posts (value of 0.75). In North Macedonia, the largest party occupied on average 50% of posts in government, which makes it a crossover point (value of 0.5).

Media policy has always been a political issue (Freedman 2008), with the regulatory solutions reflecting in many respects the political values of the parties in power at the time of the adoption of specific solutions. As a general rule, center-left parties and coalitions introduced more freedom into the media system and more support for pluralism and third sector (non-profit or community) media, while center-right or conservative/nationalist parties during the 1990s stressed the national sovereignty issue (by blocking foreign investment or ownership in relation to the media), later introduced more market liberal policies, and continuously exerted more pressure on the freedom of journalistic reporting through informal or formal means. Broader European trends show that right-wing governments in the CEE countries are not friendly toward media freedom and autonomy in general. The *dominance of right-wing parties in government* (d_rwgov) was operationalized as a share of the rule of right-wing parties in government between 2000 and 2020 (e.g., Berglund et al. 2013). If the government was in this period fully ruled by right-wing parties, the value is 1; if it was ruled by both right-wing or left or liberal parties equally, the value if 0.5; while a value of 0 signifies the full dominance of left-wing parties. For example, Montenegro's government was fully dominated by the right-wing DPS and so it was categorized as fully in the set (value of 1). In Croatia, Macedonia, and Serbia, between 60% and 70% of governments were ruled by right-wing or conservative parties during the relevant period and so these countries were categorized as more in than out (value of 0.75). Around 30% of Slovenian governments were ruled by right-wing parties, meaning that Slovenia was categorized as more out than in (value of 0.25). Bosnia and Herzegovina is an ambiguous case due to its specific political system, and so it was categorized as a crossover case with a value of 0.5.

The socio-economic field

The *socio-economic field* has also seen transformations from the feudal economy and society into early capitalist industrialization, then into socialism, and finally, post-socialist market transformations. These differences particularly played a role in relation to the dimension of the media market. The concept of inclusive and extractive institutions, as developed by Acemoğlu and Robinson (2012), explains the broad strokes of the institutional transformations seen in these fields of power, and it is also applicable to political and economic systems that were different from Western European feudalism (e.g., the sultanistic regime of the Ottoman Empire). The transformations of the socio-economic field were analyzed through the changed conditions of literacy/education and economic development. Both dimensions are, in the history of the media, related to successful media development.

In the first temporal framework, *higher literacy (m_litera)* was calculated based on data concerning illiteracy rates from 1921 (100% minus the illiteracy rate). Following the discussion in Dolenec (2013a, pp. 114–115), the thresholds for literacy were based on the level of the spread of literacy across Europe prior to 1945, and they were adjusted to accommodate the available data on trends in the spread of literacy (OECD 2014). Full participation in the set of countries with high literacy was set to at least 70% of the population being literate. The fully out category threshold was set downwards of 45%. The crossover point was set to 60%. Direct calibration was performed using data on illiteracy rates from 1921, as based on the defined thresholds, using the fsQCA software.

In the same period, the next condition was *higher industrialization (m_indust)*, which was operationalized as industrial production from 1939 (per capita, in dinars) (Bilandžić 1999). Due to the lack of other comparable external data according to which this condition could be calibrated, it was decided to use the mean of the data as a crossover value, one standard deviation up as the threshold for full membership, and one standard deviation down as the threshold for full exclusion from the set. This condition is thus calibrated on the basis of the diversity and disparities in development of only the six countries included as cases in this analysis. Although there is a lack of comparable data, when comparing Yugoslavia as a whole to other European countries, Bilandžić (1999) places it among the underdeveloped countries due to, for example, its steel production lagging 22 times behind that of Germany or 16 times behind that of the UK. The final values were directly calibrated using the fsQCA software, with Slovenia fully in the set (value of 1), Croatia more in than out (value of 0.75), and all the other countries below the threshold for membership, albeit with Serbia and Bosnia and Herzegovina somewhat better placed than the remaining two countries that are completely out of the set (see the calibration values in Table 6.1).

During the socialist period, *high literacy* (*s_litera*) was calculated as 100% minus the illiteracy rate in the SFRY (Table 4.1). Around 1970, the average illiteracy rate in Europe was 3.6%, while it was 34.2% worldwide (UNESCO 1972). According to these values, the thresholds were set to 96% for inclusion in the high literacy set and 66% or lower for exclusion from the set. Further, 80% was set as a crossover point. Direct calibration was performed based on the defined thresholds using the fsQCA software. Slovenia and Croatia are fully in the set (with values of 0.97 and 0.89, respectively), Bosnia and Herzegovina is below the crossover point and so is more out of the set than in, while the other countries are members in the set of highly literate countries, albeit with a lesser degree of membership.

The *high economic development* (*s_develo*) condition was based on the gross national income (GNI) per capita data for the SFRY countries in 1972 (Table 4.1). The threshold values were based on the World Bank database.[1] Full members of the set of highly developed countries are those that have high income economies (GNI per capita a bit below Italy's $2,500), while the fully out countries are those that have low- to middle-income economies (the threshold is set at $150). The crossover point was set as upper- to middle-income economies (a bit below Turkey's $500). Direct calibration was performed using data on the GNI per capita (Table 4.1), as based on the defined thresholds, using the fsQCA software. Slovenia and Croatia have the best placement (values of 0.76 and 0.6, respectively), Serbia is just over the threshold for membership, while the other countries are all outside the set.

In the socialist period, we also included a condition describing the type of predominant social or cultural values often claimed to (negatively) influence the development of post-socialist media systems. The set of those countries with *high post-materialist values* (*s_postmat*) was qualitatively calibrated as post-modern (value of 1), modern (value of 0.5), and traditional values (value of 0) based on discussion about Yugoslav values studies performed during the 1970s and 1980s (see Chapter 4). The calibration was based on divergences between these six cases rather than on external anchors, as it was difficult to find comparable sources to these specific Yugoslav studies. In Croatia and Slovenia, post-modern values were developing during the socialist period. Slovenia is the country with the highest modernization as operationalized in cultural terms (value of 1), while Croatia is more in than out of the set (value 0.75). Montenegro and Macedonia are categorized as fully out because, as the least developed republics, they were only in the process of developing modern values (value of 0). Bosnia and Herzegovina and Serbia had more developed modern values, although they are still categorized as more out than in the set (value of 0.25) because traditional values predominated.

In the third (or present) temporal framework, the set of countries with *high socio-economic development* (*d_develo*) was calibrated quantitatively based on World Bank GDP per capita data expressed in 1,000 US dollars. The threshold for high development was defined as a value somewhat below South Korea and Spain ($30,000). For comparison, the average of high-income economies is $44,787, while the EU average is $36,570. The threshold for full exclusion from the set was taken as a value between the low-income and lower-middle-income average – $1,500. This is a value close to the GDP per capita in Uzbekistan. The crossover value was a bit above the average of the middle-income economies ($6,000). Direct calibration was performed based on the defined thresholds using the fsQCA software. Slovenia is fully in the set (value of 0.93), Croatia is more in than out (value of 0.75), while the other countries are at the crossover point or barely over it (value of 0.5).

High post-materialist values (*d_postmat*) are, in the present temporal framework, operationalized as the acceptance of individual freedom among young people in Southeast Europe (data from Lavrič et al. 2019, p. 46). The threshold for full inclusion in the set was 40%, which means that at least 40% of young people highly accept individual freedom as a value when compared to other values (e.g., economic welfare or security). The fully out threshold was set to 10%, while the crossover value was set to 20%. According to these thresholds, Slovenia is fully in the set (value of 1), Croatia is more in than out of the set (value of 0.75), Montenegro and Serbia are more out than in the set (value of 0.25), and Bosnia and Herzegovina and Macedonia are fully excluded from the set (value of 0).

The cultural and symbolic field

The concept of the *cultural-symbolic field* enabled us to imagine the field of symbolic power during the time before the invention of printing and the media institution. There were differences in these fields within the contexts of the opposing empires. In the Ottoman Empire, the symbolic field of power that controlled public knowledge, that is, the place where the media would become critically influential in the modern age, was completely controlled by the religious authority and so was very different from the field of culture in the Western kingdoms and empires, wherein the symbolic authority of religion was being eroded by kings who established universities and secular schools and allowed the spread of printing, as well as by secular and market forces concentrated in the cities in combination with the increasingly literate populations. The arrival of the media and the formation of the nation state eventually enabled the development of the media system, whereby familiar concepts start to make sense in the original conceptualizations. The mainstream media system concepts could, without particular adaptations, be applied to the period of political pluralization and the development of party politics from the mid-19th century, when political parties were starting to be formed in the first of the six analyzed countries, until the end of the 1930s, although they required adaptation in order to make sense in the period of socialism that followed the end of World War II, as well as in the post-socialist framework of the countries undergoing democratic transformations. In the present period of digital modernity, new dimensions speaking to the digital media system were added. In addition to the dimensions of the media market, journalistic professionalism and autonomy, and media and political parallelism, the role of the state in the media system was expanded to include digital media policies. We have also added the new dimension of the globalized media culture in all the studied temporal frameworks in order to account for the importance of viewing communication/media systems in a broader transnational context rather than only as being contained within national borders.

The state and the media

With regard to the relationship between the state and the media, the concept had to be extended in the first and second temporal frameworks to include the levels of state control over the development of printing and publishing, and later on, over the establishment and operation of newspapers. While in the democratic context the role of the state extends to the levels of media policy, the organization of licensing, the protection of pluralism, the organization of PSB, and the extent of state support for the media through subsidies, in non-democratic contexts the role of the state ranges from the total abolition of printing and publishing (this was the situation in the Ottoman Empire and in four of the six countries we analyzed) to degrees of state control imposed through the licensing of newspapers and printing houses or censorship regimes (as implemented in the Habsburg Empire). These latter aspects of the state's relationship with the media were also present during the interwar period in the Kingdom of SHS/Yugoslavia, where media development was struggling against the censorship and other forms of harassment imposed by the autocratic state.

In the era of socialism, the relationship between the state and the media became more diverse. Contrary to expectations, in the case of self-management socialism the state did not manage the media directly. Instead, the media were organized as independent organizations, with their publishers (the SSRN organizations in the republics) figuring in relation to the political parallelism dimension. The state was primarily involved in media creation, subsidies, and use as a tool for propaganda/mass education only during the first period of administrative socialism (1945–1952). The state mainly played a legislative role afterwards. During the time of socialism in Yugoslavia, the republics had their own media laws based on the federal template, although the practice of certain advantages being provided by the legal framework varied. Goldstein (1996) specifies the years of increased state repression to be 1945–1949, 1954–1955, and 1971–1974, while the years that witnessed the relaxation of state pressure on the media were 1950–1954, 1963–1971, and 1984–1989. The relationship between the state and the media in this temporal framework, as well as in the first temporal framework, has been condensed in the other media system conditions, as the role of the state was present in every aspect of the media system and so could not easily be distinguished. The only exception is perhaps the level and type of censorship, which could be used as a separate condition in comparisons. The first temporal framework featured two types of censorship practices aligned with the respective empires, while after the common state framework was introduced in the early 20th century the degree of (formal) censorship of the media was similarly present or absent in respect of all the six analyzed countries/peoples. More research into the different historical practices of censorship is needed, however.

The role of the state in drawing the boundaries of the new democratic media systems was very important during the period of democratic transformations, as the legal and policy framework was expected to change in a relatively brief period of time in order to create a media system based on a market economy, with private ownership of the media, and with the freedom to establish media organizations and to publish. The speed and extent of these transformations varied among the newly independent states, and the policies that they introduced, while often following the template of Western role models in terms of mimetic policy diffusion, differed with regard to the extent that they conformed to the predominating ideas concerning the role of the media in their countries.

The role of the states in these situations of new media policies was very much in the spirit of the new social contracts (Peruško Čulek 1999a), not all of which were primarily democratic. The first decade of the democratic transition was, in all the analyzed countries, focused on nation building, with some states engaging in war. In this context, the role of the state continued to become more pronounced. Although some countries (Slovenia and Macedonia) were better placed to more quickly complete their separation from Yugoslavia, and therefore, to turn to the creation of democratic media policies, while other countries were stuck in long-term wars (Bosnia and Herzegovina, Serbia, and Montenegro), the pace of the media policy development (in terms of the new legislative framework) was not necessarily impacted by these difficulties (Croatia immediately proceeded to change its media legislature despite the ongoing war). While the policy concerning PSB is certainly an important aspect of the state's relationship with the media, in order to be as sparing as possible with regard to the number of conditions we include, the role of the public service media is included in the analysis of the media market, based on its audience share, with the understanding that it also reflects the relationship of the state to PSB.

The role of state media policy in *developing the digital infrastructure (d_dinfra)* was one of the conditions that we expected to have an influence on the present character of the media systems. The calibration is based on the discussion by Hosman and Howard (2014), and it is supported by the progress of the television broadcasting digital switchover and data concerning household Internet access (Table 5.1). Each of these aspects were calibrated separately and then the average of the calibrations was taken for the final values. In the analysis conducted by Hosman and Howard (2014), Croatia and Slovenia are front-runners in terms of their telecommunication policy (value of 1), Macedonia and Montenegro occupy a middle position (value of 0.5), while Bosnia and Herzegovina and Serbia are laggards (value of 0). Most of the six countries have completed the digital switchover process (value of 1), although the process is still ongoing in Bosnia and Herzegovina (value of 0.75). The determination of Internet access is based on the Eurostat data, with the threshold for being fully in the set standing at 90% of households with Internet access, the crossover value being 85%, and the threshold for being fully out of the set standing at 80%. The calibration for Internet access is performed directly based on the defined thresholds using the fsQCA software. The final calibration of the d_infra condition is calculated as the average of these three separate calibrations.

Media pluralism, as a policy goal, is also expected to influence the type of the media system. The *high state support for media pluralism (media and state) (d_smeplu)* condition was calibrated qualitatively. A value of 0 was coded for those countries fully out of the set where there is no, or only very weak, state support for media pluralism, while a value of 1 was coded where state support for media pluralism exists. Croatia and Slovenia are coded as 1 because they have a functioning fund for media pluralism. Serbia is coded as 0.25 because it has some support established for media pluralism, although it is considered to not be functioning properly. The other countries are coded as 0.

Finally, we posit that media freedom is, in the final analysis, an outcome of the impact of the state on the media, as well as of the media's reaction to potential threats (i.e., self-censorship, or conversely, resilience in the face of government pressure). The *high media freedom (d_mfree)* condition is based on the operationalization suggested by Kenny (2019), who used V-Dem indicators that point to different components of a broader conception of media freedom. These indicators include government censorship of the media, government censorship of the Internet, a range of media perspectives, the harassment of journalists, media self-censorship, media bias against the opposition, and the freedom of expression. A simple additive index is created from these variables using a sample of countries measured by the V-Dem 9 covering values from 2010 to 2018. The index value ranges from being the highest in Switzerland (value of 16.6) to being the lowest in North Korea (value of -17.8). The chosen thresholds are as follows: for full inclusion in the set of high media freedom, a value around that of New Zealand (12); for full exclusion from the set, a value around that of Afghanistan (2.5); and for a crossover point, a value around that of Brazil (9). Media freedom is defined as one of the key outcome conditions in the analysis that follows. Slovenia is fully in the set of countries with high media freedom (value of 0.94), Croatia is mostly in the set (value of 0.65), Montenegro and Bosnia and Herzegovina are mostly out of the set (with values of 0.23 and 0.18, respectively), while Macedonia and Serbia are fully out of the set (with values of 0.07 and 0.06, respectively).

Political parallelism

Political parallelism, as a category during the period of modernization, can be extended to the relationship between power holders and the means of communication, primarily in terms of the church and the king, where the rulers had a monopoly on public communication. With the development of printing, the monopoly was slowly eroded in the West but not in the eastern empires (both the Ottoman and Russian), where the patrimonial regimes remained in strict control of public communication. With the development of political parties during the 19th century, political parallelism arrives with its original meaning of party ownership or support for newspapers. Newspapers in Croatia and Slovenia served political functions even before the formation of political parties, especially in relation to the programs of national renewal, including the promotion of the national language and national culture (within the context of a foreign empire). Political parallelism was high in all six countries during the first period, and thus it was not a differentiating factor in our analysis.

In the era of socialism, political parallelism was also present in both formal and informal ways. Formally, the publisher of all media was the SSRN in the respective republic, as the association of the working people was supposed to represent a plurality of their interests. With such a broad and formal mandate, the link to the SK was one step removed, and the party was not involved in the running of the media. Its role remained in relation to the (informal) selection/recommendation of editors and journalists, and especially of management/CEOs, and in terms of the ideological supervision and evaluation of the media in a broad, post-publication way. The concept of political pluralism took on different shapes in different temporal frameworks, and it was found to have a recognizable variant during the era of socialism (cf. Roudakova 2012). With the passage of decades, and especially during the second half of the 1980s, the level of critique and serious public discussion in the media (especially in Croatia, Serbia, and Slovenia) did not appear to be inhibited by the possibility of party censure. Even taboo topics were debated in the media published by the SSO (the youth associations in the republics), even if this sometimes had adverse consequences for their editors. Political parallelism began to be formally reduced in the 1980s alongside the publication of alternative pop culture magazines, which were not published within the framework of the SSO. The parallelism was greater between the mainstream media and their own republican parties, and when cross republic political interests were different, they tended to side with their own parties' positions. Churches also published their own newspapers. Thus the concept of political parallelism can be applied in the context of Yugoslav self-management socialism rather than the concept of propaganda, which we would normally use for the relationship between the media and the political party in a one-party state. The degrees of parallelism varied between different media and in different republics, with the three more developed media markets exhibiting more pluralism. Pluralism also increased with the increased variety of media publishers and the exercise of the norm of objective and factual reporting and critique, which existed alongside less autonomous professional roles.

High political parallelism (s_polpa) in the socialist temporal framework reflects the differences in the levels of independence of the content and critique, as well as in the diversity of ownership and publishers. High political parallelism (value of 1) refers to those cases in which the influence of the party was felt the most (Bosnia and Herzegovina, Macedonia, and Montenegro). The value of 0.6 is given where the media were more diverse (Serbia), while the value of 0.4 is appropriate where independent publishers and churches were prominent alongside the existence of independent media (Croatia and Slovenia).

During the time of the democratic transformations after socialism, the political parallelism in this part of Europe exhibits some characteristics not traditionally (or historically) found in this region. The original idea of party-press parallelism (Seymour-Ure 1973, as adapted in Blumler and Gurevitch 1995, and in Hallin and Mancini 2004) rests on the notion that political parties (or churches, unions, etc.), through ownership or funding, influence the published content of the media in terms of the topics covered and the frames adopted, or that the media reflect certain ideological positions. In the post-socialist transformations of the media systems in this region, the political parties did not generally become owners of the media. In many countries this was expressly forbidden, especially for the broadcast media, although party ownership of newspapers is today alleged to be hidden in several countries. The key characteristic of the parallelism here is its asymmetry, something that is found with regard to contemporary political polarization and media parallelism in digital times in, for example, the United States (Faris et al. 2017). This asymmetric parallelism is characterized by the close relationship between certain political parties and the media – mainly right-wing conservative and nationalistic parties, while the center-left parties do not have their own media and so instead rely on the mainstream media to cover their activities and present their ideas. In the United States, this was recognized as the predominant relationship in connection with the 2016 presidential election, primarily with regard to the Fox cable news network and several online portals, while in the countries of Southeast Europe there is an added twist. While the right-wing parties were more commonly the governing parties, and due to the deficient democratic consolidation, the party-press parallelism turned into state-press parallelism, thereby contributing to the situation of state media capture (Bajomi-Lázár 2014), especially with regard to PSB. The center-left parties, when they were in the governing position, did not exert influence over PSB to the same degree, so these periods provided the opportunity for the further development of editorial and journalistic autonomy.

In the era of digital modernity and deep mediatization, the character of political parallelism is changing, and it is increasingly difficult to find empirical examples of the traditional structural links between left- and right-wing parties, newspapers, and audiences. We increasingly see asymmetric parallelism (Faris et al. 2017), whereby the media show favorable bias toward one political pole (usually the right), while there is no such parallelism with the left or center parties, who are represented by the objective neutral professional standards of the mainstream media. Such *asymmetric parallelism* (*d_aspar*) includes countries with this lopsided parallelism as full members of the set (value of 1); 0.75 is the value of high parallelism in countries where both political poles have significant relations with the media or journalists; 0.25 is the value for those countries where the political parallelism is not very pronounced or where there are no ownership links between the media and political parties; while 0 is the value for those countries where the media predominantly report without special privilege or affinity. Serbia and Montenegro are categorized as fully in the set (value of 1) because several mainstream media organizations in these countries have a pro-governmental bias, while "independent" or critical media organizations are relegated to the margins of the media system. Bosnia and Herzegovina and Macedonia have high political parallelism, which is aligned to the ethnic and political segmentation in these countries, and they are therefore categorized as more in than out of the set (value of 0.75). Croatia and Slovenia are categorized as more out than in the set (value of 0.25), as the mainstream media in these countries are commercially oriented and adhere to the norms of neutral reporting, while higher political parallelism is present at the (mainly digital) margins of the media system.

Media market

J.B. Thompson (1995) argues that capitalism was already in place by the time the first media organizations were established. Indeed, economic transformations had begun by the time newspapers arrived in two of the countries included in our study (Slovenia and Croatia), although they are among those countries characterized by the late demise of feudalism and by delayed modernization, which means that the media also developed later than in Western European countries, which were the leaders in this respect (e.g., Britain and France). In the other four countries, the delay in media development was even greater due to the completely different power structure seen in the Ottoman Empire, where neither field of power was free to develop independently of the political and symbolic power of the sultan. Nevertheless, after the Ottoman Empire was vanquished and reduced, and after capitalism has been introduced into the Kingdom of SHS/Yugoslavia, media markets also started to develop in these lands.

The remote condition of the *early development of printing and the press* (*m_printing*) was calibrated based on the year in which the first newspaper was published in the territory (Table 3.1) and according to the spread of printing and the press in Europe (the first newspapers started publishing in the early 17th century). Croatia and Slovenia published their first newspapers in the 18th century; Bosnia and Herzegovina, Montenegro, and Serbia in the mid-19th century; and Macedonia in the 20th century. This development is also connected to the freedom and state of printing. In Croatia and Slovenia, which published their first newspapers the earliest, printing was allowed in the 16th century, while in all the other countries it was restricted. These two countries were also where the first books and pamphlets were published. The situation of fully liberal printing and early development of the press was coded as 1 (e.g., this would pertain to France, the UK, Germany, and Italy); 0.7 was calibrated for Slovenia and Croatia and 0.3 for Bosnia and Herzegovina and Montenegro because they had early printing presses before the Turkish invasion. Macedonia and Serbia are fully out of the set (value of 0) because printing was only first allowed in the 19th century.

The very high illiteracy rate and general backwardness prior to World War II were not supportive of media development in some of these territories. The most developed lands, namely Slovenia and Croatia, developed the media the earliest. The greatest advance from the first to the second temporal framework was made in Serbia, which benefited from being at the center of the Kingdom of SHS/Yugoslavia (ruled by its dynasties). The condition of a *highly developed print market* (*m_market*), as a remote condition during the first temporal framework, includes countries characterized by the high development of the print market, and it was calibrated on the basis of the average number of published copies of newspapers from two periods (1900–1914 and 1927). These values were calibrated statistically, using the mean of the values as a crossover point, the standard deviation up as the threshold for full inclusion, and the standard deviation down as the threshold for exclusion from the set. There is a discrepancy in terms of the development of the print market between these two periods in certain countries. For example, the number of published press declined in Bosnia and Herzegovina yet significantly increased in Serbia between the early 20th century and 1920s. Direct calibration was performed using data from Table 3.1, as based on the defined thresholds, using the fsQCA software.

In the era of socialism, Serbia remained the republic that contained the capital of the federation, and because of this fact, it developed the largest press and television market, although its programming and audience preferences and social values remained predominantly traditional. Despite this development, the media systems in Slovenia and Croatia remained more advanced at that time in terms of pluralism and the diversity of the media as well as their content and alternative cultural practices. The concept of a media market can also be applied in the second temporal and spatial framework. The profit motive was the primary mover of most print media, with the exception of the political dailies, which played a primarily political role, while broadcasting was funded by a mandatory license fee collected directly by the respective republican radio and television organizations as well as by advertising, which was introduced from the start. The political dailies were also funded through the profits of the commercial editions of the daily and weekly press within their own media companies. The profiles of the audience habits historically resemble those of the Southern European countries, where journalists were writers and intellectuals and the audience was small and elite, and of the eastern lands with even more drastic delays in the development of mass audiences due to the very late development of widespread literacy. Mass audiences and the mass media market developed during the time of socialism, and they had all the regular features of capitalist media markets – advertising agencies, audience research, and competition for both advertisers and audiences. Television was the first true mass medium in all six countries, and the development of the television culture can be compared to Western developments, even if paleo television remained for longer in the eastern republics than in the western ones. The adaptation to our contemporary understanding of the market in the socialist temporal framework extends to the different type of ownership: the social ownership of companies, as in this case, allowed media competition and the pursuit of the profit motive as if it had been a private company. Of course, in practice some limitations were related to the ideological constraints placed on the media by their publishers.

The *high development of the socialist media market (s_market)* condition was calibrated quantitatively based on the average of the sum of the following standardized values: newspaper circulation divided by the population size from 1967 and by the number of television and radio users per 1,000 from 1972. Direct calibration was performed using the fsQCA software. The mean of these values was used as a crossover point, one standard deviation up as the threshold for full inclusion in the set, and one standard deviation down as the threshold for exclusion from the set. Slovenia, Serbia, and Croatia have full membership of the set, while the other three countries are fully excluded. The *highly developed advertising (s_advert)* condition was calibrated qualitatively as a dichotomous condition where the advertising centers (which developed the most in Zagreb, Belgrade, and Ljubljana) have a value of 1 and the other countries are coded as 0.

In the post-socialist era, we find that media markets can also successfully develop in the area of entertainment and popular culture in conditions of limited democratic success, as in the case of Serbia, which is the main exporter of audiovisual content (mainly reality programs) to the eastern countries in the region. The print media from the time of socialism were privatized, and many new newspaper companies were created after 1990. Some large media companies from socialist times disintegrated during the post-socialist privatization – the Croatian publishing company Vjesnik, the largest in Yugoslavia, is a case in point. Its assets (the printing press, its profitable weekly editions) were stripped and sold separately, and one of its dailies (*Večernji list*) today remains in foreign ownership. The market development in those countries with less democratic consolidation was very much reliant on the good will of the political power holders, meaning that the successful media operations in these countries belong to those who are friendly with the (usually right-wing) governing parties. Several of the smaller and less developed countries experience difficulties in terms of developing viable media markets, either because they share a language with a larger producer and are thus saturated by its content (from Serbia into Bosnia and Herzegovina and Montenegro). In some countries, significant parts of their media systems are foreign owned (Slovenia and Croatia), although some players who entered the market during the 1990s have since departed (such as the German WAZ), being replaced by domestic owners.

The *highly developed press market* (*d_press*) condition is operationalized by the reach of the dailies in Southeast Europe. The reach of the dailies in Bosnia and Herzegovina is 32.6%, in Croatia it is 59.4%, in Montenegro 41.2%, in Serbia 52.3%, and in Slovenia 50.8%. The data for North Macedonia are missing, although based on other data concerning newspaper use, which are lower than the data for Montenegro (see Figure 5.1), as well as inequalities in media use, which are the largest in North Macedonia and point to a less developed media market (see Figure 5.3), we can assume that the data for North Macedonia are closer to the data of Bosnia and Herzegovina and Montenegro. For this reason, we calculated an average of the dailies' reach in Bosnia and Herzegovina and in Montenegro as a proxy for North Macedonia. The calibration was performed using the fsQCA software, with the mean of the raw data being a crossover point (45.5), one standard deviation up being the threshold for inclusion in the set (55.8), and one standard deviation down being the threshold for exclusion from the set (35.3).

Broadcasters are generally new companies, apart from some local radio or television stations from socialist times that have either been privatized or are in the ownership of local communities, towns, or municipalities. The public service broadcasters in all the countries retained their assets despite undergoing transformations, while in some of the countries some of the broadcasting frequencies were redistributed to commercial television operators (in Croatia, for instance, prior to the digital switchover).

The *strong public service broadcasting* (*d_psb*) condition is an important distinguishing condition of contemporary CEE media systems (Castro Herrero et al. 2017). The set of countries with strong public broadcasting was operationalized through the audience share (EBU data; see Table 5.1). The threshold for those with full inclusion in the set was 34% of the audience share or more. The threshold for full exclusion from the set was 12% of the audience share or less. The crossover point was set as 20%. The final calibrated values were directly calculated using the fsQCA software. Croatia is fully in the set. Serbia, Montenegro, and Slovenia are more in than out, while Bosnia and Herzegovina is more out than in. Macedonia is fully out.

The *development of the media market* (*d_market*) in the last temporal framework is a set combining the *d-psb* and *d-print* sets, which is arrived at by averaging their respective set calibrations. As the analyzed countries are all television-centric, and because social media use is uniformly high, newspaper use combined with the importance of the public service media is also the best indicator in the period of digital modernity.

Journalistic autonomy and professionalism

The development of the journalism profession during the 18th and 19th centuries in Croatia and Slovenia followed the same pattern as that seen in Southern European countries, with intellectuals and writers with a political inclination establishing newspapers in order to promote their political ideas. Due to the low literacy rates in these countries, the discussions were conducted among the elites. Following the growth of political pluralism and the extension of the franchise to all male citizens during the latter half of the 19th century, the party press flourished and slowly moved toward the norm of neutrality, which is considered to have first been established in the daily paper *Novi list* in Rijeka (Croatia) during the early 20th century. The fact that the party press was actively suppressed by the government in the Kingdom of SHS/Yugoslavia until the mid-1930s played a significant role in turning the papers away from political commentary and the reporting of politics and toward entertainment and other lighter topics. During the era of socialism, neutral reporting as an autonomous role existed alongside the role of the journalist as a socio-political worker, part of the ruling elite, and an apologue of the regime, which predominated in the main political dailies. With the passage of time, the first role gained in prominence, while the second was reduced.

Journalists' organizations were established in these lands from the 19th century onwards, and they continued to exist during the period of the Kingdom of SHS and the socialist state. The different dynamics of establishment and different numbers of members also reflect the development of the media in the respective republics. During the post-socialist era, journalism associations continued to operate and were instrumental in the development of both the neutral/objective reporting norm and professional autonomy. However, additional associations of regime-promoting journalists were established in all the countries, albeit generally with much smaller memberships. This can be seen as a further indicator of asymmetric political parallelism in those countries where the new associations and their members gained a prominent role in the media or in media organizations' management structures.

With respect to the latter part of the first temporal framework, after the appearance of newspapers, the *high development of the journalism profession (m_journos)* condition was calibrated as a binary set, with a value of 1 signifying that journalists' associations were established before socialism and a value of 0 signifying the absence of journalists' associations before socialism.

Journalism-related university programs were developed in four of the republics in the 1960s and 1970s, while professional schools that offered brief programs had already been established in the 1950s. Still, most journalists who enrolled in higher education completed liberal arts or humanities degrees and then learned their professional standards on the job, in schools and workshops organized by the large media organizations. This self-organization of training and standard-setting disappeared after socialism, and no organized training was provided in-house by the media companies. The de-professionalization of journalism could also be noticed in relation to the digital media ecosystems.

The early establishment of journalism-related education was taken for a proxy for the *high development of the journalism profession (s_journos)*. Membership of this set was calibrated based on the year of establishment of journalism-related university programs during the socialist period. A value of 1 signifies that such programs were established by 1960, while a value of 0 signifies that there were no such programs established during the time of socialism. The year 1975 was taken as a crossover point, and the cases above or below this year have values of 0.25 or 0.75, respectively. In Slovenia, journalism-related university programs were established the earliest (in 1966), followed by Serbia in 1968, Bosnia and Herzegovina and Croatia in 1970, and North Macedonia in 1977. Montenegro did not establish any journalism-related university programs during the period of socialism.

In the last temporal framework, journalistic autonomy was operationalized as the opposite of media capture, a state increasingly invoked in regard to the backsliding of media autonomy in the CEE countries. The condition of *higher media capture (d_hmcap)* was based on the adaptation of the model created by Besley and Prat (2006). Media capture is thus defined as the undue influence of the state over the media and its democratic role, as measured by an index combining the share of foreign ownership of the main media (the top three dailies and television outlets; see Table 5.3), pressure placed on journalists (including threats and attacks; see Table 5.1), rouge state advertising (as discussed in Chapter 5), and the length of the rule of one party (as determined by the number of turns in government since 2000; from Berglund et al. 2013).[2] Besley and Prat (2006) theoretically model state capture as being endogenous and posit that the "degree of media capture influences the information of voters and their voting decisions" (p. 3). The conditions that protect against state capture include external media pluralism (a large number of media outlets), the independent ownership of media outlets (defined as the degree of difficulty experienced by the government in transferring resources to the media), and media commercialization. Media capture determines political outcomes when the reduction in political turnover is a result of higher media capture. The political polarization of the media scene reduces the risk of media capture by the state (as it becomes too expensive; Besley and Prat 2006). The final calibration is based on the average of several separate calibrations: the calibration of the share of domestic ownership of the main media, the dichotomous calibration of rouge state advertising, the calibrated length of one-party rule, and the dichotomous calibration of pressure placed on journalists. The calibration puts Croatia and Slovenia outside the set of high media capture (values of 0.29 and 0.18, respectively), and Bosnia and Herzegovina (value of 0.8), Montenegro (value of 0.78), North Macedonia (value of 0.9), and Serbia (value of 0.75) inside the set.

Globalized media culture

Media and communication systems are never closed, as they partake in the global cultural flows, and therefore, we added these dimensions to our model of media system transformation. We find that a difference in the degree of inter-state communication flows can be seen from the first period of modernization, through the socialist period, and into the period of democratic transformation, with those countries closer to the West receiving more benefits from partaking in the global flow of culture. The critique of methodological nationalism (Beck 2003; Wimmer and Schiller 2002; Livingstone 2012), as an approach whereby the nation state is seen as the natural container of society, has also been levied against the mainstream media systems model (Hardy 2012; Humphreys 2012), although nation states are still important in terms of framing both media policy and infrastructural affordances for media system development and media use (Flew and Waisbord 2015). Our research design also shifts the focus from the nation state, as we study present-day nation states in the two previous historical periods in which they were part of different political territorial units and had different administrative arrangements. We show how it is possible to travel both through time and also between different political borders so as to study cultures and peoples together with their national transformations and media system developments. This approach is somewhat unusual, although it has proved effective here in explaining the conditions and dimensions that have influenced the countries' present media arrangements, as will be demonstrated in the following section.

The condition of a *high level of globalization of communication (m_globcom)* was, in the first temporal framework, qualitatively calibrated based on the time of development of the postal service, telegraphy, and the import of books. As parts of the Habsburg Empire, Croatia and Slovenia had developed and globalized communication the earliest; however, as parts of the European periphery, they were less developed than the European center (they are assigned a value of 0.75). Bosnia and Herzegovina, Montenegro, and Serbia lagged behind and so are more out of the set than in (value of 0.25), while Macedonia is fully out of the development of globalized communication during the modernization period (value of 0).

During the time of socialism, the media system of Yugoslavia was much more a part of the global cultural flows than the media systems of the CEE countries. All the Yugoslav television stations broadcast much more Western than Eastern European content when compared to the countries that were members of the Eastern Bloc. Membership of the set of *high globalization of culture and communication (s_globcom)* during the era of socialism was based on the share of foreign programs on television (produced outside the SFRY), the share of international orientation in newspapers (focus on stories outside the SFRY), and international media cooperation. The values were calibrated statistically, and they only refer to diversity inside the SFRY. The mean was used as a crossover point, one standard deviation up as the threshold for full inclusion, and one deviation down as the threshold for full exclusion from the set. Slovenia and Croatia both have very high inclusion in the set, Serbia is just over the threshold for being in the set, while the other four countries are out of the set to varying degrees (see Table 6.1).

The *high globalization of culture and communication (d_globcom)* condition in the third temporal framework is based on data concerning the size of cultural exports (UNESCO 2017). The threshold for full inclusion in the set of countries that are influential in terms of their international exports of cultural goods is a value a bit below that of the Netherlands ($2 billion), while the threshold for exclusion from the set is a value slightly above that of Serbia ($80 million). The crossover point is a value approximately close to that of Latvia ($170 million). Due to the particular character of this set, the total size of the exports is more informative regarding international flows originated by the countries than it would be if these data were analyzed in terms of per capita exports. Direct calibration was performed based on the defined thresholds using the fsQCA software. In this temporal framework, all six countries are out of the set of highly globalized culture and communication as operationalized according to the outside measure. This condition thus proved to not have any significance in terms of differentiating the media development paths and solutions of the six countries, although it showed results when more diverse countries were included (cf. Peruško 2017). The influence of international connectivity and membership of the international

222 *Why the media systems are the way they are*

Table 6.1 Fuzzy set calibrated values

	Bosnia and Herzegovina	Croatia	Montenegro	Macedonia	Serbia	Slovenia
m_ottemp Long-term patrimonial regime in the Ottoman Empire	1	0.25	1	1	1	0
m_babemp Long term rule of absolutist or constitutional monarchy – the Habsburg Empire	0.25	1	0	0	0.25	1
m_selfrul Self-rule in 19th century	0	0.7	0	0	1	0
m_litera Higher literacy	0	0.91	0	0	0.01	1
m_indust Higher industrialization	0.23	0.75	0.08	0.08	0.34	1
m_printing Early development of printing and press	0.3	0.7	0.3	0	0	0.7
m_market Highly developed print market	0.43	0.98	0.04	0.03	0.88	0.82
m_journos High development of journalism profession	1	1	0	0	1	1
m_globcom High level of the globalization of communication	0.25	0.75	0.25	0	0.25	0.75
s_accomplur Accomodative pluralism	0	1	0	0	0.75	1
s_litera High literacy	0.34	0.89	0.64	0.59	0.64	0.97
s_develo High economic development	0.36	0.6	0.33	0.37	0.53	0.76
s_advert Highly developed advertising	0	1	0	0	1	1
s_postmat High post-materialist values	0.25	0.75	0	0	0.25	1
s_market High development of the socialist media market	0.1	0.84	0.03	0.1	0.9	0.98
s_journos High development of journalism profession	0.75	0.75	0	0.25	0.75	0.75
s_polpa High political parallelism	1	0.4	1	1	0.6	0.4

Why the media systems are the way they are   223

Variable							
(…)	0.04	0.34	0.21	0.06	0.33	0.98
High globalization of culture and communication							
d_libdem Consolidated liberal democracies	0.23	1	0.35	0.35	0.5	1
d_client High clientelism	1	0.11	1	1	1	0.1
d_mgov Majoritarian government	0.25	0.75	0.75	0.5	0.75	0.25
d_rugov Dominance of right-wing parties in government	0.5	0.75	1	0.75	0.75	0.25
d_cotran Cooperative type of transition	1	0	1	1	1	0
d_war Intensity of war	1	1	0.8	0.25	1	0.1
d_authorit Authoritarian regime in the 1990s	0.8	0.6	1	0.4	1	0
d_state Resolved stateness issues	0.4	1	1	0.6	0.4	1
d_eunit European (EU) integration	0	1	0.75	0.25	0.75	1
d_develo High socio-economic development	0.5	0.75	0.59	0.5	0.54	0.93
d_postmat High post-materialist values	0	0.75	0.25	0	0.25	1
d_globcom High globalization of culture and communication	0.01	0.03	0	0	0.04	0.15
d_dinfra Development of the digital infrastructure	0.2	0.9	0.5	0.6	0.3	1
d_psb Strong public service broadcasting	0.46	0.83	0.61	0	0.68	0.61
d_smeplu High state support for media pluralism	0	1	0	0	0.25	1
d_bmcap Higher media capture	0.8	0.29	0.78	0.9	0.75	0.18
d_aspar Asymmetric parallelism	0.75	0.25	1	0.75	1	0.25
d_press Highly developed the press market	0.02	0.98	0.22	0.07	0.88	0.82
d_mfree High media freedom	0.18	0.65	0.23	0.07	0.06	0.94
d_market Development of the media market	0.24	0.91	0.42	0.04	0.78	0.72

network of flows is more readily seen in the six countries through the condition of EU integration, which appears to be significant in several of the path solutions presented below.

Causal configurations and paths of media systems transformations in Southeast Europe

We will now proceed with the analyses intended to explain the present-day media systems. This will be achieved by uncovering the necessary conditions and the configurational paths through which certain causal conditions combine to produce certain types of media system outcomes in the present day. While a set-theoretical approach does not suffer from the problem of "many variables, small N" per se (as identified in the traditional variable-oriented research; Lijphart 1971 as quoted in De Meur and Berg Schlosser 1996, p. 425), an analysis including the trajectories of the conditions in three fields of power over three time periods in six country cases poses methodological challenges. The total number of original conditions in the study is 38 – a number impossible to include using the fsQCA software. Moreover, the theory of media system change proposed here, which rests on a permutation of critical junctures as disruptions and path dependency as institutional inertia, also needs to be adequately addressed during the data analysis phase. The separate and conjunctural roles of the three temporal frameworks, which succeed each other in the process of change and transformation of media systems, need to be unraveled. Thus the analysis had to find a way to deal with the large number of conditions as well as with the three different temporal frameworks in which the causal conditions and outcomes occur and which respond to our HI theoretical framework, which posits that the remote conditions of the *longue durée* exert an important path-dependent influence. All this adds additional complexity to the fsQCA design.

There are two approaches identified in the fsQCA literature that point to the possible ways of dealing with these issues: reducing the number of conditions in the path and addressing the conceptual problem of including the *longue durée* in the analysis. A two-step fuzzy set analysis is proposed by Schneider and Wagemann (2006), while other researchers suggest reducing the number of conditions by searching for the higher-order constructs or macro conditions (De Meur and Berg Schlosser 1996; Ragin 2000). In our analysis, we employ both approaches in order to take into account the three temporal frameworks that contain the conditions influencing the outcomes.

In the two-step analysis, the conditions are divided into *remote* and *proximate* conditions. The remote conditions are those that are more durable, or that are more distant in time, while the proximate conditions are those that refer to an actor's agency, which are less stable or more recent (Goertz and Mahoney 2005). Those conditions that are more distant in time are seen in our analysis as "remote" conditions. We also posit that the present-day media systems are shaped by the *longue durée*, which is presented in the preceding analysis of the transformations of the fields of power and the calibration of the conditions for the fsQCA analysis. All the conditions from the temporal frameworks of modernization and socialism can be viewed as remote, and we designate them as contextual conditions of the *longue durée*. To take account of these temporal frameworks and conditions, we add a third concept (from Goertz and Mahoney 2005), namely *contextual* conditions. Contextual conditions are used to denote those remote conditions from the previous temporal frameworks that provide the historical context for the subsequent development in the present temporal framework following the last critical juncture of the collapse of communism. These contextual conditions are arrived at after the first step in the analysis, and they consist of different paths for media system development in the six countries.

The total number of conditions in the first two temporal frameworks ($n = 18$) is too large to be directly included in the analysis of the causal configuration of the outcomes; therefore, higher-order constructs or macro conditions condensing these two temporal frameworks were first constructed.

The present temporal framework of digital modernity includes both remote and proximate conditions. Here, the remote conditions are those more distant conditions of the political field that describe the processes of state dissolution and transition seen during the 1990s, but that also include structural conditions as more durable conditions pertaining to the political and socio-economic fields. In all three temporal frameworks, the socio-economic and political conditions are seen as more durable conditions. The proximate conditions are those relating to the media policy as agency, as conceptualized in terms of state action and policy (i.e., the development of digital media infrastructure policy and the support for media pluralism). Other media system conditions from the present temporal framework can also be viewed as proximate conditions due to being more recent.

We approach this analysis with two complementary aims. The first aim is to explain the outcomes of the media systems developments in the six countries under study. This first aim is focused on the six countries themselves, and it provides an answer to the question of why countries that were republics within the same socialist state should have such diverse media systems some 30 years after the start of the post-socialist democratic transformations. The second aim is geared toward the broader comparative question and the attempt to contribute to our understanding of the typologies of the processes and developments involved in media system transformation over the *longue durée* and in more proximate social transformations. By differentiating between the proximate and remote conditions, as well as by acknowledging the roles of both structure (as remote conditions describing the *longue durée*, but also as conditions in the present-day media systems) and agency (as actions by state actors and by meso-level actors, such as the media or political parties, in the media capture conditions and asymmetric parallelism), we avoid the petrified "media system" logic and acknowledge the process of social change and the fact that certain processes and developments can become more entrenched as institutions and so become durable conditions influencing future developments.

We select two key outcomes from the conditions of the media systems in the six countries against which to analyze the media systems transformations: the present state of media freedom and the present state of the development of the media market. Media freedom (which in our study is calibrated in the *d_mfree* condition) is the outcome that is the key criterion for judging the quality of contemporary media systems, and it is the single most commonly compared condition (namely, different international indexes). Media market development (*d_market*) in the present day is another outcome that we chose to analyze in terms of the causal conditions and configurations that play a role in its construction. This outcome is especially interesting because it can be followed from the first temporal framework through to the last. As one particular condition, it thus speaks directly to our *longue durée* question.

Modernization path of developing media systems

During the first phase of the analysis, we focused on the modernization period, and we look for conditions that influence the development of the media/cultural field. We aimed to show how the political, social, economic, and cultural conditions influence the development of both the media market (*m_market*) and the journalism profession (*m_journos*) in the modernization period. The aim of the analysis was to identify specific paths or types of modernizations of the media system that might influence future developments during subsequent periods. We performed three different analyses with two different outcomes so as to analyze the development path in the modernization period: the development of the media market and the development of the journalism profession.

To determine the path configuration in the outcome of the highly developed print market, we first performed an analysis of the necessary conditions, as suggested by Schneider and Wagemann (2010). The analysis identified no necessary conditions for the highly developed print market during the modernization period, which indicated that there are no conditions that must always precede a highly developed print market.

The starting point for the sufficiency analysis is a truth table (all the truth tables are included in the Methodological Appendix), which shows the different configurations of conditions that produce the outcome. A standard fsQCA analysis always produces complex, parsimonious, and intermediate solutions (Ragin 2008) of the paths to the outcome. The appropriate path is chosen based on the theoretical and substantive judgment of the researcher (the type of path chosen is described in the table notes). This kind of analysis is performed for every solution regarding sufficient conditions and the appropriately consistent paths with a minimum consistency threshold of 0.75 (Schneider and Wagemann 2012; Ragin 2018). The solution consistency refers to "the degree to which membership in the solution (the set of solution terms) is a subset of membership in the outcome," while the solution coverage is "the proportion of memberships in the outcome that is explained by the complete solution" (Ragin 2018, p. 61).

Table 6.2 shows two paths that explain the development of the media markets during the period of modernization. Croatia and Slovenia have all the favorable conditions in terms of socio-economic development, higher literacy rates, industrialization, greater inclusion in global communication flows, and the earlier development of printing. They also avoided the patrimonial rule of the Ottoman Empire, and they experienced most of their modernization as members of the Habsburg Empire (however peripheral to its central flows). Serbia, however, had mostly unfavorable conditions for the development of the media market due to being under patrimonial rule and having lower industrialization, lower literacy levels, later development of printing, and less inclusion in global communication flows, although it still managed to develop a print media market thanks to the early establishment of political autonomy (i.e., an independent state). We note that Serbia was "saved" from negative development thanks to the political factor of self-rule.

As the relationships of the conditions in set theory are not linear, a negated outcome analysis needs to be performed to show why certain countries exhibit the weak development of the media market. The analysis found that there are several necessary conditions that can, in the right circumstances, produce such an outcome. The low development of the media market does not (in this context) appear without patrimonial rule, the lack of the "Habsburg factor," the lack of political autonomy, low literacy, low industrialization, low printing development, and low inclusion in global communication flows. The consistency threshold for the necessary conditions

Table 6.2 Sufficient conditions for a developed print market in modernization

Outcome	Path solution	Cases
Highly developed media market*	~m_ottemp*m_habemp* m_litera* m_industr* m_printing* m_globcom	Croatia, Slovenia
Highly developed media market**	m_ottemp*~m_habemp* m_selfrul* ~m_litera* ~m_industr* ~m_printing* ~m_globcom	Serbia
Weakly developed media market***	m_ottemp*~m_habemp* ~m_selfrul* ~m_litera* ~m_industr* ~m_printing* ~m_globcom	Bosnia and Herzegovina, Macedonia, Montenegro

Complex solution

Consistency; raw coverage; unique coverage

* 1; 0.44; 0.44 ** 1; 0.21; 0.21 *** 0.94; 0.78; 0.78

~ denotes the absence of the condition

is recommended to be at least 0.9 (Schneider and Wagemann 2012 p. 143), and all these conditions have a consistency level above 0.9. With regard to the sufficient conditions, only one condition has a recommended consistency level and also includes all the above mentioned necessary conditions (Table 6.2).

Table 6.3 presents the answer to the question of why journalism is more developed in some of the countries than in others. In the path configuration of the conditions for the outcome of the high development of the journalism profession (m_journos), the analysis found no necessary conditions. However, there are several necessary conditions for the negated outcome, with a consistency threshold of over 0.9 for the low development of the journalism profession: patrimonial rule, the lack of the "Habsburg factor," the lack of political autonomy, low levels of literacy, low industrialization, and the lower development of the media market. The analysis found no sufficient conditions for the low development of the journalism profession, although it found two paths for the high development of the journalism profession. As in the explanation concerning the higher development of the media market, Croatia and Slovenia exhibited higher literacy levels, more industrialization, greater inclusion in the global flows, the earlier development of printing, and the stronger development of the media market during the reign of the Habsburg Empire, and all without the effect of patrimonial rule. Serbia, however, had mostly unfavorable conditions, although its early political autonomy, together with the development of the media market, helped with the earlier development of journalism.

The following typology of the modernization path of media development in the six countries is advanced based on the above analysis as higher-order constructs or contextual conditions. We use an uppercase italic font to

Table 6.3 Sufficient conditions for a highly developed journalism profession in modernization

Outcome	Path solution	Cases
Highly developed journalism profession*	~m_ottemp* m_habemp* m_litera* m_industr* m_printing* m_globcom* m_market	Croatia, Slovenia
Highly developed journalism profession**	m_ottemp* ~ m_habemp* m_selfrul* ~m_litera* ~m_industr* ~m_printing* ~m_globcom* m_market	Serbia

Complex solution

Consistency; raw coverage; unique coverage.

*   1; 0.35; 0.35.
** 1; 0.17; 0.17.
~   denotes the absence of the condition.

designate the contextual conditions resulting from the path analysis. The first letter (in this case "m") is again used to denote the temporal framework.

Social and economic conditions that are favorable for the development of a rich media market and journalism profession. (Croatia and Slovenia) (*M_ECONM*)

Weak social and economic conditions, but favorable political autonomy conditions for the development of a rich media market and journalism profession. (Serbia) (*M_POLITM*)

Weak social, economic, and political autonomy conditions produce a weak media market. (Bosnia and Herzegovina, Macedonia, and Montenegro) (*M_WEAKM*)

Media systems during socialism

The same analytical approach is repeated for the socialist period, with the outcomes again being the high development of the socialist media market (*s_market*), the high development of the journalism profession (*s_journos*), and high political parallelism (*s_polpa*). Once again, the analysis seeks to determine how the different outcomes seen among the six republics can be explained.

Two necessary conditions (with consistency levels above 0.9) for the high development of the media market in socialism are high literacy levels in socialism and the development of advertising in socialism. Thus a higher level of media market development did not appear without higher literacy levels and the stronger development of advertising.

The analysis produced only one solution, which showed that Croatia, Serbia, and Slovenia all exhibited similar paths of development of their media markets. These paths were shaped by a combination of favorable conditions: a more pluralist socialist regime with some elements of accommodation of opposition views, higher literacy levels, higher economic development, stronger development of advertising, and greater inclusion in global communication flows. The analysis showed that Serbia, during the time of socialism, moved closer to Croatia and Slovenia in terms of social and economic development, which helped with the development of its media market.

In the negated outcome, the necessary conditions for a weak media market in the time of socialism result if a country does not feature the "accommodative pluralist" type of socialism, does not have a developed advertising center, does not have developed post-materialist values, and is less included in global communication flows. When we ran the analysis of the sufficient conditions for a non-highly developed media market in the time of socialism, the analysis produced only one path of unfavorable conditions that included all the necessary conditions. The solution included Bosnia and Herzegovina,

Table 6.4 Sufficient conditions for a developed media market in the era of socialism

Outcome	Path solution	Cases
Highly developed media market*	s_accomplur* s_litera* s_develo* s_advert* s_globcom*	Croatia, Serbia, Slovenia
Weaker media market**	~s_accomplur* ~s_develo* ~s_advert* ~s_postmat ~s_globcom*	Bosnia and Herzegovina, Macedonia, Montenegro

Complex solution.

Consistency; raw coverage; unique coverage.

* 1; 0.64; 0.64.
** 1; 0.64; 0.64.
~ denotes the absence of the condition.

Macedonia, and Montenegro. This path resembles the development path of the mainly unfavorable conditions from the modernization period.

What contributes to the development of journalistic professionalism in the era of socialism? The analysis found no necessary conditions. In the analysis of the sufficient conditions for the high development of the journalism profession (s_journos), a unique path was produced that showed the favorable conditions in the more amenable type of socialism, higher literacy levels, greater economic development, stronger advertising, the inclusion in the global flows, and a more developed media market contributing to the early development of journalism-related education in Croatia, Serbia, and Slovenia (Table 6.4).

What produces high political parallelism during the era of socialism? The outcome variable of high political parallelism (s_polpa) showed no necessary conditions. However, there were several necessary conditions for the absence of political parallelism in the time of socialism: the accommodative pluralist type of socialist rule, higher literacy levels, greater economic development, the stronger development of advertising, greater inclusion in global communication flows, higher post-materialist values, a stronger media market, and the earlier development of journalism-related education (Table 6.5).

The analysis found that low post-materialist values were a sufficient condition for high political parallelism in the era of socialism. With low post-materialist values, high political parallelism was always present. Countries such as Bosnia and Herzegovina, Macedonia, and Montenegro did not have any, or only very few, necessary conditions for lower political parallelism (Table 6.6). While Serbia had most of the necessary conditions for lower political parallelism, they did not prove to be sufficient. Lower post-materialist values signify the lower modernization of culture alongside lower individualism and higher authoritarian values. In Serbia, there was a large discrepancy in the modernization between urban centers and rural areas, including Kosovo as one of the least modernized areas during the time of

Table 6.5 Sufficient conditions for a developed journalism profession in socialism

Outcome	Path solution	Cases
Higher development of journalism profession*	s_accomplur* s_litera* s_develo* s_advert* s_market* s_globcom*	Croatia, Serbia, Slovenia
Weaker development of journalism profession**	~s_accomplur* s_litera* ~s_develo* ~s_advert* ~s_market* ~s_globcom*	Macedonia, Montenegro

Complex solution.

Consistency; raw coverage; unique coverage.

* 0.99; 0.58; 0.58.
** 0.94; 0.54; 0.54.
~ denotes the absence of the condition.

Table 6.6 Sufficient conditions for political parallelism in socialism

Outcome	Path solution	Cases
High political parallelism*	~s_postmat	Bosnia and Herzegovina, Macedonia, Montenegro and Serbia
Low political parallelism**	s_globccom* s_advert s_accomplur s_journal* *s_develo* s_market* s_litera*	Croatia and Slovenia

Intermediate solution.

Consistency; raw coverage; unique coverage.

* 0.96; 0.82; 0.82.
** 0.85; 1; 1.
~ denotes the absence of the condition.

socialism. A culture with high traditional values was probably not suitable for a media market based on consumerist needs, and therefore, the media market developed more in line with the needs of the political elites.

We developed the following higher-order path-related contextual conditions based on the socialist period (again marked with an uppercase italic font):

S_MARKETPROF – this condition marks the paths of achieving higher market development and the earlier development of journalism-related education in Croatia, Serbia, and Slovenia during the socialist period.

S_HIGHPARALL – this condition marks the development of higher political parallelism in Bosnia and Herzegovina, Macedonia, Montenegro, and Serbia during the socialist period.

Media systems in digital modernity

Now we will proceed with the analysis of the necessary and sufficient conditions that play a role in the different configurations of paths related to the various shapes of the media market (*d_market*) and the degrees of media freedom during the last temporal framework (*d_mfree*).

We follow several steps in order to explain whether the influences of the remote contextual conditions on the two key outcomes predominate over the influences of the structural conditions in the present temporal framework, or whether the proximate conditions related to agency at the critical juncture are the most important factor shaping contemporary media systems. We perform several analyses in both instances using different combinations of conditions so as to evaluate the different influences of the remote or proximate conditions.

The last analysis adds the combined paths of the remote conditions to the analysis of media freedom and media market development in order to show the combined influence of the *longue durée* on the present-day media systems. Macro conditions were created to render the analysis of the sufficient conditions more amenable to interpretation. The conditions from the transition period (authoritarian rule during the 1990s and the intensity of war) were combined using the compensatory approach based on averaging the scores from the different sets (Ragin 2015) to capture the extent to which the transition was marked by unfavorable conditions (*D_TRANSITION*). Liberal democracy and the resolved stateness issue were combined as two conditions that often appear together as necessary conditions, and further that point to the consolidation of political institutions. This macro condition is computed using the weakest link approach, whereby the lowest score of the sets included in the construction of the macro condition is used (*D_CONSOLIDATION*) (Ragin 2015).

Necessary conditions and different paths to the development of the media market

What combination of conditions results in membership of the set of countries with highly developed media markets (*d_market*) during the post-socialist period of digital modernity? Membership of this outcome set was calibrated on the basis of high newspaper readership and high PSB audiences as the type of media practice that allows for better informed audiences and more engaged democratic practices (Curran et al. 2014).

Stronger European integration is the only necessary condition for the higher development of the media market in digital modernity in the six analyzed countries. The EU digitalization policy, including the digitalization of television broadcasting, which was in focus during the previous decade, can be related to this finding. There are also several necessary conditions for the negated outcome of a non-highly developed media market in digital

Why the media systems are the way they are 233

modernity, including higher clientelism, weak post-materialist values, higher media capture, and asymmetric parallelism. This would tend to show the importance of action-related proximate conditions, including the policy of European integration. A lack of media policy supporting media market development is thus again found to be one of the key conditions.

SUFFICIENT MEDIA SYSTEM CONDITIONS FOR MEDIA MARKET DEVELOPMENT

With regard to the sufficient conditions, we found only two conjunctures of media system conditions that lead to the different types of media market developments seen in digital modernity. Positive support for digital infrastructure and media pluralism, as well as low levels of asymmetric parallelism and media capture, are all part of the recipe for the higher development of the media market, with Croatia and Slovenia serving as cases that follow this path. The recipe for the weaker development of the media market consists of inefficient (or a lack of) media pluralism policies, asymmetric parallelism, and media capture. Serbia appears in the second solution with weak market development, although it has a better developed market than the other three countries because it shares with them the same media system conditions in this temporal framework. Additionally, this solution has much lower consistency (although it is still above the required threshold).

SUFFICIENT STRUCTURAL AND MACRO CONDITIONS FOR MEDIA MARKET DEVELOPMENT

When the macro conditions and the structural conditions are added to the media system and policy conditions, the analysis of the sufficient conditions found three paths of higher development of the media market and no consistent specific path for weaker development of the media market. Exemplifying the equifinality of the social processes that are clearly shown by the fsQCA

Table 6.7 Sufficient media system conditions for a developed media market in digital modernity

Outcome	Path solution	Cases
High media market development*	~d_aspar* ~d_hmcap* d_smeplu* d_dinfra	Croatia, Slovenia
Weak media market development**	~d_smeplu* d_aspar* d_hmcap	Bosnia and Herzegovina, Macedonia, Montenegro, Serbia

Intermediate solution.

Consistency; raw coverage; unique coverage.

* 0.98; 0.46; 0.46.
** 0.76; 0.79; 0.79.
~ denotes the absence of the condition.

approach, media markets can develop in really diverse circumstances and with a conjuncture of different conditions (Table 6.7, Table 6.8). Slovenia had all the favorable conditions: a more favorable transition, consolidated institutions, less clientelism, more post-materialist values, greater economic development, greater European integration, positive policies toward media pluralism and digital infrastructure, and a lack of asymmetric parallelism and media capture. Croatia had unfavorable conditions during the transition period of the 1990s (e.g., war and a degree of authoritarian rule), although these unfavorable conditions in combination with the more favorable conditions that followed during the 2000s (e.g., consolidated democratic institutions, European integration, less clientelism, higher economic development when compared to other Southeast European countries, and positive state policies toward digital infrastructure and media pluralism) ultimately configured the causal outcome of a more highly developed media market. Serbia is a peculiar case whose path is characterized by unfavorable conditions: a detrimental transition, unconsolidated institutions, clientelism, a lack of effective state support for digital infrastructure and media pluralism, asymmetric parallelism, and media capture. Among the positive conditions, Serbia is now taking part in EU accession negotiations, and it is also a bit above the crossover value for economic development. However, the consistency of the path is weaker for Serbia, and the subsequent analysis will show whether historical conditions explain the development of the media market in Serbia better than just the contemporary conditions that we currently consider.

Table 6.8 Sufficient conditions for a developed media market in digital modernity – structural and agency conditions

Outcome	Path solution	Cases
High media market development*	~D_TRANSITION* D_CONSOLIDATION* ~d_client* ~d_mgov* ~d_rwgov* d_euint * d_develo *d_postmat ~d_aspar* ~d_hmcap* d_smeplu* d_dinfra	Slovenia
High media market development**	D_TRANSITION* D_CONSOLIDATION* ~d_client* d_mgov* d_rwgov* d_euint * d_develo *d_postmat d_smeplu* ~d_aspar* ~d_hmcap* d_dinfra	Croatia
High media market development***	D_TRANSITION* ~D_CONSOLIDATION* d_client* d_mgov* d_rwgov* d_euint * d_develo* ~d_postmat ~d_smeplu* d_aspar* d_hmcap* ~d_dinfra	Serbia

Intermediate solution.

Consistency; raw coverage; unique coverage.

* 0.96; 0.3; 0.22.
** 1; 0.25; 0.17.
*** 0.77; 0.32; 0.32.
~ denotes the absence of the condition.

Necessary conditions and different paths to media freedom

What causes media freedom? In the six-case universe we investigated, the necessary conditions for higher media freedom in the period of digital modernity are consolidated liberal democracy, the resolved stateness issue, European integration, economic development, state support for digital infrastructure, and a lack of media capture. The necessary conditions for weaker media freedom are clientelism, a non-cooperative transition, weak post-materialist values, asymmetric pluralism, and higher media capture.

SUFFICIENT MEDIA SYSTEM CONDITIONS FOR MEDIA FREEDOM

How do the media system characteristics from the period of digital modernity configure the final outcome of media freedom? Here the analysis is similar to most media system analyses, although it is performed using the fsQCA software (cf. Büchel et al. 2016). There is one path leading to higher media freedom in digital modernity, which consists of the higher development of the media market, positive policies toward developing digital infrastructure and media pluralism, and a lack (or lower level) of both asymmetric parallelism and media capture (Table 6.9). Two countries belong to this path, namely Croatia and Slovenia. The second path is the one to which Bosnia and Herzegovina and Serbia belong, with a lack of effective policies concerning digital infrastructure and media pluralism, as well as higher asymmetric parallelism and media capture, which produce lower media freedom. The third path is the one with the absence of a developed media market, a lack of media pluralism policies, and higher asymmetric parallelism and media capture,

Table 6.9 Sufficient media system characteristics for media freedom in digital modernity

Outcome	Path solution	Cases
High media freedom*	d_market* ~d_aspar* ~d_hmcap* d_smeplu* d_dinfra	Croatia, Slovenia
Weak media freedom**	~d_dinfra* ~d_smeplu* d_aspar* d_hmcap	Bosnia and Herzegovina, Serbia
Weak media freedom**	~d_smeplu* ~ d_market* d_aspar* d_hmcap	Bosnia and Herzegovina, Macedonia, Montenegro

Intermediate solutions.

Consistency; raw coverage; unique coverage.

* 0.96; 0.64; 0.64.
** 1; 0.61; 0.12.
*** 1; 0.6; 0.11.
~ denotes the absence of the condition.

which also produce lower media freedom. The cases belonging to this path are Bosnia and Herzegovina, Macedonia, and Montenegro. Because we are dealing with fuzzy sets, it is possible that some countries appear in two path solutions (i.e., Bosnia and Herzegovina in this example).

SUFFICIENT MACRO AND STRUCTURAL CONDITIONS IN THE PATH TO MEDIA FREEDOM

Two paths to media freedom are found when the macro and structural conditions are included in the analysis (Table 6.10). Slovenia again had the most favorable conditions, with the outcomes of higher media freedom, favorable transition factors, consolidated institutions, less clientelism, greater economic development, European integration, state support for digital infrastructure and media pluralism, a developed media market, weak media capture, and weak asymmetric parallelism. Croatia had a less favorable transition, and it also differs from Slovenia due to having a tradition of a less consensual type of government, with the largest party occupying a large share of seats in government and right-wing parties having longer dominance in government. However, although these conditions are expected to be less favorable for media freedom, consolidated institutions, less clientelism and higher economic development when compared to other SEE countries, European integration, the development of the media market, positive state policies toward digital infrastructure and media pluralism, weak media capture, and weak asymmetric parallelism are all relevant to the achievement of greater media freedom.

Table 6.10 Sufficient conditions for media freedom in digital modernity – structural and agency conditions

Outcome	Path solution	Cases
High media freedom*	~D_TRANSITION* D_CONSOLIDATION* ~d_client* ~d_mgov* ~d_rwgov* d_euint* d_develop* d_postmat * d_infra* d_smeplu ~d_hmcap* ~d_aspar* d_market	Slovenia
High media freedom**	D_TRANSITION* D_CONSOLIDATION* ~d_client* d_mgov* d_rwgov* d_euint* d_develop* d_postmat * d_infra* d_smeplu ~d_hmcap* ~d_aspar* d_market	Croatia
Weak media freedom***	D_TRANSITION* ~D_CONSOLIDATION* d_client* d_mgov* d_rwgov* d_euint* d_develop* ~d_postmat* ~d_infra * ~d_smeplu d_hmcap* d_aspar* d_market	Serbia

Intermediate solution.

Consistency; raw coverage; unique coverage.

*   1; 0.43; 0.31.
** 0.92; 0.33; 0.21.
*** 1; 0.25; 0.25.
~   denotes the absence of the condition.

Why the media systems are the way they are   237

The negated analysis of the sufficient conditions for weak media freedom found just one consistent path that only covered Serbia, which had an unfavorable transition, unconsolidated democratic institutions, higher clientelism, and weaker post-materialist values, while its state did not strongly or efficiently support either digital infrastructure or media pluralism. While Serbia did manage to create a developed media market, it is burdened by high media capture and has certain characteristics of asymmetric parallelism. Serbia's economic development is at the crossover point, and its European integration process seems to not be as effective in terms of promoting the further development of democratic institutions and the rule of law. Indeed, it seems to aid undemocratic practices and leaders (as in Montenegro) and actually supports the development of competitive authoritarianism in the name of maintaining stability (Bieber 2020).

Figure 6.1 shows how the six contemporary media systems compare with regard to their characteristics (as based on the calibrations of the relevant conditions presented in Table 6.1).

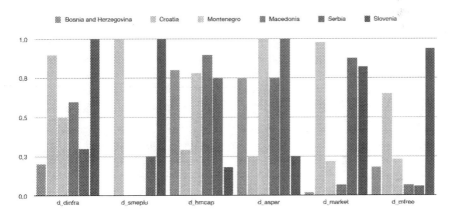

Figure 6.1 Media system conditions in the digital modernity temporal framework

The longue durée in media freedom and media market development

We now come to answer the final question by determining the influence of the *longue durée* on the media system transformations seen during the post-socialist period of democratic transformations. We first analyze the remote contextual conditions from each previous temporal framework separately in relation to the outcome of media freedom in digital modernity. There are no necessary conditions from the modernization or socialist periods for media freedom or a lack of media freedom as an outcome in the present temporal framework.

With regard to the sufficient conditions, media freedom as an outcome shows one path of conditions, with two cases sharing that path: Croatia and Slovenia (Table 6.11). They shared a similar modernization path by which the media market was developed alongside economic and social development (not like the market development under political incentives seen in Serbia, or the weak market development seen in other countries). Their path is also marked by the development of both the media market and journalism profession in the era of socialism and by weaker political parallelism in this period. Furthermore, in the period of digital modernity, another condition in this solution is the consolidation of state and democratic institutions, a more favorable political culture (i.e., less clientelism), European integration, and economic development in digital modernity. This solution shows that although Croatia had less favorable development characteristics during the transition in the 1990s (war and authoritarianism), other favorable conditions from the modernization, socialism, and digital modernity periods resulted in the greater development of media freedom.

There are two paths to weak media freedom (Table 6.11). The first is the path of Serbia, which followed a specific path of building the media market in the modernization period and developing higher political parallelism in the socialist period. In the period of digital modernity, it had mostly unfavorable conditions, including a detrimental transition, the weak consolidation of institutions, and a clientelist political culture. The case of Serbia shows that a developed media market does not necessary result in higher media freedom. The second path is that of both Bosnia and Herzegovina and Montenegro, which saw weak development of the media market in the modernization period, as well as a weaker market and journalism profession in the socialist period, but which also developed higher political parallelism during the

Table 6.11 Sufficient conditions for media freedom in digital modernity – contextual, socio-economic, and political system conditions

Outcome	Path solution	Cases
High media freedom*	M_ECONM* ~M_POLITM* ~M_WEAKM* S_MARKETPROF* ~S_HIGHPARALL* D_CONSOLIDATION* ~d_client* d_euint* d_develop*	Croatia, Slovenia
Weak media freedom**	~M_ECONM* M_POLITM* S_HIGHPARALL* D_TRANSITION* ~D_CONSOLIDATION* d_client*	Serbia
Weak media freedom***	~M_ECONM* M_WEAKM* ~S_MARKETPROF* S_HIGHPARALL* ~D_CONSOLIDATION* D_TRANSITION* d_client*	Bosnia and Herzegovina, Montenegro

Intermediate solution.

Consistency; raw coverage; unique coverage.

* 0.94; 0.73; 0.73.
** 1; 0.16; 0.16.
*** 1; 0.45; 0.45.
~ denotes the absence of the condition.

socialist period. In the period of digital modernity, these countries had a detrimental transition, weak consolidation of institutions, and a clientelist political culture. Macedonia was not explained by any configuration, although it had similar condition values as Bosnia and Herzegovina and Montenegro in the intermediate solution given below. It only differed in terms of the type of transition it underwent in the 1990s, with the more favorable conditions of a lower level of conflict and less authoritarianism. However, these favorable conditions during the early transition were degraded during the "de-consolidation" phase, which makes Macedonia more like Bosnia and Herzegovina and Montenegro. The condition of economic development did not appear in these paths, nor did the level of European integration.

Based on the presented configuration paths of the conjunctures of conditions, we develop three *remote contextual conditions* from the three analyzed periods that define the *longue durée* paths of the political, socio-economic, and cultural fields in the six analyzed countries:

> Remote path of strong markets and the consolidation of institutions (Croatia and Slovenia) R_CONSMARKET.
> Remote path of strong markets and unconsolidated institutions (Serbia) R_UNCONSMARKET.
> Remote path of weak markets and unconsolidated institutions (Bosnia and Herzegovina, Macedonia, and Montenegro) R_WMARKET.

When we add in the contextual conditions (which have resulted from the previous steps in our analysis), we again uncover three distinct paths that more or less follow the historical remote paths. Croatia and Slovenia, which exhibited the most favorable remote conditions of persistently stronger media markets and more consolidated institutions, also had more favorable media system conditions and policies in the period of digital modernity, which produced higher media freedom. Those countries that did not manage to develop their media markets in the periods of modernization and socialism also failed to do so in the period of digital modernity. Moreover, in those countries, higher parallelism developed into a form of asymmetric parallelism. The high media capture and lack of media pluralism policies showed the reluctance of the political elites to adopt media policies that might overcome the hard legacies of the contextual and remote conditions of the *longue durée*.

With the inclusion of the remote conditions in the analysis, three paths of media market development are discovered. These paths follow the historical development of the media markets in Southeast Europe. The favorable historical development path of both Croatia and Slovenia, coupled with the support for media pluralism and digital infrastructure as well as the absence of asymmetric parallelism and media capture, also explain the developed media markets seen in the period of digital modernity. The Serbian media market is also explained by a specific historical development path, although

240 Why the media systems are the way they are

Table 6.12 Sufficient conditions for media freedom in digital modernity – remote contextual and media systems conditions

Outcome	Path solution	Cases
High media freedom*	R_CONSMARKET* ~R_UNCONSMARKET* ~R_WMARKET* d_market* ~d_aspar* ~d_hmcap* d_smeplu* d_dinfra	Croatia, Slovenia
Low media freedom**	~R_CONSMARKET* ~R_UNCONSMARKET* R_WMARKET* ~d_market* ~d_smeplu* d_aspar* d_hmcap	Bosnia and Herzegovina, Macedonia, Montenegro
Low media freedom***	R_UNCONSMARKET*~R_CONSMARKET* ~d_dinfra* ~d_smeplu* d_aspar* d_hmcap	Serbia

Intermediate solution.

Consistency; raw coverage; unique coverage.

* 0.96; 0.66; 0.66.
** 1; 0.54; 0.54.
*** 1; 0.18; 0.18.
~ denotes the absence of the condition.

Table 6.13 Sufficient remote and media system conditions explaining the media market in digital modernity

Outcome	Path solution	Cases
High media market development*	R_CONSMARKET* ~R_WMARKET* ~d_aspar* ~d_hmcap* d_smeplu* d_dinfra	Croatia, Slovenia
High media market development**	R_UNCONSMARKET* ~R_WMARKET* d_aspar	Serbia
Weak media market development***	R_WMARKET* ~R_CONSMARKET* ~R_UNCONSMARKET* ~d_smeplu* d_aspar* d_hmcap	Bosnia and Herzegovina, Macedonia, Montenegro

Intermediate solution.

Consistency; raw coverage; unique coverage.

* 0.98; 0.46; 0.46.
** 0.78; 0.25; 0.25.
*** 0.91; 0.72; 0.72.
~ denotes the absence of the condition.

it is also characterized by higher asymmetric parallelism. The third group of countries are Bosnia and Herzegovina, Macedonia, and Montenegro, which all had a less favorable historical development path and are also all burdened by a lack of effective media pluralism policies and higher asymmetric parallelism and media capture.

Serbia had a somewhat more favorable path in terms of the developed media market, although it was always accompanied by higher political parallelism and unconsolidated democratic institutions in the post-socialist period. The lack of effective policies concerning the digital infrastructure and pluralism, as well as the higher media capture and asymmetric parallelism, also remain relevant conditions for the lower media freedom seen in this country.

Several analyses of post-socialist media systems reveal their similarities with polarized pluralist or Mediterranean media systems (Balčytiene 2009; Dobek-Ostrowska 2012; Peruško 2013a; Peruško et al. 2013). However, our historical institutionalist analysis also reveals significant differences in relation to the development of the media systems. As Hallin and Mancini (2004) note, the high political parallelism and weak development of the media markets in Southern Europe were tied to the later development of the bourgeoisie as well as to the longer and stronger hold of the aristocracy and church. However, in the majority of the six analyzed countries, the more serious development of the media market only evolved during the socialist period, which represents a different path to that of Southern Europe (although Greece might be the most similar case). The socialist media markets were, in some countries, developed according to the needs of the political elites, although in others they developed in accordance with new consumerist needs. The development of the media markets in the present temporal framework only succeeded if they were developed in the previous historical periods, although there are two alternative paths to their development: in the context of higher economic development, where there is greater potential for development according to the needs of both the advertising industry and consumer society; and in the opposite path, where state institutions and political elites have incentives to promote the development of the press – as the press also plays a role in forming national and political identities. When stronger market development was coupled with higher political parallelism, as was the case in Serbia, this kind of market proved to be less successful in establishing the checks and balances with other forms of power (such as political power) and in ensuring greater media freedom in later periods.

Socialism, therefore, might have played a beneficial role in strengthening the media markets and the journalism profession in some cases included in our analysis, and it could have served as a buffer against greater political instrumentalization in the democratic temporal framework. Other countries, which did not have a stronger starting point, were more vulnerable to subsequent stronger political influence. Clientelism in the present temporal framework, as an indicator of the political culture and broader societal values (higher clientelism points to a lack of post-materialist values), is shown to be an important and necessary condition for weaker media freedom, higher asymmetric parallelism, a lack of effective policies concerning media pluralism and the development of digital infrastructure, and higher media capture. Clientelism could thus be seen as a continuation of the negative impact of the weaker post-materialist values that are supportive of higher political instrumentalization. As a lack of post-materialist values was found to be a sufficient condition for higher political parallelism in the time of socialism, the thesis regarding the role of culture (i.e., social values) in (negative) media system development seems to have some traction.

The historical developmental paths were shown to be important in terms of explaining the character of the media systems in the period of digital modernity. Countries that had less favorable conditions during the previous periods did not manage to develop stronger media markets or media freedom in the contemporary period, even with certain positive policies and indicators in place from the post-socialist period. For example, although Macedonia avoided stronger inter-ethnic conflict, had a somewhat developed procedural democracy during the transitional period, and even had some positive state policies concerning the development of digital infrastructure, due to its weaker developmental starting point it did not manage to trump the deconsolidation tendencies and subsequent erosion of media freedom. The case of Macedonia shows how deeper structural factors can overcome agency. Yet, the structural factors developed in Croatia helped it to overcome certain detrimental tendencies – although it experienced war and authoritarian tendencies during the transition period in the 1990s, the positive media policy in the context of the historically inherited stronger media market and greater journalistic professionalism managed to ensure greater media freedom (in comparison to other Southeast European countries, although it lags behind Slovenia). The case of Serbia shows how agency (in terms of political will) can overcome detrimental factors related to the development of the media market, although the same conditions resulted in a politically captured media market and low media freedom.

The missing pieces and directions for future research

At the beginning of this book, we proposed that a complete sociological explanation of media system transformations would need to include both a structural analysis of institutions as well as an analysis of the actions performed by individual or collective agents. While we have focused more attention on institutions in our analysis, we have also included aspects that speak to action or agency. A related question concerned the role of the *longue durée*, as opposed to proximate or remote contemporary conditions, in the media system transformations. The impact of socialism, as one such historical source of causal conditions, was especially highlighted in our original research question. In the fsQCA, based on the substantive analyses conducted in the previous chapters, we included both structural/remote and proximate/agency conditions. The analysis presented in this chapter shows how those conditions interact in various configurations to produce specific outcomes regarding media market development and media freedom.

A brief summary of the presented analysis is that the contextual conditions of the *longue durée*, the remote structural conditions (political and socio-economic), and the proximate media system conditions all play both a positive and a negative role. Hard (unfavorable) macro conditions can be overcome through helpful actions in terms of media policy and political consolidation. Without the positive incursion of agency, the hard path of unfavorable historical conditions continues into the future. The hard *longue durée* is more vulnerable to backsliding and democratic de-consolidation. Additionally, we found that the same outcome of a developed media market can be produced by way of early political autonomy in conditions otherwise unfavorable to this result, although the market is mostly captured and not free.

In light of expectations concerning the positive role of "EU conditionality" in the media system transformations, the study found that although European integration is a necessary condition for the development of the media market, media freedom, and greater journalistic autonomy (weak media capture) in the period of digital modernity, it is not a sufficient condition. Progress in relation to European integration does not by itself guarantee higher media freedom, which was revealed in the cases of Montenegro and Serbia. While our analysis was very much centered on institutional change, as we investigated the transformations of the media system structures we could more easily notice the agency in the structuration of the new media system institutions. This direction of thought would benefit from further empirical research.

While the substantive findings regarding the media system transformations in the third wave European democracies primarily relate to the six included countries, in addition to the generalizations mentioned earlier, our approach can nonetheless also be used to study other *longue durée* media transformations in Europe and elsewhere, socialist or otherwise, albeit only with necessary conceptual adaptations to different cultures and histories. For instance, we expect that similar hard *longue durée* paths of countries under long-term patrimonial regimes would also result in the post-Soviet republics. Could the development of the media market in Russia be explained in the same way as the development in Serbia, as based on political power rather than on conditions of modernization and development?

Some of the findings of this study might be generalized even more broadly. For instance, are there examples of media systems somewhere in the world where media freedom developed without democratic consolidation, without high literacy levels, and in conditions of asymmetric parallelism and high media capture? These are just some of the findings that also require further empirical research.

How can the present results be related to the theoretical expectations of Hallin and Mancini (2004) regarding the relationships between certain dimensions and their values? Previous research conducted in the CEE countries found that the negative correlation between political parallelism and journalistic professionalism holds in contemporary CEE countries in the same way as in Western Europe (Brüggemann et al. 2014), although political parallelism does not positively correlate with higher professionalism but instead negatively correlates with press freedom (Castro Herrero et al. 2017). Our study similarly found that asymmetric parallelism is one of the necessary conditions for higher media capture (the opposite of journalistic autonomy), and further, that both these conditions are detrimental to media freedom. Our analysis also found that certain conditions shown to be important in the analysis conducted by Hallin and Mancini (2004) did not seem to be as important in this comparative analysis. For example, majoritarian government was not found to be a necessary condition for any outcome, and it also appeared in different solutions without a unique outcome.

Typically, the normative aim of media systems research in the post-socialist context is to identify recipes for the successful democratization of media systems. In our study, we also found "recipes for disaster" in the combination of conditions that produce media capture and asymmetric parallelism in hybrid and competitive authoritarian media systems. The next step in this research direction is to show how hybrid media systems are constituted beyond the six analyzed cases, which combinations of causal conditions change when compared to the development of a media system within a democratic political framework, and what actions by meso or micro actors can possibly intervene to change the hard *longue durée* path to one with a successful outcome in terms of media freedom and a developed media market.

Notes

1 GNI per capita data for 1972, World Bank, https://databank.worldbank.org/reports.aspx?source=2&series=NY.GNP.PCAP.CD&country=).
2 For later years these sources were used: https://en.wikipedia.org/wiki/Government_of_Serbia; https://en.wikipedia.org/wiki/Government_of_Slovenia; https://en.wikipedia.org/wiki/Government_of_Croatia; https://en.wikipedia.org/wiki/Government_of_the_Federation_of_Bosnia_and_Herzegovina; https://en.wikipedia.org/wiki/Government_of_Montenegro; https://en.wikipedia.org/wiki/Politics_of_North_Macedonia.

Methodological Appendix

The Methodological Appendix includes technical details concerning how the original analyses for this book were performed: content analyses, expert interviews and fsQCA. An original content analysis was conducted during the preparation of this book with the aim of documenting the media cultures in two different temporal frameworks. More specifically, content analyses were performed with regard to TV schedules and newspapers, and interviews were conducted with media professionals, media scholars, and civil society activists in the six countries of interest. The Methodological Appendix also includes truth tables related to the fsQCA in Chapter 6.

Content analysis of TV cultures

Sample

The year 1979 was represented by one constructed week ($K = 52$ days) featuring the following dates: June 27, March 20, May 11, June 2, August 23, October 14, and December 5. For 2016, we used one consecutive week (April 1–7). Although there is no definitive rule concerning the sampling procedure or the size of television schedules, Riffle et al. (1998, in Kripendorff 2004, p. 123) argue that "one constructed week adequately predicted the population mean," while Gerbner, Gross, Jackson-Beeck, Jeffries-Fox, and Signorelly (in Wimmer and Dominick 1994, p. 170) obtain comparable results from a consecutive week and a random yearly constructed week sample.

The analyzed television schedules for 1979 were published in the main republican daily newspapers (*Delo, Nova Makedonija, Oslobođenje, Pobjeda, Večernji list*, and *Večernje novosti*). As neither the newspaper archives nor the television schedules have been digitalized into publicly available databases, library archives were consulted to obtain copies of the daily newspapers for 1979, which was considered representative of the socialist period. For 1979, we analyzed all the nationwide terrestrial channels established within the country.

For all six post-Yugoslav states, TV schedules for the year 2016 were generated from the same Internet site (http://tvprofil.net). The criteria for choosing the TV channels to be included in the analysis in 2016 were the top two public service and top two commercial generalist terrestrial TV channels established in the country that covered the entire territory.

Data regarding the national markets were obtained from the MAVISE database managed by the European Audiovisual Observatory. Unfortunately, we were unable to find TV schedules for all the channels that met the above criteria on the publicly available website. Furthermore, some states only had one statewide PSB TV channel. In 2016, Macedonia only had one public service channel, while in terms of commercial television, the only available TV schedule was for ALSAT (a Macedonian commercial channel that runs programs in the Albanian language). In Bosnia and Herzegovina, Federalna Televizija (Federal Television [FTV]) was available across the entire territory, and it was the only example of a public service channel with national reach.

The final composition of the sample is presented in Table A.1. The final sample comprised 1,048 units of programs for 1979 and 4,522 units for 2016. The analyses presented in the book are based on the minutes of programs.

Unit of analysis

The unit of the content analysis was a television program as it was announced in the TV listings, with the assumption being that the listings reflect the actual reality of broadcast programs. This assumption is shared by other studies of the same type (Riffe 2008; Krippendorff 2004; Wimmer and Dominick 1994).

Table A.1 Analyzed TV channels per country for 1979 and 2016

	1979	2016 PSB	Commercial TV
Bosnia and Herzegovina	TV Sarajevo 1 TV Sarajevo 2	Federalna televizija (FTV)	OBN HAYAT TV
Croatia	TV Zagreb 1 TV Zagreb 2	Hrvatska televizija 1 program (HTV1) Hrvatska televizija 2 program (HTV)	Nova TV RTL
N. Macedonia	TV Skopje 1 TV Skopje 2	Makedonska televizija 1 (MTV1)	ALSAT
Montenegro	TV Titograd 1 TV Titograd 2	Televizija Crne Gore1 (TVCG1) Televizija Crne Gore2 (TVCG2)	PINK TV Crna Gora
Serbia	TV Beograd 1 TV Beograd 2	TV Srbji 1 (TVS1) TV Srbije 2 (TVS2)	B92 PRVA SRPSKA TV
Slovenia	TV Ljubljana 1 TV Ljubljana 2	TV Slovenija 1 (TVSLO1) TV Slovenija 2 (TVSLO2)	POP TV KANAL A

The coding

The TV schedules from 1979 were coded by Antonija Čuvalo. The schedules from 2016 were coded by trained coders who were all graduate students of journalism at the Faculty of Political Science, University of Zagreb. The two codings were reviewed and analyzed by the same coauthor.

The present study of television cultures adapted the list of program categories used in Ward's (2006) study of program diversity in four European countries, including Croatia (Peruško and Čuvalo 2014). The residual categories of *miscellaneous* (program announcements, commercials) and *other* (programs that were not identifiable) programs were excluded from the final analysis. The coding matrix included the following variables: state/republic, date, name of the channel, type of channel (public or commercial, only for 2016), program title, start time, end time, program length, and prime time (19:30–23:00). The genres were grouped into three program modes, namely information, fiction, and entertainment (Table A.3).

Table A.2 Analyzed units of programs from the TV schedules in 1979 and 2016

	1979	*2016*
Bosnia and Herzegovina	190 (19%)	671 (15%)
Croatia	177 (17%)	1,023 (23%)
N. Macedonia	173 (16%)	504 (11%)
Montenegro	179 (17%)	699 (15%)
Serbia	167 (16%)	765 (17%)
Slovenia	162 (15%)	860 (19%)
Total	1,048	4,692

Table A.3 Television genres and modes used in the television content analysis

Fiction	Comedy
	Drama (including series and miniseries)
	Film (cinema and television)
	Soap opera
Entertainment	Breakfast TV
	Chat and talk show
	Children's show
	Media and popular culture
	Music (not classical or jazz)
	Reality program
	Media and popular culture (light entertainment)
Information/factual	Cultural program (including educational program)
	Current affairs
	Documentary (on any topic, including education and science, except art and culture, which are coded in the cultural programs category)
	News
	Religion

The origin of the production was coded as EU production; US production; production of Bosnia and Herzegovina, Croatia, Montenegro, Macedonia, Serbia, Slovenia; production of other countries (outside the EU and USA); and JRT production (unspecified). The latter category refers to productions from the socialist period, when it was not possible to reliably identify the republic in which the program was produced. The majority of programs for which we could not identify the origin of production fell into the genre categories of *cartoons* and *news* in Bosnia and Herzegovina, Slovenia, and Montenegro. The daily newspapers from these republics did not consistently publish information on the origins of programs. In total, for 3% of all programs (8% in Bosnia and Herzegovina, 6% in Montenegro, and 4% in Slovenia) it was not possible to identify the republic in which they were produced. It is possible that this category also includes foreign programs edited (translation, dubbing) and transmitted by republican television stations.

For each unit of analysis, the genre and origin of the program were identified based on multiple sources: information published in TV guides and additional information obtained from newspapers' TV pages, the JRT document *JRT 79 Television Programmes*, analyzed newspapers, books (Vončina 2001, 2003), and brochures such as Andrić and Otašević (2002), and online sources, primarily the web archives of public service channels in the analyzed states, IMDb, and YouTube.

Content analysis of the daily press

Sample

The daily papers chosen for the analysis had the highest circulation in the relevant republics during the socialist period. Six daily newspapers form our sample: *Delo* from Slovenia, *Večernji list* from Croatia, *Oslobođenje* from Bosnia and Herzegovina, *Večernje novosti* from Serbia, *Pobjeda* from Montenegro, and *Nova Makedonija* from Macedonia.

The sample for the newspaper content analysis was a constructed week for the year 1979 ($K = 52$ days) featuring the following dates: January 27, March 20, May 11, July 2, August 23, October 14, and December 5. The constructed week was calculated in the following way: the number of days in the year (365) was divided by the number of days in the constructed week (7). The resulting number (52.14) was taken as the number of issues between each issue used for the sample in the analysis. If the daily paper was not published on the relevant date from the constructed week, the previous day was included (e.g., October 13, 1979, was included for *Delo* and *Večernje novosti*). In total, 42 editions were analyzed.

Unit of analysis

The unit of analysis is a newspaper article. An article was only coded if it was published or announced on the title page of the paper. The size of the sample in the analysis is 423 newspaper articles (128 in *Delo*, 59 in *Večernji list*, 77 in *Oslobođenje*, 38 in *Večernje Novosti*, 56 in *Pobjeda*, and 65 in *Nova Makedonija*).

Coding

The coding matrix for the content analysis of the newspaper articles consisted of 17 variables.

The first section was made up of technical variables (name of newspaper, date, day of the week, etc.). The second section of the coding matrix was dedicated to the technical and graphic characteristics of the analyzed newspaper articles, for example, the article size (one-quarter of a page, one-quarter to one-half a page; one-half to one page, one page or larger). The *article theme* variable measured the dominant theme of the article: art and culture, economy and business, education and science, environment, foreign policy, international politics, lifestyle, popular culture and entertainment, domestic politics, public sector and service, community and human interest story, law, security and crime, civil society, religion, sport, and other. Aside from the article theme, the *geographical focus* of each newspaper article was also measured. This variable consisted of the following categories: Western Europe, Eastern Europe, United States, other countries and global (countries outside Europe and the United States), state level (if the newspaper focuses on issues from the republic in which it was published), socialist Yugoslavia level (if the article focuses on the entire federation or other republics/states within the federation), and other (if it is impossible to determine the geographical focus). The *authorship* variable was measured based on the following categories: the article had an original author (journalist), it was translated or based on other media, the article was authored by a news agency, and finally, the authorship was unclear or the author was not named. If the article clearly stated the name of the author, then the author's gender was also coded (male, female), while if it was not clear, the coders coded the article as not signed or could not be determined.

Five coders coded newspaper articles based on their familiarity with the language and script of the sample newspapers. *Delo* is published in Slovenian, in Latin script. *Večernji list* is published in Croatian, in Latin script. *Večernje novosti*, *Pobjeda*, and *Nova Makedonija* are published in Cyrillic script. *Večernje novosti* and *Pobjeda* are published in Serbian. *Nova Makedonija* is published in Macedonian. *Oslobođenje* is partly published in Latin and partly in Cyrillic script, in Croatian and Serbian languages.

The intercoder reliability was determined using 14% of the sample, including one day for each newspaper. More specifically, the intercoder reliability was determined using a subsample of newspapers published on January 27, 1979. Krippendorff's alpha was calculated using SPSS Statistics v22.0 with Hayes's macro (De Swert 2012). The minimum recommended

Methodological Appendix

Krippendorff's alpha for good reliability is generally accepted to be 0.8 (De Swert, 2012). The results of the intercoder reliability test for the variables included in our content analysis were as follows:

- Geographical level: 0.85
- Theme of the article: 0.77
- Article size: 0.73
- Authorship: 0.81
- Author's gender: 0.8
- Text presentation: 0.88

Interviews

Interview protocol

The semi-structured interviews broadly followed the topics defined within the UNESCO Media Development Indicators. Therefore the interviewees were asked to assess the following elements of their media systems:

1 A system of regulation conductive to freedom of expression, pluralism, and diversity on the part of the media (legal and regulatory framework).
2 The plurality and diversity of the media, a level economic playing field, and the transparency of ownership (media market, concentration, and market regulation).
3 The media as a platform for democratic discourse (the role of public service media in the media field).
4 Professional capacity building and supporting those institutions that underpin the freedom of expression, pluralism, and diversity (position of the journalism profession, education, self-regulation, and the role of professional organizations and civil society.

Interviewees

Interviews were conducted by the authors of this book with experts in the media field from the six countries of interest: journalists from journalist associations, unions, media, and journalism NGOs or public media, as well as experts and media analysts from academia and civil society. The interviewees were chosen based on their expertise and availability.

Bosnia and Herzegovina

1 Mirna Buljugić, journalist, Balkan Investigative Reporting Network (BIRN), December 2016.
2 Borka Rudić, journalist, Association of BH Journalists, December 2016.

Croatia

3 Paško Bilić, academic, Institute for Development and International Relations (IRMO), March 2019.
4 Hrvoje Zovko, journalist, Croatian Journalism Association, March 2019.

North Macedonia

5 Besim Nebiu, civil society activist, December 2016.
6 Snežana Trpevska, academic, School of Journalism and Public Relations, Institute of Communication Studies in Skopje, December 2016.

Montenegro

7 Marijana Camović, journalist, Trade Union of Media, December 2016.
8 Vladan Mićunović, journalist, Radio Television Montenegro, December 2016.

Serbia

9 Dragan Janjić, journalist, Independent Association of Journalists of Serbia (NUNS), December 2016.
10 Snežana Milivojević, academic, University of Belgrade, November 2015.
11 Saša Mirković, Ministry of Culture, November 2015.
12 Antonela Riha, journalist, November 2015.
13 Aleksandar Todorović, journalist, JRT, November 2017.

Slovenia

14 Boris Bergant, journalist, former editor of TV Ljubljana and TV Slovenia, EBU, June 2017.
15 Igor Vobič, academic, University of Ljubljana, June 2017.
16 Brankica Petković, civil society activist, Peace Institute, May 2019.

fsQCA ANALYSIS

The truth tables for the fsQCA analysis in Chapter 6 are included below. The truth tables have the same numbers as the path solution tables in Chapter 6.

252 *Methodological Appendix*

Table 6.2.A Truth table for the analysis of highly developed print market in modernization as an outcome

m_otte mp	m_babe mp	m_self rul	m_lite ra	m_ind ust	m_print ing	m_globc om	N	OUT: m_mar ket	raw consist.	PRI consist.	SYM consist
0	0	1	0	1	1	1	1	1	1	1	1
0	1	1	1	1	1	1	1	1	1	1	1
1	1	0	1	0	0	0	0	1	1	1	1
1	1	0	0	0	0	0	0	3	0	0.22	0	0

Consistency threshold: 0.75

Table 6.2.B Truth table for the analysis of non-modernization

m_ott frul	m_bab era	m_sel dust	m_lit ting	m_in com	m_prin	m_glob	emp	emp	N	OUTPUT: ~m_ma rket	raw consist.	PRI consist.	SYM consist
1	0	0	0	0	0	0			3	1	0.94	0.93	1
0	1	0	1	1	1	1			1	0	0.2	0	0
1	0	1	0	0	0	1			1	0	0.18	0	0
0	1	1	1	1	1	1			1	0	0.03	0	0

Consistency threshold: 0.75

Methodological Appendix   253

Table 6.3 Truth table for the highly developed journalism profession as an outcome in modernization

m_ot temp	m_ba bemp	m_s elfru	m_l itera	m_i ndus	m_pri nting	m_m arket	m_m bcom	m_glo m_journos	N	OUTCOME	raw consis	PRI consis l	t.	t.	SYM consist
0	1	0	1	1	1	1	1	1	1	1	1	1	1	1	1
0	1	1	1	1	1	1	1	1	1	1	1	1	1	1	1
1	0	1	0	0	1	0	0	1	1	1	1	1	1	1	1
1	0	0	0	0	0	0	0	3	0	0	0.26	0.26	0.26		0.26

Consistency threshold: 0.75

Table 6.4.A Truth table for the highly developed media market in socialism as an outcome

s_acco	s_lit	s_dev	s_ad	s_post	s_glob	num	OUTCOME	raw consis	PRI	mplur	era	elo	vert	mat	com	ber	s_market consist.	consist.	SYM consist
1	1	1	1	0	1	1	1	1	1								1	1	1
1	1	1	1	1	1	2	1	1	1								1	1	1
0	0	0	0	0	0	1	0	0.16	0										0
0	1	0	0	0	0	2	0	0.15	0										0

Consistency threshold: 0.75

254 *Methodological Appendix*

Table 6.4.B Truth table with non-highly developed media market in socialism as an outcome

								~s_market
s_acco mplur	s_lit era	s_de velo	s_ad vert	s_pos tmat	s_ma rket	s_glob com	N	
0	0	0	0	0	0	1	1	1
0	1	0	1	1	0	2	1	1
1	1	1	1	0	1	1	0	0.33
1	1	1	1	1	1	2	0	0.17

Consistency threshold: 0.75

Table 6.5 Truth table with highly developed journalism profession in socialism as an outcome

s_acco mplur	s_lit era	s_de velo	s_ad vert	s_pos tmat	s_ma rket	s_glob com	N s_journos	OUTCOME: s_journos	raw consist.	PRI consist.	SYM consist
1	1	1	1	0	1	1	1	1	1	1	1
1	1	1	1	1	1	1	2	1	0.99	0.99	1
0	0	0	0	0	0	0	1	0	0.63	0.43	0.43
0	1	0	0	0	0	0	2	0	0.38	0.08	0.08

Consistency threshold: 0.75

Methodological Appendix 255

Table 6.6.A Truth table with high political parallelism in socialism as an outcome

s_acco mplur t.	s_li tera	s_de velo	s_ad vert	s_pos tmat	s_m arket	s_jou rnos	s_glo bcom	N OUTCOME E: s_polpa	OUTCOME E: s_polpa	raw consis	PRI consis t.	SYM consist
0	0	0	0	0	0	1	0	1	1	1	1	1
1	1	1	1	0	1	1	0	1	1	1	1	1
0	1	0	0	0	0	0	0	2	1	1	1	1
1	1	1	1	1	1	1	1	2	0	0.66	0	0

Consistency threshold: 0.75

Table 6.6.B Truth table with low political parallelism in socialism

s_acco rnos bcom	s_li	s_de	s_ad	s_pos	s_m	s_jou	s_glo	N mplur tera velo vert tmat arket	OUTCOME :~s_polpa	raw consis t.	PRI consis t.	SYM consist
1	1	1	1	1	1	1	1	2	1	0.91	0.73	1
1	1	1	1	0	1	1	1	1	1	0.8	0	0
0	0	0	0	0	0	1	0	1	0	0	0	0
0	1	1	0	0	0	0.	0	2	0	0	0	0

Consistency threshold: 0.75

256 *Methodological Appendix*

Table 6.7.A Truth table for highly developed media market in digital media modernity – media system conditions

d_dinfra	d_smeplu	d_bmcap	d_aspar	N	OUTCOME: d_market	raw consist.	PRI consist.	SYM consist
1	1	0	0	2	1	0.98	0.97	1
1	0	1	1	1	0	0.59	0.1	0.1
0	0	1	1	2	0	0.59	0.3	0.3

Consistency threshold: 0.75

Table 6.7.B Truth table for weakly developed media market in digital media modernity – media system conditions

d_dinfra	d_smeplu	d_bmcap	d_aspar	N	OUTCOME: ~d_market	raw consist.	PRI consist.	SYM consist
1	0	1	1	1	1	0.95	0.89	0.89
0	0	1	1	2	1	0.8	0.67	0.67
1	1	0	0	2	0	0.26	0	0

Consistency threshold: 0.75

Methodological Appendix 257

Table 6.8 Truth table for highly developed media market in digital modernity – structural and agency conditions

D_TR ANSI TION	D_CO NSOLI DATIO N	d_cli en t	d_m go v	d_rw go v	d_eu int	d_de vel o	d_pos tm at	d_dinfr a	d_smepl u	d_bm cap r	d_as pa r	N OUTC OME: d_mark et	raw con sist.	PRI con sist.	SYM cons ist
1	1	0	1	1	1	1	1	1	1	0	0	1 1	1	1	1
0	1	0	0	0	1	1	1	1	1	0	0	1	0.9 6	0.9 4	1
1	0	1	1	1	1	1	0	0	0	1	1	1	0.7 7	0.5 2	0.52

Consistency threshold: 0.75

Table 6.9.A. Truth table for high media freedom in digital modernity – media system conditions

d_dinf ra	d_smep lu	d_hmc ap	d_asp ar	d_mark et	N	OUTCOME: d_mfree	raw consist.	PRI consist.	SYM consist
1	1	0	0	1	2	1	0.96	0.94	1
0	0	1	1	1	1	1	0.36	0	0
1	0	1	1	1	0	1	0.36	0	0
0	0	1	1	1	0	1	0.29	0	0

Consistency threshold: 0.75

Table 6.9.B. Truth table for weak media freedom in digital modernity – media system conditions

d_dinf	d_smep	d_bmc	d_asp	d_mark	N	OUTCOME: ~d_mfree	raw consist.	PRI consist.	SYM consist
0	0	1	0	1	1	1	1	1	1
0	1	1	1	1	1	1	1	1	1
1	1	0	0	1	1	1	1	1	1
1	1	0	1	0	2	0	0.29	0	0

Consistency threshold: 0.75

Table 6.10.A. Truth table for high media freedom in digital modernity – structural and agency conditions

D_TRANSITION	D_CONSOLIDATION	d_client	d_rwgov	d_euint	d_develo	d_postmat	d_dinfra	d_smeplu	d_bmcap	d_d_asmarkret	N	OUTCOME: d_mfree	raw consist.	PRI consist.	SYM consist
0	1	0	0	0	1	1	1	1	0	0	1	1	1	1	1
1	1	0	1	1	1	1	1	1	0	1	1	1	0.92	0.83	1
1	0	1	1	1	1	0	0	0	1	1	1	0	0.33	0	0

Consistency threshold: 0.75

Methodological Appendix 259

Table 6.10.B Truth table for conditions media freedom in digital modernity – structural and agency

D_T RAN SITI ON	D_CO NSOLI DATI ON	d_cli ent	d_m go v	d_rw go v	d_e uint	d_ deve lo	d_po st ma t	d_ dinf ra	d_ smu epl u	d_ b m ca p	d_as pa r	d_ m ar ke t	N OUTC OME:~d_mfr ee	raw con sist.	PRI con sist.	SY M con sist
1	0	1	1	1	1	1	0	0	1	1	1	1	1	1	1	1
1	1	0	1	1	1	1	1	1	0	0	1	0	0.53	0	0
0	1	0	0	0	1	1	1	1	0	0	1	1	0	0.28	0	0

Consistency threshold: 0.75

Table 6.11.A Truth table for high media freedom in digital modernity – contextual, socio-economic and political system conditions

M_ EC ON M	M_PO LIT M	M_ WE AK M	S_MA RKET PROF	S_HI GHP ARAL L	D_CON SOLID ATION	D_TR ANSI TION	d_clien t	d_eu int	d_de vel o	N OUTC OME: d_mfre e	raw con sist.	PRI con sist.	SY M cons ist
1	0	0	1	0	1	0	0	1	1	1	1	1	1
1	0	0	1	0	1	1	0	1	1	1	0.8	0.75	1
0	0	1	0	1	0	1	1	1	1	0	0.36	0	0
0	1	0	1	1	0	1	1	1	1	0	0.1	0	0

Consistency threshold: 0.75

Table 6.11.B Truth table for weak media freedom in digital modernity – contextual, socio-economic and political system conditions

M_ECON M	M_POLIT M	M_WEAK M	S_MARKET PROF	S_HIGH ARAL L	D_CON SOLID ATION	D_TRANSI TION	d_cli ent	d_eu int	d_de velo	N OUTC raw OME: con ~d_mfrsist. ee	PRI con sist.	SYM cons ist
0	0	1	0	1	0	1	1	1	1	1 1	1	1
1	1	0	1	1	0	1	1	1	1	1 1	1	1
1	0	0	1	0	1	1	0	1	1	00.5 0	0	0
10	1	0	1	0	1	0	0	1	1	00.2 0 4	0	0

Consistency threshold: 0.75

Table 6.12.A Truth table for high media freedom in digital modernity – conditions remote and media systems

R_CON SMARK ET	R_UNCO NSMARK ET	NS	R_WMA RUNCO din fra	d_ din b	d_ ps plu	d_s me ap	d_b mc ar	d_ asp ket	d_ mar	N OUTCO ME: d_mfree	raw cons ist.	PRI consi st.	SYM consi st
1	0	0	1	1	1	0	0	1	2	1	0.95	0.9	1
0	0	1	1	0	0	1	1	0	1	0	0.4	0	0
0	0	1	0	0	0	1	1	0	1	0	0.36	0	0
0	1	0	0	1	0	1	1	1	1	0	0.09	0	0

Consistency threshold: 0.75

Methodological Appendix 261

Table 6.12.B Truth table for weak media freedom in digital modernity – conditions remote and media systems

R_CON SMARK ET	R_UNCO NSMARK ET	R_WMA RUNCO a	d_d infr lu	d_s mep p	d_b mca r	d_a spa ket	d_mar ~d_mfree	N OUTCOM E: ~d_mfree	raw consi st.	PRI consi st.	SYM consi st
0	0	0	0	1	1	0	1	1	1	1	1
0	1	1	0	1	1	0	1	1	1	1	1
0	0	0	0	1	1	1	1	1	1	1	1
1	0	1	1	0	0	1	2	0	0.29	0	0

Consistency threshold: 0.75

Table 6.13.A Truth table for highly developed media market in digital modernity – remote and media system conditions

R_CONS OUTCOM MARKET a	R_UNCON SMARKET p	R_WMAR UNCONS d_market	d_d	d_s infr	d_b mepl	d_a mca	N spa	raw consi E: st	PRI consi st	SYM consi st
0	1	0	1	1	1			1	1	1
1	0	1	0	0	1			0.98	0.98	1
0	0	0	1	1	0			0.5	0	0
0	1	0	1	1	0			0.42	0	0

Consistency threshold: 0.75

262 *Methodological Appendix*

Table 6.13.B Truth table for weak media market in digital modernity – conditions remote and media system

R_CONS MARKET	R_UNCO NSMARKET	R_WMAR UNCONS	d_d infra	d_s meplu	d_h mcap	d_a spar	N OUTCOME :~d_market	raw consi st.	PRI consi st.	SYM consi t
0	0	1	0	0	1	1	1 1	1	1	1
0	0	1	1	0	1	1	1 1	1	1	1
0	1	0	0	0	1	1	1 0	0.31	0	0
1	0	0	1	1	0	0	2 0	0.26	0	0

Consistency threshold: 0.75

References

Aalberg, T., van Aelst, P. & Curran, J. (2013) Media systems and the political information environment: A cross-national comparison. *International Journal of Press/Politics*. 15 (3), 255–271.

Acemoğlu, D. & Robinson, J. A. (2012) *Why Nations Fail: The Origins of Power, Prosperity, and Poverty*. New York, Random House.

Acemoğlu, D., Johnson, S., Robinson, J. A. & Yared, P. (2009) Reevaluating the modernization hypothesis. *Journal of Monetary Economics*. 56 (8), 1043–1058.

Adanir, F. (1989) Tradition and rural change in Southeastern Europe during Ottoman rule. In: Chirot, D. (ed.) *The Origins of Backwardness in Eastern Europe: Economics & Politics from the Middle Ages Until the Early Twentieth Century*. Berkeley, University of California Press, pp. 131–176.

Ademović, F. (1998) *Bosanskohercegovačka štampa (1918–1941)*. Sarajevo, Nezavisna unija profesionalnih novinara BiH & Soros media centar.

Ahmetašević, N. & Hadžiristić, T. (2017) *The Future of Public Service Broadcasting in Bosnia and Herzegovina*. Working Paper 6. Analitika Center for Social Research. Available from: www.analitika.ba/publications/future-public-service-broadcasting-bosnia-and-herzegovina [Accessed 30th September 2019].

Aleksić, J., Dunderović, R., Flere, S., Ilišin, V., Mihailović, S., Obradović, V., Radin, F., Ule, M. & Vrcan, S. (1986) *Položaj, svest i ponašanje mlade generacije Jugoslavije. Preliminarna analiza rezultata istraživanja*. Beograd, Zagreb, CID, IDIS.

Anderson, B. (1990) *Nacija: zamišljena zajednica- razmatranja o porijeklu i širenju nacionalizma*. Zagreb, Školska knjiga.

Andresen, K., Hoxha, A. & Godole, J. (2017) New roles for media in the Western Balkans. *Journalism Studies*. 18 (5), 614–628. https://doi.org/10.1080/1461670X.2016.1268928

Arnason, J. P. (2000) Communism and modernity. *Daedalus*. 129 (1), 61–90.

Arnautović, J. (2012) *Između politike i tržišta. Popularna muzika na Radio Beogradu u SFRJ*. Beograd, Radio-televizija Srbije.

Ashley, S. D. (2011) *Ideology of The Air: Communication Policy and the Public Interest in the United States and Great Britain, 1896–1935* [Unpublished Doctoral Thesis]. Accessed online.

Bajomi-Lázár, P. (ed.) (2017) *Media in Third-Wave Democracies: Southern and Central/Eastern Europe in a Comparative Perspective*. Budapest, L'Harmattan.

Bajomi-Lázár, P. (2015) Variations in media freedom: Why do some governments in Central and Eastern Europe respect media freedom more than other ones? *Central European Journal of Communication*. 8 (14), 4–20.

Bajomi-Lázár, P. (2014) *Party Colonisation of the Media in Central and Eastern Europe*. Budapest, CEU Press.

Bajomi-Lázár, P., Balcytiene, A., Dobreva, A. & Klimkiewicz, B. (2020) History of the media in Central and Eastern Europe. In: Arnold, K., Preston, P. & Kinnebrock, S. (eds.) *The Handbook of European Communication History*. Wiley Blackwell, pp. 277–298.

Balčytiene, A. (2009) *Small Can Also Be Multicultural: Rediscovering Baltic Media Characteristics in a Mixed Model*. International Communication Association (ICA). Keywords in Communication Conference, Chicago, May 21–25.

Banac, I. (ed.) (1992a) *Eastern Europe in Revolutions*. Ithaca, Cornell University Press.

Banac, I. (1992b). The fearful asymmetry of war: The causes and consequences of Yugoslavia's demise. *Daedalus*. 121 (2) [The Exit from Communism (Spring, 1992)], 141–174.

Banac, I. (1991/1984) *The National Question in Yugoslavia: Origins, History, Politics*. Ithaca, Cornell University Press.

Bannerman, S. & Haggart, B. (2015) Historical institutionalism in communication studies. *Communication Theory*. 25 (1), 1–22.

Bartlett, W. (2014) *Shut Out? South East Europe and the EU's New Industrial Policy. South East Europe and the EU's New Industrial Policy*. London, LEQS Paper 84. Available from: https://core.ac.uk/download/pdf/159466673.pdf [Accessed 30th September 2019].

Bartlett, W. (2009) Economic development in the European super-periphery: Evidence from the Western Balkans. *Ekonomski Anali/Economic Annals*. 54 (181), 21–44.

Bašić Hrvatin, S. & Milosavljević, M. (2001) *Medijska politika v Sloveniji v devetdesetih*. Ljubljana, Mirovni Inštitut.

Bašić Hrvatin, S. & Petković, B. (2008) *You Call This a Media Market?* Ljubljana, Mirovni Inštitut.

Bašić Hrvatin, S. & Petković, B. (2004) Regional overview. In: Bašić Hrvatin, S. & Petković, B. (eds.) *Media Ownership and Its Impact on Media Independence and Pluralism*. Ljubljana, Slovenia, Mirovni Inštitut, pp. 9–38.

Batina, G. (2006) *Počeci sociologije u Hrvatskoj*. Zagreb, Kultura i društvo.

Beck, U. (2003) Toward a new critical theory with a cosmopolitan intent. *Constellations*. 10 (4), 453–468.

Berger, A. A. (1992) *Popular Culture Genres: Theories and Texts*. Newbury Park, Sage.

Berger, P. (1986) *The Capitalist Revolution: Fifty Propositions About Prosperity, Equality and Liberty*. New York, Basic Books.

Berglund, S., Ekman, J., Deegam-Krause, K. & Knutsen, T.(ed.). (2013) *The Handbook of Political Change in Eastern Europe*. Cheltenham, Edward Elgar.

Besley, T. & Prat, A. (2006) Handcuffs for the grabbing hand? Media capture and government accountability. *American Economic Review*. 96 (3), 720–736.

Bethlehem, D. L. & Weller, M. (1997) *The "Yugoslav" Crisis in International Law*. Cambridge International Documents Series. Book 5. Cambridge, Cambridge University Press.

Bieber, F. (2020) *The Rise of Authoritarianism in the Western Balkans*. Cham, Palgrave Macmillan.

Bilandžić, D. (1999) *Hrvatska moderna povijest*. Zagreb, Golden Marketing.

References

Bilić, P. & Balabanić, I. (2016) Pluralizam ili polarizacija masovnih medija u mrežnom prostoru: slučaj monetizacije hrvatskih autocesta. *Revija za sociologiju*. 46 (2), 175–204.

Bilić, P. & Primorac, J. (2018) The digital advertising gap and the online news industry in Croatia. *Medijske studije*. 9 (18), 62–79.

Biškup, J. (1981) *Osnove javnog komuniciranja*. Zagreb, Školska knjiga.

Bjelica, M. (1969) Proučavanje istorije štampe u Jugoslaviji. In: Popović, M. (ed.) *Počeci štampe jugoslovenskih naroda. Zbornik radova sa naučnog skupa o počecima štampe jugoslovenskih naroda*. Beograd, Jugoslovenski institut za novinarstvo, pp. 245–248.

Bjelica, M. (1968) *200 godina jugoslovenske štampe. Pregled historije novinarstva*. Beograd, Sloboda.

Blekesaune, M. (2019) Can "openness-to-change" and "conservation" values predict the diffusion of the Internet into European homes? *Comparative Sociology*. 18, 735–756.

Blokker, P. (2005) Post-communist modernization, transition studies, and diversity in Europe. *European Journal of Social Theory*. 8 (4), 503–525.

Blumler, J. G. (2013) *The Fourth Age of Political Communication*. Keynote address presented at the Workshop on Political Communication Online. Berlin, Free University. Available from: www.fgpk.de/en/2013/gastbeitrag-von-jay-g-blumler-the fourth-age-of-political-communication-2/ [Accessed 15th November 2019].

Blumler, J. G. (2012) Foreword. In: Esser, F. & Hanitzsch, T. (eds) *Handbook of Comparative Communication Research*. London, Routledge, pp. xi–xiii.

Blumler, J. G. & Gurevitch, M. (1995) *The Crisis of Public Communication*. London, Routledge.

Blumler, J. G. & Kavanagh, D. (1999) The third age of political communication: Influences and features. *Political Communication*. 16 (3), 209–230.

Boduszyński, M. P. (2010) *Regime Change in the Yugoslav Successor States: Divergent Paths Toward a New Europe*. Baltimore, Johns Hopkins University Press.

Bogdanovski, A. & Lembovska, M. (2015) *Communications Interception Oversight in Macedonia – Making the Impossible Possible*. Skopje, Analytico Thinking Laboratory.

Bohle, D. & Greskovits, B. (2012) *Capitalist Diversity on Europe's Periphery*. Ithaca, Cornell University Press.

Bottomore, T. (1976) Introduction. In: Schumpeter, J. A. (ed.) *Capitalism, Socialism, Democracy*. New York, Harper and Row.

Bourdieu, P. (2005) The political field, the social science field, and the journalistic field. In: Benson, R. & Neveu, E. (eds.) *Bourdieu and the Journalistic Field*. Cambridge, Polity Press, pp. 29–47.

Bourdon, J. (2011) *Du service public a la tele-realite. Une histoire culturelle des televisions europeennes 1950–2010*. Bry-sur-Marne, INA Editions.

Briggs, A. & Burke, P. (2005) *A Social History of the Media: From Gutenberg to the Internet*. Cambridge, Polity Press.

Brkić, D. (2015) *Media Ownership and Financing in Montenegro: Weak Regulation Enforcement and Persistence of Media Control*, Peace Institute, Institute for Contemporary Social and Political Studies, Ljubljana. Available from: http://media observatory.net/radar/media-integrity-report-media-ownership-and-financing-montenegro.

Broughton Micova, S. E. (2013) *Small and Resistant: Europeanization in Media Governance in Slovenia and Macedonia* [Dissertation]. The London School of Economics and Political Science (LSE), London. Available from: http://etheses.lse.ac.uk/800/1/BroughtonMicova_Small_and_Resistant.pdf [Accessed 30th September 2019].

Brüggemann, M., Engesser, S., Büchel, F., Humprecht, E. & Castro, L. (2014) Hallin and Mancini revisited: Four empirical types of Western media systems. *Journal of Communication.* 64 (6), 1037–1065.

Brüggemann, M. & von Königslöw, K. (2013) Explaining cosmopolitan coverage. *European Journal of Communication.* 28 (4), 361–378.

Bryant, J. & Oliver, M. B. (eds.) (2009) *Media Effects: Advances in Theory and Research.* Third Edition. New York, Routledge.

Büchel, F., Humprecht, E. & Castro-Herrero, L. (2016) Building empirical typologies with QCA: Toward a classification of media systems. *The International Journal of Press/Politics.* 21 (2), 209–232.

Bunce, V. (2010) *Subversive Institutions: The Design and the Destruction of Socialism and the State.* Cambridge, Cambridge University Press.

Bunce, V. (2000) Comparative democratization: Big and bounded generalizations. *Comparative Political Studies.* 33 (6–7), 703–734.

Bunce, V. (1999) The political economy of postsocialism. *Slavic Review.* 58 (4), 756–793.

Burg, S. L. (1983) *Conflict and Cohesion in Socialist Yugoslavia: Political Decision Making Since 1966.* Princeton, Princeton University Press.

Burić, I. (2017) Teorijske refleksije o mogućim uzrocima inertnosti egalitarog sindroma. *Revija za sociologiju.* 47 (3), 335–359.

Calic, M.-J. (2019) *A History of Yugoslavia.* West Lafayette, IN, Purdue University Press.

Camaj, L. (2016) Between a rock and a hard place: Consequences of media clientelism for journalist – politician power relationships in the Western Balkans. *Global Media and Communication* 12 (3), 229–246.

Capoccia, G. & Kelemen, R. D. (2007) The study of critical junctures: Theory, narrative and counterfactuals in historical institutionalism. *World Politics.* 59 (3), 341–369.

Car, V. (2016) Comparative perspective: The common challenges in South East Europe. In: Car, V., Radojković, M. & Zlatevare, M. (eds.) *Requirements for Modern Journalism Education – The Perspective of Students in South East Europe.* Berlin, Konrad Adenauer Stiftung, pp. 163–191.

Carothers, T. (2002) The end of the transition paradigm. *Journal of Democracy.* 13 (1), 5–21.

Carruthers, S. L. (2011) *The Media at War.* Second Edition. London, Palgrave Macmillan, Red Globe Press.

Carter, A. (1982) *Democratic Reform in Yugoslavia: The Changing Role of the Party.* London; Pinter.

Castells, M. (2009) *Communication Power.* Oxford, Oxford University Press.

Castro Herrero, L., Humprecht, E., Engesser, S., Brüggemann, M. & Büchel, F. (2017) Rethinking Hallin and Mancini beyond the West: An analysis of media systems in Central and Eastern Europe. *International Journal of Communication.* 11 (27), 4797–4823.

Chadwick, A. (2013) *The Hybrid Media System: Politics and Power.* Oxford, Oxford University Press.

Chalaby, J. K. (1996) Politička komunikacija u predsjedničkim porecima u destrukturiranim i nekonsolidiranim demokracijama. Globalna komparativna perspektiva. *Medijska istraživanja*. 2, 115–137.
Chang, T.-K., Berg, P., Ying-Him Fung, A., Kedl, K. D., Luther, C. A. & Szuba, J. (2001) Comparing nations in mass communication research, 1970–97: A critical assessment of how we know what we know. *Gazette*. 63 (5), 415–434.
Chapman, J. J. (2005) *Comparative Media History. An Introduction 1789 to the Present*. Cambridge, Polity.
Chirot, D. (1989) Causes and consequences of backwardness. In: Chirot, D. (ed.) *The Origins of Backwardness in Eastern Europe: Economics & Politics from the Middle Ages Until the Early Twentieth Century*. Berkeley, University of California Press, pp. 1–15.
Christians, C. G., Glasser, T. L., McQuail, D., Nordenstreng, K. & White, K. A. (2009) *Normative Theories of the Media: Journalism in Democratic Societies*. Urbana, University of Illinois Press, pp. 1–135.
Cianetti, L., Dawson, J. & Hanley, S. (2018) Rethinking "democratic backsliding" in Central and Eastern Europe – looking beyond Hungary and Poland. *East European Politics*. 34 (3), 243–256.
Cipek, T. (2006) Ideologija i nacije. Političke stranke u Austro-Ugarskoj Monarhji. In: Cipek, T. & Matković, S. (eds.) *Programatski dokumenti hrvatskih političkih stranaka i skupina 1842–1914*. Zagreb, Disput, pp. 15–49.
Coppedge, M., Gerring, J., Lindberg, S. I., Skaaning, S., Teorell, T., Altman, D., Bernhard, M. et al. (2017) *"V-Dem Codebook v7." Varieties of Democracy (V-Dem) Project*. Available from: https://www.v-dem.net/en/ [Accessed 7th May 2020].
Coşgel, M. M., Miceli, T. J. & Rubin, J. (2012) The political economy of mass printing: Legitimacy and technological change in the Ottoman empire. *Journal of Comparative Economics*. 40 (3), 357–371. https://doi.org/10.1016/j.jce.2012.01.002
Couldry, N. (2012) *Media, Society, World: Social Theory and Digital Media Practice*. Cambridge, Polity Press.
Couldry, N. & Hepp, A. (2017) *The Mediated Construction of Reality*. Cambridge, Polity Press.
Couldry, N. & Hepp, A. (2012) Comparing media cultures. In: Esser, F. & Hanitzsch, T. H. (eds.) *The Handbook of Comparative Communication Research*. New York, Routledge.
Couldry, N. & Mejias, U. A. (2019) *The Costs of Connection: How Data Is Colonizing Human Life and Appropriating It for Capitalism*. Stanford, Stanford University Press.
Crowley, S. & Stanojević, M. (2011) Varieties of capitalism, power resources, and historical legacies: Explaining the Slovenian exception. *Politics & Society*. 39 (2), 268–295.
Curran, J., Coen, S., Soroka, S., Aalberg, T., Hayashi, K., Hichy, Z., Iyengar, S., Jones, P., Mazzoleni, G., Papathanassopoulos, S. & Rhee, J. W. (2014) Reconsidering "virtuous circle" and "media malaise" theories of the media: An 11-nation study. *Journalism*. 15 (7), 815–833.
Curran, J. & Park, M.-J. (2000) *De-Westernizing Media Studies*. London, Routledge.
Cvek, S. D. (2017) Class and culture in Yugoslav factory newspapers. In: Jelača, D., Kolanović, M. & Lugarić, D. (eds.) *The Cultural Life of Capitalism in Yugoslavia: (Post)Socialism and Its Other*. Cham, Palgrave Macmillan, pp. 101–119.

Czepek, A., Hellwig, M. & Nowak, E. (eds.) (2009) *Press Freedom and Pluralism in Europe: Concepts and Conditions*. Bristol, Intellect Book.

Čepulo, D. (2000) Sloboda tiska i porotno suđenje u banskoj Hrvatskoj 1948–1918. *Hrvatski ljetopis za kazneno parvo i praksu*. 7 (20), 923–975.

Daskalovski, Z. (1999) Elite transformation and democratic transition in Macedonia and Slovenia. *Balkanologie*. 3 (1), 5–32.

De Meur, G. & Berg-Schlosser, D. (1996) Conditions of authoritarianism, fascism, and democracy in interwar Europe: Systematic matching and contrasting of cases for "small N" analysis. *Comparative Political Studies*. 29 (4), 423–468.

Denitch, B. (1990) *Limits and Possibilities: The Crisis of Yugoslav Socialism and State Socialist System*. Minneapolis, University of Minnesota Press.

De Smaele, H. (1999) The applicability of Western media models on the Russian media system. *European Journal of Communication*. 14 (2), 173–189.

Diamandouros, N. & Gunther, R. (eds.) (2001) *Parties, Politics, and Democracy in the New Southern Europe*. Baltimore, Johns Hopkins University Press.

Diamond, L. (2015) Facing up to the democratic recession. *Journal of Democracy*. 26 (1), 141–155.

Diamond, L. (2002) Thinking about hybrid regimes. *Journal of Democracy*. 13 (2), 21–35.

Dimnik, M. (1984) Gutenberg, humanism, the reformation, and the emergence of the Slovene literary language, 1550–1584. *Canadian Slavonic Papers/Revue Canadienne des Slavistes*. 26 (2–3), 141–159.

Dobek-Ostrowska, B. (2015) 25 years after communism: Four models of media and politics in Central and Eastern Europe. In: Dobek-Ostrowska, B. & Glowacki, M (eds.) *Democracy and Media in Central and Eastern Europe 25 Years on*. Frankfurt, Peter Lang, pp. 11–45. https://doi.org/10.3726/978-3-653-04452-2

Dobek-Ostrowska, B. (2012) Italianization (or Mediterraneanization) of the Polish media system? Reality and perspective. In: Hallin, D. & Mancini, P. (eds.) *Comparing Media Systems Beyond the Western World*. Cambridge, Cambridge University Press, pp. 26–50.

Dobek-Ostrowska, B. & Glowacki, M. (2014) *Party Colonisation of the Media in Central and Eastern Europe*. Budapest, CEU Press.

Dobek-Ostrowska, B., Jakubowicz, J., Glowacki, M. & Sükösd, M. (eds.) (2010) *Comparative Media Systems: European and Global Perspectives*. Budapest, CEU Press.

Dolenec, D. (2014) Preispitivanje "egalitarnog sindroma" Josipa Županova. *Politička misao*. 51 (4), 41–64.

Dolenec, D. (2013a) *Democratic Institutions and Authoritarian Rule in Southeast Europe*. Budapest, ECPR Press.

Dolenec, D. (2013b) QCA metoda u političkoj znanosti: ključne karakteristike, doprinosi i ograničenja. *Politička misao*. 50 (1), 104–126.

Dolenec, D. & Širinić, D. (2018) Još uvijek teorijska fantazija: egalitarni sindrom Josipa Županova. *Politička misao*. 55 (3), 7–42.

Dolowitz, D. P. & Marsh, D. (2000) Learning from abroad: The role of policy transfer in contemporary policy-making. *Governance: An International Journal of Policy and Administration*. 13 (1), 5–24.

Donais, T. (2013) Bosnia. In: Burgelund, S., Ekman, J., Deegan-Krause, K. & Knutsen, T. (eds.) *The Handbook of Political Change in Eastern Europe*. Third Edition. Northampton, MA, Edward Elgar, pp. 481–522.

Downey, J. & Mihelj, S. (eds.) (2012) *Central and Eastern European Media in Comparative Perspective*. Farnham, Ashgate.

Downey, J. & Stanyer, J. (2013) Exposing politicians' peccadilloes in comparative context: Explaining the frequency of political sex scandals in eight democracies using fuzzy set qualitative comparative analysis. *Political Communication.* 30 (3), 495–509.

Downey, J. & Stanyer, J. (2010) Comparative media analysis: Why some fuzzy thinking might help. Applying fuzzy set qualitative comparative analysis to the personalization of mediated political communication. *European Journal of Communication.* 25 (4), 331–347.

Dragičević-Šešić, M. (1994) *Neofolk kultura. Publika i njene zvezde.* Sremski Karlovci, Izdavačka knjižarnica Zorana Stojanovića.

Dragomir, M., Reljić, D., Thompson, M. & Grünwald, A. (2005) Overview. In: *Television Across Europe: Regulation, Policy and Independence.* Budapest, Open Society Institute.

Duda, I. (2010) *Pronađeno blagostanje. Svakodnevni život i potrošačka kultura u Hrvatskoj 1970-ih i 1980-ih.* Zagreb, Srednja Europa.

Dunatov, Š. (2010) Začeci višestranačja u Hrvatskoj 1989. godine. *Radovi Zavoda za povijesne znanosti HAZU u Zadru.* 52 (10), 381–397.

Džebo, S. (2019) *The Business of Misinformation: Bosnia and Herzegovina.* Center for Media, Data and Society Central European University School of Public Policy. Available from: https://cmds.ceu.edu/sites/cmcs.ceu.hu/files/attachment/basicpage/1652/businessofmisinformationbosnia.pdf [Accessed 30th September 2019].

Džihana, A., Ćendić, A. & Tahmaz, M. (2012) *Mapping Digital Media: Bosnia and Herzegovina.* Open Society Foundations. Available from: https://www.opensocietyfoundations.org/publications/mapping-digital-media-bosnia-and-herzegovina [Accessed 17th July 2019].

Eco, U. (1983) La Transparance Perdue. In: *La Guerre de Faux.* Paris, Grasset & Fasquelle, pp. 141–158.

Eisenstein, E. L. (1993/1979) *The Printing Press as an Agent of Change: Communications and Cultural Transformation in Early-Modern Europe: Volumes I and II.* Cambridge, Cambridge University Press.

Ekiert, G. & Hanson, S. (2003) *Capitalism and Democracy in Central and Eastern Europe: Assessing the Legacy of Communist Rule.* Cambridge, Cambridge University Press.

Ekiert, G. & Ziblatt, D. (2013) Democracy in Central and Eastern Europe one hundred years on. *East European Politics and Societies.* 27 (1), 90–107.

Elvestad, E. & Blekesaune, A. (2008) Newspaper readers in Europe: A multilevel study of individual and national differences. *European Journal of Communication.* 23 (4), 425–447.

Erdei, I. (2012) *Čekajući Ikeu. Potrošačka kultura u postsocijalizmu i pre njega.* Beograd, Filozofski fakultet Univerziteta u Beogradu.

Esser, F. & Hanitzsch, T. (eds.) (2012) *Handbook of Comparative Communication Research.* London, Routledge.

Esser, F. & Pfetsch, B. (2004) *Comparative Political Communication.* Cambridge, Cambridge University Press.

Esser, F. & Strömback, J. (2014) *Mediatization of Politics: Understanding the Transformation of Western Democracies.* Basingstoke, Palgrave Macmillan.

Fabris, H. H. (1995) Westification? In: Paletz, D. L., Jakubowicz, K. & Novosel, P. (eds.) *Glasnost and After: Media and Change in Central and Eastern Europe.* Cresskill, NJ, Hampton Press, pp. 221–232.

Faris, R. M., Roberts, H., Etling, B., Bourassa, N., Zuckerman, E. & Benkler, Y. (2017) *Partisanship, Propaganda, and Disinformation: Online Media and the 2016 U.S. Presidential Election*. Berkman Klein Center for Internet & Society Research Paper. Available at: https://dash.harvard.edu/handle/1/33759251 [Accessed 7th May 2020].

Feldman, A. (2017) Kállay's dilemma on the challenge of creating a manageable identity in Bosnia and Herzegovina (1882–1903). *Review of Croatian History*. 13 (1), 103–117.

Finnemann, N. O. (2014) Digitization: New trajectories of mediatization? In: Lundby, K. (ed.) *Mediatization of Communication*. Berlin, De Gruyter.

Finnemann, N. O. (2011) Mediatization theory and digital media. *Communications*. 36 (1), 67–89.

Fisher, S. (2006) *Political Change in Post-Communist Slovakia and Croatia: From Nationalist to Europeanist*. New York: Palgrave Macmillan.

Flew, T. & Waisbord, S. (2015) The ongoing significance of national media systems in the context of media globalization. *Media, Culture & Society*. 37 (4), 620–636.

Fortunati, L. (2005) Mediatization of the net and internetization of the mass media. *International Communication Gazette*. 67 (1), 27–44.

Freedman, D. (2008) *The Politics of Media Policy*. Cambridge, Polity Press.

Freedom House (2019) Freedom in the world 2019: Democracy in Retreat. Freedom House: Washington DC and New York.

Galić, M. (2016) *Leksikon radija i televizije*. Zagreb, HRT i Ljevak.

Geertz, C. (1973) *The Interpretation of Cultures*. New York, Basic Books.

Giddens, A. (2012) *Understanding Society – A Sociologists' Perspective* [Lecture]. Centre for Research in the Arts, Social Sciences and Humanities, University of Cambridge, Imperial College London, October 16. Available from: www.youtube.com/watch?v=xl6FoLrv4JQ [Accessed 30th September 2019].

Giddens, A. (1984) *The Constitution of Society: Outline of the Theory of Structuration*. Cambridge, Polity Press.

Giddens, A. (1981a). Time and space in social theory. In: Matthes, J. (ed.) *Lebenswelt und soziale Probleme: Verhandlungen des 20. Deutschen Soziologentages zu Bremen 1980*. Frankfurt, Campus Verlag, pp. 88–97.

Giddens, A. (1981b) *Contemporary Critique of Historical Materialism*. London, Palgrave Macmillan.

Goati, V., Marković, V., Pantić, D., Vasović, M., Oegan, S., Bačević, Lj., Mihailović, S. & Vujović, J. (1989) *Jugosloveni o društvenoj krizi. (istraživanje javnog mnenja 1985. godine)*. Beograd, Centar za društvena istraživanja CKSKJ.

Goertz, G. & Mahoney, J. (2005) Two-level theories and fuzzy-set analysis. *Sociological Methods & Research*. 33 (4), 497–538.

Goldstein, S. (1996) Javna riječ u Hrvatskoj. *Erasmus*. 17, 2–6.

Golubović, Z. (1988) *Kriza identiteta savremenog jugoslovenskog društva. Jugoslovenski put u socijalizam viden iz različitih uglova*. Beograd, Filip Višnjić.

Gorsuch, A. E. & Koenker, D. P. (2013) *The Socialist Sixties: Crossing Borders in the Second World*. Bloomington, Indiana University Press.

Greskovits, B. (2015) Capitalist diversity and the media. In: Zielonka, J. (ed.) *Media and Politics in New Democracies: Europe in a Comparative Perspective*. Oxford, Oxford University Press.

Gross, M. (1985) *Počeci nstit Hrvatske*. Zagreb, Globus, Centar za povijesne znanosti.

Gross, P. (2004) Between reality and dream: Eastern European media transition, transformation, consolidation, and integration. *East European Politics and Societies*. 18 (1), 110–131.

Gross, P. (2002) *Entangled Evolutions: Media and Democratization in Eastern Europe*. Washington, DC, Woodrow Wilson Center Press, Johns Hopkins University Press.
Habermas, J. (1962/1989) *The Structural Transformation of the Public Sphere*. Cambridge, Polity Press.
Halilović, M. & Nadaždin-Defterdarević, M. (2012) Freedom of expression- normative framework. In: Halilović, M. & Džihana, A. (eds.) *Media Law in Bosnia and Herzegovina*. Sarajevo, Internews Network, pp. 33–52.
Hall, P. A. & Taylor, C. R. (1996) Political science and the three new institutionalisms. *Political Studies*. 44 (5), 936–957.
Hallin, D. C. (1984) The media, the war in Vietnam, and political support: A critique of the thesis of an oppositional media. *Journal of Politics*. 46 (1), 2–24.
Hallin, D. C. & Mancini, P. (eds.) (2012) *Comparing Media Systems Beyond the Western World*. New York, Cambridge University Press.
Hallin, D. C. & Mancini, P. (2004) *Comparing Media Systems: Three Models of Media and Politics*. Cambridge, Cambridge University Press.
H-Alter. (2015) *Novine kao ambalaža za reklame*. Available from: www.volim-losinj.org/politika/2531-novine-kao-ambalaza-za-reklame [Accessed 15th November 2019].
Hanitzsch, T. & Donsbach, W. (2012) Comparing journalism cultures. In: Esser, F. & Hanitzsch, T. (eds.) *The Handbook of Comparative Communication Research*. New York, Routledge, pp. 262–275.
Hanitzsch, T., Hanusch, F., Mellado, C., Anikina, M., Berganza, R., Cangoz, I., Coman, M., Hamada, B., Hernandez, M.-E., Karadjov, C. D., Moreira, S. V., Mwesige, P. G., Plaisance, P. L., Reich, Z., Seethaler, J. A., Vardiansyah Noor, D. & Wang Yuen, E. K. (2011) Mapping journalism cultures across nations: A comparative study of 18 countries. *Journalism Studies*. 12, 273–293.
Hanley, S. & Vachudova, M. A. (2018) Understanding the illiberal turn: Democratic backsliding in the Czech Republic. *East European Politics*. 34 (3), 276–296.
Hanson, P. (1974) *Advertising and Socialism: The Nature and Extent of Consumer Advertising in the Soviet Union, Poland, Hungary and Yugoslavia*. London, Palgrave Macmillan.
Hardy, J. (2012) Comparing media systems. In: Esser, F. & Hanitzsch, T. (eds.) *The Handbook of Comparative Communication Research*. London, Routledge.
Hasebrink, U. & Domeyer, H. (2012) Media repertoires as patterns of behaviour and as meaningful practices: A multimethod approach to media use in converging media environments. *Participations: Journal of Audience & Reception Studies*. 9 (2), 757–779.
Hebrang Grgić, I. (2000) Zakoni o tisku u Hrvatskoj od 1945. do danas. *Vjesnik bibliotekara Hrvatske* 43 (3), 117–134.
Hećimović, A. (2019) *Media Pluralism in Six Former Yugoslavian Republics*. Unpublished manuscript.
Henjak, A., Zakošek, N. & Čular, G. (2013) Croatia. In: Burgelund, S., Ekman, J., Deegan-Krause, K. & Knutsen, T. (eds.) *The Handbook of Political Change in Eastern Europe*. Third Edition. Northampton, MA, Edward Elgar, pp. 443–480.
Hillve, P., Majanen, P. & Rosengren, K. E. (1997) Aspects of quality in TV programming. structural diversity compared over time and space. *European Journal of Communication*. 12 (3), 291–318.

Hislope, R. (2013) Macedonia. In: Burgelund, S., Ekman, J., Deegan-Krause, K. & Knutsen, T. (eds.) *The Handbook of Political Change in Eastern Europe*. Third Edition. Northampton, MA, Edward Elgar, pp. 607–650.

Historija jugoslovenskog novinarskog udruženja (1927) *Novinar (Organ jugoslovenskog novinarskog udruženja)*. 4 (7).

Hjarvard, S. (2014) From mediation to mediatization: The institutionalization of new media. In: Hepp, A. & Krotz, F. (eds.) *Mediatized Worlds: Culture and Society in a Media Age*. Basingstoke, Palgrave Macmillan, pp. 123–142.

Hjarvard, S. (2012) Three forms of mediatized religion: Changing public face of religion. In: Hjarvard, S. & Lövheim, M. (eds.) *Mediatization and Religion*. Goteborg, Nordicom, pp. 21–44.

Hjarvard, S. (2008) The mediatization of society. *Nordicom Review*. 29, 102–131.

Hobsbawm, E. (2011) *On History*. Kindle Edition. Weidenfeld & Nicholson.

Hodžić, S. (2014) Bosnia and Herzegovina. In: Petković, B. (ed.) *Media Integrity Matters: Reclaiming Public Service Values in Media and Journalism*. Ljubljana, Peace Institute, pp. 327–390.

Hodžić, S. & Pajnik, M. (2016) *Communicating Citizens' Protests, Requiring Public Accountability: Case Studies from Albania, Bosnia and Herzegovina and Macedonia*. Sarajevo: Mediacentar Sarajevo.

Horvat, B. (1971) Yugoslav economic policy in the post-war period: Problems, ideas, institutional developments. *American Economic Review*. 61 (3), 69–169.

Horvat, J. (2003/1962) *Povijest novinstva Hrvatske 1771–1939*. Zagreb: Golden Marketing.

Hosman, L. & Howard, P. N. (2014) Telecom policy across the former Yugoslavia: Incentives, challenges, and lessons learned. *Journal of Information Policy*. 4, 67–104.

Hozić, A. A. (2008) Democratizing media, welcoming big brother: Media in Bosnia and Herzegovina. In: Jakubowicz, K. & Sükösd, M. (eds.) *Finding the Right Place on the Map: Central and Eastern European Media Change in a Global Perspective*. Bristol, Intellect Books, pp. 145–163.

Hrženjak, M. (2019) Prekarizacija v novinarstvu: požrešne institucije, podjetniške subjektivitete in vidik spola, In: Pajnik, M. & Luthar, B. (eds.) *Mediji in spol: strukture in prakse neenakosti*. Ljubljana, Fakulteta za družbene vede, pp. 31–54.

Humphreys, P. (2012) A political scientist's contribution to the comparative study of media systems in Europe: A response to Hallin and Mancini. In: Just, N. & Puppis, M. (eds.) *Trends in Communication Policy Research: New Theories, Methods and Subjects*. Bristol, Intellect, pp. 141–158.

Humprecht, E. & Büchel, F. (2013) More of the same or marketplace of opinions? A cross-national comparison of diversity in online news reporting. *International Journal of Press/Politics*. 18 (4), 436–461.

Huntington, S. P. (1991) *The Third Wave: Democratization in the Late Twentieth Century*. Norman, University of Oklahoma Press.

Ilišin, V. (1986) Interesiranja i slobodno vrijeme mladih. In: Aleksić, J., Dunđerović, R., Flere, S., Ilišin, V., Mihailović, S., Obradović, V. L., Radin, F., Ule, M. & Vrcan, S. (eds.) *Položaj, svest i ponašanje mlade generacije Jugoslavije. Preliminarna analiza rezultata istraživanja*. Beograd, Zagreb, CID, IDIS, pp. 114–130.

Ilišin, V., Radin, F. & Županov, J. (1986) *Kultura radničke omladine. Prilog istraživanju položaja, vrijednosti i aktivnosti mladih radnika u SR Hrvatskoj*. Zagreb, Centar društvenih djelatnosti SSOH.

Imre, A. (2014) Postcolonial media studies in postsocialist Europe. *Boundary 2*. 41 (1), 113–134. https://doi.org/10.1215/01903659-2409694
Imre, A., Havens, T. & Lustyik, K. (eds.) (2012) *Popular Television in Eastern Europe During and Since Socialism*. First Edition. London, Routledge.
Inglehart, R. (1995) *Value Change in Global Perspective*. Ann Arbor, University of Michigan Press.
Inglehart, R. & Welzel, C. H. (2005) *Modernization, Cultural Change, and Democracy: The Human Development Sequence*. Cambridge, Cambridge University Press.
Innis, H. A. (1951) *The Bias of Communication*. Toronto, University of Toronto Press.
Irion, K. & Jusić, T. (2018) *Media Constrained by Context, International Assistance and the Transition to Democratic Media in the Western Balkans*. Budapest, CEU Press.
Irion, K. & Jusić, T. (2014) International assistance and media democratization in the Western Balkans: A cross-national comparison. *Global Media Journal*. 4 (2).
Jakubowicz, K. (2008) Public service broadcasting in post-communist countries: Finding the right place on the map. In: Jakubowicz, K. & Sükösd, M. (eds.) *Finding the Right Place on the Map: Central and Eastern European Media Change in a Global Perspective*. Bristol, Intellect Books, pp. 101–124.
Jakubowicz, K. (2007) The Eastern-European post-communist media system: An introduction. In: Terzis, G. (ed.) *European Media Governance: National and Regional Dimensions*. Bristol, Intellect Books, pp. 303–312.
Jakubowicz, K. (2004) Ideas in our heads: Introduction of PSB as part of media system change in Central and Eastern Europe. *European Journal of Communication*. 19 (1), 53–74.
Jakubowicz, K. (1995) Media within and without the state: Press freedom in Eastern Europe. *Journal of Communication*. 45 (4), 125–139.
Jakubowicz, K. & Gross, P. (eds.) (2013) *Media Transformations in the Post-Communist World: Eastern Europe's Tortured Path to Change*. Lanham, Lexington Books.
Jakubowicz, K. & Sükösd, M. (eds.) (2008) *Finding the Right Place on the Map: Central and Eastern European Media Change in Global Perspective*. ECREA Book Series. Bristol, Intellect Books.
Jebril, N., Stetka, V. & Loveless, M. (2013) *Media and Democratization: What Is Known About the Role of Mass Media in Transitions to Democracy*. Oxford, Reuters Institute for the Study of Journalism. Report.
Jergović, B. (2003) Zakonske promjene i tisak u Hrvatskoj od 1990. do 2002. *Politička misao*. 40 (1), 92–108.
Jones, H. D. (2014). *The Media in Europe's Small Nations*. Cambridge, Cambridge Scholars.
Jović, D. (2009) *Yugoslavia: A State that Withered Away*. West Lafayette, IN, Purdue University Press.
JRT 79 Television Programmes (1979) JRT.
Jugoslovenski institut za novinarstvo (1975) *Informisanje u društveno-ekonomskom i političkom sistemu*. Belgrade, Institut za novinarstvo.
Jugoslovenska štampa (1911) *Referati i bibliografija*. Belgrade, Izdanje Srpskog novinarskog udruženja.

Jusić, T. (2005) Bosnia and Herzegovina. In: *Television Across Europe: Regulation, Policy and Independence*. Budapest, Open Society Institute.

Jusić, T. & Ahmetašević, N. (2018) Media reform through intervention: International media assistance in Bosnia and Herzegovina. In: Irion, K. & Jusić, T. (eds.) *Media Constrained by Context, International Assistance and the Transition to Democratic Media in the Western Balkans*. Budapest, CEU Press.

Kalanj, R. (1990) *Modernost i modernizacija*. Zagreb, Sociološko društvo Hrvatske.

Kaleši, H. (1969) Prve tursko-srpske štamparije i počeci štampe na Kosovu. In: Popović, M. (ed.) *Počeci štampe jugoslovenskih naroda. Zbornik radova sa naučnog skupa o počecima štampe jugoslovenskih naroda*. Beograd, Jugoslovenski institut za novinarstvo, pp. 223–229.

Kamalipour, Y. R. & Snow, N. (2004) *War, Media and Propaganda: A Global Perspective*. London, Rowman and Littlefield.

Kanižaj, I. (2016) Mapping media literacy in Croatia – national summary. In: Insights, M. & Chapman, M. (eds.). *Mapping of Media Literacy Practices and Actions in EU-28*. Strasbourg: European Audiovisual Observatory, pp. 206–217.

Karaman, I. (2000) *Hrvatska na pragu modernizacije /1750–1918/*. Zagreb, Naklada Ljevak.

Karaman, I. (1991) *Industrijalizacija građanske Hrvatske (1800–1941)*. Zagreb, Naprijed.

Karl, T. L. & Schmitter, Ph. C. (1995) From an iron curtain to a paper curtain: Grounding transitologists or students of postcommunism? *Slavic Review*. 54 (4), 965–978.

Keane, John. 1991. *The Media and Democracy*. Cambridge, Polity Press.

Kenny, P. D. (2019) "The enemy of the people": Populists and press freedom. *Political Research Quarterly*. 1–15. https://doi.org/10.1177/1065912918824038

Kerševan Smokvina, T. (2016) Mapping media literacy in Slovenia – national summary. In: Insights, M. & Chapman, M. (eds.). *Mapping of Media Literacy Practices and Actions in EU-28*. Strasbourg, European Audiovisual Observatory, pp. 348–359.

Kirbiš, A. (2013) Political participation and non-democratic political culture in western Europe, East-Central Europe and post-Yugoslav countries. In: Demetriou, K. N. (ed.) *Democracy in Transition*. Berlin, Heidelberg, Springer, pp. 225–251.

Kitschelt, H. (1995) Formation of party cleavages in post-communist democracies: Theoretical propositions. *Party Politics*. 1 (4), 447–472.

Kitschelt, H., Mansfeldova, Z., Markowski, R. & Toka, G. (1999) *Post-Communist Party Systems: Competition, Representation, and Inter-party Cooperation*. Cambridge, Cambridge University Press.

Klasić, H. (2012) *Jugoslavija i svijet 1968*. Zagreb, Naklada Ljevak.

Klimkiewicz, B. (2005) *Media Pluralism: European Regulatory Policies and the Case of Central Europe*. EUI-RSCAS Working Papers 19. European University Institute (EUI), Robert Schuman Centre of Advanced Studies (RSCAS). Available from: https://ideas.repec.org/p/erp/euirsc/p0156.html [Accessed 30th September 2019].

Knezović, Z. (1992) Obilježja boljševizacije hrvatske kulture (1945–1947). *Časopis za suvremenu povijest*. 24 (1), 101–133.

Kokushkin, M. (2011) Transitional societies in Eastern Europe: Moving beyond the Washington consensus paradigm in transitology. *Sociology Compass*. 5 (12), 1044–1057.

Kolanović, M. (2013) Utopija pod upitnikom. Predodžba "Amerike" u stihovima dekadentnog socijalizma. In: Duraković, L. & Matošević, A. (eds.) *Socijalizam na klupi. Jugoslavensko društvo očima nove postjugoslavenske humanistike.* Pula, Srednja Europa, Sveučilište Jurja Dobrile, Sanjam knjige u Istri.

Kollmorgen, R. (2013) Theories of postcommunist transformation, approaches, debates, and problems of theory building in the second decade of research. *Studies of Transition States and Societies.* 5 (2), 88–105.

Kramberger, T., Mihelj, S. & Rotar, D. B. (2004) Representations of the nation and of the other in the Slovenian periodical press before and after 1991: Engagements and implications. In: Spassov, O. (ed.) *Quality Press in Southeastern Europe.* Sofia, Southeast European Media Centre, pp. 276–305.

Krippendorff, K. (2004) *Content Analysis: An Introduction to Methodology.* Second Edition. Thousand Oaks, CA, Sage.

Križan, M. (1989) Of "civil society" and socialism in Yugoslavia. *Studies in Soviet Thought.* 37 (4), 287–306. Available from: www.jstor.org/stable/20100432 [Accessed 29th September 2019].

Krležijana (2012) *Govor na kongresu književnika u Ljubljani, Zagreb, Leksikografski zavod Miroslav Krleža.* Available from: http://krlezijana.lzmk.hr/clanak.aspx?id=373 [Accessed 29th September 2019].

Krotz, F. (2014) Mediatization as a mover in modernity: Social and cultural change in the context of media change. In: Lundby, K. (ed.) *Mediatization of Communication.* Berlin, De Gruyter Mouton, pp. 131–162.

Krotz, F. (2009) Mediatization: A concept with which to grasp media and societal change. In: Lundby, K. (ed.) *Mediatization: Concept, Changes, Consequences.* New York, Peter Lang, pp. 21–40.

Kunelius, R. & Reunanen, E. (2016) Changing power of journalism: The two phases of mediatization. *Communication Theory.* 26 (4), 369–388.

Lah, P. & Žilič-Fišer, S. (2012) Journalism in Slovenia. In: Weaver, D. H. & Willnat, L. (eds.) *The Global Journalist in the 21st Century.* New York, Routledge, pp. 283–294.

Lampe, J. R. (2014) *Balkans into Southeastern Europe, 1914–2014: A Century of War and Transition.* London, Palgrave Macmillan.

Lampe, J. R. (2000) *Yugoslavia as History: Twice There Was a Country.* Second Edition. Cambridge, Cambridge University Press.

Lampe, J. R. (1989) Imperial borderlands or capitalist periphery? Redefining Balkan backwardness. 1520–1914. In: Chirot, D. (ed.) *The Origins of Backwardness in Eastern Europe: Economics & Politics from the Middle Ages Until the Early Twentieth Century.* Berkeley, University of California Press, pp. 177–209.

Lamza Posavec, V. & Rihtar, S. (2003) Neke osobine publike informativno političkog tiska, *Društvena istraživanja.* 126 (68), 927–956.

Lavrič, M., Jusić, M. & Tomanović, S. (2019) *Youth Study Southeast Europe 2018/2019.* Friedrich-Ebert-Stiftung. Available from: https://mlad.si/uploads/objave/NOVICE%20UREDNISTVO/Youth%20Study%20Southeast%20Europe%202018-2019.pdf.pdf [Accessed 30th September 2019].

Lechner, F. J. (2008) *The Netherlands: Globalization and National Identity.* New York, Routledge.

Leković, Z. & Bjelica, M. (1976) *Communication Policies in Yugoslavia.* Paris, UNESCO.

Levi, P. (2009) *Raspad Jugoslavije na filmu*, Belgrade, Biblioteka XX vek.

Levitsky, S. & Way, L. A. (2002) Elections without democracy: The rise of competitive authoritarianism. *Journal of Democracy*. 11 (2), 51–65.

Lijphart, A. (1971) Comparative politics and comparative method. *Comparative Political Studies*. 8, 158–177.

Lilly, C. S. (1994) Problems of persuasion: Communist agitation and propaganda in post-war Yugoslavia, 1944–1948. *Slavic Review*. 53 (2), 395–413.

Linz, J. J. & Stepan, A. (1996) *Problems of Democratic Transition and Consolidation: Southern Europe, South America, and Post-Communist Europe*. Baltimore, Johns Hopkins University Press.

Livingstone, S. (2012) Challenges to comparative research in a globalizing media landscape. In: Esser, F. &. Hanitzsch, T. (eds.) *Handbook of Comparative Communication Research*. New York, Routledge, pp. 415–429.

Logan, R. K. (2002) The five ages of communication. *Explorations in Media Ecology*. 1 (1), 13–20. Available from: http://openresearch.ocadu.ca/id/eprint/891/1/ [Accessed 15th November 2019].

Lučić, J. (1962) PTT Arhiv 1958–1961. *Arhivski vjesnik*. 4–5 (1), 413–418.

Luketić, K. (2013) *Balkan: od geografije do fantazije*. Zagreb, Algoritam.

Lundby, K. (ed.) (2014) *Mediatization of Communication*. Berlin, De Gruyter Mouton.

Luthar, B. & Pušnik, M. (2010) *Remembering Utopia: The Culture of Everyday Life in Socialist Yugoslavia*. Washington, DC, New Academia.

Macan, T. (1995) *Hrvatska povijest*. Zagreb, Matica hrvatska.

MacBride, S. (1984) *Many Voices, One World*. Paris, UNESCO.

Madianou, M. (2014) Polymedia communication and mediatized migration: An ethnographic approach. In: Lundby, K. (ed.) *Mediatization of Communication*. Berlin/Boston, De Gruyter Mouton, pp. 323–346.

Maestas, C. D. (2018) Expert surveys as a measurement tool: Challenges and new frontiers. In: Atkeson, L. R. & Alvarez, M. R. (eds.) *Oxford Handbook of Pooling and Survey Methods*. New York, Oxford University Press, pp. 583–607.

Magin, M. (2015) Shades of mediatization: Components of media logic in German and Austrian elite newspapers (1949–2009). *International Journal of Press/Politics*. 20 (4), 415–437.

Mahoney, J. (2001) Path-dependent explanations of regime change: Central America in comparative perspective. *Studies in Comparative International Development*. 36 (1), 111–141.

Mahoney, J. (2000) Path dependence in historical sociology. *Theory and Society*. 29 (4), 507–548.

Malešević, S. (2002). *Ideology, Legitimacy and the New State: Yugoslavia, Serbia and Croatia*. London, Routledge.

Mance, G. (1985) *Istraživanje novina: Iskustvo izdavačke kuće Vjesnik 1973–1983*. Zagreb, Vjesnik.

Mance, G. (1976) *Profili čitalačkih publika*. Zagreb, NIŠP Vjesnik.

Marko, D. (2017) Public services without a public? How public service broadcasters in the Western Balkans interact with their audiences. *IC – Revista Científica de Información y Comunicación*. 14, 217–242. Available from: http://icjournal-ojs.org/index.php/IC-Journal/article/view/373/338 [Accessed 30th September 2019].

Marko, D. (2012) *Citizenship in Media Discourse in Bosnia and Herzegovina, Croatia, Montenegro, and Serbia*. CITSEE Working Paper 2012/25. SSRN.

Available from: https://ssrn.com/abstract=2388673 or http://dx.doi.org/10.2139/ssrn.2388673.

Marko, D. & Veljanovski, R. (2018) *Recommendations for Strengthening the Independence of Public Broadcasters in Serbia*. Analitika Center for Social Research. Available from: http://analitika.ba/publications/recommendations-strenghtening-independence-public-broadcasters-serbia [Accessed 30th September 2019].

Markus, T. (1998) Dokumenti o hrvatskom pokretu iz 1849. godine. *Časopis za suvremenu povijest*. 30 (3), 577–595.

Martić, M., Vuković, S., Ćurgus Kazimir, V., Rosić, B., Đurić Mišović, I. & Đerić, A. (2011) *Poslednja mladost u Jugoslaviji: epizoda Beograd*. Beograd, Muzej istorije Jugoslavije.

Martinović, N. (1965) *Razvitak štampe i štamparstva u Crnoj Gori: 1493–1945*. Beograd, Jugoslovenski institut za novinarstvo.

Matić, J. & Valić Nedeljković, D. (2014) Serbia. In: Petković, B. (ed.) *Media Integrity Matters: Reclaiming Public Service Values in Media and Journalism*. Ljubljana, Peace Institute, pp. 327–390.

Marx, K. (1875) *Critique of the Gotha Programme*. Available from: www.marxists.org/archive/marx/works/1875/gotha/ch01.htm [Accessed 30th September 2019].

Marx, K. & Engels, F. (2005/1888) *The Communist Manifesto*. Available from: www.gutenberg.org/cache/epub/61/pg61.html [Accessed 30th September 2019].

Mattoni, A. & Ceccobelli, D. (2018) Comparing hybrid media systems in the digital age: A theoretical framework for analysis. *European Journal of Communication*. 33 (5), 540–557.

Mazzoleni, G. & Schulz, W. (1999) "Mediatization" of politics: A challenge for democracy? *Political Communication*. 16 (3), 247–261.

McChesney, R. W. (2007a). *Communication Revolution: Critical Junctures and the Future of Media*. New York, New Press.

McChesney, R. W. (2007b) Freedom of the press for whom? The question to be answered in our critical juncture. *Hofstra Law Review*. 23 (3), 1433–1455.

McChesney, R. W. (2000) *Rich Media, Poor Democracy: Communication Politics in Dubious Times*. New York, The New Press.

McLuhan, M. (1964) *Understanding Media: The Extensions of Man*. London, Routledge.

McQuail, D. (2007) *McQuail's Mass Communication Theory*. London, Sage.

McQuail, D. (1995) *Media Performance: Mass Communication and the Public Interest*. London, Sage.

Mechkova, V., Lührmann, A. & Lindberg, S. I. (2017) How much democratic backsliding? *Journal of Democracy*. 28 (4), 162–169.

Menke, M., Kinnebrock, S., Kretzschmar, S., Aichberger, I., Broersma, M., Hummel, R., Kirchhoff, S., Prandner, D., Ribeiro, N. & Salaverría, R. (2016) Convergence culture in European newsrooms. *Journalism Studies*. 1469–1699 [Online]. https://doi.org/10.1080/1461670X.2016.1232175

Merkel, W. (2011) *Transformacija političkih sustava*. Zagreb, Biblioteka politička misao Fakulteta političkih znanosti Sveučilišta u Zagrebu.

Meyen, M. & Scwer, K. (2007) Credibility of media offerings in centrally controlled media systems: A qualitative study based on the example of East Germany. *Media, Culture & Society*. 29 (2), 284–303.

Meyrowitz, J. (1985). *No Sense of Place. The Impact of the Electronic Media on Social Behavior*. New York and Oxford, Oxford University Press.

Mihaljević, J. (2015) Liberalizacija i razvoj medija u komunističkoj Hrvatskoj 1960-ih i na početku 1970-ih. *Društvena istraživanja: časopis za opća društvena pitanja*. 24 (2), 239–258.

Mihelj, S. (2014) Understanding socialist television: Concepts, objects, methods. *View, Journal of European Television History & Culture*. 3 (5).

Mihelj, S. (2013) The Politics of privatization: Television entertainment and the Yugoslav sixties. In: Gorsuch, A. E. & Koenker, D. P. (eds.) *The Socialist Sixties: Crossing Borders in the Second World*. Bloomington, Indiana University Press, pp. 251–267.

Mihelj, S. (2012) Television entertainment in socialist Eastern Europe: Between Cold War politics and global developments. In: Imre, A., Havens, T. & Lustyk, K. (eds.) *Popular Television in Eastern Europe During and Since Socialism*. London, Routledge.

Mihelj, S. (2011) Negotiating cold war culture at the crossroads of East and West: Uplifting the working people, entertaining the masses, cultivating the nation. *Comparative Studies in Society and History*. 53 (3), 509–539.

Mihelj, S. & Huxtable, S. (2018) *From Media Systems to Media Cultures: Understanding Socialist Television*. Cambridge, Cambridge University Press.

Milivojević, S. (2018) *Slučaj Savamala*. Belgrade, Civil Rights Defenders.

Milivojević, S. (2005) Serbia. In: *Television Across Europe: Regulation, Policy and Independence*. Budapest, Open Society Institute.

Milivojević, S., Milenković, D. & Raković, M. (2012) *Medijski sistem Srbije: UNESCO indikatori medijskog razvoja*. Belgrade: Faculty of Political Science, University of Belgrade. Available from: http://centarzamedije.fpn.bg.ac.rs/wp-content/uploads/2020/03/unesco-indikatori-medijskog-razvoja.pdf [Accessed 23th October 2019].

Milojević, A. & Krstić, A. (2018) Hierarchy of influences on transitional journalism – corrupting relationships between political, economic and media elites. *European Journal of Communication*. 33(1), 37–56.

Milosavljević, M., Biljak Gerjević, B. & Petković, B. (2018*) Monitoring Media Pluralism in Europe: Application of the Media Pluralism Monitor 2017 in the European Union*. FYROM, Serbia & Turkey. Country Report, Slovenia, EUI CMPF.

Milosavljević, M. & Broughton Micova, S. (2013) Because we have to: Digitalization of terrestrial television in South East Europe. *International Journal of Digital Television*. 4 (3), 261–277.

Milosavljević, M. & Kerševan Smokvina, T. (2012) *Mapping Digital Media: Slovenia. A Report by the Open Society Foundations*. Available from: www.opensocietyfoundations.org/publications/mapping-digital-media-slovenia#publications_download [Accessed 17th July 2019].

Milosavljević, M. & Poler, M. (2018) Balkanization and pauperization: Analysis of media capture of public service broadcasters in the Western Balkans. *Journalism*. 19 (8), 1149–1164.

Milošević, A. (2019) Playing memory games with Europe's totalitarian history. *Balkan Insight*. Available from: www.balkaninsight.com/en/article/memory-games-moving-the-iron-curtain-01-28-2019 [Accessed 17th July 2019].

Milutinović, I. (2014) Uloga radiodifuzne regulative u oblikovanju novije istorije srpske kulture (1944–1990). *Megatrend revija*. 11 (1), 101–126.

Mirković, M. (1958) *Ekonomska historija Jugoslavija*. Zagreb, Ekonomski pregled.

References 279

Missika, J.-L. (2006) *La fin de télévision*. Seuil, La République des Idées.

Mladina (2019) *Hungary's Attempt to Control Slovenian Media*. Available from: www.mladina.si/190431/hungary-s-attempt-to-control-slovenian-media/ [Accessed 15th December 2019].

Mokrov, B. (1969) Počeci makedonske štampe. In: Popović, M. (ed.) *Počeci štampe jugoslovenskih naroda. Zbornik radova sa naučnog skupa o počecima štampe jugoslovenskih naroda*. Beograd, Jugoslovenski institut za novinarstvo, pp. 141–152.

Moore, B. (1966) *Social Origins of Dictatorship and Democracy: Lords and Peasant in Making of the Modern World*. Boston, Beacon Press.

Morley, D. (2009) For a materialist, non-media-centric media studies. *Television & New Media*. 10 (1), 114–116.

Mrduljaš, M. & Kulić, V. (2012) *Unfinished modernizations. Between utopia and pragmatism*. Zagreb, UHA/CCA.

Mučalo, M. (2010) *Radio – medij 20. stoljeća*. Zagreb, AGM.

Napoli, P. M. (1999) Deconstructing the diversity principle. *Journal of Communication*. 49 (4), 7–34.

Naroll, R. (1961) Two solutions to Galton's problem. *Philosophy of Science*. 28 (1), 15–39.

Nebiu, B., Selmani, N. & Sekulovski, D. (2016) *Indicators on the Level of Media Freedom and Journalists' Safety (Macedonia), Independent Journalists' Association of Serbia*. Available from: http://safejournalists.net/wp-content/uploads/2016/12/MACEDONIA-Summary-Indicators-on-the-level-of-media-freedom-and-journalists%E2%80%99-safety-in-the-Western-Balkans-1.pdf [Accessed 30th September 2019].

Nikodinoska, V. & Šopar, V. (2012) *Development of the Media in Macedonia According to UNESCO Indicators*. Skopje, Macedonian Institute for Media.

Nikolić, K., Cvetković, S. & Tripković, Đ. (2010) *Bela knjiga – 1984. Obračun sa "kulturnom kontrarevolucijom u SFRJ."* Beograd, Službeni glasnik.

Nimrod, G., Adoni, H. & Nossek, H. (2015) The Internet as a cultural forum: A European perspective. *International Journal of Communication*. 9, 321–341.

Nixon, R. B. & Bryan, C. R. (1966) The press system of Yugoslavia: Communism with a difference. *Journalism Quarterly*. 43(2), 291–299.

Nordenstreng, K. & Varis, T. (1974) *Television Traffic: A One Way Street? A Survey and Analysis of the International Flow of Television Programme Material*. Paris, UNESCO.

Norris, P. (2009) Comparative political communications: Common frameworks or Babelian confusion? *Government and Opposition*. 44 (3), 321–340.

Norris, P. & Inglehart, R. (2009) *Cosmopolitan Communications: Cultural Diversity in a Globalized World*. New York, Cambridge University Press.

Novak, B. (2005) *Hrvatsko novinarstvo u 20. stoljeću*. Zagreb, Golden Marketing.

Novosel, P. (1976) Specifikacije delegatskih komunikacijskih sistema. *Politička misao: časopis za politologiju*, 13 (2–3).

Obradović, S. & Stupan, A. (1968) Gledaoci o centralnim informativnim dnevnim emisijama. In: *Novinarstvo 1968 (3–4)*. Beograd, Jugoslovenski institut za novinarstvo, pp. 105–110.

Offe, C. (1991) Capitalism by democratic design? Democratic theory facing the triple transition in East Central Europe. *Social Research*. 58 (4), 865–892.

Open Society Institute (2012) *Mapping Digital Media*. Budapest, Open Society Institute.

Open Society Institute (2005) *Television Across Europe: Regulation, Policy and Independence*. Monitoring Reports. Budapest, Open Society Institute.

Osolnik, B. (1960) *Zakon o štampi: i drugim vidovima informacija*. Belgrade, Službeni list FNRJ.
Paletz, D. L. & Jakubowicz, K. (eds.) (2003) *Business as Usual: Continuity and Change in Central and Eastern European Media*. Cresskill, Hampton Press.
Paletz, D. L., Jakubowicz, P. & Novosel, P. (eds.) (1995) *Glasnost and After: Media and Change in Central and Eastern Europe*. Cresskill, Hampton Press.
Papić, M. (1969) Počeci štampe u Bosni i Hercegovini. In: Popović, M. (ed.) *Počeci štampe jugoslovenskih naroda. Zbornik radova sa naučnog skupa o počecima štampe jugoslovenskih naroda*. Belgrade, Jugoslovenski institut za novinarstvo, pp. 121–126.
Parrott, B. (1997) Perspectives on postcommunist democratization. In: Dawisha, K. & Parrott, B. (eds.) *The Consolidation of Democracy in East-Central Europe*. Cambridge, Cambridge University Press, pp. 1–39.
Parsons, T. (1971) *The Systems of Modern Societies*. Englewood Cliffs, NJ, Prentice Hall.
Patterson, P. H. (2011) *Bought and Sold: Living and Losing the Good Life in Socialist Yugoslavia*. Ithaca, Cornell University Press.
Patterson, P. H. (2003) Truth half told: Finding the perfect pitch for advertising and marketing in socialist Yugoslavia, 1950–1991. *Enterprise and Society*. 4 (2), 179–225. https://doi.org/10.1017/s1467222700012222
Patterson, P. H. (2000) The east is read: The end of communism, Slovenian exceptionalism, and the independent journalism of Mladina. *East European Politics & Societies*. 14 (2), 411–459.
Pejanović, Đ. (1961) *Bibliografija štampe Bosne i Hercegovine 1850–1941*. Sarajevo, Veselin Masleša.
Peruško, Z. (2017) Mediatization: From structure to agency (and back again). In: Driessens, O., Hepp, A., Hjarvard, S. & Bolin, G. (eds.) *Dynamics of Mediatization: Institutional Change and Everyday Transformations in a Digital Age*. Basingstoke, Palgrave Macmillan, pp. 57–83.
Peruško, Z. (2016) Historical institutionalist approach in comparative media systems research: The case of post-Yugoslavia. *Javnost – The Public*. 23 (3), 255–272.
Peruško, Z. (2014) Great expectations: On experiences with media reform in post-socialist Europe (and some unexpected outcomes). *Central European Journal of Communication*. 7 (13), 241–252.
Peruško, Z. (2013a). Rediscovering the Mediterranean characteristics of the Croatian media system. *East European Politics and Societies*. 27(4), 709–726. https://doi.org/10.1177/0888325413494770
Peruško, Z. (2013b). Media pluralism policy in a post-socialist Mediterranean media system: The case of Croatia. *Central European Journal of Communication*. 6 (11), 204–218.
Peruško, Z. (2013c). Komparativna analiza post-socijalističkih medijskih sustava, *Politička misao (Croatian Political Science Review)*, 50(2). 38–59.
Peruško, Z. (2012) *Medijski sustav i medijska politika u Hrvatskoj 2010–2011. Prema UNESCO-ovim indikatorima medijskog razvoja, Monitoring medija, 1*. Zagreb, Centar za istraživanje medija i komunikacije, Fakultet političkih znanosti, Sveučilište u Zagrebu.
Peruško, Z. (2011) *Assessment of Media Development in Croatia Based on UNESCO Media Development Indicators*. Paris, UNESCO.

Peruško, Z. (2007) Media and civic values. In: Ramet, P. & Matić, D. (eds.) *Democratic Transition in Croatia: Value Transformation, Education and Media*. College Station, Texas A&M University Press, pp. 224–246.

Peruško, Z. (2005) Croatia. In: *Television Across Europe: Regulation, Policy and Independence*. Budapest, Open Society Institute.

Peruško Čulek, Z. (2003) Croatia: The first ten years. In: Paletz, D. & Jakubowicz, K. (eds.) *Business as Usual*. Cresskill, Hampton Press, pp. 111–145.

Peruško Čulek, Z. (1999a) *Demokracija i mediji*. Zagreb, Barbat.

Peruško Čulek, Z. (1999b) Nova medijska agenda: za europsku medijsku politiku u Hrvatskoj. *Medijska istraživanja*. 5 (2), 285–301.

Peruško Čulek, Z. (1993) Broadcasting environment and legislature in Croatia. In: Kleinwachter, W. (ed.) *Broadcasting in Transition: The Changing Legal Framework in the Eastern Part of Europe*. Working Papers. Electronic Media Seminar, Warsaw, March 17–20, Netcom Papers No. 3. Leipzig, pp. 96–105.

Peruško, Z. & Čuvalo, A. (2014) Comparing socialist and post-socialist television culture: Fifty years of television in Croatia. *View – Journal of European Television & Culture*. 3 (5), 131–150. Available from: www.viewjournal.eu/articles/86/ [Accessed 30th September 2019].

Peruško, Z., Čuvalo, A. & Vozab, D. (2017) Mediatization of journalism: Influence of the media system and media organization on journalistic practices in European digital mediascapes. *Journalism: Theory, Practice & Criticism*. https://doi.org/10.1177/1464884917743176

Peruško, Z., Čuvalo, A. & Vozab, D. (2016) Journalists in Croatia. *WJS Country Report*. Available from: https://epub.ub.uni-muenchen.de/29703/1/Country_report_Croatia.pdf [Accessed 25th September 2019].

Peruško, Z., Perišin, T., Topić, M., Vilović, G. & Zgrabljić Rotar, N. (2011) *Hrvatski medijski sustav prema UNESCO-ovim indikatorima medijskog razvoja (Croatian media system according to UNESCO media development indicators)*. Biblioteka Hrvatska politologija. Zagreb, Politička misao, FPZG.

Peruško, Z. & Popović, H. (2008) From transmission to the public good: Media policy for the digital age in Croatia. In: Sukosd, M. & Isanović, A. (eds.) *Public Service Television in the Digital Age: Strategies and Opportunities in Five South-East European Countries*. Sarajevo, Mediacentar, pp. 141–190.

Peruško, Z. & Vozab, D. (2016) The field of communication in Croatia: Toward a comparative history of communication studies in Central and Eastern Europe. In: Simonson, P. & Park, D. W. (eds.) *The International History of Communication Study*. New York, Routledge.

Peruško, Z., Vozab, D. & Čuvalo, A. (2015) Digital mediascapes, institutional frameworks, and audience practices across Europe. *International Journal of Communication*. 9, 342–364. Available from: https://ijoc.org/index.php/ijoc/article/view/3447 [Accessed 30th September 2019].

Peruško, Z., Vozab, D. & Čuvalo, A. (2013) Audiences as a source of agency. *Mediální Studia/Media Studies*. 7 (2), 137–154. Available from: www.medialnistudia.fsv.cuni.cz/front.file/download?file=2013_02_02_perusko.pdf [Accessed 30th September 2019].

Peters, B. G. (2000) *Institutional Theory in Political Science: The "new institutionalism."* London, Continuum.

Petković, B. (ed.) (2004) *Media Ownership and Its Impact on Media Independence and Pluralism*. Ljubljana, Peace Institute.

Petković, B. & Bašić Hrvatin, S. (2019) Izgubljeni emancipatorni potencial medijske politike. In: Pajnik, M. & Luthar, B. (eds.) *Mediji in spol: strukture in prakse neenakosti*. Ljubljana, Fakulteta za družbene vede, pp. 171–195.

Petković, B., Bašić Hrvatin, S., Londo, I., Hodžić, S., Nikodinoska, V., Milenkovski, S., Pavlović, P., Valić Nedeljković, D. & Janjatović Jovanović, M. (2019) *Media and Information Literacy in the Western Balkans: Unrealized Emancipatory Potential*, Sarajevo, Mediacentar.

Petković, B., Panić, S. & Bašić Hrvatin, S. (2016) *Comparing Models and Demanding Reforms of Public Service Media – Funding and Governing Models of the Public Service Media in the Countries of South East Europe*. SEE Media Observatory. Available from: https://seenpm.org/wp-content/uploads/Comparing-Models-and-Demanding-Reforms-of-Public-Service-Media.pdf [Accessed 30th September 2019].

Pfetsch, B. & Esser, F. (2012) Comparing political communication. In: Esser, F. & Hanitzsch, T. (eds.) *Handbook of Comparative Communication Research*. New York, Routledge, pp. 25–47.

Pfetsch, B. & Esser, F. (2008) Conceptual challenges to the paradigms of comparative media systems in globalized world. *Journal of Mass Communication*. 1 (3–4), 118–131.

Pickard, V. (2015) Media activism from above and below: Lessons from the 1940s American reform movement. *Journal of Information Policy*. 5, 109–128.

Pierson, P. (2004) *Politics in Time: History, Institutions and Social Analysis*. Princeton, Princeton University Press.

Pjesivac, I. & Imre, I. (2018) Perceptions of media roles in Serbia and Croatia: Does news orientation have an impact? *Journalism Studies*. 20 (13), 1864–1882. https://doi.org/10.1080/1461670X.2018.1539627

Polojac, F. (2011) Novinske agencije. In: Peruško, Z. (ed.) *Uvod u medije*. Zagreb, Jesenski i Turk.

Popescu, M., Toka, G., Gosselin, T. & Santana Pereira, J. (2011) *European Media Systems Survey 2010: Results and Documentation*. Colchester, University of Essex.

Popović, M. V. (ed.) 1969. *Počeci štampe jugoslovenskih naroda. Zbornik radova sa naučnog skupa o počecima štampe jugoslovenskih naroda*. Beograd, Jugoslovenski institut za novinarstvo.

Popović, M. V. et al. (1977) *Društveni slojevi i društvena svest: sociološko istraživanje interesa, stilova života, klasne svesti i vrednosno-ideoloških orijentacija društvenih slojeva*. Beograd, Centar za sociološka istraživanja, Institut društvenih nauka.

The Population of Yugoslavia (1974) Demographic Research. Belgrade, Center, Institute for Social Sciences.

Poulantzas, N. (2000/1978) *State, Power, Socialism*. London, Verso.

Primorac, J. (2004) Mapping the position of cultural industries in Southeastern Europe. In: Švob-Ðokić, N. (ed.) *Cultural Transitions in Southeastern Europe*. Zagreb, Institute for International Relations, pp. 59–78.

EBU (2018) *PSM Barometer*. Media Intelligence Series, EBU.

Puppis, M., d'Haenens, L., Steinmaurer, T. & Künzler, M. (2009) The European and global dimension taking small media systems research to the next level. *International Communication Gazette*. 71 (1–2), 105–112.

Pušnik, M. & Starc, G. (2008) An entertaining (r)evolution: The rise of television in socialist Slovenia. *Media, Culture, Society*. 30 (6), 777–793.

Radenić, A. (1969) Prve novine u Srbiji. In: Popović, M. (ed.) *Počeci štampe jugoslovenskih naroda. Zbornik radova sa naučnog skupa o počecima štampe jugoslovenskih naroda.* Belgrade, Jugoslovenski institut za novinarstvo, pp. 59–120.

Radin, F. (1986a) Vrijednosti Jugoslavenske omladine. In: Aleksić, J., Dunđerović, R., Flere, S., Ilišin, V., Mihailović, S., Obradović, Vl., Radin, F., Ule, M. & Vrcan, S. Položaj, svest i ponašanje mlade generacije Jugoslavije. *Preliminarna analiza rezultata istraživanja.* Beograd, Zagreb, CID, IDIS, pp. 55–75.

Radin, F. (1986b) Vrijednosti i vrijednosne orijentacije. In: Ilišin, V., Radin, F. & Županov, J. *Kultura radničke omladine. Prilog istraživanju položaja, vrijednosti i aktivnosti mladih radnika u SR Hrvatskoj.* Zagreb, Centar društvenih djelatnosti SSOH, pp. 117–164.

Radojković, M. (1994) Mass media between state monopoly and individual freedom: Media restructuring and restriction in former Yugoslavia. *European Journal of Communication.* 9 (2), 137–148.

Ragin, C. C. (2018) *User's Guide to Fuzzy-Set/Qualitative Comparative Analysis 3.0.* Irvine, Department of Sociology, University of California.

Ragin, C. C. (2015) *Qualitative Comparative Analysis WORKSHOP.* Available from: www.charlesragin.com, www.fsqca.com, www.compasss.org.

Ragin, C. C. (2008) *Redesigning Social Inquiry: Fuzzy Sets and Beyond.* Chicago, University of Chicago Press.

Ragin, C. C. (2000) *Fuzzy Set Social Science.* Chicago, University of Chicago Press.

Ragin, C. C. (1987) *The Comparative Method: Moving Beyond Qualitative and Quantitative Strategies.* Berkeley, University of California Press.

Ragin, C. C., Drass, K. A. & Davey, S. (2006) *Fuzzy-Set/Qualitative Comparative Analysis 2.0.* Tucson, Department of Sociology, University of Arizona.

Ramet, S. P. (2009) *Tri Jugoslavije. Izgradnja države i izazov legitimacije 1918–2005.* Zagreb, Golden Marketing Tehnička knjiga.

Ramet, S. P. (2003) Shake, rattle and self-management: Rock music and politics in socialist Yugoslavia and after. In: Ramet, S. P. & Crnković, G. P. (eds.) *Kazaaam! Splat! Ploof! The American Impact on European Popular Culture Since 1945.* Lanham, Rowman and Littlefield.

Ramet, S. P. (2002) *Balkan Babel: The Disintegration of Yugoslavia from the Death of Tito to the Fall of Milosevic.* Boulder, Westview Press.

Ranković, L. (2019) *Serbia – Media Landscape.* European Journalism Centre (EJC) 2019. Available from: https://medialandscapes.org/country/serbia [Accessed 30th September 2019].

Referendum o Zakonu o RTV Slovenia (2010) Available from: www.dvk-rs.si/index.php/si/arhiv-referendumi/referendum-o-zakonu-o-rtv-slovenija-2-12-december-2010 [Accessed 15th November 2019].

Reifova, I. & Pavličkova, T. (2013) Invisible audiences: Structure and agency in post-socialist media studies. *Mediální studia/Media Studies.* 2, 130–136.

Riffe, D., Lacy, S. & Fico, F. G. (2008) *Analyzing Media Messages: Using Quantitative Content Analysis in Research.* Second Edition. New York, Routledge.

Rimac, I., Burić, I. & Štulhofer, A. (2017) Višerazinsko modeliranje egalitarnog sindroma i validacija kratke skale SEMA-5. *Politička misao.* 54 (3), 64–79.

Rizman, R. M. (2001) *Slovenia's Path Towards Democratic Consolidation.* RFE/RL East European Perspectives. Available from: www.rferl.org/eepreport/.

Robinson, G. (1977) *Tito's Maverick Media: Communication Policy in Yugoslavia.* Urbana, University of Illinois Press.

Roig-Tierno, N., Gonzalez-Cruz, T. F. & Llopis-Martinez, J. (2017) An overview of qualitative comparative analysis: A bibliometric analysis. *Journal of Innovation & Knowledge*. 2, 15–23.

Roth-Ey, K. & Zakharova, L. (2019) Communications and media in the USSR and Eastern Europe. *Cahiers du monde russe*. 56 (2–3). Available from: http://journals.openedition.org/monderusse/8182 [Accessed 30th September 2019].

Roudakova, N. (2017) *Losing Pravda: Ethics and the Press in the Post-Truth Russia*. Cambridge, Cambridge University Press.

Roudakova, N. (2012) Comparing processes. In: Hallin, D. & Mancini, P. (eds.) *Comparing Media Systems Beyond the Western World*. New York, Cambridge University Press, pp. 246–277.

RTV Zagreb. *Radiotelevizija Zagreb*. Available from: https://obljetnica.hrt.hr/leksikon/r/radiotelevizija-zagreb/ [Accessed September 25, 2019].

RTV Zagreb. Radio i televizija u 1970. Informacija o anketnom istraživanju. *"Naš studio"*. List kolektiva Radio-televizije Zagreb. 25.

Ružić, N. (2017) *Public Service Broadcasting in Montenegro*. Analitika, Center for Social Research. Available from: https://seenpm.org/public-service-broadcasting-montenegro/ [Accessed 30th September 2019].

Ryfe, D. M. (2006) Guest editor's introduction: New institutionalism and the news. *Political Communication*. 23 (2), 135–144.

Ryfe, D. M. (2001) History and political communication: An introduction. *Political Communication*. 18 (4), 407–420.

Sarikakis, K. & Ganter, S. (2014) Priorities in global media policy transfer: Audio-visual and digital policy mutations in the EU, MERCOSUR and US triangle. *European Journal of Communication*. 29 (1), 17–33.

Schierup, C. U. (1992) Quasi-proletarians and a patriarchal bureaucracy: Aspects of Yugoslavia's re-peripheralisation. *Soviet Studies*. 44 (1), 79–99.

Schmitter, P. C. & Karl, T. L. (1994) The conceptual travels of transitologists and consolidologists: How far to the East should they attempt to go? *Slavic Review*. 53 (1), 173–185.

Schneeberger, A. (2019) *The Internationalisation of TV Audience Markets in Europe*. Strasbourg, European Audiovisual Observatory (Council of Europe). Available from: https://rm.coe.int/the-internationalisation-of-tv-audience-markets-in-europe/168094ea72 [Accessed 10th December 2019].

Schneider, C. Q. & Schmitter, P. C. (2004) Liberalization, transition and consolidation. Measuring the components of democratization. *Democratization*. 11 (5), 59–90.

Schneider, C. Q. & Wagemann, C. (2012) *Set-Theoretic Methods for the Social Sciences: A Guide to Qualitative Comparative Analysis (QCA)*. Cambridge, Cambridge University Press.

Schneider, C. Q. & Wagemann, C. (2010) Standards of good practice in qualitative comparative analysis (QCA) and fuzzy-sets. *Comparative Sociology*. 9 (3), 397–418.

Schneider, C. Q. & Wagemann, C. (2006) Reducing complexity in qualitative comparative analysis (QCA): Remote and proximate factors and the consolidation of democracy. *European Journal of Political Research*. 45 (5), 751–786.

Schumpeter, J. A. (1976/1942) *Capitalism, Socialism, Democracy*. New York, Harper and Row.

Schwartz, S. H. & Bardi, A. (1997) Influences of adaptation to communist rule on value priorities in Eastern Europe. *Political Psychology*. 18 (2), 385–410.

Scuteri, L. G. (2016) TV as a linguistic issue in Yugoslavian Slovenia: A brief chronology from the 1960s to the 1980s. In: Bönker, K., Obertreis, J. & Grampp, S. (eds.) *Television Beyond and Across the Iron Curtain.* Newcastle upon Tyne, Cambridge Scholars.

Seizova, S. & Rupar, V. (2016) *Journalists in Serbia: Country Report.* LMU Munich, Institut für Kommunikationswissenschaft, Research Report. https://doi.org/10.5282/ubm/epub.31033

Sekulić, D. (2011) Vrijednosno-ideološke orijentacije kao predznak i posljedica društvenih promjena. *Politička misao: časopis za politologiju.* 48 (3), 35–64.

Sekulić, D. (2010) Vrijednosti i društvene promjene. In: Kregar, J., Sekulić, D., Ravlić, S., Malenica, Z., Jeknić, R. & Petričušić, A. (eds.) *Izgradnja institucija: Etika i korupcija.* Zagreb, Pravni fakultet u Zagrebu, pp. 131–156.

Sekulić, D., Massey, G. & Hodson, R. (2006) Ethnic intolerance and ethnic conflict in the dissolution of Yugoslavia. *Ethnic and Racial Studies.* 29 (5) 797–827. https://doi.org/10.1080/01419870600814247

Senjković, R. (2008) *Izgubljeno u prijenosu: pop iskustvo soc kulture.* Zagreb, Institut za etnologiju i folkloristiku.

Seymour-Ure, C. (1973) Media systems, political culture and party. *Il Politico.* 38 (2), 217–231.

Shehata, A. (2010) Pathways to politics: How media system characteristics can influence socioeconomic gaps in political participation. *International Journal of Press/Politics.* 15 (3), 295–318.

Shehata, A. & Strömbäck, J. (2011) A Matter of context: A comparative study of media environments and news consumption gaps in Europe. *Political Communication.* 28 (1), 110–134.

Siebert, F. S., Peterson, T. & Schramm, W. (1956) *Four Theories of the Press.* Urbana, University of Illinois Press.

Skocpol, T. (1985) Cultural idioms and political ideologies in the revolutionary reconstruction of state power: A rejoinder to Sewell. *Journal of Modern History.* 57 (1), 86–96.

Skocpol, T. & Pierson, P. (2002) Historical institutionalism in contemporary political science. In: Katznelson, I. & Milner, H. V. (eds.) *Political Science: State of the Discipline.* New York, W.W. Norton, pp. 693–721.

Slovenian Statistical Yearbook (1974) *Pregled po republikah, Povzetni pregled za SFRJ in druge republike.* Available from: www.stat.si/doc/letopis/1974/1974_33.pdf [Accessed 25th September 2019].

Smithson, M. & Verkuilen, J. (2006) *Fuzzy Set Theory: Applications in the Social Sciences.* Thousand Oaks, CA, Sage.

Soifer, H. D. (2012) The causal logic of critical junctures. *Comparative Political Studies.* 45 (12), 1572–1597.

Sokolović, S., Mišović, M., Lukač, S. & Lazović, A. (1967) *Organizacija redakcija u Jugoslaviji.* Beograd, Jugoslavenski institut.

Šonje, V. (2016) Egalitarni sindrom: ekonomska perspektiva. *Politička misao.* 53 (1), 153–163.

Šopar, V. & Latifi, V. (2005) Macedonia. In: *Television Across Europe: Regulation, Policy and Independence.* Budapest, Open Society Institute, pp. 1168–1230.

Sparks, C. (2012) Beyond political communication: Toward a broader perspective on the Chinese press. *Chinese Journal of Communication.* 5 (1), 61–67.

Sparks, C. (2008) Media systems in transition: Poland, Russia, China. *Chinese Journal of Communication*. 1 (1), 7–24.
Sparks, C. (1998) *Communism, Capitalism and the Mass Media*. London, Sage.
Spaskovska, L. J. (2014) The Yugoslav chronotope – histories, memories and the future of Yugoslav studies. In: Bieber, F., Galijaš, A. & Archer, R. (eds.) *Debating the Dissolution of Yugoslavia*. London, Ashgate, pp. 241–253.
Spasovska, Lj. (2017). *The Last Yugoslav Generation: The Rethinking of Youth Politics and Cultures in Late Socialism*. Manchester, Manchester University Press.
Spasovska, K. (2011) *Journalism Under Siege: An Investigation into How Journalists in Macedonia Understand Professionalism and Their Role in the Development of Democracy* [Dissertation]. University of Tennessee. Available from: https://trace.tennessee.edu/utk_graddiss/1128 [Accessed 30th September 2019].
Spehnjak, K. & Cipek, T. (2007) Disidenti, opozicija i otpor – Hrvatska i Jugoslavija 1945–1990. *Časopis za suvremenu povijest*. 39 (2), 249–513.
Splichal, S. (2001) Imitative revolutions changes in the media and journalism in East Central Europe. *Javnost – The Public*. 8 (4), 31–58.
Splichal, S. (1994) *Media Beyond Socialism: Theory and Practice in East-Central Europe*. London, Routledge.
Splichal, S. (1989) Indigenization versus ideologization: Communication science on the periphery. *European Journal of Communication*. 4 (3), 329–359.
Surćulija Milojević, J. (2018) *Monitoring media pluralism in Europe: Application of the media pluralism monitor 2017 in the European Union, FYROM, Serbia & Turkey*. Country report: Serbia. EUI The Centre for Media Pluralism and Media Freedom. Available from: https://cadmus.eui.eu/bitstream/handle/1814/61154/2018_Serbia_EN.pdf [Accessed 15th July 2019].
Šrot, V. (2008) Zgodovina raziskovanja RTV programov in občinstva: Služba za študij programa in njeni nasladniki. *Javnost – The Public* 15 (Supplement), 133–150.
Stanyer, J. & Mihelj, S. (2016) Taking time seriously? Theorizing and researching change in communication and media studies. *Journal of Communication* 66, 266–279.
Stępińska, A. & Ossowski, S. (2012) Three generations of Polish journalists: Professional roles and identities. *Journalism Studies*. 13 (5–6), 857–867.
Štetka, V. (2012) From multinationals to business tycoons: Media ownership and journalistic autonomy in Central and Eastern Europe. *International Journal of Press/Politics*. 17 (4), 433–456.
Stojanovski, F. (2018) *Hungary's Regime Is Exporting Instability and Propaganda to the Balkans*. Available from: https://seenpm.org/hungarys-regime-exporting-instability-propaganda-balkans/ [Accessed 15th December 2019].
Stokes, G. (1989) The social origins of East European politics. In: Chirot, D. (ed.) *The Origins of Backwardness in Eastern Europe: Economics & Politics from the Middle Ages Until the Early Twentieth Century*. Berkeley, University of California Press, pp. 210–252.
Štulhofer, A., Bačak, V. & Šuljok, A. (2010) Provincijalni karakter hrvatske sociologije. *Revija za sociologiju*. 40 (1), 103–108.
Štulhofer, A. & Burić, I. (2015) Je li egalitarni sindrom samo teorijska fantazija? Empirijski hommage Josipu Županovu. *Politička misao*. 52 (3), 7–31.
Stradiotto, G. A. & Guo, S: (2010) Transnational modes of democratization and democratic outcomes. *International Journal on World Peace*. 27 (4), 5–40.

Strate, L. (2004) A media ecology review. *Communication Research Trends*. 23 (2). Available from: http://cscc.scu.edu [Accessed 15th November 2019].
Strömbäck, J. (2008) Four phases of mediatization: An analysis of the mediatization of politics. *International Journal of Press/Politics*. 13 (3), 228–246.
Sükösd, M. & Bajomi-Lázár, P. (2003) *Reinventing Media: Media Policy Reform in East-Central Europe*. Budapest, CEU Press.
Surowiec, P. & Štětka, V. (2019): Introduction: Media and illiberal democracy in Central and Eastern Europe. *East European Politics*. 1–9.
Šonje, V. & Polšek, D. 2019. *Prešućeni trijumf liberalizma: o praktičnoj važnosti slobode 1989–2019*. Zagreb, Arhivanalitika.
Švoger, V. (2013) Ban Josip Jelačić u očima svojih suvremenika. *Zbornik Odsjeka povijsnih znanosti Zavoda povijesnih društvenih znanosti*. 31, 247–271.
Swindler, A. (1986) Culture in action: Symbols and strategies. *American Sociological Review*. 51 (2), 273–286.
Sztompka, P. (1993) *The Sociology of Social Change*. Oxford, Blackwell.
Tadić Mijović, M. & Šajkaš, M. (2016) *Captured News Media: Bosnia and Herzegovina, Serbia, and Montenegro*. CIMA Center for International Media Assistance, National Endowment for Democracy. Available from: www.cima.ned.org/wp-content/uploads/2016/06/CIMA-Balkans-Captured-Media.pdf [Accessed 25th September 2019].
Tanner, M. (1997) *Croatia: A Nation Forged in War*. New Haven, Yale University Press.
Terzis, G. (2009) *European Journalism Education*. Bristol, Intellect Books.
Terzis, G. (ed.) (2007) *European Media Governance: National and Regional Dimensions*. Bristol, Intellect Books and University of Chicago Press.
Thompson, J. B. (1995) *The Media and Modernity: A Social Theory of the Media*. Cambridge, Polity Press.
Thompson, M. (1995) *Kovanje rata: mediji u Srbiji, Hrvatskoj i Bosni i Hercegovini*. Zagreb, Hrvatski helsinški odbor za ljudska prava Građanska inicijativa za slobodu javne riječi.
Tilly, C. (1997) *Suočavanje sa društvenom promenom*. Beograd, Filip Višnjić.
Tilly, C. (1995) *European Revolutions, 1492–1992*. Oxford, Blackwell.
Tilly, C. (1992) *Coercion, Capital and European State AD 990–1992*. Oxford, Blackwell.
Tilly, C. (1984) *Big Structures, Large Processes, Huge Comparisons*. New York, Russell Sage Foundation.
Todorova, M. (2009 [1997]) *Imagining the Balkans*. New York, Oxford University Press.
Todorova, M. (2004) What is or is there a Balkan culture, and do or should the Balkans have a regional identity? *Southeast European and Black Sea Studies*. 4 (1), 175–185.
Todorović, N. (1987) *Ženska štampa i kultura ženstvenosti*. Beograd, Naučna knjiga.
Todosijević, B. (2013) Serbia. In: Burgelund, S., Ekman, J., Deegan-Krause, K. & Knutsen, T. (eds.) *The Handbook of Political Change in Eastern Europe*. Third Edition. Northampton, MA, Edward Elgar, pp. 523–566.
Tomić-Koludrović, I. (1993) Alternativna kultura kao oblik otpora samoupravnom socijalizmu. *Društvena istraživanja*. 6–7 (4–5), 835–862.
Tracy, J. D. (2016) *Balkan Wars. Habsburg Croatia, Ottoman Bosnia, and Venetian Dalmatia. 1499–1617*. New York, Rowman and Littlefield.

Trpevska, S. (2017) Ethnocentric coverage: Audiences comfy zone in Macedonia. *New Europe's: Our World in 2017*. 24 (1193). Available from: www.neweurope. eu/article/ethnocentric-coverage-audiences-comfy-zone-macedonia/ [Accessed 30th September 2019].

Trpevska, S. & Micevski, I. (2018) *Country Report: Former Yugoslav Republic of Macedonia. Monitoring Media Pluralism in Europe: Application of the Media Pluralism Monitor 2017 in the European Union, FYROM, Serbia & Turkey*. The Centre for Media Pluralism and Media Freedom. Available from: https://cmpf. eui.eu/media-pluralism-monitor/mpm-2017-2/ [Accessed 30th September 2019].

Trpevska, S. & Micevski, I. (2014) Macedonia. In: *Media Integrity Matters: Reclaiming Public Service Values in Media and Journalism*. Ljubljana, Peace Institute, pp. 257–326.

Trpevska, S., Micevski, I., Adilagic, R., Nebiu, B., Selmani, N., Sekulovski, D., Camovic, M., Qollaku, P. & Vukasovic, M. (2018*) Indicators on the Level of Media Freedom and Journalists' Safety in the Western Balkans*. Comparative Analysis 2018. Independent Journalists' Association of Serbia. Available from: http://safejournalists.net/wp-content/uploads/2018/12/indicators_on_the_level_of_media_freedom_WB_2018.pdf [Accessed 30th September 2019].

Tumber, H. & Palmer, J. (2004) *Media at War: The Iraq Crisis*. London, Sage.

Udovičić, R. (2015) *Journalists in a Gap Between Devastated Media and Legal Insecurity*. Sarajevo, Mediacentar.

Ule, M. (1988) *Mladina in ideologija*. Ljubljana, Delavska enotnost.

UNESCO (2008) Media Development Indicators: A Framework for Assessing Media Development. *Intergovernmental Council of the IPDC*. Twenty-sixth session. UNESCO, Paris.

Van Cuilenburg, J. (2007) Media diversity, competition and concentration: Concepts and theories. In: de Bens, E. (ed.) *Media Between Culture and Commerce*. Changing Media – Changing Europe Series Vol. 4. Bristol, Intellect, pp. 25–53.

Van Cuilenburg, J. & van der Wurff, R. (2007) Toward easy-to-measure media diversity indicators. In: de Bens, E. (ed.) *Media Between Culture and Commerce*. Changing Media – Changing Europe Series Vol. 4. Bristol, Intellect, pp. 99–113.

Van Dijck, J., Poell, T. & De Wall, M. (2018) *The Platform Society: Public Values in a Connective World*. New York, Oxford University Press.

Vatovec, F. (1969) Prva pojava slovenačke periodičke štampe. In: Popović, M. (ed.) *Počeci štampe jugoslovenskih naroda. Zbornik radova sa naučnog skupa o počecima štampe jugoslovenskih naroda*. Beograd, Jugoslovenski institut za novinarstvo, pp. 27–40.

Vesnić-Alujević, L. & Bajić, N. S. (2013) Media consumption patterns: Watching TV in former Yugoslav states. *Medialni Studia/Media Studies*. 7 (2), 192–211.

Vliegenthart, R. (2012) Advanced strategies for data analysis: Opportunities and challenges of comparative data. In: Esser, F. & Hanitzsch, T. (eds.) *Handbook of Comparative Communication Research*. New York, Routledge, pp. 486–500.

Vobič, I. & Milojević, A. (2014) "What we do is not actually journalism": Role negotiations in online departments of two newspapers in Slovenia and Serbia. *Journalism*. 15 (8), 1023–1040.

Vobič, I. & Milojević, A. (2012) Societal roles of online journalists in Slovenia and Serbia. *Participations*. 9 (2). Available from: www.participations.org/Volume%209/ Issue%202/26%20Vobic.pdf [Accessed 30th September 2019].

Volčić, Z. (2013) Connecting the disconnected: Balkan culture studies. *Communication and Critical/Cultural Studies*. 10 (2–3), 333–339. https://doi.org/10.1080/14791420.2013.812597

Voltmer, K. (2013) *The Media in Transitional Democracies, Contemporary Political Communication*. Cambridge, Polity Press.

Voltmer, K. (2012) How far can media systems travel? Applying Hallin and Mancini's comparative framework beyond the Western world. In: Hallin, D. & Mancini, P. (eds.) *Comparing Media Systems Beyond the Western World*. Cambridge, Cambridge University Press, pp. 224–245.

Voltmer, K. (2008) Comparing media systems in new democracies: East meets South meets West. *Central European Journal of Communication*. 1, 23–40.

Vončina, N. (2005) *Emisije RTV Zagreb: 1964–1971: prilozi za povijest radija i televizije u Hrvatskoj VI*. Zagreb, Hrvatski Radio.

Vončina, N. (2003) *Najgledanije emisije: 1964–1971: prilozi za povijest radija i televizije u Hrvatskoj V*. Zagreb, Hrvatski Radio.

Vončina, N. (2001) *RTV Zagreb 1959–1964: prilozi za povijest radija i televizije u Hrvatskoj IV*. Zagreb, Hrvatski Radio.

Vončina, N. (1999) *TV osvaja Hrvatsku: prilozi za povijest radija i televizije u Hrvatskoj III. (1954–1958)*. Zagreb, Hrvatski Radio.

Vozab, D. (2017) Pristrani i neprijateljski mediji te polarizacija u novom medijskom okolišu. *Političke analize*, 8 (30).

Vozab, D. & Majstorović, D. (2017) *Journalism Profession as Seen in Scientific Journals in Socialist and Post-Socialist Croatia* [Presentation]. CEECOM 2017, Critique of/at/on Periphery, Ljubljana, Slovenia, June 15–17.

Vujnović, M. (2008) *Forging the Bubikopf Nation: A Feminist Political-Economic Analysis of Ženski List, Interwar Croatia's Women's Magazine, for the Construction of an Alternative Vision of Modernity* [Dissertation]. University of Iowa. https://doi.org/10.17077/etd.5ivieavo

Vukasovich, C. & Boyd-Barrett, O. (2012) Whatever happened to Tanjug? Reloading memory for an understanding of the global news system. *International Communication Gazette*. 74 (8), 693–710.

Vuković, V., Štulhofer, A. & Burić, I. (2017) Je li Županov imao pravo? Testiranje podrijetla i perzistencije egalitarnog sindroma. *Društvena istraživanja*. 26 (2), 207–225.

Walker, C. & Orttung, R. W. (2014) Breaking the news: The role of state-run media. *Journal of Democracy*. 25 (1), 71–85.

Weik, E. (2015) A return to the enduring features of institutions: A process ontology of reproduction and endurance. *Philosophy of the Social Sciences*. 45 (3), 291–314.

Williams, C. C. & Horodnic, I. A. (2015) Tackling the informal economy in Southeast Europe: An institutional approach. *Southeast European and Black Sea Studies*. 15 (4), 519–539.

Wimmer, R. D. & Dominick, J. R. (2004) *Mass Media Research: An Introduction*. Fourth Edition. Belmont, CA, Wadsworth.

Wimmer, A. & Schiller, N. G. (2002) Methodological nationalism and beyond: Nation-state building, migration and the social sciences. *Global Networks*. 2 (4), 301–334.

YRT Yearbook (1971–1972). Jugoslovenska televizija Belgrade 1972.

Zajec, D. (2013) Slovenia. In: Burgelund, S., Ekman, J., Deegan-Krause, K. & Knutsen, T. (eds.) *The Handbook of Political Change in Eastern Europe*. Third Edition. Northampton, MA, Edward Elgar, pp. 339–368.

Zakon o štampi i drugim oblicima informacija (1960) Izdanje službenog lista FNRJ.

Zakošek, N. (2008) Democratization, state-building and war: The cases of Serbia and Croatia. *Democratisation*. 15 (3), 588–610.

Zeh, R. & Hopmann, D. N. (2013) Indicating mediatization? Two decades of election campaign television coverage. *European Journal of Communication*. 28 (3), 225–240.

Zielonka, J. (2015) *Media and Politics in New Democracies: Europe in a Comparative Perspective*. Oxford, Oxford University Press.

Žikić, B. (2010) Dissidents liked pretty girls: Nudity, pornography and quality press in socialism. *Medijska istraživanja*. 16 (1), 53–71.

Zubak, M. (2018) *The Yugoslav Youth Press (1968–1980): Student Movements, Youth Subcultures and Alternative Communist Media*. Zagreb, Srednja Europa.

Zubak, M. (2012) Pop-express (1969–1970): Rock-kultura u političkom omladinskom tisku. *Časopis za suvremenu povijest*. 44 (1), 23–35.

Zubčevič, A. R., Bender, S. & Vojvodić, J. (2017) *Media Regulatory Authorities and Hate Speech in the Western Balkans*. Council of Europe. Available from: https://rm.coe.int/media-regulatory-authorities-and-hate-speech/16807338f5 [Accessed 15th November 2019].

Županić, N. (1911) *Slovenačka štampa/ Slovenci, njih zgodovina i časnikarstvo in Jugoslovenska štampa. Referati i bibliografija*. Beograd, Izdanje Srpskog novinarskog udruženja, pp. 257–281.

Županov, J. (1996) The social legacy of communism. *Društvena istraživanja*. 5 (2), 425–455.

Županov, Josip. (1995) *Poslije potopa*. Zagreb, Globus.

Županov, J. (1987) *Sociologija i samoupravljanje*. Zagreb, Školska knjiga.

Županov, J. (1986) Radnička omladina i društvena stabilnost. In: Ilišin, V., Radin, F. & Županov, J. (eds.) *Kultura radničke omladine. Prilog istraživanju položaja, vrijednosti i aktivnosti mladih radnika u SR Hrvatskoj*. Zagreb, Centar društvenih djelatnosti SSOH, pp. 165–192.

Županov, J. (1983) *Marginalije o društvenoj krizi*. Zagreb, Globus.

Index

accommodative pluralism (s_accomplur) condition 202
administrative period 93–95
advertising 112–113, 164, 175
Afghanistan 212
afternoon programs 122
Albania 7
alternative civil society media, 103
apologetic reporting 101
asymmetric parallelism (d_aspar) condition 172, 213–214, 225, 233–237, 239–241, 243–244
atavistic value orientation 152
audience research 113
Audiovisual Media Services Directive (AVMSD) 152–153
Austria 49, 50
Austro-Hungarian Empire 47, 52, 56
authoritarian model 4
authoritarian regime in the 1990s (d_authorit) condition 203–204

Balkan wars 46
BBC public service model 166
Black Wave films 88–89, 126
Bohemia-Czechoslovakia 49
book publishing 52–54, 74
Bosnia and Herzegovina: clientelism and corruption 140; consociational regime, 140; cultural field transformation 150; digital media policy 165, 211; elections during regime conversions. 136; freedom of expression 107, 159–160; genre distribution 184; global communication flows 221; independence 137; interviews 250; journalism culture/professional autonomy 72; media capture 220; media freedom 212; media markets 174–177, 215–216, 229; media pluralism policy 164; media policy 156–157; media system transformations 188–190; nationalist writings 99; newspapers 61–62, 69, 103, 171–172, 215–216; original media production 110; political cleavages 87, 140; political communication 69; political field transformation 43–44, 48, 202–206; political parallelism 171, 230; post-socialist democratic transition 188; potential candidate country of EU 8; public service broadcasting 166, 185; public service media governance 168; regulatory system for broadcasting 161–162; religious press 169; socialism in 84–85; socio-economic field transformation 207; state advertising 164; stateness issues 140; sufficient macro and structural conditions in path to media freedom 238–239; sufficient media system conditions for media freedom 235–240; telegraph services 73; television 110, 115, 118–119, 183–186; television schedules 124; war 138
Brazil 212
broadcasting frequency distribution 156
Bulgaria 5, 46, 136
bureaucratic-authoritarian communism 81
business parallelism 71

calibration 195–200
capitalism 148
Catholic Church 44, 51–52, 169
Catholic radio 169

Index

censorship 30, 52–55, 59, 69, 72, 94–95, 97, 108, 139, 158, 181, 183, 209–211
Central and Eastern European (CEE) countries: analysis of post-socialist capitalism in 148–149; approaches to comparing media systems of 3–5; cluster with Western European countries 190; democratic consolidation of 203; democratization of media systems in 151; Eurovision Song Contest 1; freedom of expression and censorship in 158–161; global communication flows 220–221; governance of public service media 166–168; impact of European integrations 11; impact of socialism on media systems 7–9; influence of digital communication revolution 133; institutional development models 22; journalism culture/professional autonomy 218–219, 243; liberalization-transition-consolidation processes of democratization 135; media developments in 90; media freedom 188, 205; media market after self-management socialism 173–187; media policy 152–158; media systems analysis 2–5; media systems cluster with Western European countries 5–7; media system transformations in 198; political culture 150; political frameworks 74; political parallelism 168–173, 243; post-socialist democratic transitions 134–147; post-socialist media policy of 152–153, 156; public service media 37–38, 218; rise of right-wing movements in 160–161; socialism in 26; transformations of media systems 18
centralized command socialism 81
China 49, 81
citizen engagement 150
civic governance model 167
class 84
clientelism 47, 81, 85, 140, 167, 204–205, 233–238, 241–242
communication change 14–15
communication juncture 28–32

comparative analysis: fuzzy set qualitative comparative analysis (fsQCA) 33–34; problems of 32; qualitative comparative analysis 33
comparative political science approach 134
consolidated liberal democracies (d_libdem) condition 204
consolidation phase 147
content analysis: daily press 109–110, 248–250; television cultures 183, 245–248
conversion transition 136
cooperative transitions 136, 203
cooperative type of transition (d_cotran) condition 203
corporatist governance model 167
corruption 140
critical junctures: communication revolution 28–32; concept of 22; modernization 25–26; post-socialist democratizations 27–28; revolutionary 200; socialism 26–27
critical reporting 101
Croat-Hungarian Nagodba (Agreement, Settlement) 45, 53
Croatia: Catholic Church 52, 57, 169; clientelism and corruption 140; cooperative transition 136; cultural field transformation 150, 189; cultural journals 109; democratic consolidation 145, 147; development of printing 56–58; digital media policy 165, 211; economic field transformation 148–149; freedom of expression 107, 158–160; genre distribution 184; global communication flows 187, 221; independence 137; interviews 251; journalism culture/professional autonomy 72, 180, 218; journalism-related education 230; journalists' associations 182; literacy rates 58–59, 62–63; media capture 220; media freedom 212; media literacy 165–166; media markets 173–177, 215–216, 229; media pluralism policy 163, 211; media policy 156–157; media systems 5; media system transformations 188–189; as member of EU 8; modernization path of developing media systems 227; music 124; nationalist

Index   293

writings 99; newspapers 59–60, 62, 67–69, 103, 170, 215; original media production 110; political cleavages 87–88, 140–145; political communication 67–69; political field transformation 43–45, 47, 48, 202–206; political parallelism 169, 170; political parties 67, 74, 86, 88, 167, 170; political pluralism 87; postal authority 73; postal service 73; post-socialist democratic transition 188; Protestant Reformation 56–57; public service broadcasting 185; public service media governance 167; publishing companies 63–66; radio 66; reform movements 86–87; regulatory system for broadcasting 161; socialism in 84–85; socio-economic field transformation 207–208; state involvement in media system 52–53, 55; sufficient macro and structural conditions in path to media freedom 236–237; sufficient media system conditions for media freedom 235; telegraph services 63; television 110, 114, 118–119, 126, 183–186; television schedules 124; war 137–138; workers' papers 70
cultural field: conditions shaping outcomes 37–39, 208–224; Habsburg Empire 52–53, 57, 59; Kingdom of SHS/Yugoslavia, 54–56; Ottoman Empire 51–54, 56–59, 61–63; in post-socialist media systems 149–187; in socialist modernity 88–124; Yugoslavia 88–127
cultural journals 108–109
cultural programs 117–118
culture 20–22
Czechia (Czech Republic) 139, 173
Czechoslovakia 1, 7, 81, 136

Dalmatia 44, 48, 50
decadent socialism 98–99
de-democratization 23, 135, 147, 157
defamation 160
democracy index 190
democratic backsliding 146–147
democratic consolidation 134–135, 145–147, 153, 157, 189, 203–204, 214, 243

democratization: in Croatia 88, 150, 189; failed 23; in Greece 148; hybrid regimes 145–147; in Italy 148; media 2, 11, 24, 135–136, 139, 151, 153, 244; in Portugal 148; post-socialist trajectories 1–2, 27–28, 36, 125, 134–147, 199; relationship between modernization and 10; in Slovenia 108, 145–146; in Spain 149
developing the digital infrastructure (d_dinfra) condition 211
development of the media market (d_market) condition 218
digital literacy 181
digital media 31, 181
digital media outlets 170–171
digital media policy 164–166, 211, 232
dominance of right-wing parties in government (d_rwgov) condition 205–206

early development of printing and the press (m_printing) condition 215
economic field: conditions shaping outcomes 35–36, 206–208; Habsburg Empire 49–51; Kingdom of SHS/Yugoslavia, 51; Ottoman Empire 49–51, 74; in post-socialist media systems 147–149; in socialist modernity 82–84; Yugoslavia 82–84
educational programs 116
egalitarian syndrome 90
embedded neoliberal capitalism 148
entertainment programs 116–118
Estonia 173
European Broadcasting Union (EBU) 1, 100, 123
European [EU] integration (d_euint) condition 204
European mainstream media system model 5, 189
European peripheral media system cluster 190
European Union (EU): candidate countries 8, 165, 188, 204; digital media policy 232; economic field 148–150; Eurovision Song Contest 1; freedom of expression 158; funding of journalism 170, 181; harmonization 152–153; integration 204; media systems 6; political cleavage 145; role in media system transformations 243; rule of law 140;

television content 118–119, 186, 248; threshold for *high globalization of culture and communication* 224; threshold for *high socio-economic development* 208
Eurovision Song Contest 1
extractive institutions 35–36

factory newspaper 113–114
federal-level transition (Yugoslavia) 136
feudalism 49
fiction programs 116–118
films 88–89, 124, 126
foreign investment 173
foreign media 152
foreign news agencies 73
France 114
freedom of expression 107, 156, 158–161, 211–212
freedom of the press 4, 52–53, 55, 59, 71, 94, 99, 150, 156–158, 211–212
fuzzy set qualitative comparative analysis (fsQCA) 33–34, 195–200

gender imbalance 100
German Democratic Republic (GDR) 81, 123, 136
Germany 207
global communication flows 39, 72–73, 122–124, 133, 183–187, 220–223
governance models (public service media) 166–167
Greece 114, 148, 149, 189–190

Habsburg Empire: cultural field transformation 52–53, 55, 57, 59; development of media markets 57, 59; economic field transformation 49–51, 74; global communication flows 221; imperial rule of 43–44; newspapers 59–62; political field transformation 41, 43–45, 202; political institutions 44; postal service 72–73; Press Law of the Dual Monarchy 55
"Habsburg factor" 227–228
hate speech 158–159
high clientelism (d_clien) condition 204–205
high development of the journalism profession (m_journos) condition 219
high development of the journalism profession (s_journos) condition 219
high development of the socialist media market (s_market) condition 216
high economic development (s_develo) condition 207
higher industrialization (m_indust) condition 206–207
higher literacy (m_litera) condition 206
higher media capture (d_hmcap) condition 219–220
high globalization of culture and communication (d_globcom) condition 221
high globalization of culture and communication (s_globcom) condition 221
high level of globalization of communication (m_globcom) condition 221
high literacy (s_litera) condition 207
highly developed advertising (s_advert) condition 216–217
highly developed press market (d_press) condition 217
highly developed print market (m_market) condition 215–216
high media freedom (d_mfree) condition 211
high political parallelism (s_polpa) condition 213
high post-materialist values (d_postmat) condition 208
high post-materialist values (s_postmat) condition 207–208
high socio-economic development (d_develo) condition 208
high state support for media pluralism (media and state) (d_smeplu) condition 211
historical institutionalism (HI) 8, 10, 19–20, 22, 25, 32, 194, 198, 241
human values 91
Hungary 5, 49, 136
hybrid liberal model 4, 190
hybrid regimes 145–147, 183

idealistic value orientation 152
illiteracy rates 63, 82, 206–207, 215
imitation (mimesis) thesis 152
inclusive institutions 35–36, 37
Industrial Revolution, 40
informational/factual programs 116–117
institutional development models 22

intensity of war (d_war) condition 203
interviews 250–251
Istria 48, 50
Italianization model 152
Italy 5, 48, 114, 148

journalism associations 102
journalism culture/professional autonomy 38, 41, 67, 71–72, 99–102, 126, 133, 177–183, 218–219, 226–229
journalism-related education 219, 230–231
journalism-related university programs 219
journalistic roles 101
journalists' associations 102, 182–183, 218–219

Kingdom of SHS/Yugoslavia: economic field transformation 51; formation of 47–48; journalism culture/professional autonomy 71; media development 209, 215; newspapers 62–66; political field transformation 46–47; political parallelism 70–71; state involvement in media system 54–56
Kosovo 8, 43, 47, 62, 87, 107, 136, 138, 140, 147, 188, 204, 230
Kruševo Republic 46

law suits (SLAP) 160–161
liberalization stage 147
literacy rates 25, 29, 45, 50, 58–59, 62–63, 74, 206–207, 216, 218, 227–230, 243
Lithuania 5, 173
long-term patrimonial regime in the Ottoman Empire (m_ottemp) condition 202
long-term rule of an absolutist or constitutional monarchy – the Habsburg Empire (m_habemp) condition 202
longue durée 17, 21, 24, 133, 194, 195, 224–226, 232, 237–244

Macedonia: candidate country of EU 8; censorship 55; cultural field transformation 150; democratic consolidation 145; digital media policy 211; elections during regime conversions. 136; establishment of schools 61; freedom of expression 107, 158–160; global communication flows 221; independence 137; journalism culture/professional autonomy 180–181; journalists' associations 182; media freedom 212; media literacy 165; media markets 215–216, 230; media policy 156–157; media systems cluster with Western European countries 5; media system transformations 189–190; nationalist writings 99; newspapers 61, 70, 215; original media production 110; political cleavages 87, 140; political communication 70; political field transformation 43, 46, 47, 202–206; political parallelism 170, 171, 230; public service broadcasting 185; regulatory system for broadcasting 162; socialism in 84–85; socio-economic field transformation 208; stateness issues 140; sufficient macro and structural conditions in path to media freedom 239–240, 242; sufficient media system conditions for media freedom 236; television 110, 115, 118–119, 183–186; television schedules 124
majoritarian government (d_mgov) condition 205
market economy 147–149
marketing agencies 172
market socialism 111
mass communication 26, 30
mass media 27
media capture 219–220, 244
media culture 7, 31, 39, 122–124, 126, 183–187
media ecology approach 30
media freedom: impact of the state on media and 211–212; inclusive institutions and 36; as key criterion for judging quality of contemporary media systems 226; necessary conditions and different paths to 235–242; negative influence of populist rule on 146; as part of political criteria for EU accession 153; political parallelism and 168; in post-socialist media systems 156–160, 162, 182; protest in support of 150; regulation and 97; right-wing governments and 205;

Index

sufficient macro and structural conditions in the path to 236–237; sufficient media system conditions for 235–236; war and 139
media freedom (d_free) condition 226
media in transition model 4, 190
media legislation 97–99, 125, 158–161
media literacy 164–166
media market development (d_market) condition 226
media markets: after self-management socialism 173–177; conditions shaping outcomes 38–39, 214–218; development of printing 56–59; global communication 72–73; Habsburg Empire 214–218; journalism culture/ professional autonomy 71–72; modernization path of 226–229; necessary conditions and different paths to development 232–233; newspapers 59–70; political communication 67–71; in post-socialist media systems 133, 152, 173–177, 217–218; radio 66–67; sufficient media system conditions for development 233; sufficient structural and macro conditions for development 233–234
media pluralism policy 162–164, 211
media systems: conditions shaping outcomes in 34–39, 200–224; critical junctures 22–32; cultural field 37–39, 88–124; economic field 78–81, 82–84; economic field transformation 35–36; global communication flows 39, 72–73, 122–124, 133, 183–187, 220–223; impact of socialism on 7–9; influence of democratic consolidation 147; journalism culture/professional autonomy 38, 41, 67, 71–72, 99–102, 126, 133, 177–183, 218–219; making socialist media 92–99; media culture 7, 31, 39, 122–124, 126, 209, 220–223; media field 38–39, 51; media market/ infrastructure 38–39, 133; media policy 152–158, 205; political field transformation 35–36, 84–88, 194, 198, 201–206; political parallelism 38, 67–70, 125–126, 168–173; post-socialist 132–190; role in the wars of former Yugoslavia 138–139; in socialist modernity 88–127; socio-economic field 36–37, 194, 198, 206–208; state involvement 30, 37–38, 52–55, 69, 72, 92–99, 108, 139, 151, 181, 183, 209–212; symbolic field 37–39, 42, 56, 194, 198, 208–224; types in post-communist part of Europe 4; United States 24
media systems analysis: aims 225–226; approaches to comparing media systems of CEE countries 3–5; causal configurations and paths of media systems transformations 224–242; CEE countries cluster with Western European countries 5–7, 189–190; challenges associated with 201; comparative monitoring projects 151; contextual conditions 225, 239; country-by-country monographs 151; fuzzy set qualitative comparative analysis (fsQCA) 33–34, 195–200; historical institutionalist approach 19–20; media systems during socialism 229–231; media systems in digital modernity 232–242; modernization path of developing media systems 226–229; problem of comparison 32; problem of studying media change 14–22; proximate conditions 224–225; quantitative comparative studies 151; recent studies 151; remote conditions 224–225; sufficiency analysis 226–227
mediatization theory 28–32, 41, 133
Mediterranean model 5, 152, 177, 241
modernization: concept of 40–41, 132–133; as critical juncture 25–26; as form of social change 17–18; path of developing media systems 226–229; relationship between democratization and 10; socialist values and 89–92
Montenegro: candidate country of EU 8; clientelism and corruption 140; cultural field transformation 150; democratic consolidation 145, 147; digital media policy 211; elections during regime conversions. 136; establishment of

schools 61; freedom of expression 107, 158–160; genre distribution 185; global communication flows 221; interviews 251; journalists' associations 182–183; media capture 220; media freedom 212, 243; media literacy 165; media markets 174–177, 215–216, 230; media system transformations 189–190; nationalist writings 99; newspapers 60–61, 70, 215; original media production 110; political cleavages 87, 145; political communication 70; political field transformation 43, 46, 202–206; political parallelism 171, 230; political parties 70; post-socialist democratic transition 189–190; radio 66; regulatory system for broadcasting 162; socialism in 84–85; socio-economic field transformation 208; state advertising 164; sufficient macro and structural conditions in path to media freedom 238–240; sufficient media system conditions for media freedom 236; television 110, 115, 118–119, 183–186; television schedules 124; war 138
multi-party parliamentary systems 140
music 89, 123–124, 126

national accommodative communism 81, 84–85
nationalist writings 99
neo-corporatist capitalism 148
neoliberal capitalism 148
neo-modernization theory 18
neo-television 30
Netherlands 19, 221
newspapers: Bosnia and Herzegovina 61–62, 69, 103, 171–172, 215–216; content analysis 109–110, 248–250; Croatia 59–60, 62, 67–69, 103, 170, 215; factory newspaper 113–114; Habsburg Empire 59–62; Kingdom of SHS/Yugoslavia 62–66, 70–71; Macedonia 61, 70, 215; Montenegro 60–61, 215; Ottoman Empire 53–54, 59–62; political communication 67–70, 102–103; political public spheres in 59–62, 109–110; Serbia 60–61, 62, 69, 103, 169–171, 215–216; Slovenia 59, 62, 69, 215; television schedules 124; Yugoslavia 103–110, 122
New Zealand 212
Nordic countries 148
Nordic model 5
North Korea 212
North Macedonia: clientelism and corruption 140; democratic consolidation 147; development of printing 56–57; EU candidate countries 152; freedom of expression 159; genre distribution 184; interviews 251; journalists' associations 182; media capture 220; media markets 174–177; media pluralism policy 163, 164; political field transformation 43, 46, 47, 48, 51; political parallelism 171; public service broadcasting 185; public service media governance 168; state advertising 164

Orthodox Church 44, 52
Ottoman Empire: book publishing 74; cultural field transformation 51–54, 56–59, 61–63, 208; development of media markets 56–62; economic field transformation 74; imperial rule of 43–44; media development 215; newspapers 53–54, 59–62; patrimonial regime 202, 227; political field transformation 41, 74, 202; political institutions 44; state involvement in media system 52–54
ownership 111

parliamentary governance model 167
party loyalty 101
party-press parallelism 172, 213
path dependency framework 10, 19–20, 22, 32, 149, 153, 195, 224
patrimonial regimes 202, 212, 227, 243
patrimonial socialism 81, 84–85
peasant revolution 49
periodization: communication juncture 28–32; critical junctures 22–28
Poland 1, 49, 136
political cleavage 140–145
political cleavages 86–87, 107, 140–145, 171–172
political communication 30–31, 67–70, 102–103

Index

political culture 28
political engagement 107
political field: between 15th and 18th centuries 45; analysis 194; conditions shaping outcomes 35–36, 201–206; Habsburg Empire 43–45; Kingdom of SHS/Yugoslavia 46–47; Ottoman Empire 42–47, 74; in post-socialist media systems 132–147; in socialist modernity 78–81, 84–88; Yugoslavia 84–88
political papers 67–70
political parallelism 38, 67–70, 125–126, 168–173, 182, 212–214, 230–231
political parties: Central and Eastern European countries 132, 168–169, 172; Croatia 67, 74, 86, 88, 167, 170; development of 209; Kingdom of SHS/Yugoslavia 47–48, 62–63; links between media and 212–214; Montenegro 70; partisan media in US 172; public service media governance 166–167; Serbia 69, 172, 182; Slovenia 45, 69, 167, 172
political pluralism 86–88, 202, 218
political protests 150
politicized media model 4, 190
popular culture 88–89
Portugal 114, 134, 148
postal service 72–73
post-socialist capitalism 148
post-socialist democratizations: case study approach 134; comparative political science approach 134; critical juncture 27–28; cultural field transformation 149–150; democratic consolidation 134–135, 145–147, 153, 157, 189, 203–204, 214, 217, 243; economic field transformation 147–149; exiting socialism 136–137; in fuzzy set qualitative comparative analysis 199; political cleavages 140–145; political field transformation 1–2, 35–36, 125, 134–147; state building 139–140; state intuitions 139–140; transition in Yugoslavia 137–139; transition paradigm 134–137
post-socialist media systems: creating democratic 151–190; cultural field transformation 150–187; digital media policy 164–166; freedom of expression 107, 158–161; global communication flows 183–187; journalism culture/professional autonomy 177–183, 219; media culture 183–187; media market after self-management socialism 133, 173–177, 217–218; media pluralism policy 162–164; political parallelism 168–173; political party influence 168–173; post-socialist makeovers 152–158; public service media governance 166–168; regulatory system for broadcasting 161–162
post-television 30
press agencies 73
prime time programs 117
print 27, 29–30, 41, 156, 174–176, 215, 226–227
printing press 36, 41, 43, 48, 51, 53–54, 57–58, 60, 199, 215, 217
privacy protection 160
professional governance model 167
Protestant Reformation 52, 56–57
public opinion 107–108
public service broadcasting (PSB) 5, 37–38, 156, 166–168, 170, 172, 174, 180, 185, 209, 211, 218
public service radio 122
public sphere 59–66, 103–110
publishing companies 63–66, 112

qualitative comparative analysis (QCA) 33–34, 196–197

radio: Catholic Church 169; contents of 122; Croatia 66; introduction of 24, 56; Kingdom of SHS/Yugoslavia 66–67; large audiences for 27; Montenegro 66; public service radio 122; Serbia 66; Yugoslavia 82, 97–98, 115, 122
record companies 123–124
reform movements 86–87
religion 84
religious institutions 169
religious press 169
Republika Srpska 138, 140, 147, 164, 172, 204
resolved stateness issues (d_state) condition 204
right of correction 107
right of reply 107
right to information 98

right to publish opinion 107
right-wing media 170
Romania 5, 136
rule of law 81, 125, 140
Russia 5, 49
Russian Empire 43, 52

self-management socialism: development of media in 11, 27, 92; development of television in 114–122; political parallelism and 103, 125; positive example of 81; of socialist media market 95–98; socialist public sphere and 107; socialist values and 90–91
Serbia: candidate country of EU 8, 234; clientelism and corruption 140; regime collapse and foreign intervention 136; cultural field transformation 150; democratic consolidation 145, 147; development of printing 57–58; digital media policy 165, 211; establishment of universities 59; freedom of expression 107, 158–160; genre distribution 184; global communication flows 187, 221; interviews 251; journalism culture/professional autonomy 72, 126, 180–181; journalism-related education 230; journalists' associations 182; literacy rates 58; media capture 220; media culture 183–187; media freedom 212, 243; media markets 173–177, 215–216, 229; media pluralism policy 164; media policy 157; media systems cluster with Western European countries 5; media system transformations 188–189; music 124; nationalist writings 99; newspapers 60–61, 62, 69, 103, 169–171, 215–216; original media production 110; political cleavages 87–88, 145; political communication 67, 69; political field transformation 43, 46, 202–206; political parallelism 169–170, 171, 230; political parties 69, 172, 182; political pluralism 87–88; political protests 150; postal service 73; post-socialist democratic transition 189–190; press agencies 73; public service broadcasting 185; public service media governance 168; publishing companies 66; radio 66; reform movements 86–87; regulatory system for broadcasting 162; religious press 169; socialism in 84–85; socio-economic field transformation 208; state advertising 164; state involvement in media system 54, 55; stateness issues 140; sufficient macro and structural conditions in path to media freedom 236–237; telegraph services 63; television 110, 115, 118–119, 183–186; war 137–138
Sicily 48
Slovakia 139
Slovenia: Catholic Church 52, 169; clientelism and corruption 140; cooperative transition 136; cultural field transformation 150, 189–190; cultural journals 108–109; democratic consolidation 145, 147; development of printing 56–58; digital media policy 165, 211; economic field transformation 148; establishment of universities 59; freedom of expression 107, 159; global communication flows 187, 221; independence 137; interviews 251; journalism culture/professional autonomy 72, 181–182, 218; journalism-related education 230; journalists' associations 182; literacy rates 58–59, 63; media capture 220; media freedom 212; media literacy 165–166; media markets 173–177, 215–218, 229; media pluralism policy 163–164, 211; media policy 156–157; media system transformations 188–189; as member of EU 8; modernization path of developing media systems 227; music 124; nationalist writings 99; neo-corporatist capitalism 148; newspapers 59, 62, 69, 215; original media production 110; political cleavages 87–88, 140; political communication 67, 69; political field transformation 43–45, 48, 202–206; political parallelism 169, 170; political parties 45, 69, 167, 172; political pluralism 86, 87; postal service 73; Protestant Reformation 52;

public service broadcasting 185; public service media governance 167; publishing companies 66; radio 66; regulatory system for broadcasting 161; socialism in 84–85; socio-economic field transformation 207–208; state advertising 164; sufficient macro and structural conditions in path to media freedom 236; sufficient media system conditions for media freedom 235; telegraph services 63; television 110, 115, 118–119, 126, 183–186; television schedules 124; war 137–138; workers' papers 70
social change: in communication research 14–15; as evolution 17–18; processual approach to 18–20; role of culture 18–20; role of technology 29–30; social theories on 15–17
socialism: in Central and Eastern European countries 26; class structure 84; as critical juncture 26–27; decadent 98–99; economic inefficiency, 90; idea of 79–81; impact on media systems 7–9; introduction of 26–27; media systems during 229–231; media transformation following 152–158; political field transformation 202; types in Europe 81; in Yugoslavia 7, 26–27, 76, 79, 81–88
Socialist Federal Republic of Yugoslavia (SFRY) see Yugoslavia
socialist media: administrative period 93–95; mature period of decadent socialism 98–99; self-management of market 95–98; socialist media 92–99
socialist public sphere 103–110
socialist values 89–92
social media 218
social realism 27, 88–89, 95
social responsibility theory 99
social structure 16
social values 22
socio-economic field 36–37, 194, 198, 206–208
socio-political workers 101, 126
Southeast European model 5, 189
South Korea 208
Soviet economic model 82–83
Spain 5, 114, 134, 149, 208
state advertising 164

state building 139–140
state collapse 136
state consolidation 45
state intuitions 139–140
state media control: censorship 30, 52–54, 59, 69, 72, 94–95, 97, 108, 139, 181, 183; conditions shaping outcomes 37, 209–212; creating democratic media systems 151; making socialist media 92–99, 125
stateness issues 204
strong public service broadcasting (d_psb) condition 218
sufficiency analysis 226–227
Swiss public service model 166
Switzerland 212
symbolic field 37–39, 42, 56, 194, 198, 208–224
systems theory 16

telecommunication policy 211
telegraph 30, 40, 42, 56, 63, 73, 114
television: afternoon programs 122; audience research 113; content analysis 183, 245–248; content from other republics 118–119; cultural programs 117–118; developing in self-management socialism 114–122; digital 165; educational programs 116; entertainment programs 116–118; fiction programs 116–118; genre distribution 183–187; global communication flows 122–124; influence on creation of common public sphere 110; introduction of 11, 24; large audiences for 27; media markets 175–176; as medium of political communication 31; prime time programs 117; role in wars of former Yugoslavia 138–139; schedules 124
Television Without Frontiers Directive (TWFD) 152
time 17
transition paradigms 134–135, 203
Turkey 207

Union of Soviet Socialist Republics (USSR) 23, 45, 48, 78, 82, 85, 92, 95–96, 115, 123, 125, 139
United Kingdom (UK) 19, 48, 114, 207
United States 19, 24, 59, 109, 118, 123, 125, 172, 186, 187, 213–214, 249

universities 59
Uzbekistan 208

value orientations 152
Venetian Empire 43
"verbal delict, the" 98

war 137–139, 140
Warsaw Pact 1
workers' councils 112
workers' papers 70
World War I 46
World War II 11, 26, 41, 46, 48, 49, 66–67, 74, 76, 82, 93, 114, 200, 209, 215

youth organizations 85, 213
youth-oriented media 108
Yugoslavia: audience research 113; class structure 84; communications policy 96–97; concentration of media outlets 114; cultural field transformation 88–127; cultural policy 96; development of art and literature 88–89; development of television in 114–122; economic field transformation 82–84, 207; establishment of universities 59; Eurovision Song Contest 1; films 88–89; financial autonomy of media 112–113; freedom of expression 158; global communication flows 122–124, 221; historical revisionism and false narratives 78–79; illiteracy rates 82; journalism culture/professional autonomy 99–102, 126; making socialist media 92–99; media legislation 97–99, 125; media system development 24–25; music 89; newspapers 103–110, 114; ownership of media system 111; political cleavages 86–88; political field transformation 84–88; political parallelism 102–110, 125–126, 213; political pluralism 87–88; popular culture 88–89; post-socialist democratic transition 135, 137–139, 188; public spheres 103–110, 125–126; radio 82, 97–98; record companies 123–124; right to publish opinion 107; role of media in war 138–139; self-management of media market 111–127; socialism in 7, 26–27, 76, 79, 81–88, 126–127; socialist public sphere 103–110; socialist values 89–92; state involvement in media system 210; unification of states 46–47; "verbal delict, the" 98; war 137–139, 140; *see also* Kingdom of SHS/Yugoslavia

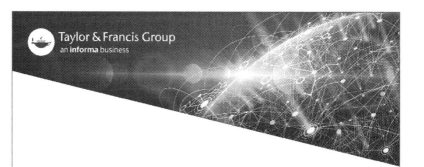

Printed in the United States
By Bookmasters